公路施工新技术与工程管理研究

赵利军 张 毅 马英杰 主编

哈尔滨出版社
HARBIN PUBLISHING HOUSE

图书在版编目（CIP）数据

公路施工新技术与工程管理研究 / 赵利军，张毅，马英杰主编． — 哈尔滨：哈尔滨出版社，2023.1
ISBN 978-7-5484-6735-9

Ⅰ．①公… Ⅱ．①赵… ②张… ③马… Ⅲ．①道路施工－工程技术②道路施工－施工管理 Ⅳ．①U415.6 ②U415.1

中国版本图书馆CIP数据核字（2022）第173680号

书　　名：公路施工新技术与工程管理研究
GONGLU SHIGONG XINJISHU YU GONGCHENG GUANLI YANJIU

作　　者：	赵利军　张　毅　马英杰　主编
责任编辑：	韩伟锋
封面设计：	张　华
出版发行：	哈尔滨出版社（Harbin Publishing House）
社　　址：	哈尔滨市香坊区泰山路82-9号　邮编：150090
经　　销：	全国新华书店
印　　刷：	廊坊市广阳区九洲印刷厂
网　　址：	www.hrbcbs.com
E－mail：	hrbcbs@yeah.net
编辑版权热线：	（0451）87900271　87900272
开　　本：	787mm×1092mm　1/16　印张：12.75　字数：280千字
版　　次：	2023年1月第1版
印　　次：	2023年1月第1次印刷
书　　号：	ISBN 978-7-5484-6735-9
定　　价：	68.00元

凡购本社图书发现印装错误，请与本社印制部联系调换。
服务热线：（0451）87900279

前 言

传统工艺和技术导向下的公路施工建设为我国的公路事业做出巨大的贡献，在很多条件艰苦、山峰险峻的地区进行公路建设的尝试，事实证明我国公路建设是具有一定的进步和发展的。随着社会经济水平的发展和提高，民众对于交通便利的需求越来越大，并且在偏远地区生活的人民更加需要有畅通的公路来支撑日常生活采购和物流行为，这对公路建设施工的建设范围和建设量有了较为明显的需求。在这一基础上就需要公路施工技术和工艺在原有程度上进行创新性改进和突破性完善，以此来提高公路施工时的工作效率和工作质量，为我国公路建设事业增添一份新的能量。

随着我国市场经济的日趋完善，公路作为发展国民经济的重要基础设施，发挥着不可替代的作用。高速公路的建设是一个系统化的工程，是需要规范的技术、正确的决策思想、高水平的管理及各个部分的互相监督为支撑的。管理者要根据高速公路施工的特点，加强施工管理，实现高速公路施工工程项目快速、优质、低耗的目标。

现代桥梁建设施工企业要加强自身管理水平与技术水平，不断采用更新的技术，通过对技术人员的培训，提高项目的质量；通过对管理人员的培训，提高项目的综合管理水平，这些都是为了保障桥梁工程施工质量，为我国公路运输事业的发展奠定坚实的基础。

本书是一本关于公路施工新技术与工程管理研究的专著，共八章。首先，对公路路基的构造与施工进行了阐述；其次，对公路路面的施工技术与流水施工组织进行了分析；最后，对公路施工的质量与安全进行了分析，以期我国的公路施工技术水平不断提高，管理系统逐步完善。

需要说明的是，本书在具体的编写过程中，参考并借鉴诸多相关专业的书籍与资料，在此对相关作者表示感谢。由于笔者水平所限，书中不妥之处在所难免，在此恳请广大读者朋友不吝批评，并提出宝贵意见，不胜感激。

编 者
2022 年 5 月

编委会成员

主 编　赵利军　张　毅　马英杰
副主编　聂宇晨　王金玲　张敏敏
　　　　张晓坤　赵丽瑾　张铭志

目 录

第一章 路基构造与要求 ... 1
- 第一节 公路的分级、技术标准及组成部分 ... 1
- 第二节 路基的基本构造与要求 ... 7
- 第三节 公路自然区划与路基土的干湿类型 ... 14

第二章 土质路基施工 ... 18
- 第一节 土质路基填筑 ... 18
- 第二节 土质路堑开挖 ... 25
- 第三节 土质路堤压实 ... 29

第三章 石质路基施工 ... 33
- 第一节 填石路堤施工 ... 33
- 第二节 石质路堑施工 ... 37

第四章 水泥混凝土路面施工 ... 42
- 第一节 小型机具施工 ... 42
- 第二节 轨模式摊铺机施工 ... 47
- 第三节 滑模式摊铺机施工 ... 54
- 第四节 特殊气候条件下施工 ... 56
- 第五节 施工质量检查与竣工验收 ... 61

第五章 沥青路面施工 ... 67
- 第一节 多级嵌挤密级配沥青混合料路面施工 ... 67
- 第二节 SMA 沥青路面施工 ... 73
- 第三节 SMA 施工质量管理和验收 ... 86
- 第四节 透层、黏层和封层施工 ... 97

　　　　第五节　沥青路面基层冷再生施工新技术…………………………………… 99
　　　　第六节　废旧橡胶沥青路面施工技术…………………………………………… 102

第六章　流水施工（流水作业）组织 …………………………………… 109
　　　　第一节　施工组织方法与流水施工的概念 ……………………………………… 109
　　　　第二节　平面流水施工组织 …………………………………………………… 120
　　　　第三节　空间流水施工组织 …………………………………………………… 125
　　　　第四节　无节拍流水施工段次（顺）序的优化 ………………………………… 129
　　　　第五节　公路工程流水施工的特点 …………………………………………… 135

第七章　公路工程质量管理 ………………………………………………… 141
　　　　第一节　公路工程质量控制的常用方法 ………………………………………… 141
　　　　第二节　公路工程质量缺陷处理方法 …………………………………………… 148
　　　　第三节　路基工程质量检验 …………………………………………………… 149
　　　　第四节　路面工程质量检验 …………………………………………………… 152
　　　　第五节　桥梁工程质量检验 …………………………………………………… 153
　　　　第六节　隧道工程质量检验 …………………………………………………… 160
　　　　第七节　质量检验评定 ………………………………………………………… 165

第八章　公路工程项目施工安全标准化管理 …………………………… 172
　　　　第一节　特殊工序作业安全作业要点 …………………………………………… 172
　　　　第二节　临时用电安全技术要求 ……………………………………………… 175
　　　　第三节　机械设备安全操作要点 ……………………………………………… 182
　　　　第四节　安全专项方案编制 …………………………………………………… 185
　　　　第五节　公路工程安全风险分级管控与隐患排查治理 ………………………… 190
　　　　第六节　公路工程施工应急管理 ……………………………………………… 192

结　语 ………………………………………………………………………… 194

参考文献 …………………………………………………………………… 195

第一章　路基构造与要求

公路路基的施工在公路工程的整体质量中有着非常重要的意义，为了使公路路基工程的建设质量得到一定保证，必须对其施工引起重视。本章主要分析了公路路基的构造与施工要求，从而进一步促进公路工程建设与公路运输业的发展。

第一节　公路的分级、技术标准及组成部分

一、公路分类

（一）按行政等级划分

公路按行政等级可分为：国家公路、省公路、县公路、乡公路（简称为国、省、乡道）以及专用公路五个等级。一般把国道和省道称为干线，县道和乡道称为支线。

1. 国道是指具有全国性政治、经济意义的主要干线公路，包括重要的国际公路、国防公路；连接首都与各省、自治区、直辖市首府的公路；连接各大经济中心、港站枢纽、商品生产基地和战略要地的公路。国道中跨省的高速公路由交通运输部批准的专门机构负责修建、养护和管理。

2. 省道是指具有全省（自治区、直辖市）性政治、经济意义，并由省（自治区、直辖市）公路主管部门负责修建、养护和管理的公路干线。

3. 县道是指具有全县（县级市）性政治、经济意义，连接县城和县内主要乡（镇）、主要商品生产和集散地，以及不属于国道、省道的县际间公路。县道由县、市公路主管部门负责修建、养护和管理。

4. 乡道是指主要为乡（镇）村经济、文化、行政服务，以及不属于县道以上公路的乡与乡之间及乡与外部联络的公路。乡道由人民政府负责修建、养护和管理。

5. 专用公路是指专供或主要供厂矿、林区、农场、油田、旅游区等与外部联系的公路。专用公路由专用单位负责修建、养护和管理，也可委托当地公路部门修建、养护和管理。

（二）按功能和适应的交通量划分

1. 根据公路使用任务、功能和适应的交通量，将公路分为五个等级：高速公路、一级公路、二级公路、三级公路、四级公路。

（1）高速公路为专供汽车分向、分车道行驶并应全部控制出入的多车道公路。

四车道高速公路应能适应将各种汽车折合成小客车的年平均日交通量2.5~5.5万辆；

六车道高速公路应能适应将各种汽车折合成小客车的年平均日交通量4.5~8万辆；

八车道高速公路应能适应将各种汽车折合成小客车的年平均日交通量6~10万辆。

（2）一级公路为供汽车分向、分车道行驶并可根据需要控制出入的多车道公路。

四车道一级公路应能适应将各种汽车折合成小客车的年平均日交通量1.5~3万辆；

六车道一级公路应能适应将各种汽车折合成小客车的年平均日交通量2.5~5.5万辆。

（3）二级公路为供汽车行驶的双车道公路。

双车道二级公路应能适应将各种汽车折合成小客车的年平均日交通量0.5~1.5万辆。

（4）三级公路为主要供汽车行驶的双车道公路。

双车道三级公路应能适应将各种车辆折合成小客车的年平均日交通量2000~6000辆。

（5）四级公路为主要供汽车行驶的双车道或单车道公路。

双车道四级公路应能适应将各种车辆折合成小客车的年平均日交通量2000辆以下；

单车道四级公路应能适应将各种车辆折合成小客车的年平均日交通量400辆以下。

2. 各级公路设计交通量的预测应符合下列规定

（1）高速公路和具干线功能的一级公路的设计交通量应按20年预测；具集散功能的一级公路，以及二、三级公路的设计交通量应按15年预测；四级公路可根据实际情况确定。

（2）设计交通量预测的起算年应为该项目可行性研究报告中的计划通车年。

（3）设计交通量的预测应充分考虑走廊带范围内远期社会、经济的发展和综合运输体系的影响。

3. 公路等级的选用

公路等级的选用应根据公路功能、路网规划、交通量，并充分考虑项目所在地区的综合运输体系、远期发展等，经论证后确定。

一条公路可分段选用不同的公路等级或同一公路等级不同的设计速度与路基宽度，但不同公路等级的设计速度与路基宽度间的衔接应协调，过渡应顺适。

预测的设计交通量介于一级公路与高速公路之间时，当拟建公路为干线公路时，宜选用高速公路；拟建公路为集散公路时，宜选用一级公路。

干线公路宜选用二级及二级以上的公路。

4. 车辆折算系数

交通量换算采用小客车为标准车型。确定公路等级的各汽车代表车型和车辆折算系数规定。

5. 公路工程技术标准

公路工程技术标准是指对公路路线和构造物的设计与施工在技术性能、几何形状和尺寸、结构组成上的具体要求，把这些要求以指标和条文的形式确定下来，即形成公路工程的技术标准。

技术标准是根据汽车的行驶性能、数量、荷载等方面的要求，在总结公路设计、施工、养护和汽车运输经验的基础上，经过调查研究和理论分析制定出来的。它反映了我国公路建设的技术政策和技术要求，是公路设计和施工的基本依据和必须遵守的准则。

各级公路的技术指标是根据路线在公路网中的功能、规划交通量和交通组成、设计速度等因素确定的。其中，设计速度是技术标准中最重要的指标，它对公路的几何形状、工程费用和运输效率影响最大，在考虑路线的使用功能和规划交通量的基础上，根据国家的技术政策制定设计速度。路线在公路网中具有重要经济与国防意义者，交通量较大者，技术政策规定采用较高的设计速度，反之规定较低的设计速度。对于某些公路通向机场、经济开发区、重点游览区用途的公路，尽管其交通量不是很大，但具有重要的政治、经济、国防意义，也须采用较高的设计速度。

一条公路可分段选用不同的公路等级或同一公路等级不同的设计速度、路基宽度（车道数），但应注意以下四个方面。

（1）为保持公路技术指标的均衡、连续，一条公路的等级或设计速度分段不应频繁变更。设计速度相同的路段应为同一设计路段，高速公路设计路段不宜小于15km，一、二级公路设计路段不宜小于10km。

（2）等级或标准的变更处，原则上应选在交通量发生较大变化或驾驶员能够明显判断前方需要改变行车速度处；高速公路、一级公路宜设在互通式立体交叉或平面交叉处；二、三、四级公路宜设在交叉路口、桥梁、隧道、村镇附近或地形明显变化处。

（3）在标准变更的相互衔接处前、后一定长度范围内主要技术指标应逐渐过渡，避免发生事故，设计速度高的一端应采用较低的平、纵技术指标，反之则应采用较高的平、纵技术指标，以使平、纵线形技术指标较为均衡。

（4）应采用连续、均衡的技术指标。

二、城市道路分类与技术分级

1. 城市道路分类

按照道路在城市道路网中的地位、交通功能以及对沿线建筑物的服务功能，将城市道路分为以下四类。

（1）快速路：为城市中长距离快速交通服务的道路。快速路上的机动车道两侧不应设置非机动车道。快速路对向行车道之间应设置中间分隔带，其进出口应全控制或部分控制。快速路沿线两侧不能设置吸引大量车流、人流的公共建筑物的进出口，对一般建筑物的进出口应加以控制，当进出口较多时宜在两侧另建辅道。

（2）主干路：为连接城市各主要分区的干线道路，以交通功能为主的道路。非机动车交通量大时应设置分隔带与机动车分离行驶，两交叉口之间分隔机动车与非机动车的分隔带宜连续。主干路两侧不宜设置吸引大量车流、人流的公共建筑物的进出口。

（3）次干路：与主干路共同组成城市道路网，起集散交通的作用，兼有服务功能的道路。次干路两侧可设置公共建筑物的进出口，并可设置机动车和非机动车的停车场，公共交通站点和出租车服务站。

（4）支路：为次干路与居民区、工业区、市中心区、市政公用设施用地和交通设施用地等内部道路的连接线，解决局部区域交通，以服务功能为主的道路。支路可与平行于快速路的道路相接，但不得与快速路直接相接。支路需要与快速路交叉时应采用分离式立体交叉跨过或穿过快速路。

2.城市道路分级

根据城市规模、规划交通量和地形等因素，除快速路外，各类道路可划分为Ⅰ、Ⅱ、Ⅲ级。大城市应采用各类道路中的Ⅰ级标准，中等城市应采用Ⅱ级标准，小城市应采用Ⅲ级标准。

在选用城市道路分级时，受地形限制的山城可降低一级，特殊发展的中、小城市可提高一级。当有特殊情况需要变更级别时，应做技术经济论证，报规划审批部门批准。城市道路规划交通量达到饱和状态时的设计年限，快速路、主干路为20年，次干路为15年，支路为10~15年。城市规模可按照其市区和近郊区（不包括所属县）的非农业人口总数划分为：大城市（指人口50万以上的城市）、中等城市（20~50万人）和小城市（20万人以下）。

三、公路的基本组成部分

公路的基本组成部分包括：路基、路面、桥梁、涵洞、隧道、防护与加固工程、排水设施和山区特殊构造物等。此外，为保证汽车行驶的安全、畅通和舒适，还需要有各种附属工程，如公路标志、路用房屋、加油站及绿化栽植等。

路基是公路的基本结构，是支撑路面结构的基础。它与路面共同承受行车荷载的作用，一同承受着气候变化和各种自然灾害的侵蚀和影响。

路面是用各种筑路材料铺筑在公路路基上供汽车行驶的结构层，直接承受和传递车轮荷载，承受磨耗，经受自然气候和各种自然灾害的侵蚀和影响。

桥涵是指公路跨越水域、沟谷和其他障碍物时修建的构造物。

公路隧道通常是指建造在山岭、江河、海峡和城市地面下，供车辆通过的工程构造物。

为防止路基填土或山坡土体坍塌而修筑的承受土体侧压力的墙式构造物称挡土墙，它是路基加固工程的一种结构形式。

为保持路基的稳定和强度而修建的地表和地下排水设施称为路基排水设施，包括边沟、截水沟、排水沟、急流槽、跌水、渗沟和渗井等。

公路交通工程及沿线设施是保证公路功能、保障安全行驶的配套设施，是现代公路的重要标志。

公路工程的进度横道图是以时间为横坐标，以各分部（项）工程或工作内容为纵坐标，按一定的先后施工顺序，用带时间比例的水平横线表示对应工作内容持续时间的进度计划图表。公路工程中常常在横道图对应分项的横线下方表示当月计划应完成的累计工程量或工作量百分数，横线上方表示当月实际完成的累计工程量或工作量百分数。

S 曲线是以时间为横轴，以累计完成的工程费用的百分数为纵轴的图表化曲线。一般在图上标注有一条计划曲线和实际支付曲线，实际线高于计划线则实际进度快于计划，否则就慢；曲线本身的斜率也反映进度推进的快慢。有时为反映实际进度会另增加一条实际完成线（支付滞后于完成）。在公路工程中，常常将 S 曲线和横道图合并于同一张图表中，称为"公路工程进度表"。它既能反映各分部（项）工程的进度，又能反映工程总体的进度。

垂直图是以公路里程或工程位置为横轴，以时间为纵轴，而各分部（项）工程的施工进度则相应地以不同的斜线表示。在图中可以辅助表示平面布置图和工程量的分布，垂直图很适合表示公路、隧道等线形工程的总体施工进度。斜线越陡进度越慢，斜线越平进度越快。

斜率图是以时间（月份）为横轴，以累计完成的工程量的百分数为纵轴，将分项工程的施工进度相应地用不同斜率表示的图表化曲（折）线。事实上就是分项工程的 S 曲（折）线，主要是作为公路工程投标文件中施工组织设计的附表，以反映公路工程的施工进度。

1. 顺序作业法（也称为依次作业法）的主要特点

（1）没有充分利用工作面进行施工，（总）工期较长。

（2）每天投入施工的劳动力、材料和机具的种类比较少，有利于资源供应的组织工作。

（3）施工现场的组织、管理比较简单。

（4）不强调分工协作，若由一个作业队完成全部施工任务，不能实现专业化生产，不利于提高劳动生产率；若按工艺专业化原则成立专业作业队（班组），各专业队是间歇作业，不能连续作业，材料供应也是间歇供应，劳动力和材料的使用可能不均衡。

2. 平行作业法的主要特点

（1）充分利用了工作面进行施工，（总）工期较短。

（2）每天同时投入施工的劳动力、材料和机具数量较大，材料供应特别集中，所需作业班组很多，影响资源供应的组织工作。

（3）如果各工作面之间需共用某种资源时，施工现场的组织管理比较复杂，协调工作量大。

（4）不强调分工协作，各作业单位都是间歇作业，此点与顺序作业法相同。这种方法的实质是用增加资源的方法来达到缩短（总）工期的目的，一般适用于需要突击性施工时施工作业的组织。

3. 流水作业法的主要特点

（1）必须按工艺专业化原则成立专业作业队（班组），实现专业化生产，有利于提高劳动生产率，保证工程质量。

（2）专业化作业队能够连续作业，相邻作业队的施工时间能最大限度地搭接。

（3）尽可能地利用了工作面进行施工，工期比较短。

（4）每天投入的资源量较为均衡，有利于资源供应的组织工作。

（5）需要较强的组织管理能力。这种方法可以充分利用工作面，有效地缩短工期，一般适用于工序繁多、工程量大而又集中的大型构筑物的施工，如大型桥梁工程、立交桥、隧道工程、路面等施工组织。

一般路面各结构层施工的速度不同，从而持续的时间也往往不相同。组织路面流水施工时应注意以下要点：

（1）各结构层的施工速度和持续时间。要考虑影响每个施工段的因素，水泥稳定碎石的延迟时间、沥青拌和能力、温度要求、摊铺速度、养护时间、最小工作面的要求等。

（2）相邻结构层之间的速度决定了相邻结构层之间的搭接类型，前道工序的速度快于后道工序时选用开始到开始搭接类型。否则选用完成到完成搭接类型。

（3）相邻结构层工序之间的搭接时距的计算。时距＝最小工作面长度/两工序中快的速度。

在实际的公路通道和涵洞施工中，全等节拍流水较少见，更多的是异节拍流水和无节拍流水。对于通道和涵洞的流水组织主要是以流水段方式组织流水施工，而流水段方式的流水施工往往会存在窝工（资源的闲置）或间歇（工作面的闲置）。根据流水施工的组织原理，异步距异节拍流水实质上是按无节拍流水组织，引入流水步距概念的目的就是为了消除流水施工中存在的窝工现象。消除窝工和消除间歇的方法都采用累加数列错位相减取大差的方法，构成累加数列的方法。当不窝工的流水组织时，其流水步距计算是同工序各节拍值累加构成数列；当不间歇（无多余间歇）的流水组织时，其施工段的段间间隔计算是同段各节拍值累加构成数列；错位相减取大差的计算方法，两种计算方法相同。

不窝工的无节拍流水工期 = 流水步距和 + 最后一道工序流水节拍的和技术间歇和

无多余间歇的无节拍流水工期 = 施工段间间隔和 + 最后一个施工段流水节拍的和 + 技术间歇和

有窝工并且有多余间歇的无节拍流水工期，一般通过绘制横道图来确定。如果是异节拍流水时往往是不窝工或者无多余间歇流水施工中的最小值，此时一般是无多余间歇流水工期最小。

多跨桥梁的桥梁基础或桥梁下部结构施工由于受专业设备数量的限制，不宜配备多台，因此，只能采取流水施工。桥梁的流水施工也是属于流水段法流水施工，应注意尽可能地组织成有节拍的形式。工期计算与通道涵洞相同。

第二节　路基的基本构造与要求

一、路基的类型

为了满足行车的要求，路线有些部分高出地面，需要填筑；有些部分低于原地面，需要开挖。因此，路基横断面形状各不相同。典型的路基横断面分为路堤、路堑、填挖结合及零填零挖四种类型。

1. 路堤

高于原地面的填方路基称路堤。路堤在结构上分为上路堤和下路堤，上路堤是指路面底面以下 0.80~1.50m 范围内的填方部分，下路堤是指上路堤以下的填方部分。按其填土高度划分：填土高度低于 1~1.5m 的路堤属矮路堤，填土高度在 1.5~18m（土质）或 20m（石质）范围内的路堤为一般路堤，填土高度超过 18m（土质）或 20m（石质）的路堤属于高路堤。按其所处的条件及加固类型的不同还有沿河路堤、陡坡护脚路堤及挖渠填筑路堤等。

路堤通风良好，排水方便，且为人工或机械填筑，对填料的性质、状态和密实程度可以按要求加以控制。因此，路堤式路基病害较少，是经常采用的一种形式。平坦地区往往是耕地，地势较低、水文条件差，设计时要特别注意控制最小填土高度，使路基处于干燥或中湿状态。

填方高度在 1.5~12.0m 范围内，一般情况下属于正常的路堤，可按常规设计，采用规定的横断面尺寸，一般不做特殊处置。原地面倾斜的全填路堤，当倾斜度陡于 1∶5 时，需将原地面挖成台阶（土质地面）台阶宽度大于或等于 1.0m，向内倾斜 1%~2%，或将原地面凿毛（石质地面）；原地面倾斜度陡于 1∶2 时，则宜设置石砌护脚等横断面形式。矮路堤因易受地面水的影响，有时难以满足最小填土高度要求，故其两侧均应设置边沟。有时，基底需加特殊处置与加固，如清除基底、换土、设隔离层、排除地下水等。一般路堤可不设边沟。沿河路堤浸水部分，其边坡应按规定放缓或采取防护与加固措施。地面横坡较陡时，为防止填方沿山坡向下滑动并节省用地，可设置石砌护脚或挡土墙。填土高度超过 20m 的路堤，应进行个别设计。

2. 路堑

低于原地面的挖方路基称为路堑。

最典型的路堑为全挖断面，路基两侧均需设置边沟。在陡峭山坡上可挖成台口式路基，即在山坡上，以山体自然坡面为下边坡，其他部分全部由开挖形成。三、四级公路建在整体坚硬的岩石坡面上时，为减少石方工程，有时可采用半山洞路基，前提要确保安全可靠，不得滥用。

路堑边坡形式及坡率应根据工程地质与水文地质条件、边坡高度、排水措施、施工方法，并结合自然稳定的山坡和人工边坡的调查及力学分析综合确定，必要时可采用稳定性分析方法予以验算。

路堑开挖后，在一定范围内破坏了原地面的天然平衡状态，其边坡的稳定性主要取决于地质与水文条件，以及边坡坡度和边坡高度。一般情况下，地质条件较差（如岩层倾向边坡、岩性软弱极易风化、岩石破碎或为土夹石等）、水文状况不利（如地层含有地下水、当地暴雨量集中或地面排水不畅）时，深路堑边坡的稳定性较差，路基的后遗病害较多。所以，深路堑的设计，需要根据地质及水文条件，选用合适的边坡坡率，并且自下而上逐层放缓形成折线形边坡或台阶形边坡。

水文状况对路堑的影响较大，地质条件越差，水的破坏作用越明显。因此，路堑排水至为重要。路堑必须设置边沟，以排除边坡和路基表面的降水。为防止大量地面水流向路基，造成坡面冲刷或边沟溢流，应在路堑两侧坡面上方规定的距离以外（不小于 5m），设置一道或多道截水沟。

如果挖方路基位于含水土层，因地下水文状况不利，会经常产生水分聚积现象，可能导致路面破坏。所以，路堑以下的天然土层要压实至规定的密实程度，必要时还需翻挖并重新分层填筑或换土，也可采取加铺隔离层，设置必要的地下排水设施等措施予以处理。

路堑由天然地层开挖而成，其构造取决于当地的自然条件，如岩土类型、地质构造、水文等。此外，路堑成巷道式，受排水、通风、日照影响，病害多于路堤，且行车视距差、行车条件和景观要求亦有所降低，施工难度大。所以，设计时应尽量少用很深的长路堑，必需时要选用合适的边坡坡率及边坡形式，以确保边坡的稳定可靠。同时，加强排水，处置基底，保证基底不致产生水文情况的恶化。在确定路线走向和进行路线平、纵面设计时，要兼顾日照、积雪、通风等因素，尽可能地选用大半径平竖曲线和缓和的纵、横坡度等技术指标。等级较高的公路，还必须进行平、纵面线形的组合设计，兼顾道路景观和环境协调，以改善路堑的行车条件。

3. 填挖结合路基

在一个断面内，部分为路堤、部分为路堑的路基称为填挖结合路基。陡坡上的填挖结合路基，可根据地形、地质条件，采用护肩、砌石或挡土墙，当山坡高陡或稳定性差，不宜多挖时，可采用桥梁或悬出路台等构造物。这种类型的工程量最小，是路基横断面设计时应当首先考虑的一种断面形式。如若处理得当，路基稳定可靠，这种形式是比较经济的。但由于开挖部分路基为原状土，而填方部分为扰动土，往往这两部分密实程度不相同。另外，填方部分与山坡结合不够稳定，若处理不当，路基会在填挖交界面处出现纵向裂缝，填方沿基底滑动等病害，因此，应加强填挖交界面结合处的处理。

从路基稳定性方面考虑，陡坡路基一般应"宁挖勿填"或"多挖少填"；在陡峭山坡上，尤其是沿溪路线，为减少石方的开挖数量，避免大量废方阻塞溪流，有时又需要"少挖多填"。因此，填挖结合的路基，在选定路线和线形设计时，应予以统一安排。

4. 零填零挖路基

这种路基虽然节省土石方，但对排水非常不利，且原状土密实程度往往不能满足要求，容易发生水淹、雪埋、沉陷等病害，因此，应尽量少用或不用该类路基（干旱的平原区和丘陵区、山岭区的山脊线方可考虑）。为保证路基的稳定性，需要检查路床顶面以下30cm 范围内原状土的密实程度，必要时翻松原状土重新分层碾压，或换填土层。同时，路基两侧应设置边沟，以利排水。

二、路基的构造

路基由宽度、高度和边坡坡度构成。路基宽度取决于公路技术等级；路基高度取决于路线的纵坡设计及地形；路基边坡坡度取决于土质、地质构造、水文条件及边坡高度，并由边坡稳定性和横断面经济性等因素比较确定。下面分别叙述其确定方法。

1. 路基宽度

路基宽度是在一个横断面上两路肩外缘之间的宽度。各级公路路基宽度为车道宽度与路肩宽度之和，当设有中间带、加（减）速车道、爬坡车道、紧急停车带、错车道等时，应计入这些部分的宽度。

高速公路、一级公路的路基横断面分为整体式和分离式两类。整体式断面包括车道、中间带（中央分隔带及左侧路缘带）、路肩（硬路肩及土路肩）以及紧急停车带、爬坡车道、加（减）速车道等；分离式断面包括车道、路肩（硬路肩及土路肩）以及紧急停车带、爬坡车道、加（减）速车道等。

二、三、四级公路的路基横断面包括车道、路肩以及错车道等。二级公路位于中、小城市城乡接合部、混合交通量大的连接线路段，实行快、慢车道分开行驶时，可根据当地实际情况设置车道或加宽右侧硬路肩。

2. 路基高度

路基高度与路基强度和稳定性有关，也与工程量的大小密切相关。所以，它既是路线纵断面设计的重点，也是路基设计的重点。

路基高度是路基设计标高和中桩地面标高的差值。路堤为填筑高度，路堑为开挖深度。路基设计标高：一般公路指路肩外缘的设计标高，高速公路和一级公路指中央分隔带外侧边缘的设计标高。此外，由于除平原区外，路基自然横纵面多为倾斜面，所以，在路基宽度范围内，两侧的高差有较大差别。而路基两侧边坡高度是指填方坡脚或挖方坡顶与路基边缘的相对高差，这一高差通常称为边坡高度。当地面横坡度较大时，该边坡高度将严重影响路基的稳定，所以在路基设计时应引起重视。

路基高度的确定，是在路线纵断面设计时，综合考虑路线纵坡要求、路基稳定性和工程经济等因素后确定的。从路基的强度和稳定性要求出发，路基上部土层应处于干燥或中湿状态，并满足最小填土高度的要求。对于高路堤和深路堑，由于土石方数量大、占地多、施工困难、边坡稳定性差、行车不利等因素影响，应尽量避免使用。矮路堤和浸水路堤，还要考虑排水和设计洪水频率的要求。

3. 路基边坡坡度

确定路基边坡坡率是路基设计的基本任务。为保证路基稳定，路基两侧应做成具有一定坡度的坡面。公路路基边坡坡率可用边坡高度 H 和边坡宽度 b 之比值表示。将高度定为 1，则边坡坡率一般写成 1:m（路堤）或 1:n（路堑）。

路基边坡坡率的大小，关系边坡的稳定和路基工程的数量。边坡越陡，稳定性越差，若处理不当，易造成坍方等路基病害；边坡过缓，土石方数量增大，裸露面积增大，自然影响面加大，如果不能快速恢复生态，也会影响路基边坡的稳定。所以，在确定边坡坡率时，要根据实际情况，综合考虑路基边坡的稳定、国家及地方环保政策、工程造价等因素后合理确定。

路基边坡坡率的大小，主要取决于地质、土壤与水文等自然因素。影响路基边坡稳定的因素是多方面的，除上述因素外，边坡的高度也是一个重要方面。在陡坡或填挖较大的路段，边坡稳定不仅会影响土石方工程量的大小，也涉及工程施工的难易，是路基整体稳定的关键。一般路基的边坡坡度可根据多年工程实践经验和设计规范推荐的数值来确定。

（1）路堤边坡

沿河路堤边坡坡度，要求在设计水位以下部分视填料情况，可采用 1:1.75~1:2.0；常水位以下部分可采用 1:2.0~1:3.0。当公路沿线有大量天然石料或路堑开挖的废石方时，可用于填筑路堤。填石路堤坡面应用由不易风化的较大（大于 25cm）石块砌筑，边坡坡度可用 1:1。

当沿着比较陡峻的山坡填筑路堤时，填方边坡接近平行于山坡，以至于填方量过大或占地太宽，甚至无法填筑。此时，可以利用当地石料，分别砌筑护肩、护脚、边坡砌石及挡土墙等路基断面。

对边坡高度超过 20m 的路堤或地面斜坡坡率陡于 1:2.5 的路堤，以及不良地质，特殊地段的路堤，应进行个别勘察设计，对重要的路堤应进行稳定性监控。

（2）路堑边坡

路堑边坡根据路堑开挖的岩土性质可分为土质和石质两大类，其边坡形式也因高度和岩性的不同而有所区别。

在进行路堑边坡设计时，首先应从地貌和地质构造上判断其整体稳定性。遇到工程地质或水文地质条件不良的地层时，应尽量使路线绕避它；而对于稳定的地层，则应考虑开挖后，土部岩体是否会由于失去支撑，坡面风化加剧而引起失稳的因素。

影响路堑边坡稳定的因素非常复杂，路堑开挖深度、地质构造、岩性、岩石风化破碎程度、地下水和地表水的影响、土体结合的密实程度、土壤的性质、当地的自然气候、施工方法等因素都会影响路堑边坡的稳定性，所以，在进行路堑边坡设计时必须综合考虑。

在确定岩石路堑边坡时，除考虑上述影响路堑边坡稳定性的因素外，由于存在地区自然差异，所以，还要不断积累当地的实践经验。结合施工方法进行综合分析，结合当地的工程地质和水文条件，参考当地相应类型稳定的成型边坡度，加以对比选用。同时，还要根据环保设计要求修正边坡值。对于定性比较困难的地段，必要时还要进行个别设计与验算，并结合采用排水、防护与加固等技术措施。

土质挖方边坡高度超过 20m，岩质挖方边坡高度超过 30m 以及不良地质，特殊岩土地段的挖方边坡，应进行个别勘察设计。

三、路基的附属设施

为保证路基的稳定和行车的安全畅通，除应认真搞好路基结构及必要的排水、加固与防护等主体工程外，路基设计应重视排水设施与防护设施的设计，取土、弃土应进行专门设计，防止水土流失，堵塞河道和诱发路基病害，还应同时合理设置取土坑、弃土堆、护坡道、碎落台、堆料坪、错车道及护栏等。这些附属设施也是路基设计的组成部分，正确合理的设置是十分重要的。

1. 取土坑与弃土堆

路基土石方的挖填平衡是公路路线设计的基本原则之一，但往往难以做到完全平衡。土石方数量经过合理调配后，还会在全线出现不可避免的借方和弃方（又称废方）。路基土石方的借或弃，首先要合理选择地点，即确定取土坑或弃土堆的位置。选点时要兼顾土质、数量、用地及运输条件等因素，还必须结合沿线区域规划，因地制宜，综合考虑，维护自然平衡，防止水土流失，做到借之有利、弃之无害。借、弃所形成的取土坑或弃土堆，要求尽量结合当地地形，力争得以充分利用，并注意外形规整，弃堆稳固，对高等级公路或位于城郊附近的干线公路，尤其应注意。

平坦地区，如果用土量较少，可以沿路两侧设置取土坑，与路基排水和农田灌溉相结合。路旁取土坑，深度约 1.0m 或更深一些，宽度用土数量和用地允许而定。为防止坑内积水危害路基，当堤顶与坑底高差不足 2.0m 时，在路基坡脚与坑之间需要设宽度不小于 1.0m 的护坡平台，坑底设纵横排水坡及相应设施。

河水淹没地段的桥头引道近旁一般不设取土坑，如设取土坑要距河流中水位边界 10m 以外，并与结构物位置相适应。此类取土坑要求水流畅通，不得长期积水危及路基或构造物的稳定。

路基开挖的废方，应尽量加以利用，如用以加宽路基或加固路堤，填补坑洞或路旁洼地，也可兼顾农田水利或基建等所需，不得任意倾倒。做到变废为用，弃而不乱，并采取必要的防护措施。

废方一般选择路旁低洼地，就近弃堆。当地面横坡缓于1：5时，弃土堆可以设在路堑两侧；地面较陡时，宜设在路基下方。沿河路基爆破后的废石方，往往难以远运，条件许可时可以占用部分河道，但要注意河道压缩后，不致壅水危及上游路基及附近农田等。

路旁弃土堆的设置，要求堆弃整平，顶面具有适当的横坡，并设置排水沟，宽度d与地面土质有关，最小3.0m，最大可按路堑深度加5.0m，即d≥H+5.0m。弃土堆表面应进行绿化设计，以使其尽快恢复生态。

积沙或积雪地区的弃土堆，宜有利于防沙防雪，可设在迎风面一侧，并且保持足够的距离。

2. 护坡道与碎落台

设置护坡道是保证路基边坡稳定的一项措施。护坡道一般设置在路堤坡脚，如取土坑与坡脚之间，高路堤边坡中部的变坡处等。护坡道是沿原地面或边坡坡面纵向做成的有：1、弃土堆，2、三角平台，3、边沟，4、截水沟，5、弃土堆内侧坡脚与路堑坡顶的距离；H——路堑高度定宽度的平台。设置的目的是加宽边坡横向距离，减少边坡平均的坡度，增加边坡整体稳定性。护坡道越宽，越有利于边坡的稳定，但工程量也随之增加。护坡道宽度至少为1.0m，兼顾路基稳定与经济合理，通常护坡道宽度d视边坡高度h而定，h≥3.0m时，d=1.0m；h=3~6m时，d=2.0m；h=6~12m时，d=2~4m。浸水路基的护坡道，可设在浸水线以上的边坡上。

在岩石破碎，土质较差或土夹石地段开挖路堑，由于雨水的作用，路堑边坡经常发生碎落坍方，容易堵塞边沟或阻碍交通。因此，可在边沟外侧或路堑边坡中间预设碎落台，以供风化碎落土石块积聚，养护时再做定期清除。设置碎落台，同时，提高了边坡的稳定性，兼有护坡道和视距台（弯道）的作用。碎落台宽度一般为1.0~1.5m。

3. 堆料坪与错车道

二级以下公路，路面养护所用集料，可以就近选择路旁合适地点堆置备用。也可以在路肩外侧设置堆料坪，其面积可结合地形与材料数量而定，一般每隔50~100m设置一个，其长为5.0~8.0m、宽2.0m左右。

四级公路采用4.5m路基时，应设置错车道。设置错车道道路的路基宽度不得短于6.5m，通常应每隔200~500m设置一处错车道。按规定，错车道的长度不得短于30m，两端各有长为10m的出入过渡段，中间10m供停车用。错车道是单车道路基的一个组成部分，应与路基同时设计与施工。

4. 护栏

护栏是公路附属的安全设施。不封闭的各级公路，当路堤高度大于或等于6m，急弯、陡峻山坡、桥头引道等危险路段应设置护栏。设置护栏路段的路基，一侧应加宽0.5m，以保持设置护栏后的路肩宽度。护栏分墙式和柱式两种：重力式挡土墙、砌石、填石路基应该采用墙式护栏，其他情况可以设置柱式护栏。

墙式护栏的内侧为路肩边缘，外侧距路基边缘应为10cm。墙式护栏应采用浆砌片（块）石或混凝土块砌筑，宽40cm，高出路肩50~60cm，每段长200cm，净间距200cm。墙式护栏应用M7.5水泥砂浆砌筑、抹面，外涂白色。

柱式护栏中心距内侧路肩边缘应为20cm，距外侧路基边缘应为30cm。柱式护栏宜采用钢筋混凝土制作，直径为15~20cm，高出路肩70~80cm，埋深约70cm。柱式护栏中心距在平曲线路段为200cm，直线路段为300cm。柱式护栏应用涂料标出红白相间的条纹或加反光材料。

四、对路基的基本要求

1. 符合规范要求

路基横断面形式及尺寸应符合交通运输部的有关规定。

2. 具有足够的整体稳定性

路基的整体稳定性是指路基整体在车辆及自然因素的作用下，不会产生不允许的变形和破坏。路基是直接在地面上填筑或挖去一部分地面建筑而成的。路基修筑后，改变了原地面的天然平衡状态。因此，为防止路基结构在行车荷载及自然因素作用下发生不允许的变形和破坏，必须因地制宜地采取定措施来保证路基整体结构的稳定性。

3. 具有足够的强度和刚度

路基的强度和刚度是指在行车荷载作用下，路基抵抗破坏与变形的能力。因为行车荷载及路基路面的自重对路基下层和地基产生一定压力，这些压力可使路基产生一定的变形，当其超过某一限度时，将导致路基自身的损坏并直接损坏路面的使用品质。为保证路基在外力作用下，不致产生超过容许范围内的变形，要求路基应具有足够的强度和刚度。

4. 具有足够的水温稳定性

路基的水温稳定性是指路基在水和温度的作用下保持其强度的能力，包括水稳定性和温度稳定性。路基在地面水和地下水的作用下，其强度将会显著降低。特别是季节性冰冻地区，由于水温状况的变化，路基将发生周期性冻融作用，形成冻胀和翻浆，使路基强度急剧下降。为保证路基的正常工作状态，路基应具有足够的水温稳定性。

第三节　公路自然区划与路基土的干湿类型

一、公路自然区划

（一）划分自然区划的目的和原则

1. 划分自然区划的目的：我国各地气候、地形、地貌、水文地质等自然条件相差很大，而这些自然条件与公路建设密切相关。为区分不同地区的自然条件对公路工程影响的差异性，并在路基路面的设计、施工和养护中采取适当的技术措施和采用合适的设计参数，以体现各地公路设计与施工的特点和侧重必须解决的问题，更有利于保证公路的质量和经济合理。

2. 公路自然区划的原则

（1）道路工程特征相似的原则。在同一区划和同样的自然因素下筑路具有相似性，如北方不利季节主要是春融时期，有翻浆病害；南方不利季节在雨季，有冲刷、水毁等病害。

（2）地表气候区划差异性的原则。地表气候是地带性差异与非地带性差异的综合结果。通常，地表气候随着当地纬度的不同而变，如北半球，北方寒冷，南方温暖，这称为地带性差异。除此之外，还与高程的变化有关，即沿垂直方向的变化，如青藏高原，由于海拔高，与纬度相同的其他地区相比，气候更加寒冷。

（3）自然气候因素既有综合作用又有主导作用的原则。自然气候的变化是各种因素综合作用的结果，但其中又有某种因素起着主导作用，如道路冻害是水和热综合作用的结果。但是在南方，只有水而没有寒冷气候的影响，不会有冻害，说明温度起主要作用；西北干旱区与东北潮湿区，同样都有负温度，但前者冻害轻于后者，说明水起主导作用。

（二）我国自然区划的划分

为使自然区划便于在实践中应用，结合我国的地理、气候特点，将全国的公路自然区划分为三个等级。首先将全国划分为多年冻土、季节冻土和全年不冻土三大地带，然后根据水热平衡和地理位置，划分为冻土、湿润、干湿过渡、湿热、潮暖和高寒七个大区。

1. 一级区划：根据不同地理、气候、构造、地貌界限的交错和叠合，将我国分为七个一级区划。即

　　Ⅰ区——北部多年冻土区；

　　Ⅱ区——东部温润季冻区；

　　Ⅲ区——黄土高原干湿过渡区；

Ⅳ区——东南湿热区；

Ⅴ区——西南潮湿区；

Ⅵ区——西北干旱区；

Ⅶ区——青藏高寒区。

2. 二级区划：二级区划仍以气候和地形为主导因素，以潮湿系数 K 为主的一个标志体系（潮湿系数 K 值为年降水量与年蒸发量之比）。根据二级区划的主导因素与标志，在全国七个一级自然区划内又分为 33 个二级区和 19 个副区（亚区），共有 52 个二级自然区。

3. 三级区划：三级区划是二级区划的进一步划分。三级区划的方法有两种：一种是按照地貌、水文和土质类型将二级自然区进一步划分为若干类型单元；另一种是继续以水热、地理和地貌等为标志将二级区划细分为若干区划。各地可根据当地的具体情况选用。

二、路基的干湿类型

路基的强度与稳定性和路基的干湿状况有密切关系，并在很大程度上影响路面结构设计。为此，在进行路基设计时应严格区分其干湿类型。

（一）路基干湿类型及湿度来源

路基按其干湿状态可分为干燥、中湿、潮湿和过湿四类。为保证路基路面结构的稳定性，一般要求路基处于干燥或中湿状态。潮湿和过湿状态的路基必须经过处理后方可铺筑路面。

路基土所处的状态是由土体的含水量或相对含水量决定的，含水量取决于湿度的来源及作用的延续时间。

1. 大气降水：大气降水通过路面、路肩和边坡渗入路基；
2. 地面水：边沟水及排水不良时的地表积水，以毛细水的形式渗入；
3. 地下水：靠近地面的地下水，通过毛细管作用上升到路基内部；
4. 凝结水：在土颗粒空隙中流动水蒸气，遇冷凝结为水。

（二）路基干湿类型划分

1. 根据平均稠度划分

路基干湿类型可以实测不利季节路床顶面以下 800mm 深度内土的平均稠度 W_c。干燥、中湿、潮湿和过湿四类干湿类型以分界稠度 ω_{c1}、ω_{c2} 和 ω_{c3} 来划分。土的平均稠度 ω_c 定义为土的液限 W_L 与土的平均含水量 $\bar{w}$ 之差与土的液限 W_L 与塑限 W_p 之差的比值。即

$$\omega = \frac{\omega_L - \bar{\omega}}{\omega_L - \omega_P}$$

式中：

ω_c——土的平均稠度；

ω_L——土的液限，单位为%；

$\bar{\omega}$——土的平均含水量，单位为%；

ω_p——土的塑限，单位为%。

土的稠度较准确地表示了土的各种形态与湿度的关系，稠度指标综合了土的塑性特性，包含液限与塑限，全面直观地反映了土的硬软程度，物理概念明确。

（1）$\omega_c=1.0$，即$\bar{\omega}=\omega_p$，为半固体与硬塑状的分界值；

（2）$\omega_c=0$，即$\bar{\omega}=\omega_p$，为流塑与流动状的分界值；

（3）$1.0>\omega_c>0$，即$\omega_L>\omega_c>\omega_p$，土处于可塑状态。

以稠度作为路基干湿类型的划分标准是合理的，路面设计应根据路基土的分界稠度确定路基的干湿类型。

在新建公路勘测设计中，确定路基的干湿类型需要现场进行勘查，根据当地稳定的平均天然含水量、液限、塑限计算平均稠度，并考虑填土高度，有无地下水、地表积水的影响，论证地确定路基土的干湿类型。对于原有公路，按不利季节路床顶面以下0.80m深度内土的平均稠度确定。路床面以下0.80m内，每0.10m取土样测定其天然含水量，按以下公式求算：

$$\bar{\omega}C = \frac{\sum_{i=1}^{8}\omega_{ci}}{8}$$

式中：$\bar{\omega}$——土的平均含水量，%；

ω_{ci}——路床顶面以下0.80m内，每0.10m为一层，第i层上的天然含水量，%。

根据$\bar{\omega}C$判别路基的干湿类型，要按照道路路基土的类型，与分界稠度做比较，确定道路所属路基的干湿类型。

2. 根据临界高度划分

对于新建道路，路基尚未建成，无法按上述方法现场勘查路基的湿度状况，可以用路基临界高度作为判别标准。在路基的地下水位或地表积水水位一定的情况下，路基的湿度由下而上逐渐减小。临界高度是指在不利季节，与分界稠度相对应的路床顶面距地下水位或地表积水水位的高度称为路基临界高度H。即

H1相对应于ω_{C1}，为干燥与中湿状态的分界标准；

H2相对应于ω_{C1}，为中湿与潮湿状态的分界标准；

H3相对应于ω_{C1}，为潮湿与过湿状态的分界标准。

在设计新建道路时，如能确定路基临界高度值，则可以以此作为判别标准，与路基设计高度做比较，由此确定路基的干湿类型。

为了保证路基的强度和稳定性不受地下水或地表积水的影响。在设计路基时，要求路基保持干燥或中湿状态，路槽底距地下水或地表积水的距离，要大于或等于干燥、中湿状态所对应的临界高度。

预计到2030年，交通运输需求量、主要通道交通量或将有3~4倍的增长。10.6万公里的普通国道显然已不能支撑和适应，对国道建设进行深入、细致的研究，提出一个覆盖全国所有县的基础性公路网络，将会为社会提供一种更高标准的基本交通出行服务。为此，根据《规划》，今后十几年，中国将投入4.7万亿元，到2030年建成总规模约40万公里的国家公路网。中国普通国道总规模约26.5万公里，将原有规划量翻了一番还多；高速公路约11.8万公里，增加3.3万公里。目前全国仍有900多个县没有国道覆盖，有18个新增的城镇人口在20万以上的城市和29个地级行政中心未实现与国家高速公路相连接。根据《规划》，普通国道将新建8000公里、升级改造10万公里，国家高速公路将新建2.5万~3.3万公里。未来的高速公路网络重心将从东部沿海地区逐渐向中西部地区转移，为GDP总值的稳健上升做出"卓越贡献"。

第二章 土质路基施工

理想的设计要通过施工来实践。对于公路工程来说，路基施工往往是施工组织管理的关键，土质路基的施工在施工方法和操作上具有其特点，本章将对土质路基施工的填筑、开挖以及路基的压实做分析介绍。

第一节 土质路基填筑

一、施工取土

各类公路用土具有不同的工程性质，在选择作为路基的填筑材料时，应根据不同的土类分别采取不同的工程技术措施。

（一）路基土的工程性质

1. 不易风化的石块

不易风化的石块主要包括漂石和卵石，有很高的强度和稳定性，使用场合和施工季节均不受限制，为最好的填筑路基材料，也可用于砌筑边坡。但石块之间要嵌锁密实，以免在自重和行车荷载作用下，石块松动产生沉陷变形。

2. 碎（砾）石土

碎（砾）石土强度能满足要求，内摩擦系数高、水稳定性好、透水性大、施工压实方便，能达到较好的密实程度，为很好的填筑材料。但若细粒含量增多，则透水性和水稳定性就会下降。

3. 沙土

沙土无塑性，透水性和水稳定性均良好，毛细管水上升高度很小，具有较大的内摩擦系数。但沙土黏结性小，易于松散，对流水冲刷和风蚀的抵抗能力很弱，压实困难。

4. 沙性土

沙性土既含有一定数量的粗颗粒，又含有一定数量的细颗粒，级配适宜，强度、稳定性等都能满足要求，是理想的路基填筑材料。

5. 黏性土

黏性土细颗粒含量多，内摩擦系数小而黏聚力大，透水性小而吸水能力强，毛细现象显著，有较大的可塑性，干燥时坚硬而不易挖掘，施工时不易破碎，浸水后强度下降较多，干湿循环因胀缩引起的体积变化较大，过干或过湿时都不便施工。

6. 粉性土

粉性土因含有较多的粉粒，毛细现象严重，干时易被风蚀，浸水后很快湿透，在季节性冰冻地区常引起冻胀和翻浆，水饱和时有振动液化问题。粉性土特别是粉土，属于不良的公路路基用土。

7. 膨胀性重黏土

膨胀性重黏土几乎不透水，黏结力特强，湿时膨胀性和塑性都很大。其工程性质受黏土矿物成分影响较大，黏土矿物主要包括蒙脱土、伊里土、高岭土。蒙脱土其塑性大，吸湿后膨胀强烈，干燥时收缩大，透水性极低，压缩性大，抗剪强度低；高岭土其塑性较低，有较高的抗剪强度和透水性，吸水和膨胀量较小；伊里土性质介于上述两者之间。

8. 易风化的软质岩石（如泥灰岩、硅藻岩等）

易风化的软质岩石浸水后易崩解，强度显著降低，变形量大，一般不宜做路堤填筑材料。总之，路基用土中，沙性土最优，黏性土次之，粉性土属不良材料，容易引起路基病害，膨胀性重黏土，特别是蒙脱土更是不良的路基土。

（二）规范中对路基用土的规定

1. 路堤填料不得使用淤泥、沼泽土、冻土、有机土、含草皮土、生活垃圾、树根和含有腐朽物质的土。采用盐渍土、黄土、膨胀土填筑路堤时，应遵照有关规定执行。

2. 液限大于50%、塑性指数大于26以及含水量超过规定的土，不得直接作为路堤填料。需要应用时，必须采取满足设计要求的技术处理，经检查合格后方可使用。

3. 钢渣、粉煤灰等材料，可用做路堤填料。其他工业废渣在使用前应进行有害物质含量试验，避免有害物质超标，污染环境。

4. 捣碎后的种植土，可用于路堤边坡表层。

5. 路基填料最小强度和最大粒径应符合国家的有关规定。

（三）施工前的复查和试验工作

路基工程需要大量的填料。在施工前的准备工作中，必须对路基工程范围内的地质、水文情况进行调查，并通过取样、试验，确定相关材料如土、工业废渣等的性质和数量，以保证施工所需。其要点如下：

1. 施工技术人员应根据设计文件提供的资料，对取自挖方、借土场、料场的路堤填料进行复查和取料试验。如设计文件提供的料场不足时，应自行勘察寻找，以保证施工用料可靠和数量充足。

2. 挖方借土场和料场用作填料的土应进行下列项目的试验：

（1）液限、塑限、塑性指数、天然稠度或液性指数试验；

（2）颗粒大小分析试验；

（3）含水量试验；

（4）密度试验；

（5）相对密度试验；

（6）击实试验；

（7）强度试验（CBR值）；

（8）一级公路、高速公路应做有机质含量试验及易溶盐含量试验。

（四）铺筑试验路段

高等级公路以及在特殊地区或采用新技术、新工艺、新材料进行路基施工时，应采用不同的施工方案做试验路段，从中选出路基施工的最佳方案指导全线施工试验路段的位置应选在地质条件、断面形式均具有代表性的路段，长度不宜小于100m。通过试验路段施工应包括以下七点内容：

1. 填料试验、检测报告等；

2. 压实工艺主要参数有机械组合、压实机械规格、松铺厚度、碾压遍数、碾压速度，最佳含水量及碾压时含水量允许偏差等；

3. 过程质量控制方法、指标；

4. 质量评价指标、标准；

5. 优化后的施工组织方案及工艺；

6. 原始记录、过程记录；

7. 对施工设计图的修改建议等。

二、路基填筑施工

（一）路基填筑施工的主要工序

路基填筑施工的主要工序有料场选择、基底处理、填筑和碾压。

1. 料场选择

填筑路堤的材料以采用强度高，水稳定性好，压缩变形小，便于施工压实以及运距短的土、石材料为宜。在选择填料时，一方面要考虑料源和经济性，另一方面要顾及填料的性质是否合适。

2. 基底处理

路堤基底的处理是保证路堤稳定、坚固极为重要的措施。在路堤填筑前进行基底处理,能使填土与原来的表土密切结合;能使初期填土作业顺利进行;能使地基保持稳定,增加承载能力;能防止因草皮、树根腐烂而引起的路堤沉陷。

(1)伐树、除根及表层土处理

1)路基用地范围内的树木、灌木丛等均应在施工前砍伐或移植清理,砍伐的树木应移置于路基用地之外,进行妥善处理。高速公路、一级公路和填方高度小于1m的其他公路应将路基范围内的树根全部挖除并将坑穴填平夯实,填方高度大于1m的其他公路允许保留树根但根部露出地面不得超过20cm。

2)路堤基底为耕地土或松土时,应先清除种植有机土,平整后按规定要求压实。清除深度应达到设计要求(一般不小于1cm),平整后按规定要求压实。在深耕地段,必要时,应将松土翻挖,土块打碎,然后回填、整平压实。

3)路堤基底原土强度不符合要求时,应进行换填,对深度不小于30cm的路堤基底,应子分层压实到规定要求。

①高速公路、一级公路、二级公路路堤基底压实度不小于90%。

②当路堤填土高度小于路面和路床厚度(80cm)时,应将地基表层土进行超挖并分层回填压实,其处置深不应小于重型汽车荷载作用的工作区深度,基底的压实度不宜小于路床的压实度标准。

4)路堤修筑范围内,原地面的坑、洞、墓穴等,应用原地的土或沙性土回填,并按规定进行压实。路堤经过水田、池塘、洼地时,应根据具体情况采用排水疏干、换填水稳性好的土、抛石挤淤等处理措施,确保路堤基底具有足够的稳定性。

(2)坡面基底的处理

填方路堤。如基底为坡面时,填方路堤在荷载作用下,极易失稳而沿坡面产生滑移,因此,在施工前必须对基底坡面处理后方能填筑。

1)地面横坡在1:10~1:5之间时,需清除坡面上的树、草、杂物,将翻松的表层土压实后即可保证坡面的稳定。

2)地面横坡枯1:5~1:2.5之间时,对于土质地基,原地面应挖成台阶,台阶宽度不小于1m,台阶顶面做成向堤内倾斜2%~4%的坡度;对于石质地基,应将岩面凿成台阶后再分层填土夯实修筑路堤。

3)地面横坡陡于1:2.5时,应做特殊处理,以防止路堤沿基底滑动。常用的处理措施有:

①经验算下滑力不大时,先清除基底表面的薄层松散土,再挖宽1~2m台阶,坡脚附近的台阶宜再宽一些,通常为2~3m;

②经验算下滑力较大或边坡下部填筑土层太薄时,先将基底分段挖成不陡于1:2.5的缓坡,再在缓坡上挖宽1~2m的台阶,最下一级台阶宜更宽一些。

3. 填筑方法

路堤填筑必须考虑不同的土质，从原地面逐层填筑，并分层压实，每层厚度随压实方法而定。

（1）填筑方式

1）水平分层填筑。填筑时按横断面全宽分成水平层次，逐层向上填筑。

2）纵坡分层填筑适用于推土机或铲运机从路堑取土填筑，运距较短的路堤，依纵坡方向分层、逐层推土填筑。

3）竖向填筑。从路基一端按各横断面的全部高度，逐步推进填筑，适用于无法自下而上，分层填土的陡坡、断岩或泥沼地区。

4）混合填筑。当高等级公路路线穿过深谷或陡坡，尤其是要求上部的压实度标准较高时，施工时下层采用横向填筑，上层采用水平分层填筑。

（2）沿横断面一侧填筑的方法

旧路拓宽改造需加宽路堤时，所用填土应与原路堤用土尽量接近或为透水性好的土，并将原边坡挖成向内倾斜的台阶，分层填筑，碾压到规定的密实度，严禁将薄层新填土贴在原边坡的表面。

高速公路和一级公路在横坡陡峻地段的半填半挖路基，必须在山坡上从填方坡脚向下挖成向内倾斜的台阶，台阶宽度不应小于1m。其中沿横断面挖方的一侧，在行车范围之内的宽度不足一个行车道宽度时，应挖够一个行车道宽度，其上路床深度范围之内的原地面土应予以挖除换填，并按上路床填方的要求施工。

填方分几个作业段施工，两段交接处不在同一时间填筑时，则先填地段应按1:1坡度分层留台阶；若两个地段同时填，则应分层相互交叠衔接，其搭接长度不得小于2m。

（3）不同土质混填时的方法

对于不同性质的土混合填筑时，应视土的透水能力大小，进行分层填筑压实，并采用有利于排水和路基稳定的方式。一般应遵循以下三点原则：

1）以透水性较小的土填筑路堤下层时，其顶面应做成4%的双向横坡；与用于填筑上层时，不应覆盖在由透水性较好的土所填筑的路堤边坡上。

2）不同性质的土应分别填筑，不得混填，每种填料层累计总厚度不宜小于0.5m。

3）凡不因潮湿及冻融而变更其体积的优良土应填在上层，强度较小的土应填在下层。

（4）桥涵及其他构造物处的填筑施工要点

为了保证桥涵及其他构造物（主要指桥台背、锥坡、挡土墙墙背等）的稳定和使用要求，必须认真细致地进行填筑施工。其要点如下：

1）必须坚持在隐蔽工程经监理工程师检查验收认可后，才能进行回填土施工。

2）桥涵及其他构造物处的填料，除设计文件另有规定外，应采用沙类土或透水性土。当采用非透水性土时，应在土中增加外掺剂，如石灰、水泥等，待改良其性质后再使用。

3）台背填土顺路线方向长度要求：顶部为距翼墙尾端不小于台高2m，底部距基础内缘不小于2m，拱桥台背填土长度不应小于台高的3~4倍，涵洞填土长度每侧不应小于2

倍孔径长度。

4）做好压实工作。结构物处的填土应分层填筑，每层松铺厚度不宜超过 15cm。

5）在回填压实施工中，应做到对称回填压实，并保持结构物完好无损。压路机压不到的地方，应使用小型机动夯具夯实并达到规定要求的密实度。

6）施工中应安排桥台背后填土与锥坡填土同时进行，以取得更佳效果。

7）涵洞缺口填土，应在两侧对称均匀分层回填压实。如使用机械回填，则涵台胸腔部分及检查井周围应先用小型压实机具压实后，方可用大机械进行大面积回填。

8）涵洞顶面填土压实厚度大于 50cm 后，方可允许重型机械和汽车通过。

9）挡土墙填料宜选用砂石土或沙类土。墙趾部分的基坑，应注意及时回填，并做成向外倾斜的横坡。填土过程中，应采取相应的措施，防止水害。回填结束后，挡土墙顶部应及时封闭。

10）严格控制和保证达到压实标准。

高速公路与一级公路的桥台和涵身背后、涵洞顶部的填土压实度标准，从填方基底或涵洞顶部至路床顶面均为 96%，其他公路为 95%。

(5) 土方路基填筑压实要求

路基必须分层填筑压实，使每层都表面平整，路拱合适，排水良好。

路堤填筑压实的施工要点如下：

1）填筑路堤宜采用水平分层填筑法施工。

2）严格控制碾压最佳含水量。用透水性不良的土填筑路堤时，应控制其含水量在最佳含水量 ±2% 之内。

3）严格控制松铺厚度。采用机械压实时，高速公路和一级公路的分层最大松铺厚度不应超过 30cm；其他公路，按土质类别、压实机具功能、碾压遍数等，经过试验确定，最大松铺厚度不宜超过 50cm。填筑至路床顶面最后一层的最小压实厚度，不应小于 8cm。

4）严格控制路堤几何尺寸和坡度。路堤填土宽度每侧应比设计宽度宽出 30~50m，压实宽度不得小于设计宽度，压实合格后，最后削坡。

5）掌握压实方法。

6）加强土的含水量检查。

4. 碾压

碾压是路基填筑工程的一个关键工序，有效地压实路基填筑土，才能保证路基工程的施工质量。

（二）路基施工的要求

路基施工时，除了要满足设计的断面尺寸及纵段高程之外，还要满足强度、整体稳定性和水温稳定性的基本要求。

路基施工有以下几点要求：

1. 保证足够的整体稳定性；

2. 强度符合设计要求；

3. 保持足够的水温稳定性；

4. 必须精心施工，确保工程质量；

5. 推行机械化施工；

6. 合理用地，保护生态环境；

7. 严格执行路基施工技术规范。

（三）路基施工的方法

路基土石方的施工作业主要包括开挖、运输、铺填、压实和修整等工作。有时为了提高挖土的效率，还要先松土。路基施工的基本方法可分为以下四种：

1. 人工和半机械化施工

人工和半机械化施工是主要依靠人力，使用手工工具和简易的机械设备进行施工的方法。适用于缺乏机械的地方道路工地和工程量小而分散的零星工程点，以及某些辅助性工作。

2. 水力机械施工

水力机械施工是运用水泵、水枪等水力机械，喷射强力水流，把土冲散并泵送到指定地点沉积的方法。这种方法可用来挖掘比较松散的土层和进行软土地基加固的钻孔工作，但施工现场需有充足的水源和电源。

3. 爆破施工

爆破施工是开挖岩石路堑的基本方法。如采用钻岩机钻孔，爆破后机械清理运碴，便是岩石路基机械化施工的必备条件。除岩石路堑开挖之外，爆破法还可用于冻土（硬土）、泥沼等特殊路基施工和开采石料；定向爆破可将路基挖方直接移做填方。

4. 机械化施工

机械化施工是采用推土机、铲运机、平地机、挖掘机、压路机及松土机等机械，经过选配，共同协调地进行施工的方法。它可以极大地提高劳动生产率，显著地加快施工进度，并有效地保证了工程质量。

上述施工方法的选择，应根据工程性质条件、施工期限、现有施工条件等因素确定，同时要综合考虑、因地制宜和综合配套地使用各种方法。

第二节　土质路堑开挖

路堑施工就是按设计要求进行挖掘，并将挖掘的土石方运到路堤地段作为填料，或者运往弃土堆处；有时也可经加工，作为自采材料，用于结构物或其他工程部位。

路堑由天然地层构成，开挖后边坡易发生变形和破坏，路基的病害常发生在路堑挖方地段，如滑坡、崩塌、落石、路基翻浆等。因此，施工方法与路堑边坡的稳定有密切关系，开挖方式应根据路堑的深度、纵向长度以及地形、地质、土石方调配情况和机械设备条件等因素确定，以加快施工进度，提高工作效率。

一、土方路堑的开挖方式

土方路堑开挖根据路堑深度和纵向长度，开挖方式可分为全断面横挖法、纵挖法及混合式开挖法三种。

1. 全断面横挖法

路堑整个横断面的宽度和深度从一端或两端逐渐向前开挖的方式称为全断面横挖法。全断面横挖法可分为一层横向全宽挖掘法和多层横向全宽挖掘法两种方式。

一层横向全宽挖掘法适用于开挖深而短的路堑；

多层横向全宽挖掘法适用于开挖深而短的路堑。

2. 纵挖法

纵挖法是沿道路的纵向进行挖掘。纵挖法分为分层纵挖法、通道纵挖法及分段纵挖法三种方式。

（1）分层纵挖法

分层纵挖法适用于较长的路堑开挖。当路堑长度不超过100m，开挖深度不大于3m，地面较陡时，宜采用推土机作业，当地面横坡较缓时，表面宜横向铲土，下层的土宜纵向推运。

（2）通道纵挖法

沿路堑纵向挖掘一通道，然后将通道向两侧拓宽，上层通道拓宽至路堑边坡后，再开挖下层通道，按此方向进行土方挖掘和外运的流水作业，直至开挖到挖方路基顶面标高，称为通道纵挖法。通道可作为机械通行、运输土方车辆的道路。

（3）分段纵挖法

分段纵挖法适用于路堑过长，弃土运距过远的傍山路堑或一侧堑壁不厚的路堑开挖，同时还应满足其中间段有弃土场、土方调配计划有多余的挖方废弃的条件。

（4）混合式开挖法

将横挖法与通道纵挖法混合使用称为混合式开挖法。适用于纵向长度和挖深都很大的路堑，先将路堑纵向挖通后，然后沿横向坡面挖掘，以增加开挖坡面。每个坡面应设一个机械班组进行作业。

二、路堑开挖施工应注意的问题

1. 路堑排水

不论采用何种方法开挖，均应保证开挖过程中及竣工后能顺利排水。为此，施工时应先在适当的位置开挖截水沟，并设置排水沟，以排除地面水和地下水。施工中要在路堑的路线方向保持一定的纵坡。

2. 废方处理

路堑挖出的土方，除利用外，多余的土方应按设计的弃土堆进行废弃，不得妨碍路基的排水和路堑边坡的稳定。同时，弃土应尽可能地用于改地造田，美化环境。

3. 注意边坡的稳定并及时设置必要的支护工程

路堑开挖时，不论开挖工程量和开挖深度的大小，均应按照横断面自上而下进行，随挖随修边坡，不得乱挖、超挖。防止因开挖不当导致坍方，尤其在地质不良地段，应分段开挖，分段支护。

4. 禁止超挖

土方路基开挖施工过程中，应经常测量高程和路基宽度，通过计算检验其是否符合设计要求。

三、冬、雨期开挖路堑注意事项

1. 雨期开挖

（1）土质路堑开挖前，在路堑边坡坡顶2m以外开挖截水沟并接通出水口。

（2）开挖土质路堑宜分层开挖，每挖一层均应设置排水纵横坡。挖方边坡不宜一次挖到设计标高，应沿坡面留30cm厚，待雨期过后整修到设计坡度；以挖做填的挖方应随挖、随运、随填。

（3）土质路堑挖至设计标高以上30~50cm时应停止开挖，并在两侧挖排水沟，待雨期过后再挖到路床设计标高并压实。

（4）土的强度低于规定值时应按设计要求进行处理。

（5）雨期开挖岩石路堑，炮眼应尽量水平设置。边坡应按设计坡度自上而下，层层刷坡，坡度应符合设计要求。

2. 冬期开挖

（1）当破开冻土层挖到未冻土后，应连续作业、分层开挖，中间停顿时间较长时，应在表面覆雪保温，避免重复被冻。

（2）挖方边坡不应一次挖到设计线，应预留30cm厚台阶，待到正常施工季节再削去预留台阶，整理达到设计边坡。

（3）路堑挖至路床面以上1m时，挖好临时排水沟后，应停止开挖并在表面覆以雪或松土，待到正常施工时，再挖去其余部分。

（4）冬期开挖路堑必须从上向下开挖，严禁从下向上掏空挖"神仙土"。

（5）每日开工时选挖向阳处，气温回升后再挖背阴处，如开挖时遇地下水源，应及时挖沟排水。

（6）冬期施工开挖路堑的弃土要远离路堑边坡坡顶堆放。弃土堆高度般不应大于3m，弃土堆坡脚到路堑边坡顶的距离一般不得小于3m，深路堑或松软地带应保持5m以上。弃土堆应摊开整平，严禁把弃土堆于路堑边坡顶上。

四、路基施工机械和设备

路基施工机械包括土石方机械和压实机械两大类，本章仅做土石方机械的介绍，压实机械将在路基压实部分叙述。

土石方机械包括推土机、装载机、挖掘机、铲运机、平地机和凿岩机等几个重要机种，是路基施工中用途最广泛的施工机械，它们担负着土石方的铲装、填挖、运输和整平等作业。

（一）推土机

1. 性能

推土机是以工业拖拉机或专用牵引车为主机，前端装有推土装置，依靠主机的顶推力，对土石方或散装物料进行切削或搬运的铲土运输机械。推土机担负着切削、推运、开挖、填积、回填、平整、疏松和压实等多种土石方作业，其特点是作业面小，机动灵活，转移方便，短距离运土方便。因此，推土机是路基施工中必不可少的机械设备。

2. 适用性

推土机一般适用于季节性较强、工程量集中、施工条件较差的工程环境，主要用于50~100m的短距离作业，如路基修筑、基坑开挖、平整场地、清除树根、堆积散料等，并可为铲运机与挖装机械松土和助铲及牵引各种拖式工作装置等作业。

履带式推土机，适用于Ⅳ级以下土的推运。当推运Ⅳ级和Ⅳ级以上土和冻土时，须先进行松土。

3. 作业方式

推土机的基本作业是铲土、运土、卸土和空回四个过程，通常有以下五种作业方法：

（1）波浪式铲土法；

（2）接力式推土法；

（3）槽式推土法；

（4）并列推土法；

（5）下坡推土法。

（二）铲运机

铲运机主要用于较大运距的土方工程，如填筑路堤、开挖路堑和大面积的平整场地等。由于它本身能完成铲装、运输和卸铺作业，并兼有一定的压实和平整能力，所以在公路工程施工中，铲运机是一种使用范围很广的土方施工机械。

1. 适用性

铲运机的适用范围主要取决于土质特性、运距、机器本身的性能和道路状况。

2. 作业方式

（1）一次铲装法；

（2）交替铲装法（跨铲法）；

（3）波浪式铲土法；

（4）下坡铲土法。

（三）平地机

平地机是一种装有以铲土刮刀为主，配备其他多种可换作业装置，进行刮平和整形连续作业的工程机械。平地机的铲土刮刀较推土机的推土铲刀灵活，它能连续进行改变刮刀的平面角和倾斜角，使刮刀向一侧伸出的作业；也可以连续进行铲土、运土及大面积平地、挖沟和刮边坡的作业等。

1. 适用性

平地机的主要用途：从路线两侧取土，填筑不高于1cm的路堤；修整路堤的横断面；旁刷边坡；开挖路槽和边沟，以及大面积平整等。此外，还可以在路基上拌和、摊铺路肩上的杂草及冬季道路除雪等。

2. 作业方式

（1）选择铲土角；

（2）选择刮刀回转角；

（3）斜行作业；

（4）刮刀侧移；

（5）刮刀移土作业。

（四）挖掘机

挖掘机在公路工程中是用于挖掘和装载土、石、沙砾和散粒材料的重要施工机械。挖掘机是土石方工程施工的主要机械，特点是效率高、产量大，但机动性较差。在公路工程施工中，遇到开挖量较大的路堑和填筑高路堤等大工程量时，用挖掘机配合运输车辆组织施工是比较合理的选择。

（五）装载机

装载机是一种工作效率较高的铲土运输机械，它兼有推土机和挖掘机两者的工作能力，可以进行铲掘、推运、整平、装卸和牵引等多种作业。

装载机的适应范围主要取决于使用场所、土石料特性和工作环境，选用时应注意以下三点：

1. 装载机的经济合理运距；
2. 装载机的斗容与汽车车厢容积的匹配；
3. 充分发挥装载机的效率。

第三节　土质路堤压实

一、路基压实的意义

路基施工破坏了土体的天然状态，使结构松散的颗粒需要重新组合。为使路基具有足够的强度与稳定性，必须予以压实，以提高其密实程度。所以路基的压实工作是路基施工过程中一个重要工序，亦是提高路基强度与稳定性的根本技术措施之一。

土是三相体，土粒为骨架，颗粒之间的孔隙为水分和气体所占据。压实的目的在于使土粒重新组合，彼此挤紧，孔隙缩小，让土的单位质量提高，形成密实整体，最终使其强度增加、稳定性提高。

通过大量的试验和工程实践证明，土基压实后，路基的塑性变形、渗透系数、毛细水作用及隔温性能等，均有明显改善。

二、影响压实效果的因素

对于细粒土的路基，影响压实效果的因素有内因和外因两方面。内因指土质和湿度，外因指压实功能(如机械性能、压实时间与速度、土层厚度)及压实时自然和人为的其他外界因素等。下面就影响压实效果的主要因素进行讨论。

1. 含水量对压实的影响

(1) 含水量 w 与密实度(以干容重/度量)的关系。

(2) 含水量 w 与土的水稳定性的关系。

2. 土质对压实效果的影响

土质对压实效果的影响很大。通过对比可见,沙性土的压实效果优于黏性土。其机理在于土粒越细,比表面积大的土粒,表面水膜所需的含水量越多,加之黏土中含有亲水性较高胶体物质,使得沙性土的压实效果优于黏性土。另外,至于沙土的颗粒组,由于呈松散状态,水分极易散失,对其最佳含水量的概念就没有多大的实际意义。

3. 压实功能对压实的影响

压实功能(指压实工具的质量、碾压次数或锤落高度、作用时间等)对压实效果的影响,是除含水量之外的另一个重要因素。据此规律,工程实践中可以增加压实功能(选用重碾、增加次数或延长作用时间等),以提高路基强度或降低最佳含水量。但必须指出,用增加压实功能的办法提高土基强度的效果,要有一定限度。压实功能增加到一定限度以后,效果提高变得缓慢,在经济效益和施工组织上,不是很合理。甚至当压实功能过大时,一是会破坏土基结构,二是相对应含水量减少而使水稳定性变差,其压实效果会适得其反。相比之下,严格控制最佳含水量,要比增加压实功能收效大得多。当含水量不足,洒水有困难时,适当增大压实功能可以收效,如果土的含水量过大,此时若增大压实功能,必将出现"弹簧现象",即压实效果很差,造成返工浪费。

4. 压实厚度对压实效果的影响

相同压实条件下(土质、含水量与压实功能不变)实测土层不同深度的密实度(γ 或压实度)可得知,密实度随深度递减,表层 5cm 最高。不同压实工具的有效压实深度有所差异,根据压实工具类型、土质及土基压实的基本要求,路基分层压实的厚度有具体的规定数值。一般情况下,夯实不宜超过 20cm;12~15t 光面压路机,不宜超过 25cm;振动压路机或夯击机,宜以 50cm 为限。实际施工时的压实厚度应通过现场试验确定合适的摊铺厚度。

三、压路机的选择与操作

1. 压实机具的选择

压实机具的选择及合理的操作,是影响土基压实效果的另一综合因素。土基压实机具的类型较多,大致分为碾压式、夯实式和振动式三大类型。碾压式(又称静力碾压式),包括光面碾(普通的两轮和三轮压路机)、羊足碾和气胎碾等几种;夯击式中除人工使用的石碾、大夯外,机动设备中有夯锤、夯板、风动夯及蛙式夯机等;振动式中有振动器、振动压路机等。此外,运土工具中的汽车、拖拉机及土方机械等,也可用于路基压实。

不同压实机具，适用于不同土质及土层厚度等条件，这些都是选用何种压实机具的主要依据。正常条件下，对于沙性土的压实效果，振动式较好，夯击式次之，碾压式较差；对于黏性土，则宜选用碾压式或夯击式，振动式较差甚至无效。不同压实机具，在最佳含水量条件下，适应于一定的最佳压实厚度及通常的压实遍数。

2. 压实要求

实践经验证明，土基压实时，在机具类型、土层厚度及行程遍数已经选定的条件下，压实操作时宜先轻后重、先慢后快、先边缘后中间（超高路段等需要时，则从内侧至外侧宜先低后高）。压实时，相邻两次的轨迹应重叠轮宽的1/3，保持压实均匀，不漏压，对于压不到的边角，应辅以人力或小型机具夯实。压实全过程中，经常检查含水量和密实度，以达到符合规定压实度的要求。

四、土基压实标准及其应用

1. 土基压实标准

土基的压实程度用压实度来表示，以此来检查和控制压实的质量。压实度是指土被压实后的干密度与该土的标准最大干密度之比，用百分率表示。标准最大干密度是指按照标准击实试验法得到的土在最佳含水量时的干密度。土被压实后的干密度是指在施工条件下，获取施工压实后的土样通过试验所得到的干密度。压实度按以下公式计算：

$$K = \frac{\rho_d}{\rho_0} \times 100\%$$

式中：

K——压实度，%；

ρ_d——压实土的干密度，kg/m³；

ρ_0——压实土的标准最大干密度，kg/m³。

2. 压实标准规定的应用

（1）土质路基压实度应符合国家相关的规定。

（2）填石路堤，包括分层填筑路堤和倾填爆破石块的路堤，不能用土质路基的压实度来判定路基的密实程度。

五、碾压工序的控制

1. 确定不同种类填土最大干密度和最佳含水量

用于填筑路基的沿线土石材料，性质往往有较大的变化。在路基填筑施工前，必须对主要取土场采集代表性土样，进行土工试验，用规定方法求得各个土场土样的最大干密度和最佳含水量，以便指导路基土的施工。

2. 检查控制填土含水量

由于含水量是影响路基土压实效果的主要因素，故需检测欲填入路基中的土的含水量。用透水性不良的土做填料时，应控制其含水量在最佳含水量 ±2% 之间。

3. 分层填筑、分层压实

土压实层的密度随深度递减，表面 5cm 的密度最高。填土分层的压实厚度和压实遍数与压实机械类型、土的种类和压实度要求有关，应通过试验路来确定。一般认为，对于细粒土，用 12~25t 光轮压路机时压实厚度不超过 20cm；用 22~25t 振动压路机时（包括激振力），压实厚度不超过 50cm。

4. 全宽填筑、全宽碾压

填筑路基时，应要求从基底开始在路基全宽范围内分层向上填土和碾压，尤其应注意路堤的边缘部分。路堤边缘往往得不到压实，处于松散状态，雨后容易滑坍，故两侧可采取宽填 30~50 cm，压实工作完成后在按设计宽度和坡度予以刷齐整平。

5. 压实原则

掌握"先轻后重、先慢后快"进行压实的原则组织压实，轨迹重叠达到规定要求。一般应在 30~50cm 以上。

6. 加强测试检验及压实控制

检查压实度一般采取灌砂法、环刀法、蜡封法、水带法和核子密度仪法。环刀法适用于细粒土，灌砂法适用于各类土。采用核子仪时应先进行标定，并于灌砂法做对比试验，找出相关的压实度修正系数。尤其是当填土种类发生变化时，必须重新标定，方能保证压实度检测的准确可靠性。

填筑路基时，应分层碾压并分层检查压实，并要求填土层压实度达到要求后方填筑上一层填土，只有分层控制填土的压实度，才能保证全深度范围内的压实质量。

当工地实测压实度小于要求压实度时，应检查填土含水量，当填土含水量 w 与最佳含水量 w0 之差在 ±2% 以内，说明压实功能不够，应增加碾压遍数，如果压实遍数超过 10 遍仍达不到压实度要求，继续增加遍数效果很小，不如减少压实层厚度；当 w>w0 时，将填土挖松，晾干至 w0 再重新碾压；当 w<w0 时，应洒水使填土含水量接近 w0 再进行碾压。

许多地段都是由于路基压实度未能达到规定要求而导致路基出现翻浆、沉陷等破坏现象。因此，路基填筑时压实度必须达到规定的要求，这样才能保证路基的稳定性。

第三章　石质路基施工

本章主要针对石质路基工程的施工展开探讨，以期能为有关方面的需要提供有益的参考和借鉴。

第一节　填石路堤施工

一、填石路堤的施工方法

填石路堤的施工方法如下：

1. 填石路堤的基底处理同填土路堤。

2. 高速公路、一级公路和铺设高级路面的其他等级公路的填石路堤均应分层填筑，分层压实。二级及二级以下且铺设低级路面的公路在陡峻山坡段施工特别困难或需大量爆破以挖做填时，可采用倾填方式将石料填筑于路堤下部，但倾填路堤在路床底面下不小于1.0m范围内仍应分层填筑压实。

3. 填石路堤的压实度检验包括分层填筑岩块及倾填爆破石块填筑的路堤，在规定深度范围内，以12t以上振动压路机进行压实试验，当压实层顶面稳定，不再下沉（无轨迹）时，可判为密实状态。

二、填石路堤的施工要求

1. 填料的选择

填石路堤是指用粒径大于40mm，含量超过70%的石料填筑的路堤。

膨胀性岩石、易溶性岩石、崩解性岩石和盐化岩石等均不应用于路堤填筑。用强风化石料软质岩石填筑路堤时，应按土质路堤施工规定先检验其CBR值是否符合要求，CBR

值不符合要求时不得使用，符合使用要求时应按土质筑堤的技术要求施工。

填石路堤的石料强度不应小于15MPa（用于护坡的不应小于20MPa）。填石路堤石料最大粒径不宜超过层厚的2/3。

2. 施工中应将石块逐层水平填筑

分层松铺厚度：高速公路及一级公路不宜大于0.5m，其他公路不宜大于1.0m。大面向下摆放平稳，紧密靠拢，所有缝隙填以小石块或石屑。高速公路及一级公路填石路堤路床顶面以下50cm范围内应填筑符合路床要求的土并分层压实，填料最大粒径不得大于10cm；其他公路填石路堤路床顶面以下30cm范围内宜填筑符合路床要求的土并压实，填料最大粒径不应大于15cm。超粒径石料应进行破碎，使填料颗粒符合要求。

3. 填石路堤压实

填石路堤应使用重型振动压路机分层洒水压实，压实时继续用小石块或石屑填缝，直到压实层顶面稳定、不再下沉且无轨迹、石块紧密、表面平整为止。

4. 路堤边坡坡脚码砌

填石路基倾填前，路堤边坡坡脚应用粒径大于30cm的硬质石料码砌。

当无设计规定时，填石路堤高度小于或等于6m时，其码砌厚度大于1m；大于6m时，不应小于2m。

软质岩石的高破碎率会产生很多的小粒径填料，因此，采用软质岩石作为填石料时，其结构主要是骨架密实型。坚硬岩石的破碎率则比较低，因而会产生较少的小粒径石料，所以，如果采用坚硬岩石作为填石料的话，其结构主要是骨架孔隙型。

填料的粒径如果比较大的话，其均匀性就会比较差，离析现象经常会发生，使路基各个不同部位的密实度存在较大的差别。石料在被压实的过程中，其原有的料径组成结构就会发生改变，从而对路基的强度密度及稳定性等都会带来重大的影响。

造成路基施工工程性质出现大差别的原因不是填料石料的粒径，而是填料石料不同的强度、岩性、吸水性和抗风化程度。

填石料的压缩模量比普通填料的压缩模量要大得多，正是因为填石料这种强大的压缩模量性质，才不易致填石路堤发生变形。使用压缩模量大的填石料的填石路堤不但变形比较小，而且变形的速度比较快，正常情况下，填石路堤大部分的变形在施工期内就可以完成。

大颗粒填料在长时间的使用中容易被风化，一旦风化，其稳定性能就会大大下降。

为了确保路堤的压实度，需要严格控制好填料的粒径。由于用于填石路堤的石料的强度一定要超过15Mpa。所以，在施工前，就要选择符合要求的石料，主要是在隧道弃渣或路基挖方中选择。但实际上只要是中硬岩以上的岩石都可以选作填石料。所以，为了获取满足填筑要求的石料，在开挖石方时就要进行爆破试验，以确保获得合适的爆破参数，这样就可以保证爆破的粒径。石块的粒径一旦过大的话，还要再进行人工解小。

在进行路堤填石时，由于填料的粒径比较大，而且填层的厚度也要确保在40~50cm之间，因此，要选择合适的机械设备，即大吨位振动压路机。

在完成施工放样工作后,就要对表土、树根的草皮、腐殖土等进行清除。地基要经过压实且压实度要保证在85%以上,方可再进行填筑。为了确保基底的压实度满足路床的标准,填土的高度一定要大于路床的厚度。

基底松散层的厚度如果超过了30cm,就要进行重新翻挖然后再分层进行回填并压实,严重增加工作量和工程成本。

在填筑前第一步就是进行人工分层的码砌边坡。码砌边坡必须要符合以下八个要求:第一,垂直于路基中线的方向的每填层码砌的宽度要大于0.5m;第二,在码砌时,边坡的每侧都要加宽0.2m;第三,选择较大的石块进行码砌,并要呈直角梯形,并确保大面要朝下,为了确保放实摆稳,还要用碎石填塞密实好空隙,保证坡面的平顺;第四,砌好边坡码后,要进行相关的工艺实验,以此来确定层厚,然后再进行堆卸石料数量的计算并进行标点,最后根据路堤的横断面进行纵向分层的填筑,而填筑时要按照先两侧后中央和先低后高的原则来进行;第五,在对半填半挖的地段和需要帮填石质的路堤的施工中,要先开挖好台阶并且要进行分层搭接,在形成一个整体后,才能进行填筑工序施工;第六,为了保证质量,每层填料的石质要尽量一致,而且要确保好级配要求和厚度,如果填料石块的层厚大于2/3的,还要进行再解小工作;第七,在纵向的方位上每隔20m就设置一个断面,而且每个断面要布设3~5个的测点;第八,利用大型的推土机来整平初压卸下的石质填料,各石块间要大致平衡,局部不平的地段利用细颗粒料进行人工填平。

第一,石料运输路线的安排和专人指挥协调的工作要在填筑分层时就要完成,而且必须要根据先低后高的原则来进行。第二,如果是自动卸载车上的填石料时,只需要在粗平石料的表面上直接卸载堆放就可以了;但如果是自卸车需要进行倒退卸料,则要根据从路基两侧边坡码砌的接合部位再到中间堆料摊铺的顺序原则;而边坡码砌和路基结合部位的填料则要选用细料或小碎块石;为了确保石料间的初步密实,要用功率比较大的推土机进行向前推平。第三,石料级配差且粒径大的,要先进行大粒径块石料的摊铺并利用人工进行分开摆平放稳,在摆放的过程中要尽可能地贴近底层,然后再利用小石块找平;用推土机来摊平每层表面嵌缝隙中的石屑和碎石土;大粒径的块石不能在同一位置上进行重叠摆放;为了避免石块,尤其是大石块的过度集中和控制内部密实度出现有空洞的情况,就要随时随地检查相关还填料的均匀性。第四,对不符合设计要求的粒径要进行二次破解,或者利用挖掘机来分拣出可用于边坡码砌的大粒径石块;如果个别段落的表面存在比较少细料时,还需要铺撒一层山皮土或细石料,并以人工嵌缝的方式来填满大粒料间的缝隙;如果路段存在有明显的空洞空隙,还要进行细料的补充,这样才可以确保摊铺层面可以相对平顺。第五,在推土机以及人工的作用下,石料摊铺得到初步的平整,但要保证其石料摊铺的厚度在40cm内,并对初平后的石料表面再填筑大约10cm的山皮土;每层路基顶面的标高要现场进行测量,通过平地机对横坡进行找平并调整,使其平整度要符合规范的要求,这样也有利于压路机下一步的碾压夯实效果。

在摊铺整平好填石路堤并确保其表面的平整度满足要求后,再进行压实的工序。由于填石路堤的稳定性与填石料的密实程度有密切的关系，因此，为保证填石路堤的压实效果，需要选择大吨位的振动型压路机进行碾压，主要作用有以下几种：第一，碾压产生的振动会使颗粒的填石料处于运动的状态，这样可以减少填料内部的空隙，提高填料的压实度；第二，剪应力和压应力之所以会在填料中出存在，主要是因为振动压路机会产生地静重及压力波，会形成一定的动力，有效地减少颗粒间的阻力，并使路堤得到有效的压实。

公路工程项目进度管理是以现代科学管理原理作为其理论基础的，主要有动态控制原理、系统控制原理、信息反馈原理、弹性原理、封闭循环原理、网络计划技术原理。

1. 进度计划的提交

（1）总体性进度计划。

在中标通知书发出后合同规定的时间内，承包人应向监理工程师书面提交以下文件：一份详细和格式符合要求的工程总体进度计划及必要的各项关键工程的进度计划；一份有关全部支付的现金流动估算；一份有关施工方案和施工方法的总说明（通过施工组织设计提出）。

（2）阶段性进度计划。

在将要开工前或在开工后合理的时间内，承包人应向监理工程师提交以下文件：年、月（季）度进度计划及现金流动估算和分项（或分部）工程的进度计划。

2. 进度计划的审查要点

施工单位编制完进度计划后，应重点从以下几方面对进度计划进行审查：

（1）工期和时间安排的合理性。

1）施工总工期的安排应符合合同工期；

2）各施工阶段或单位工程（包括分部、分项工程）的施工顺序和时间安排与材料和设备的进场计划相协调；

3）易受冰冻、低温、炎热、雨季等气候影响的工程应安排在适宜的时间，并应采取有效的预防和保护措施；

4）对动员、清场、假日及天气影响的时间，应充分考虑并留有余地。

（2）施工准备的可靠性。

1）所需主要材料和设备的运送日期已有保证；

2）主要骨干人员及施工队伍的进场日期已经落实；

3）施工测量、材料检查及标准试验的工作已经安排；

4）驻地建设、进场道路及供电、供水等已经解决或已有可靠的解决方案。

（3）计划目标与施工能力的适应性

1）各阶段或单位工程计划完成的工程量及投资额应与设备和人力实际状况相适应；

2）各项施工方案和施工方法应与施工经验和技术水平相适应；

3）关键线路上的施工力量安排应与非关键线路上的施工力量安排相适应。

3.进度计划的调整

当公路工程项目施工实际进度影响到后续工作时，总工期需要对进度计划进行调整时，通常采用以下两种方法：

（1）改变某些工作间的逻辑关系。

当工程项目实施中产生的进度偏差影响到总工期，且有关工作的逻辑关系允许改变时，可以改变关键工作或超过计划工期的原非关键工作（新关键工作）之间的逻辑关系，达到缩短工期的目的。例如，将顺序进行的工作改为平行作业、搭接作业及分段组织流水作业等，都可以有效地缩短工期。

但要注意压缩过程中关键线路会随着压缩关键工作而改变或增加条数。

（2）缩短某些工作的持续时间。

这种方法是不改变工程项目中各项工作之间的逻辑关系，而是通过采取增加资源投入、提高劳动效率等措施来缩短某些工作的持续时间，使工程进度加快，以保证按计划工期完成该工程项目。这些被压缩持续时间的工作是位于关键线路上的（关键工作，还包括原来是非关键工作但是现在已经超过计划工期的新关键工作）。同时，这些工作又是其持续时间可被压缩的工作。这种调整方法通常可以在网络图上直接进行。

第二节　石质路堑施工

石质路堑开挖最有效的方法是爆破。爆破可以大大提高施工效率，缩短工期，节约劳力，提高公路的使用质量。

1.炸药性能和药包量

（1）炸药性能

一般在坚石中，宜采用粉碎力大的炸药，如 TNT、胶质炸药等；在次坚石、软石、裂缝大而多的岩石中，以及在松动爆破中，宜采用爆炸力较大而粉碎力较小的炸药；开采料石时，宜采用爆炸力和粉碎力都较小的炸药，如黑火药。

（2）药包量

药包量的多少，必须根据具体条件和爆破目的来决定。

2.地形条件

地形不同，其爆破的特征及效果也不同。地形越陡，炸药用量越省。地形倾斜时，爆破土方的岩石因振动而松裂，在自重的作用下脱离岩体而坍塌，从而扩大爆破漏斗的范围，增加爆破方量。此外，炮位的临空面的数目对爆破效果的影响也很大，临空面越多，爆破效果就越好。

3. 地质条件

当岩石的密度大、强度高、整体性好时，单位耗药量较高，对爆破后的边坡稳定有利，适宜采用大爆破；反之，密度小、力学强度低，节理、层理发达，较易破碎，单位用药量低，不宜采用大爆破。

一、石质路堑的开挖方式

石质路堑的开挖通常采用爆破法，有条件时宜采用松土法，局部情况可采用破碎法。

施工时，采用的爆破方法，要根据石方的集中程度，地质、地形条件及路基断面形状等具体条件而定。爆破的主要方法有钢钎炮、深孔爆破、葫芦炮、光面爆破与预裂爆破和抛坍爆破。

（一）常用爆破方法的特点及优点

1. 综合爆破

综合爆破是根据石方的集中程度，地质、地形条件，公路路基断面的形状，综合配套使用的一种比较先进的爆破方法。

综合爆破一般包括小炮和洞室炮两大类。小炮主要包括钢钎炮、深孔爆破等钻孔爆破；洞室炮主要包括药壶炮和猫洞炮，洞室炮则随药包性质、断面形状和地形的变化而不同。用药量1t以上为大炮，1t以下为中小炮。

（1）裸露药包法

裸露药包法是将药包置于被炸物体表面或经清理的岩缝中，药包表面用草皮或稀泥覆盖，然后进行爆破。

（2）钢钎炮（炮眼法）

在路基工程中，钢钎炮（炮眼法）是指炮眼直径小于70mm和深度小于5m的爆破方法。一般情况下，单独使用钢钎炮爆破石方是不经济的，原因有以下两点。

1）炮眼直径小、炮眼浅、用药少，一般最多装药为眼深的1/3~1/2，每次爆破的石方量不大（通常不超过10m），并全靠人工清除，所以工效较低；

2）不利于爆破能量的利用，但比较灵活，因而它又是一种不可缺少的炮型，在综合爆破中是一种改造地形、为其他炮型服务的铺炮型。

（3）药壶炮（葫芦炮）

药壶法是指在深2.5~3.0m以上的炮眼底部用小量炸药经一次或多次烘膛，使底成葫芦形，将炸药集中装入药壶中进行爆破。葫芦炮炮眼较深，适用于均匀致密黏土（硬土）、次坚石、坚石。对于炮眼深度小于2.5m，节理发育的软石，地下水较多或雨季施工时，不宜采用。

（4）猫洞炮

猫洞炮是炮洞直径为0.2~0.5m，洞穴成水平或略有倾斜（台眼），深度小于5m，将药集中于炮洞中进行爆破的一种方法。它适用于硬土、胶结良好的石古河床、冰渍层、软石和节理发育的次坚石，坚石可用其间的裂隙修成导洞或药室，这种炮型对大孤石、独岩包等爆破效果更佳。

（5）爆破（洞室）的施工方法

大爆破是采用导洞和药室装药，用药量在1000kg以上的爆破方法。

2. 光面爆破

光面爆破是在开挖限界的周边，适当排列一定间隔的炮孔。在有侧向临空面的情况下，用控制抵抗线和药量的方法进行爆破，使之形成一个光滑平整的边坡。

3. 预裂爆破

预裂爆破是在开挖限界处按适当间隔排列炮孔，在没有侧向临空面和最小抵抗线的情况下，用控制药量的方法，预先炸出一条裂缝，使拟爆体与山体分开，作为隔振减振带，消除或减弱开挖限界以外山体或建筑物的地震破坏作用。

4. 抛掷爆破

抛掷爆破运用于自然地面坡度大于30°，地形地质条件复杂的半填半挖路堑。

5. 微差爆破

相邻两药包或前后排药包以毫秒的时间间隔（一般为15~75ms）依次起爆，称为微差爆破，亦称毫秒爆破。多发一次爆破最好采用毫秒雷管。多排孔微差爆破是浅孔深孔爆破发展的方向。

6. 定向爆破

在公路工程中用于以借为填或以挖做填地段，特别是在深挖高填相间、工程量大的鸡爪形地区，宜采用定向爆破。

（二）松土法

为了有利于开挖边坡的稳定和保护既有建筑物的安全，大马力推土机不断普及，用松土法开挖岩石被越来越广泛地采用。

二、爆破开挖路堑的施工方法

1. 恢复路基中线，放出边线，钉牢边桩。
2. 根据地形、地质及挖深选择适宜的开挖爆破方法，制订爆破方案，做出爆破施工组织设计，报有关部门审批。
3. 用推土机整修施工便道，清理表层覆盖土及危石。
4. 在地面上准确放出炮眼（井）位置，竖立标牌，标明孔（井）号、深度、装药量。
5. 用推土机配合爆破，创造临空面，使最小抵抗线面向回填方向。
6. 炮眼在布置整体爆破时采用"梅花形"或"方格形"，预裂爆破时采用"一字形"，洞室爆破根据设计确定药包的位置和药量。

7. 在居民区及地质不良可能引起坍塌后遗症的路段，原则上不采用大中型洞室爆破。在石方集中的深挖路堑采用洞室爆破时，应认真设计分集药包位置和装药量，精确测算爆破漏斗，防止超爆、少爆或振松边坡，留下后患。

8. 爆破施工要严格控制飞石距离，采取切实可行的措施，确保人员和建筑物的安全，如采用毫秒微差爆破技术。

9. 控制爆破也可以采用分段毫秒爆破方法。

10. 为确保边坡爆破质量，可采用预裂爆破技术、光面爆破技术和排眼毫秒爆破技术。同时，配合选择合理的爆破参数，减少冲击波影响，降低石料大块率，以减少二次破碎，有利于装运和填方。

11. 装药前要布好警戒，选择好通行道路，认真检查炮孔、洞室，吹净残渣，排除积水，做好爆破器材的防水保护工作。雨季或有地下水时，可考虑采用乳化防水炸药。

12. 装药分单层、分层装药，预裂装药及洞室内集中装药。炮眼装药后用木杆捣实，填塞黏土；洞室装药时，将预先加好的起爆体放在药包中心位置，周围填以硝酸安全炸药，用砂黏土填塞，填塞时要注意保护起爆线路。

13. 认真设计，严密布设起爆网络，防止发生短路及二响重叠现象。

14. 顺利起爆，并清除边坡危石后，用推土机清出道路，用推土机、铲运机纵向出土填方；运距较远时，用挖掘机械装土，自卸汽车运输。

15. 随时注意控制开挖断面，切勿超爆，适时清理整修边坡和暴露的孤石。

三、石质路基质量控制

（一）一般规定

1. 土方路基和石方路基的实测项目技术指标的规定值或允许偏差按高速公路、一级公路和其他公路（指二级及二级以下公路）两档设定，其中土方路基压实度按高速公路和一级公路，二级公路，三、四级公路三档设定。

2. 本节规定的实测项目的检查频率，如果检查路段以延米计时，则为双车道公路每一检查段内的最低检查频率（多车道公路必须按车道数与双车道之比，相应增加检查数量）。

3. 路基压实度须分层检测，并符合规范规定。路基其他检查项目均在路基顶面进行检查测定。

4. 路肩工程可作为路面工程的一个分项工程进行检查评定。

5. 服务区停车场、收费广场的土方工程压实标准可按土方路基要求进行监控。

（二）石方路基的基本要求

1. 石质路堑的开挖宜采用光面爆破法。爆破后应及时清理险石、松石，确保边坡安全、稳定。

2. 修筑填石路堤时应进行地表清理，逐层水平填筑石块，摆放平稳、码砌边部。填筑层厚度及石块尺寸应符合设计和施工规范规定，填石空隙用石碴、石屑嵌压稳定。上、下路床填料和石料最大尺寸应符合规范规定。采用振动压路机分层碾压，压至填筑层顶面石块稳定，18t 以上压路机振压两遍无明显标高差异。

3. 路基表面应整修平整。

4. 外观鉴定

（1）上边坡不得有松石。不符合要求时，每处减 1~2 分。

（2）路基边线直顺，曲线圆滑。不符合要求时，单向累计长度每 50m 减 1~2 分。

第四章 水泥混凝土路面施工

水泥混凝土路面是指以水泥混凝土板和基（垫）层所组成的路面，亦称为刚性路面。水泥混凝土路面以其抗压、抗弯、抗磨损、高稳定性等诸多优势，在各级路面上得到广泛应用，在我国高等级公路中水泥混凝土路面日渐增多，加上近年来农村公路建设中普遍采用水泥混凝土路面，使得水泥混凝土路面科学化、规范化施工成为广大公路建设者关注的问题。本节将对公路水泥混凝土路面施工的工艺流程进行探讨。

第一节 小型机具施工

一、施工前的准备工作

施工准备工作是路面施工质量保证体系的重要一环，是保证路面施工顺利进行、按期完成任务的关键。因此，必须做好施工前的一切准备工作。

1. 编制施工组织设计

施工单位根据设计文件及施工条件，确定施工方案，编制施工组织设计，包括施工工艺、材料使用计划、劳动计划、机械选型及使用计划、临时设施、现场组织管理计划、安全措施等。

2. 选择混凝土拌和场地

拌和场地的选择既要考虑交通便利、运距最短，又要考虑水电供应方便，并且有足够的场地堆放材料和搭建办公生活用房、工棚仓库和消防等设施，一般情况下宜设置在施工路段的中部。

3. 进行材料试验和混凝土配合比检验及调整

按公路等级的要求及工地的具体情况在现场建立工地试验室，并依据相应的试验规程和检测频率对混凝土面层所用的各种原材料进行检验，并根据检验结果调整混凝土的配合比和改善施工工艺。

4. 基层检查与整修

基层检查是检查基层的宽度、高程、横坡、弯沉、平整度等是否符合要求。在混凝土摊铺施工前，应清理基层表面，并充分洒水湿润，以防混凝土底部的水分被干燥基层吸去，使混凝土变得疏松以致产生细小裂缝。

5. 模板安装

常用模板有木模和钢模。模板应平直，装、拆方便，而且加载后挠度小。同时，其高度应与混凝土板厚相同。高速公路、一级公路混凝土路面施工，应采用钢模板，这样不仅保证工程质量，而且可多次重复使用。钢模板可用4~5 mm厚钢板冲压制作，或用3~4 mm厚钢板与边宽40~50mm的角（槽）钢组合构成。模板一般长为3m，接头处应设置牢固的拼装配件。

安装模板前，应根据设计图纸定出路面中心及路面边缘线，模板顶面应与路面设计高程一致。如果因基层局部低洼而造成模板下出现空隙，可在空隙处模板两边填入砂浆等材料。

模板两侧用铁钎打入基层以固定位置，接头处拼装应牢固紧密。安装完毕后，应再检查一次模板相接处的高差和模板内侧是否有错位和不平整等情况，高度差大于3mm或有错位和不平整的模板应拆掉重新安装。确认安装合格的模板内侧表面应刷涂隔离剂，以利于拆模。两侧模板安装就位后，应横跨路面拉线，用直尺检测拉线至基层表面的距离是否满足混凝土板厚的要求，基层局部高出部分应予以铲除。

模板准确定位是保证混凝土路面质量的重要因素，因此，施工时必须经常检查、严格控制。

二、混凝土的制备和运输

1. 混凝土的制备

混凝土混合料应采用机械搅拌，搅拌站的位置应根据施工和运输工具选定，容量由工程量大小和施工进度确定。进行拌和时，掌握好混凝土施工配合比，严格控制加水量，应根据砂、石料的实测含水量，调整拌和时的实际用水量。混合料组成材料的计量允许误差为：水泥为±1%，粗、细骨料为±5%，水为±1%，外加剂为±2%。搅拌机装料顺序宜为砂、水泥、碎（砾）石，进料后，边搅拌边加水。每锅混合料的搅拌时间取决于搅拌机的性能和混合料的和易性，一般为1.5~3.0min，干硬性混凝土搅拌时间略长一点，一般为2.0~4.0min。常用的搅拌机械有自落式搅拌机和强制式搅拌机两大类。

自落式搅拌机是通过搅拌鼓的转动，将混合料提到一定高度后自由落下而达到拌和目的。

其优点是能耗小、价格较便宜，但仅适用于搅拌塑性和半塑性混凝土。而对于干硬性混凝土，由于坍落度小，粒料容易黏附在叶片上，难以拌和均匀，出料也有困难，因而不宜使用。强制式搅拌机是在固定不动的搅拌筒内，用高速旋转的多组搅拌叶片对筒内材料进行强制搅拌。它的优点是搅拌时间短、效率高、操纵系统灵活、卸料干净；缺点是需要较大的动力，搅拌叶片及搅拌筒磨耗大。它适用于搅拌干硬性混凝土及细粒料混凝土。强制式搅拌机从构造上分为立轴式和卧轴式，立轴强制式搅拌机由于其叶片、衬板磨耗量较大，其使用受到一定限制。双卧轴强制式搅拌机拌和均匀，轴和叶片更换方便、省电，有较好的技术经济指标。因此，水泥混凝土搅拌设备选型时应尽可能选用双卧轴强制式搅拌机。

2. 混凝土的运输

混合料宜采用翻斗车或自卸车运输，当运距较远时，宜采用水泥混凝土搅拌运输车运输。混合料从搅拌机出料后，运至铺筑施工现场进行摊铺、振捣、整平，直至铺筑结束的允许时间，可根据水泥初凝时间及施工气温确定。装运混合料，应防漏浆和离析，夏季和冬季施工，应有遮盖或保温设备，卸料高度不宜超过1.5m。若出现明显离析时，铺筑时应重新拌匀。

三、混凝土的摊铺和振捣

1. 混凝土的摊铺

摊铺混凝土前，应对模板的位置、高度、支承情况及拉杆的放置再进行一次全面检查，确认满足要求后，即可进行混凝土的摊铺。

混凝土混合料由运输车辆直接卸在基层上。卸料时应不使混合料离析，且应尽可能将其卸成几小堆，以便于摊铺。如发现离析现象，应在铺筑时用铁锹拌均匀，但严禁第二次加水。

混凝土板厚度不大于24 cm时可一次摊铺；大于24 cm时宜分两次摊铺，下层厚度宜为总厚的3/5。摊铺时应考虑混凝土振捣后的下落高度，而预留一定厚度，松铺厚度通过现场试验确定，一般为设计厚度的1.1~1.15倍。

人工用铁锹摊铺时，应采用"扣锹"的方法，严禁抛掷和搂耙，以防止混合料离析。

2. 钢筋设置

当混凝土板中根据设计要求需要设置钢筋时，应配合摊铺工作一起进行。

安放单层钢筋网片时，应在其底部先摊铺一层混凝土，其高度按钢筋网片设计位置预加一定的下落高度。待钢筋网片就位后，再继续浇注混凝土。

安放双层钢筋网时，对厚度不大于25 cm的板，上、下两层钢筋网可事先用架立筋扎成骨架后，一次安放就位；厚度大于25cm的，按单层网片的方法，上、下两层网片分两次安放。

钢筋网的接头应搭接，其搭接长度应为一个网格或者20 cm，搭接处应用细铁丝绑扎。

安放角隅钢筋时，先在角隅处摊铺一层混凝土拌和物，摊铺厚度应按钢筋设计位置预加一定的下落度，角隅钢筋就位后，用混凝土拌和物压住；安放边缘钢筋时，先沿边缘铺筑一条混凝土拌和物，拍实至钢筋位置，然后放置边缘钢筋，在钢筋两端弯起，用混凝土拌和物压住。

3. 混凝土的振捣

混合料摊铺后，应迅速振捣密实。常用振捣器有插入式振捣器、平板式振捣器和振动梁。对厚度不大于24 cm的铺层，应先用插入式振捣器对边角及安置钢筋的部位依顺序振捣，再用不小于2.2kW的平板式振捣器纵横交错全面振捣。振捣器在每一位置振捣的持续时间以混合料停止下沉、不再冒气泡并泛出水泥浆为准，不宜过振，一般为10~15s。水灰比小于0.45时，用平板振捣器，不宜少于30s；用插入式振捣器时，不宜少于20s。

平板式振捣器作业完成后，用带有振动器且底面平直的振动梁进一步拖拉振实并初步整平。振动梁移动的速度要缓慢均匀，一般以每分钟1.2~1.5m为宜，不允许中途停留。拖振过程中，多余的混合料随着振动梁的拖移而刮去。低陷处应及时人工填补，填补时应用较细的混合料，但严禁用纯砂浆。再用直径为130~150 mm的平直无缝钢管滚杠进一步滚揉表面，使表面进一步提浆并整平。滚杠既可滚拉又可平推提浆赶浆，使混凝土表面均匀保持5~6 mm的砂浆层，以有利于密封和做面。

对采用两次摊铺的混凝土板（厚度>24cm），应特别注意上层混凝土拌和料的振捣必须在下层拌和料初凝之前完成。另外，在振捣上层拌和料时，插入式振捣器应插入下层拌和料5 cm，以使两层很好地融合。

在整个振捣过程中，要随时注意检查模板，如发现问题，应及时处理。

四、接缝施工

接缝是混凝土路面施工的难点，接缝施工质量的好坏直接影响到混凝土路面的使用寿命和行车的舒适性，因此，需特别认真加以对待。

1. 胀缝施工

胀缝应与混凝土路面中心线垂直，缝壁垂直于板面，宽度均匀一致，缝中不得有黏浆或坚硬杂物，相邻板的胀缝应设在同一横断面上。胀缝传力杆的准确定位是胀缝施工成败的关键。为了保证传力杆位置的正确（平行于混凝土板面及路面中心线，其误差不得大于5 mm），可采用两种固定方式：顶头木模固定法和支架固定法。

（1）顶头木模固定法，适用于混凝土一天施工终了时设置的胀缝。传力杆长度的一半穿过端头挡板，固定于外侧定位模板中。在混凝土拌和料浇筑前先检查传力杆位置，浇筑时先摊铺下层拌和料，用插入式振捣器振实，并在校正传力杆位置后，再浇筑上层拌和料。第二天浇筑邻板前，拆去顶头木模，并及时设置胀缝板、木制嵌条和传力杆套管等。

（2）支架固定法，适用于混凝土板连续浇筑过程中设置的胀缝。传力杆长度的一半穿过胀缝板和端头挡板，并用钢筋支架固定就位。浇筑时先检查传力杆的位置，再在胀缝两侧摊铺混凝土拌和料至板面，振捣密实后，抽出端头挡板，空隙部分填补混凝土拌和料，并用插入式振捣器振实，然后整平。

胀缝中嵌条的尺寸及拆除时间应把握好。嵌条尺寸应比设计接缝稍宽些、稍低些，最好做成上宽下窄的楔形，以便拔出。嵌条拆除时间以混凝土初凝前、泌水后为宜。嵌条取出后，再将缝槽抹平整。

2. 横向缩缝施工

横向缩缝一般采用锯切缝或压入缝。与压入缝相比，切缝法做出的缩缝质量较好，接缝处质量均匀。因此，缩缝施工应尽量采用切缝法。为防止切缝不及时可能出现的早期裂缝，也可每隔几条切缝做一条压缝。

（1）切缝

混凝土结硬后应及时用金刚石或碳化硅锯片切缝。切缝时间的早晚一定要控制好，切得过早（混凝土抗压强度<10 MPa）粗骨料容易从砂浆中脱落，不能切出整齐的缝；切得过迟，不但造成切缝困难，增加切缝刀片的消耗，而且会使因混凝土的温度下降和水分减少而产生的收缩因板较长而受到阻碍，导致收缩应力超出其抗拉强度在非预定位置出现不规则的早期裂缝。施工中较多采用"温度-小时"法来控制切缝的合适时间。即混凝土浇筑到切割开始的间隔小时与气温的乘积一般控制在250~300"温度-小时"。当然，这只是一种粗略估算的方法。最佳切缝时间除与施工温度有关外，还与混凝土质量，特别是集料的质量、水泥类型及水灰比等因素有关，施工时应通过试切后确定。切缝可采用一次切割成型或两次切割成型的方法。一次切割成型的槽口窄而深，进行嵌缝料施工不易填实，且当缝隙因板的伸缩稍有变化时，嵌缝料便会在深度上出现较大的起落，引起嵌缝料被挤出槽口外或槽口内嵌缝料不足；两次切割成型即先用薄锯片进行深锯切再用厚锯片做浅锯切以加宽上部槽口。这种两次切割成型的槽口工作性能较前种好。

（2）压缝

为防止出现早期裂缝，每隔3~4条切缝做一条压缝。压缝的做法是：当混凝土拌和料做面后，立即用振动压缝刀压缝，当压至规定深度后提出压缝刀，用原浆修平缝槽，然后放入铁制或木制的嵌条，再次修平缝槽，待混凝土初凝前、泌水后，取出嵌条，便形成了缝槽。施工时应特别小心，尽量避免接缝两边的混凝土结构受到扰动，并应保证两边平整。如难以做到这点，缩缝也可仅由切缝形成，但应保证不出现早期裂缝。

缩缝传力杆的安装一般采用支架固定法，传力杆长度的一半再加5 cm范围内涂上沥青，保证其在混凝土中自由滑动。

3. 纵缝施工

纵缝一般为平缝加拉杆形式。纵缝施工应符合设计规定的构造，保持顺直、美观。拉杆可采用三种方式设置。

（1）根据拉杆的位置在模板上留孔，立模后在浇筑混凝土之前将拉杆穿在孔内。但拆模时较为费事。

（2）事先将拉杆弯成直角，沿模板按设计位置放置，并将其一半浇筑在板内。在浇筑临板时再将拉杆扳直。当拉杆较粗时，采用此方法易损坏拉杆相接处的混凝土。

（3）采用带螺丝的拉杆。一半拉杆用支架固定在基层上，然后浇筑混凝土，摊铺相邻板前将另一半带螺丝接头的拉杆接上。施工时应注意使拉杆螺纹接头端面紧靠板侧面，且套节的螺纹部分不能进入混凝土或砂浆（用黄油等材料封填），以免另一半拉杆无法接上。此方法在日本广泛使用，效果良好。

4. 施工缝

施工缝宜设于胀缝或缩缝处，多车道路面及民航机场道面的施工缝应避免设在同一横断面上。传力杆一半锚固于混凝土中，另一半应涂上沥青，传力杆必须平行于板面、垂直于缝壁。

5. 灌注嵌缝料

混凝土养护期满即可灌注嵌缝料，嵌缝料必须清洁、干燥，并与缝壁黏附紧密、不渗水，灌注高度一般比板面低 2 mm 左右。当使用加热施工型嵌缝料时，应加热到规定的温度并搅匀，采用灌缝机或灌缝枪灌缝；气温较低时应用喷灯加热缝壁，使嵌缝料与缝壁结合良好。

第二节　轨模式摊铺机施工

一、施工准备

1. 材料准备及性能检验

混凝土路面施工前的准备工作包括材料准备及质量检验、混合料配合比检验与调整、基层的检验与整修、施工放样及机械准备等。

根据混凝土路面施工进度计划，施工前应分批备好所需的各种材料，并在使用前进行核对、调整，各种材料应符合规定的质量要求。新出厂的水泥应至少存放一周后方可使用。路面在浇筑前必须对混凝土拌和物的工作性进行检验并做必要的调整。

2. 基层检查与整修

混凝土路面施工前，应对混凝土路面板下的基层进行强度、密实度及几何尺寸等方面的质量检验。基层质量检查项目及其标准应符合基层施工规范要求。基层宽度应比混凝土路面板宽 30~35 cm 或与路基同宽。

3. 施工放样

施工放样是用轨模式摊铺机施工混凝土路面的重要准备工作。首先，根据设计图纸恢复路中心线和混凝土路面边线，在中心线上每隔20m设一中心桩，同时，布设曲线主点桩及纵坡变坡点、路面板胀缝等施工控制点，并在路边设置相应的边桩，重要的中心桩要进行拴桩。每隔100m左右应设置一临时水准点，以便复核路面高程。由于混凝土路面一旦浇筑成功就很难拆除，因此，测量放样必须经常复核，在浇捣过程中也要进行复核，做到勤测、勤核、勤纠偏，确保混凝土路面的平面位置和高程符合设计要求。

4. 机械配套及检修

混凝土路面施工前必须做好各种机械的检修工作，以便施工时能正常运行。用轨道式摊铺机施工时，主要工序是混凝土的拌和与摊铺成型，因此，应把混凝土摊铺机作为第一主导机械，搅拌机作为第二主导机械。选择的主导机械应能满足施工质量和工程进度要求。搅拌机与摊铺机应互相匹配，拌和质量、拌和能力、技术可靠性及工作效率等应能满足要求。在保证主导机械发挥最大效率的前提下，选用的配套机械要尽可能少。

二、拌和与运输

1. 混凝土拌和

确保混凝土拌和质量的关键是选用质量符合规定的原材料、搅拌机技术性能满足要求、拌和时配合比计量准确。采用轨道式摊铺机施工时，拌和设备应附有可自动准确计量的供料系统；无此条件时，可采用集料箱加地磅的方法进行计量。各种组成材料的计量精度应不超过下列范围：水和水泥 ±1%，粗、细集料 ±3%，外加剂 ±2%。拌和过程中加入外加剂时，外加剂应单独计量。最佳拌和时间应控制为：立轴式强制搅拌机为90~180s；双卧轴强制式搅拌机为60~90s，最短拌和时间不低于低限，最长拌和时间不超过高限的3倍。

2. 混凝土运输

通常采用自卸汽车运输混凝土拌和物，拌和物坍落度大于5cm时应采用搅拌车运输。从开始拌和到浇筑的时间应满足下列要求：用自卸汽车运输时，不得超过1h；用搅拌车运输时，不得超过1.5 h。若运输时间超过上述时间限制或在夏季浇筑时，拌和过程中应加入适量的缓凝剂。运输时间过长，混凝土拌和物的水分蒸发和离析现象会增加，因此，应尽量缩短混凝土拌和物的运输时间，并采取措施防止水分损失和混合料离析。拌和物运到摊铺现场后倾卸于摊铺机的卸料机内，摊铺机卸料机械有侧向和纵向两种。侧向卸料机在路面摊铺范围外操作，自卸汽车不进入路面铺摊范围卸料，设有供卸料机和汽车行驶的通道；纵向卸料机在摊铺范围内操作，自卸汽车后退供料，施工时不能像侧向卸料机那样在基层上预先安设传力杆。

三、摊铺与振捣

1. 轨道与模板（轨模）安装

轨道式摊铺机的整套机械在轨道上前后移动，并以轨道为基准控制路面的高程。摊铺机的轨道与模板同时进行安装，固定在模板上，然后统一调整定位，形成的轨模既是路面边模又是摊铺机的行走轨道。

模板应能承受机组的质量，横向要有足够的刚度。轨模数量应根据施工进度配备并能满足周转要求，连续施工时至少需配备三个全工作量的轨模。

轨模安装时必须精确控制高程，做到轨模平直、接头平顺，否则将影响路面的外观质量和摊铺机的行驶性能。

2. 摊铺

轨道式摊铺机有刮板式、箱式或螺旋式三种类型，摊铺时将卸在基层上或摊铺箱内的混凝土拌和物按摊铺厚度均匀地充满轨模范围内。刮板式摊铺机本身能在轨道上前后自由移动，刮板旋转时将卸在基层上的混凝土拌和物向任意方向摊铺。这种摊铺机质量轻、容易操作、易于掌握、使用较普遍，但摊铺能力较小。箱式摊铺机摊铺时，先将混凝土拌和物通过卸料机一次卸在钢制料箱内，摊铺机向前行驶时料箱内的混合料摊铺于基层上，通过料箱横向移动按松铺厚度准确、均匀地刮平拌和物。螺旋式摊铺机由可以正向和反向旋转的螺旋布料器将拌和物摊平，螺旋布料器的刮板能准确调整高度。螺旋式摊铺机的摊铺质量优于前两种摊铺机，摊铺能力较大。

摊铺过程中应严格控制混凝土拌和物的松铺厚度，确保混凝土路面的厚度和高程符合设计要求。一般应通过试铺来确定拌和物的松铺厚度。

3. 振捣

摊铺机摊铺时，振捣机跟在摊铺机后面对拌和物做进一步的整平和捣实。在振捣梁前方设置一道长度与铺筑宽度相同的复平梁，用于纠正摊铺机初平的缺陷并使松铺的拌和物在全宽范围内达到正确的高度，复平梁的工作质量对振捣密实度和路面平整度影响很大。复平梁后面是一道弧面振动梁，以表面平板式振动将振动力传到全宽范围内。拌和物的坍落度及集料粒径对振动效果有很大影响，拌和物的坍落度通常不大于 2.5 cm，集料最大粒径应控制在 40 mm 以下。当混凝土拌和物的坍落度小于 2cm 时，应采用插入式振捣器对路面板的边部进行振捣，以达到应有的密实度和均匀性。振捣机械的工作行走速度一般应控制在 0.8 m/min，但随拌和物坍落度的增减可适当变化，混凝土拌和物坍落度较小时可适当放慢速度。

根据施工项目的施工环境，合理选择项目经理部的设置地点，确定设备停放场地、仓库、办公室和宿舍等的平面布置，项目部设置地点应因地制宜、方便施工，尽量减少对环境的影响。

住址选址由项目经理负责在进场前组织相关人员按照施工、安全和管理的要求进行调查，确定选址方案。

驻地选址宜靠近工程项目现场的中间位置，应远离地质自然灾害区域，用地合法，周围无塌方、滑坡、落石、泥石流、洪涝等自然灾害隐患，无高频、高压电源及油、气、化工等其他污染源，满足安全、环保、水保的要求，交通、通信便利，水电设施齐全。

离集中爆破区500 m以外，不得占用独立大桥下部空间、河道、互通匝道区及规划的取弃土场。

1. 可自建或租用沿线合适的单位或民用房屋，但应坚固、安全、实用、美观，并满足工作和生活需求，自建房还应安装拆卸方便且满足环保要求。

2. 自建房屋最低标准为活动板房，建设宜选用阻燃材料，搭建不宜超过两层。每组最多不超过10栋，组与组之间的距离不小于8 m，栋与栋之间的距离不小于4m，房间净高不低于2.6m。驻地办公区、生活区应采用集中供暖设施，严禁电力取暖。

3. 宜为独立式庭院，四周设有围墙，有固定出入口。有条件的，可在出入口设置保卫人员。

4. 办公、生活用房建筑面积和场地面积应满足办公和生活需要。

5. 办公区、生活区及车辆、机具停放区等布局应科学合理，分区管理，合理规划人车路线，尽可能减少不同区域间的互相干扰。区内场地及主要道路应做硬化处理，排水设施完善，庭院适当绿化，环境优美整洁，生活、生产污水和垃圾集中收集处理。

在适当位置设置临时室外消防水池和消防沙池，配置相应的消防安全标志和消防安全器材，并经常检查、维护、保养。

驻地内应设置消防通道，并保证消防车道的畅通，禁止在消防车道上堆物、堆料或挤占消防通道。

生活污水排放应进行规划设计，设置多级沉淀池，通过沉淀过滤达到排放标准。厕所污水应通过集中独立管道进入化粪池，封闭处理。

驻地内应设置一个大型垃圾堆积池，容积不小于3m×2m×1.5m，将各种垃圾集中存放，定期按环保要求处置。

驻地内应设有必要的防雷设施，在条件允许的情况下驻地应设置报警装置和监控设施。

1. 场地选址

（1）以方便、合理、安全、经济及满足工期为原则，结合施工合同段所属预制梁板的尺寸、数量、架设要求以及运输条件等情况进行综合选址。

（2）应满足用地合法，周围无塌方、滑坡、落石、泥石流、洪涝等地质灾害；无高频、高压电源及其他污染源；离集中爆破区500 m以外；不得占用规划的取、弃土场。

（3）原则上不宜设在主线征地范围内。若确实存在用地困难等特殊情况需要将预制场设于主线征地范围内时，应报项目建设单位审批。

2. 场地布置形式

预制场的布置取决于现场的面积、地形、工程规模、安装方法、工期及机械设备情况等，条件不同，布置方法差异较大。

（1）路基外预制场

该类型预制场比较普遍，制梁区使用大型龙门吊，在路基一侧设置预制场；如一般工程量不大，则不采用龙门吊，但要有足够存放全部梁片的场地，必要时可在路基两侧制梁。

（2）路基上预制场

在其他地方设置预制场困难时可将预制场设在路基上，要求桥头引道上有较长的平坡，并且路基比较宽（一般应大于24m）。但此类预制场严重影响引道路基的施工。布置时首先要留足桥头架桥机的拼装场地，并偏向一侧设置梁区，以便留出道路。

（3）桥下预制场

在很多跨河桥下都有高出河面的场地，但这些场地都比较窄长，不可能像河滩上那样大面积布置预制场。可根据场地情况，沿一孔垂直线路方向顺桥平行布置。

（4）桥上预制场

桥梁施工在市内时，现场没有预制场地，若在城外预制梁片，运梁十分困难，可考虑在桥墩之间拼装支架，制作安装2~3孔主梁，然后把施工完成的跨径部分作为预制场，并依次使预制场扩展出去。它要求预制台座可活动，大梁安装采用跨墩龙门吊较方便。

（5）远距离预制场

远距离预制场可在与施工现场完全无关的条件下预制梁，有利于集中管理，场地面积不受限制，梁片数量大时尤为有利；但梁运输距离远、运输费用高。这种预制场一般适用于城市立交桥，其布置可因地制宜，充分利用现有机械，场地尽可能扩大，提前预制多片梁。

3. 场地建设

（1）场地建设前施工单位应将梁场布置方案报监理工程师审批，方案内容应包含各类型梁板的台座数量、模板数量、生产能力、存梁区布置及最大存梁能力等。

（2）宜采用封闭式管理，场地内应设办公区、生活区、构件加工区、制梁区和存梁区、废料处理区等科学合理设置，功能明确、标志清晰。生活区应与其他区隔开，生活用房按照驻地建设相关标准建设。

（3）各项目预制场应统筹设置，建设规模和设备配备应结合预制梁板的数量和预制工期相适应。

（4）场内路面宜做硬化处理，主要运输道路应采用不小于20cm厚的C20混凝土硬化，基础不好的道路应增设碎石掺石屑垫层。场内不允许积水，四周设置砖砌排水沟，并采用M7.5砂浆抹面。

（5）预制梁场应尽量按照"工厂化、集约化、专业化"的要求规划、建设，每个预制梁场预制的梁板数量不宜少于300片。若个别受地形、运输条件限制的桥梁梁板需单独预制，规模可适当减小，但钢筋骨架定位胎膜、自动喷淋养护等设施仍应满足施工生产要求。

（6）预制梁场钢筋加工、混凝土拌和应尽量使用合同段既有的钢筋加工厂、拌和站。

（7）预制梁板钢筋骨架应统一采用定位胎模进行加工，并设置高强度砂浆垫块确保钢筋保护层。

（8）设置自动喷淋养护设备，预制梁板采用土工布包裹喷淋养护（北方地区应根据气候情况采用蒸汽保湿养护），养护水应循环使用。

4. 预制梁板台座布设

（1）预制梁板的台座强度应满足张拉要求，台座尽量设置于地质较好的地基上，在不良地基路段，应先进行地基处理。为防止发生张拉台座不均匀沉降、开裂事故，影响预制梁板的质量，先张法施工的张拉台座不得采用重力式台座，应采用钢筋混凝土框架式台座。

（2）底模宜采用通长钢板，不得采用混凝土底模。推荐使用不锈钢底模板，钢板厚度不小于 6 mm，并确保钢板平整、光滑，防止黏结造成底模"蜂窝""麻面"，底模钢板应采取防止变形措施。

（3）存梁区台座混凝土强度等级不低于 C20，台座尺寸应满足使用要求。用于存梁的枕梁应设在离梁两端面各 50~80 m 处，且不影响梁片吊装，支垫材质应采用承载力足够的非刚性材料，且不污染梁底。

（4）梁板预制完成后，移梁前应对梁板喷涂统一标志和编号，标志内容应包括预制时间、张拉时间、施工单位、梁体编号、部位名称等。

（5）空心板、箱梁最多存放层数应符合设计文件和相关技术规范要求。设计文件无规定时，空心板叠层不得超过 3 层，小箱梁堆叠存放不超过 2 层。预制梁存放时（特别是叠层存放）应采取支撑等措施确保安全稳定。

场地应满足用地合法，周围无塌方、滑坡、落石、泥石流、洪涝等地质灾害；无高频、高压电源及其他污染源；离集中爆破区 500 m 以外；不得占用规划的取、弃土场。

拌和站选址应根据本合同段的主要构造物分布、运输、通电和通水条件等特点综合选址，尽量靠近主体工程施工部位，做到运输便利、经济合理；并远离生活区、居民区，尽量设在生活区、居民区的下风向。

拌和站应根据工程实际情况集中布置，宜采用封闭式管理，四周设置围墙，入口设置大门和值班室。

拌和站建设应综合考虑施工生产情况，合理划分拌和作业区、材料计量区、材料库、运输车辆停放区、试验区、集料堆放区及生活区，内设洗车池（洗车台）、污水沉淀池和排水系统。生活区应与其他区隔离，生活用房按照"驻地建设"相关标准建设。

拌和站场地面积、搅拌机组配置及产能应满足生产、施工需求和工程进度要求。

场地（含堆料区、加工区）应做硬化处理，主要运输道路应采用不小于 20cm 厚的 C20 混凝土硬化，基础不好的道路应增设碎石掺石屑垫层，场内排水宜按照中间高四周低的原则预设不小于 1.5% 的排水坡度，四周宜设置砖砌排水沟，并采用 M7.5 砂浆抹面。

拌和站各罐体宜连接成整体，安装缆风绳和防雷设施，每一个罐体应喷涂成统一的颜色，并绘制项目名称及施工单位名称，二者竖向平行绘制。

1. 凡用于工程的砂石料应按级配要求，不同粒径、不同品种分场存放，每区醒目位置设置材料标志牌，并采用不小于30 cm厚的混凝土或厚度不小于60 cm的浆砌片石隔墙等构造物分隔，隔墙高度应确保不串料（一般不小于2.5m），储料仓预留一定空间方便装载机上料。

2. 水泥混凝土、路面面层储料场应用混凝土进行硬化处理，路面基层储料场可用水稳材料进行硬化处理。料场底应高于外部地面，修筑成向外顺坡（不小于3%），并在料场口设置排水沟，防止料场积水。

3. 水泥混凝土、路面面层储料场应搭设顶棚，防止太阳直接照晒或雨淋，顶棚宜采用轻型钢结构，高度应满足机械设备操作空间（一般不宜小于7 m），并满足受力、防风、防雨、防雪等要求，路面基层、底基层储料场地中细集料堆放区宜搭设防雨大棚，防止石料雨淋。

4. 所有拌和机的集料仓应搭设防雨棚，并设置隔板，隔板高度不宜小于100 cm，确保不串料。

混凝土拌和应采用强制式拌和机，单机生产能力不宜低于90 m/h。拌和设备应采用质量法自动计量，水、外加剂计量应采用全自动电子称量法计量，禁止采用流量或人工计量方式，保证工作的连续性、自动性，且具备电脑控制及打印功能。减水剂罐体应加设循环搅拌水泵。

水稳拌和应采用强制式拌和机，设备具备自动计量功能，一般设自动计量补水器加水。

沥青混合料采用间歇式拌和机，配备计算机及打印设备。

拌和站计量设备应通过当地有关部门标定后方可投入生产，使用过程中应不定期进行复检，确保计量准确。

拌和站应根据拌和机的功率配备相应的备用发电机，确保拌和站有可靠的电源使用。

作业平台、储料仓、集料仓、水泥罐等涉及人身安全的部位均应设置安全防护装置，传动系统裸露的部位应有防护装置和安全检修保护装置。

每次拌和作业完成后，及时清洗机具、清理现场，做到场地整洁。

应根据需要设置机动车辆、设备冲洗设施、排水沟及沉淀池，施工污水处理达标后方可排入市政污水管网或河流。

砂石料场底部、上料台、上料输送带下部废料应经常性清理并保持清洁，严禁装载机铲料时铲底。地面应定期洒水，对粉尘源进行覆盖遮挡。

水泥、粉煤灰等材料进料时，应保证材料罐顶的密封性能，预留通气孔应设有降尘措施；当粉尘较大时，应暂时停止上料，待处理完后方可继续。

沥青混合料拌和站推荐设置碎石加工除尘与石灰水循环水洗，确保细集料洁净无杂质。

纤维材料、抗车辙剂、抗剥落剂等外加剂必须采用仓库存放，地面设置架空垫层，高度为离地面30 cm，以免受潮。

第三节　滑模式摊铺机施工

一、施工工艺

　　滑模式摊铺机施工混凝土路面不需要轨模，摊铺机支承在4个液压缸上，两侧设置有随机移动的固定滑模，摊铺厚度通过摊铺机上下移动来调整。滑模式摊铺机一次通过即可完成摊铺、振捣、整平等多道工序。铺筑混凝土时，首先，由螺旋式布料器将堆积在基层上的混凝土拌和物横向铺开，刮平器进行初步刮平；然后，振捣器进行捣实，随后刮平板进行振捣后的整平，形成密实而平整的表面；再使用搓动式振捣板对拌和物进行振实和整平，最后用光面带进行光面。整面作业与轨道式摊铺机施工基本相同，但滑模摊铺机的整面装置均由电子液压系统控制，精度较高。

　　滑模式摊铺机比轨道式摊铺机更高度集成化，整机性能好、操纵方便、生产效率高，但对原材料混凝土拌和物的要求更严格，设备费用较高。

二、施工过程

1. 准备工作

　　滑模式摊铺机施工水泥混凝土路面的准备工作包括以下内容：

　　（1）基层质量检查与验收。滑模式摊铺机施工对基层的检验项目及质量验收标准与轨模式摊铺机施工相同。一般情况下滑模式摊铺机施工的长度不少于4km。基层应留有供摊铺机施工行走的位置，因此，基层应比混凝土面层宽出50~80 cm。

　　（2）测量放样，悬挂基准绳。滑模式摊铺机的摊铺高度和厚度可实现自动控制。摊铺机一侧有导向传感器，另一侧有高程传感器。导向传感器接触导向绳，导向绳的位置沿路面的前进方向安装。高程传感器接触高程导向绳，导向绳的空间位置根据路线高程的相对位置来安装。摊铺机摊铺的方向和高程准确与否，取决于导向绳的准确程度，因此，导向绳经准确定位后固定在打入基层的钢钎上。

　　（3）混凝土配合比与外加剂。滑模式摊铺机对混凝土拌和物的品质要求十分严格，集料最大粒径应小于40 mm，拌和物摊铺时的坍落度应控制在4~6cm之间。为了增加混凝土拌和物的施工和易性，以达到所需要的坍落度，常需要使用外加剂。所掺外加剂品种、数量应先通过试验确定。

　　（4）选择摊铺机类型。高速公路、一级公路宜选配一次能摊铺2~3个车道宽度

（7.5~12.5m）的滑模摊铺机；二级及二级以下公路路面最小摊铺宽度不得小于单车道设计宽度。

硬路肩的摊铺宜选配中、小型多功能滑模摊铺机，并连体一次摊铺路缘石。

2. 施工过程

滑模式摊铺机摊铺混凝土拌和物时，用自卸汽车将拌和物运至现场并卸在摊铺机料箱内。螺旋布料器前拌和物的高度保持在螺旋布料器高度的1/2~2/3，过低会造成拌和物供应不足，过高摊铺机会因阻力过大而造成机身上翘。滑模式摊铺机的工作速度应根据拌和物稠度、供料多少和设备性能控制在 0.8~3.0 m/min，一般宜在 1 m/min 左右。拌和物稠度发生变化时，应先调整振捣频率，后改变摊铺速度。混凝土强度初步形成后，用刻纹机或拉毛机制作表面纹理。混凝土路面的养护、锯缝、灌缝等施工方法与轨道式摊铺机施工相同。

使用纹理养生机对新铺水泥混凝土路面拉毛，并随后进行养生薄膜液体的洒布。纹理养生要在 30 min 之内摊铺段完成。刷子应调整到低于水泥混凝土路面表面 8~10 mm。趁新铺水泥混凝土路面表面还发亮时，就应进行薄膜液体的喷洒。喷嘴应调整到距离路表面 40~50cm 高度。

用洒布机在新铺路面喷洒薄膜材料应分两层进行。第一层是在混凝土路面精整并除去水泥浆后，当湿润的路面表面逐渐变得无光泽时进行；第二层是在第一次喷洒之后，过 30~60 min 后进行。养生膜的总厚度应为 0.4~0.7 mm。

为了避免热天阳光直接照射，在第二层养生膜喷洒之后，给路面铺上一层厚度 2~4 cm 的沙子，或洒布一层石灰浆。石灰浆装在洒布机的料罐里，由洒布机进行喷洒。

滑模式摊铺机摊铺混凝土路面板时，可能会出现板边塌陷、麻面、气泡等问题，应及时采取措施进行处理。塌陷的主要形式为边缘坍落、松散无边或倒边。造成塌边的主要原因是模板边缘调整角度不正确、摊铺速度过慢。边缘坍落会影响路面的平整度，横坡达不到设计要求；双幅施工时，会造成路面排水不畅。因此，应根据混凝土拌和物的坍落度调整出一定的预抛高，使混凝土坍落变形后恰好符合设计要求。造成倒边和松散无边的主要原因是集料针片状或圆状颗粒含量较多而造成拌和物成型性差、离析严重。此外，混凝土配合比不当、摊铺机的布料器将混凝土稀浆分到两侧也会导致倒边。为防止各种原因造成的倒边，应采用拌和质量好的搅拌机；施工过程中出现集料集中时，应将集料分散、除去或进行二次布料。麻面主要是由于混凝土拌和物坍落值过低造成的，混合料拌和不均匀也是原因之一。因此，应严格控制混凝土拌和物的坍落度，使用计量准确且拌和效果好的搅拌机，同时对混凝土的配合比做适当调整。

第四节 特殊气候条件下施工

要做好水泥混凝土路面，不仅对材料质量、配合比、各工序的施工技术和工艺要求严格掌握、控制，而且施工时气温高低和气候情况也都应注意。例如，雨季施工要比旱季施工困难，冬夏施工要比春秋季施工不便，因此，在不同的季节施工就应分别采取不同的措施以确保工程质量。

一、雨季施工

我国有些地区，特别是江南地区，每年有一定时间的雨季或梅雨，尤其在路面当天浇筑的中途突然下雨，将会给施工带来很多不便。特别是对混凝土的质量，由于水分增大而无法控制，造成强度降低，表面磨耗层砂浆会被雨水冲洗，日后可能出现露砂露石。因此，必须做好以下各点：

1. 经常与当地气象台取得联系，了解近期的天气形势预报，抓紧在不下雨的时候施工。尤其是对当天的晴雨情况要及时掌握，一般有雨不施工。

2. 预先搭设一定数量的工作雨棚。移动式工作雨棚可用小竹及铅丝绑扎而成，或木条制成。专业筑路单位，建议采用 p25mm~$40mm 的自来水管制成晴雨棚较妥，其铁管节点处用螺栓固定，使用拆装方便，反复使用时间长，棚上覆盖塑料布或油布。目前工地已广泛采用。

3. 对刚铺筑的路面，遇下雨时，即以工作雨棚放上，也可以利用它继续铺筑。一般在下雨时，应铺筑完未浇完的一块板，并停工做工作缝，不要再另行铺筑另一块。

4. 如局部面层砂浆已被雨水冲掉，可另拌少量同级配砂浆及时加以修补。如表面被雨水冲刷严重、面积较大，并且石子已经显露，将工作雨棚放好后，立即拌制 1:1.5~1:2.0 水泥砂浆加以粉面，厚度不超过 4mm，水灰比为 0.4，不许用纯干水泥或干拌水泥黄砂材料（正常情况是禁止另加水泥砂浆抹面的）。

二、夏季施工

夏季气温高，混凝土中水分容易蒸发，特别是在高温烈日下可以带来以下几个问题。

1. 高温情况下可以出现坍落度严重降低，失去原有施工和易性，给混凝土操作、振捣密实等带来困难。

2. 水分过快蒸发，混凝土表面很难振出足够的砂浆磨耗层（约 3mm 厚），并对表面整平和收水抹面带来困难。

3.高温烈日下可以使混凝土表面产生严重收缩裂缝。缩缝形状一般为直线形，缝长为20~100cm，裂缝深度可达3~5cm。这种情况的出现，主要是混凝土内水分蒸发量超过混凝土出现裂缝前的每小时容许蒸发1~1.5L/m。

夏季施工为防止水分过早大量蒸发，一般应采取以下措施。

（1）预先估计到混凝土在运输、摊铺过程中水分过快蒸发所造成的坍落度的降低，事先调整好配合比，适当增加用水量。至于用水量增加多少，应根据运距、气候、日照、风力大小来决定，一般在30℃气温下，要保持气温20℃时的坍落度，就要增加单位用水量4~7kg。

（2）混凝土在运输时要遮盖，及时运送至工地，中途不许延搁过久。

（3）摊铺、振捣收水抹面与养护各道工序应衔接紧凑，尽可能缩短施工时间。

（4）在已摊铺好的路面上，可搭设凉棚（用雨季施工的雨棚代替），以避免混凝土表面遭到烈日暴晒。

（5）建筑防风墙，以减弱吹到混凝土表面的风速，减少水分蒸发。

（6）遇到高温烈日和大风时，在已振捣的混凝土面层，可适当喷洒少量水加以湿润，能防止混凝土内水分过量蒸发。同样，在收水抹面时，因表面过分干燥而无法操作的情况下容许喷洒少量水于表面进行收水扫毛或滚槽。

三、冬季施工

混凝土强度的增长主要依靠水泥的水化作用。温度高混凝土水化作用迅速完成，强度增长快；温度低，水化作用缓慢，强度增长慢。若在日平均温度低于5℃或最低气温低于0℃时施工，必须采取冬季施工措施。若日平均气温低于0℃，一般应停止施工。

冬季温度降到0℃以下时（一般混凝土冻结温度为-3℃），具有和易性的混凝土即产生冰冻，表面则产生冰晶混凝土解冻后，这种印迹仍然存在。早期受冻的混凝土强度可降低40%~50%，强度大幅度降低的原因为：结冰时混凝土中水的体积增加9%，解冻后则不再恢复；集料周围有层水膜或水泥浆膜，在结冰后其黏结力被破坏。

严重受冻的混凝土可以形成一堆互不起作用的混合物。因此，混凝土路面应尽可能在气温高于5℃时进行施工，当昼夜平均气温在5℃与-5℃之间时，为保证混凝土受冻前至少能达到设计强度的70%左右，应采取下列措施。

1.原材料加热法

拌制混凝土的水加热至80℃，应在加入水泥以前先放入集料，或者把水和砂石料一齐加热至60℃~70℃，保证混凝土在拌制时的温度不超过40℃，摊铺后的温度不低于10℃~20℃。收水抹面结束后，即覆盖双层干草帘保温，冬季负温时不必洒水，水泥板要在0℃以上的温度条件下保持7h以上，即可达到28d强度的50%~60%。如果气温更低，或不具备材料加热条件，可考虑添加总量不超过 2% 氯化钙或氯化钠，同时，掺入等量的亚硝酸钠。

2. 外加混凝土早强剂

（1）氯化钙和其它氯盐

这是一种常用的早强剂。其掺量为：普通混凝 ±2%；钢筋混凝 ±1%；预应力混凝土中禁止使用氯化钙和其它氯盐（以水泥重量计）。使用前溶成 30%~35% 的溶液同拌和水一起加入搅拌机内。掺量过多，会使混凝土结构破坏引起凝结过快，造成无法施工，同时，会引起混凝土体积收缩、产生裂缝、降低强度。在电讯和电力电缆导电范围内，不得使用氯化物，以防导电。使用氯化钙早强剂有许多优点，使用方便、易溶于水、价廉易得，能防止混凝土早强冻结，有利于冬季施工；主要缺点是加剧钢筋锈蚀（锈胀可引起结构的破坏）。因此，有些国家禁用于钢筋混凝土中，在我国规定在钢筋混凝土中，掺量不得超过水泥重量的 2%，也不得超过 6kg/m。氯化钙和氯化钠两种早强剂不得同时使用。

（2）三乙醇胺复合早强剂（方案一）

配合比为三乙醇胺 0.05%+ 氯化钠 0.5%（以水泥重量计）。其特点是早强效果好，在正温条件下养生，比不掺早强剂的 2d 强主可提高 30%~50%，达到 28d 强度的 70% 的时间缩短一半。

（3）三乙醇胺复合早强剂（方案二）

配合比为三乙醇胺 0.05%+ 氯化钠 0.5%+ 亚硝酸钠 0.5%~1.0%（以水泥重量计）。早强效果同方案一，因掺有 0.5% 的亚硝酸钠，故能有效地阻止由于掺入 0.5% 氯化钠而引起的钢筋锈蚀，并能起到早强和防冻作用，是冬季施工较为理想的外加剂。

三乙醇胺和亚硝酸钠单掺时早强效果并不显著，但当与氯化钠复合后，早强效果显著增加。在使用三乙醇胺复合早强剂时，按规定比例，如 100kg 水泥需 500g 氯化钠，500~100g 亚硝酸钠、50g 三乙醇胺溶成 6kg 的水溶液，然后在使用时同拌和水一起加入搅拌机内即可。有一点必须注意，掺有外加剂的混凝要保证不少于 2.5min 的拌和时间，一般比正常拌和时间多 1~1.5min。适当增加拌和时间是冬季施工应特别注意的问题。

（4）硫酸盐复合早强剂

用配合比为 2% 的硫酸钠 +1%~2% 的亚硝酸钠 +1%~2% 的二水石膏（以水泥重量计）配制硫酸复合早强剂，早强效果好。在 -8℃ 至自然正温条件下，掺硫酸钠复合早强剂的混凝土比不掺早强剂的混凝 ±2d 强度能提高 60% 以上，达到 28d 强度 70% 的时间也能缩短 1/2~3/4，其 28d 强度还能增加 15% 左右，硫酸钠和亚硫酸钠对钢筋均能起保护和防锈作用，但亚硝酸钠对砂石集料有侵蚀作用。故应严禁在含有活性集料（如蛋白石）的混凝土中使用。

另外，早强剂的使用不但对水泥混凝土路面的冬季施工具有重要的意义，而且在正常情况下，特别对城市道路局部路面的损坏修复起积极的作用。因水泥混凝土路面修筑成后需较长时间的养生，才能开放使用，这样会中断交通而影响车辆的正常行驶，而掺了早强剂后，一般 5d 左右即可开放使用。

3. 保温电热法

保温棚四周用油布遮好，在离浇筑好的混凝土地面 1.5m 处高的地方每隔 3m 间隔各挂一支 100W 的灯泡，连续通电 72h 后，其强度也能达到设计强度的 50% 以上。

在冬季采用矿渣水泥做胶结料时，收水抹面也常遇到这种情况，使水泥凝结时间大大推迟，收水抹面的整个过程可以拖得很长，且表层出现大量泌水。因此，在收水抹面前，应用芦花扫帚将面层泌水顺横纹方向排除，然后按抹面的顺序和要求进行。

另外，应当指出收水抹面不许另加干水泥或干拌水泥黄沙，否则日后易起壳脱落。下午浇筑的混凝土，应在防雨保温棚内进行收水抹面工作。保温棚周围应用塑料布密封，不使混凝土水化过程中放出的热量和水汽散失，以保持一定温度（不得低于 0℃）和湿度，保证混凝土强度的增长。

混凝土浇筑后，表面有相当硬度（用手指轻轻揿上去没有痕迹）时，应铺 1~2 层草包。若遇雨雪，必须再加盖油布保温，保温期为 3~5d。

混凝土的浇水养生工作一般宜在第二天上午进行，下午不宜浇水，若温度低于 5℃ 也不宜浇水。

1. 进度计划执行中的跟踪检查

对进度计划的执行情况进行跟踪检查是计划执行信息的主要来源，是进度分析和调整的依据，也是进度控制的关键步骤。

跟踪检查的主要工作是定期收集反映工程实际进度的有关数据，收集的数据应当全面、真实、可靠，不完整或不正确的进度数据将导致判断不准确或决策失误。为了全面、准确地掌握进度计划的执行情况，监理工程师应该认真做好以下三个方面的工作。

（1）定期收集进度报表资料。进度报表是反映工程实际进度的主要方式之一。进度计划执行单位应按照进度监理制度规定的时间和报表内容，定期填写进度报表。监理工程师通过收集进度报表资料掌握工程实际进展情况。

（2）现场实地检查工程进展情况。派监理人员常驻现场，随时检查进度计划的实际执行情况，这样可以加强进度监测工作，掌握工程实际进度的第一手资料，以便使获取的数据更加及时、准确。

（3）定期召开现场会议。定期召开现场会议，既可以了解工程实际进度状况，又可以协调有关方面的进度关系。一般情况下，进度控制的效果与收集数据资料的时间间隔有关。如果不经常地、定期地收集实际进度数据，就难以有效地控制实际进度。进度检查的时间间隔与工程项目的类型、规模、监理对象及有关条件等多方面因素相关，可视工程的具体情况，每月、每半月或每周进行一次检查。在特殊情况下，甚至需要每日进行一次进度检查。

2. 实际进度数据的加工处理

为了进行实际进度与计划进度的比较，必须对收集到的实际进度数据进行加工处理，形成与计划进度具有可比性的数据。

3. 实际进度与计划进度的对比分析

将实际进度数据与计划进度数据进行比较，可以确定建设工程实际执行状况与计划目标之间的差距。为了直观反映实际进度偏差，通常采用表格或图形进行实际进度与计划进度的对比分析，从而得出实际进度比计划进度超前、滞后还是一致的结论。

通过实际进度与计划进度的比较，发现进度偏差时，为了采取有效措施调整进度计划，必须深入现场进行调查，分析产生进度偏差的原因。

当查明进度偏差产生的原因之后，要分析进度偏差对后续工作和总工期的影响程度，以确定是否应采取措施调整进度计划。

当出现的进度偏差影响到后续工作或总工期需要采取进度调整措施时，首先应当确定可调整进度的范围，主要包括关键节点、后续工作的限制条件以及总工期允许变化的范围。这些限制条件往往与合同条件有关，需要认真分析后确定。

采取进度调整措施，应该以后续工作和总工期的限制条件为依据，确保要求的进度目标得到实现。

进度计划调整之后，应该采取相应的组织、经济、技术措施执行，并继续监测其执行情况。

1. 改变某些工作间的逻辑关系

当工程项目实施中产生的进度偏差影响到总工期，且有关工作的逻辑关系允许改变时，可以改变关键线路和超过计划工期的非关键线路上的有关工作之间的逻辑关系，达到缩短工期的目的。

2. 缩短某些工作的持续时间

这种方法是不改变工程项目中各项工作之间的逻辑关系，而通过采取增加资源投入、提高劳动效率等措施来缩短某些工作的持续时间，使工程进度加快，以保证按计划工期完成该工程项目。这些被压缩持续时间的工作是位于关键线路和超过计划工期的非关键线路上的工作。同时，这些工作又是其持续时间可被压缩的工作。

这种调整方法通常可以在网络图上直接进行。其调整方法根据限制条件及对其后续工作的影响程度不同而有所不同，一般有以下三种情况。

（1）网络计划中某项工作进度拖延的时间已超过其自由时差但未超过其总时差。此时该工作的实际进度不会影响总工期，而只对后续工作产生影响。因此，在进行调整前，需要确定后续工作允许拖延的时间限制，并以此作为进度调整的限制条件。该限制条件的确定常常较复杂，尤其是当后续工作由多个平行的承包单位负责实施时更是如此。后续工作如果不能按原计划进行，在时间上产生的任何变化都可能使合同不能正常履行，从而导致蒙受损失的一方提出索赔。因此，寻求合理的调整方案，把进度拖延对后续工作的影响减少到最低限度是监理工程师的一项重要工作。

（2）网络计划中某项工作进度拖延的时间超过其总时差。如果网络计划中某项工作进度拖延的时间超过其总时差，则无论该工作是否为关键工作，其实际进度都将对后续工作和总工期产生影响。此时，进度计划的调整方法又可分为以下三种情况。

1）项目总工期不允许拖延。如果工程项目必须按照原计划工期完成，则只能采取缩短关键线路上后续工作持续时间的方法来达到调整计划的目的。

2）项目总工期允许拖延。如果项目总工期允许拖延，则只需要以实际数据代替原计划数据，并重新编制实际进度检查日期之后的简化网络计划即可。

3）项目总工期允许拖延的时间有限。如果项目总工期允许拖延，但允许拖延的时间有限，则当实际进度拖延的时间超过此限制时，也需要对网络计划进行调整，以便满足要求。具体的调整方法是以总工期的限制时间作为规定工期，对检查日期之后尚未实施的网络计划进行工期优化，即通过缩短关键线路上后续工作持续时间的方法来使总工期满足规定工期的要求。

以上三种情况都是以总工期为限制条件调整进度计划的。

需要注意的是，当某项工作实际进度拖延的时间超过其总时差而需要对进度计划进行调整时，除需考虑总工期的限制条件外，还应考虑网络计划中后续工作的限制条件，特别是对总进度计划的控制更应注意这一点。因为在这类网络计划中，后续工作也许就是一些独立的合同段。时间上的任何变化，都会带来协调上的麻烦或者引起索赔。因此，当网络计划中某些后续工作对时间的拖延有限制时，同样需要以此为条件，按前述方法进行调整。

（3）网络计划中某项工作进度超前。监理工程师对建设工程实施进度控制的任务就是在工程进度计划的执行过程中，采取必要的组织协调和控制措施，以保证建设工程按期完成。

在建设工程计划阶段所确定的工期目标，往往是综合考虑了各方面因素而确定的合理工期。因此，时间上的任何变化，无论是进度拖延还是超前，都可能造成其他目标的失控。

第五节　施工质量检查与竣工验收

混凝土路面施工质量应符合设计和施工规范要求。为此应加强施工前的原材料质量检验，施工过程中应对每一道工序进行严格的质量检查和控制。对已完成的混凝土路面进行外观检查，测量其几何尺寸，并根据设计文件进行校核。此外，还要查阅施工记录，包括原材料试验和试件强度资料、配合比及隐蔽构造等，以检查结果作为评定工程质量的依据。

一、施工质量控制

1. 原材料质量检验

施工前应对各种原材料进行质量检验，以检验结果作为判定材料质量是否符合要求的依据。在施工过程中，当材料规格和来源发生变化时应及时对材料进行质量检验。材料质量检验的内容包括：材料质量是否满足设计和规范要求；数量供应能否满足工程进度；材料来源是否稳定可靠；材料堆放和储存是否满足要求等。质量检查时以"批"为单位进行，通常将同一料源、同一次购进的同品种材料作为一批，取样方法按试验规程进行。混凝土所用的水泥、粗细集料、水、外加剂、钢材、接缝材料等原材料的质量检查项目和标准应符合有关要求。

2. 施工过程中的质量控制

在混凝土路面施工过程中，应检查混凝土拌和物的配合比是否符合设计要求，对拌和、摊铺、振捣的质量等进行检查，并做好记录。混凝土的抗折强度以养护28 d龄期的小梁试件来测定，以试验结果计算的抗折强度作为评定混凝土质量的依据。强度试验应按下列规定进行：

（1）用正在摊铺的混凝土拌和物制作试件，若施工时采用真空脱水工艺，则试件亦采用真空脱水工艺成型。

（2）每台班或每铺筑200m混凝土，应同时制作两组试件，龄期分别采用标准养生7d和28d；每铺筑1000~2000m混凝土拌和物需增制一组试件，用于检查后期强度，龄期不少于90d。

（3）当普通硅酸盐水泥混凝土在标准养护条件下养生7d的强度达不到28 d强度的60%时，应分析原因，并对混凝土的配合比做适当调整。

（4）铺筑完毕的混凝土路面，应抽检实际强度、厚度，可采用现场钻取圆柱试件测定，并进行圆柱劈裂强度试验，以此推算小梁抗折强度。

二、竣工验收

混凝土路面施工完毕，施工单位应将全线以1 km作为一个检查段，按随机取样的方法选择对每检查段的测点，按混凝土面层质量验收和允许偏差的规定进行自检，并向监理部门和建设单位提供全线检测结果及施工总结报告。施工质量监理单位应会同施工单位一起按随机抽样的办法选择一定数量的检查段进行抽样检查，抽样总长度不宜少于全程的30%，检查的内容和频度应符合规范规定。检查指标的评定标准为：对于高速公路和一级公路，可考虑a_1=95%的保证率；对于其他等级公路可考虑a_n=90%的保证率。检查段应不少于3个，每段长度为1 km。

混凝土路面完工后，应根据设计文件、交工资料和施工单位提出的交工验收报告，按国家建设工程竣工验收的办法组织验收。验收时应提交设计文件和交工资料、交工验收报告、混凝土强度试验报告、材料检查及材料试验记录、基层检查记录、工程重大问题处理文件、施工总结报告、工程监理总结报告等。

施工组织是指项目施工前，根据工程设计文件、建设单位的要求，以及主客观条件，对工程施工全过程采用科学的方法所进行的一系列筹划、安排活动。施工组织要从工程的全局出发，按照客观的施工规律和当时当地的施工条件，统筹考虑施工活动的人力、资金、材料、机械和施工方法这五个主要因素之后，对整个工程的施工进度和资源消耗等做出科学的安排。施工组织的目的是使工程建设在一定的时间和空间内，实现有组织、有计划、有秩序的施工，以期达到工程施工的相对最优效果。

公路的养护工作不同于一般工程，这是由公路自身的快速、经济、安全、舒适等特点所决定的，因此，公路养护施工具有及时性、快速性、高质量性等特点。这就对公路养护施工组织具有特定的要求。

1. 维修保养工作的施工组织要求

由于维修保养工作是为保持公路及其附属设施的正常使用功能而安排的经常性保养和修补其轻微损坏部分的作业，这就决定了其经常性、周期性、计划性等特点。因此，施工组织的要求为：

（1）施工组织方式必须贯穿常备不懈的特点，可采取属段化的组织方式，50km左右设置一个养护管理单元，随时进行维修。

（2）充分认识和掌握维修保养工作的周期性规律，合理安排施工设备、人员等。

（3）由于日常维修保养工作的内容较多而固定，所以应根据实际情况制订施工组织计划，合理安排工作内容。

2. 专项工程的施工组织要求

专项养护是对管养范围内的公路及其工程设施的集中性缺陷、局部损坏或普遍性病害进行有针对性的专门处理加固，以基本恢复原状或使用效果，并在一定程度上提高公路抗病害能力、美化路容路貌的小型工程项目。由于其针对性较强，施工范围较集中，所以要求在施工组织设计中做好主要工艺流程、设备管理等工作。

3. 大修工程的施工组织要求

大修工程是对管养范围内的公路及其工程设施的较大缺陷、较大损坏、路段性的严重病害等，进行周期性的或针对性的综合修理，以恢复和提高公路运营能力的工程项目。由于其具有时效性、安全性等特点，所以施工组织要求：

（1）尽可能减少对交通的干扰，尽量减少养护作业时间，快速地准备好现场，并在大修工作完成后快速撤离现场、恢复交通。

（2）做好安全组织工作，最大限度地降低大中修工程施工中的危险性。不同季节的气候因素可能对公路的路容、路貌、行车条件、道路病害、道路设施损坏带来阶段性或集中性的养护需求。由于季节性因素的影响，养护工作分布不均衡，不仅造成了资金、人员、材料使用的不均衡，对养护装备配置也带来了很多困难。例如北方地区，大批的专用除雪设备夏天用不上，而大量的绿化设备冬天又不能使用，这无疑降低了设备的利用率，增加了养护成本。公路养护工作要结合地域的气候、交通需求，充分考虑季节性的特点。人员应一专多能，装备应一机多用，以此提高作业效率，降低养护成本。

在公路养护工作中，对于突发事件，要采取紧急抢修措施，尽快恢复交通。这就要求养护组织能够适应突发性抢修的特点。养护组织应能够满足应急抢险的要求，人员、材料、设备和指挥调度系统常备不懈，并有应对的预案。在路网内具有随时可以调动的机动人员，并将公路沿线地方政府、医疗机构和社会力量组织起来作为处理突发事件的后备力量。为保证突发事件的顺利处理，需要安排一定数量的应急、抢修专项资金，以备急需时专用。

在公路养护作业中，相当一部分工作是通过流动作业的方式来完成的，如清扫、保洁、除雪、防滑等是在养护设备行进中完成的。另外，还有一些工作，虽然需要养护机械停下来工作，但停下来作业的时间很短，而行走却占用更多的时间，这种作业也属于流动性作业。如为沿线的树木浇水、喷药、草坪修剪、路面坑槽修补、残缺标记修补等。养护施工组织要适应流动性作业的特点，不仅要在装备配置上走机械化养护的道路，在作业方式上也应有一套有针对性的作业组织方法，其中包括行走方式、作业方式、安全措施等。

在公路养护施工过程中，日常养护作业是不关闭交通的，高速的交通流和复杂的现场作业环境构成了养护作业安全隐患多的特点。施工组织不当是安全隐患的原因之一，比如设备进场顺序错乱会导致交通堵塞引发交通事故等。因此，施工组织过程中应结合养护作业安全隐患多的特点，合理组织施工。

在养护管理中，公路的业主主要负责以下工作：

1. 路况调查，掌握道路、桥梁、结构的工作状态。
2. 编制养护工作计划。
3. 筹集养护经费。
4. 选择养护施工单位。
5. 做好养护工程项目管理。
6. 编制公路运营技术状况报告。

业主管理机构可以分为两种情况：一种情况是业主将养护工作全面委托出去，交由公路养护公司负责养护。路况调查、养护工程设计和监理工作也分别委托具有从业资质的单位实施。业主的管理机构主要有两个部门：计划财务部门，负责筹划和掌握养护资金的使用；养护管理部门，负责养护工作的协调、组织和养护成果的考核；另一种情况是业主全面承担养护工程的组织工作，这样，业主机构要相应地增设养护技术和生产部门以满足养护工作的需要。

在公路网级管理机构中，还要根据区域路网的大小、交通流量、路况、养护工作量的特点来设置业主的养护机构。为了适应公路养护专业化、机械化的特点，很多路网级的业主单位，在管理机构中主要设置以下部门：

1. 养护部，负责日常养护的组织和管理；

2. 工程部，负责专项和大修工程的组织和管理；

3. 材料设备部，负责大型保障性设备的采购和管理；

4. 机电维护部，负责机电系统的维护和管理。

以养护专项工程为例，公路业主养护管理工作如下：

1. 编制养护专项工程项目建议书。主要工作有：交通流量调查，路况调查，协调养护工程预安排，编制养护工程建议书，审查建议书，并纳入养护计划；

2. 项目施工图设计。主要工作有：绘制图纸，编制施工预算，履行设计审批程序；

3. 项目实施准备。主要工作有：编制合同文件，确定施工单位，签署合同文件；

4. 项目实施。主要工作有：项目质量控制，项目进度控制，项目安全控制，项目费用控制，项目履约；

5. 项目验收。主要工作有：数量验收，质量评价，项目总结。

项目总结的内容包括：道路运营技术状况报告，养护专项工程组织情况报告，养护专项工程成本情况报告，养护专项工程质量情况报告。

养护公司管理的目标是在养护工程合同中体现出来的，不仅包括造价，还包括质量、工期、安全责任目标以及一般工程合同中包括的责任和义务。

1. 工前准备阶段的主要工作

（1）签署工程合同；

（2）编制施工组织设计；

（3）场地临时建设；

（4）组织材料进场，施工配合比设计；

（5）设备进场、安装、调试；

（6）查看现场；

（7）工前技术交底、安全培训；

（8）成本及管理目标分解；

（9）准备标志设施；

（10）办理施工作业许可；

（11）申请开工。

2. 养护施工阶段的主要工作

（1）材料管理：控制进场材料的规格、数量、质量和价格；贵重材料、易损、易潮、易燃、易爆材料还要做好安全管理；对出场材料特别是场内拌制的混合料要把好质量检验关。

（2）设备管理：包括施工车辆、大型设备使用、运行、安全和成本管理，应根据生产的需要，合理配置和调度设备，提高装备的使用率，加强对设备使用及工作量的考核，并组织好维修和保养。

（3）劳动力管理：通过劳动合同的方式对养护维修作业人员进行管理。临时工人应有试用阶段，在试用阶段考核其技能；在正式聘用阶段，考核出勤情况和完成的劳动定额。

（4）技术和质量管理：养护公司内部要建立质量责任制，从进场材料开始控制，工序间要有质量自检、互检和交接。直至工程成品，都应该满足合同和技术规范确定的质量标准。

（5）成本和合同管理：公司要取得利润，应该十分重视成本和合同管理。要掌握工程数量和合同确定的工期，通过人工、机械和劳动力的合理投入，按照完成的数量和质量，计量和支付各种工程费用。

（6）现场组织管理：主要是现场的作业秩序、组织和调度，使其合理、紧凑，以最恰当的消耗、最佳的时间来做好计划内的工程，避免人员误工、机械待料和出现安全事故。

3. 工后责任履约阶段的主要工作

工程完工后要确认工程缺陷责任期，履行缺陷责任期内的责任和采取的修复措施，以及验收、计量标准，以保证缺陷责任期内发现的工程缺陷能够得到及时补救，以最终履行合同所确定的质量责任。

一般情况下，施工组织机构分为两层。高层为施工组织的决策层，主要岗位有项目经理、负责生产组织的项目副经理和技术、质量管理的项目总工程师；中层为施工组织的操作层，其中，履行管理职责的有综合部、合同部、财务部、技术质量部和材料设备部。履行生产职责的有拌和场、（摊铺）机械队、运输队、试验室、测量班和施工队。

2021年2月24日，《国家综合立体交通网规划纲要》（以下简称《纲要》）对外发布，规划期为2021—2035年。《纲要》提出，到2035年，国家综合立体交通网实体线网总规模合计70万公里左右（不含国际陆路通道境外段、空中及海上航路、邮路里程）。其中铁路20万公里左右、公路46万公里左右、高等级航道2.5万公里左右。

2020年年末全国公路总里程519.81万公里，比2019年年末增加18.56万公里。公路密度54.15公里/百平方公里，增加1.94公里/百平方公里。公路养护里程514.40万公里，占公路总里程99.0%。2020年年末全国四级及以上等级公路里程494.45万公里，比2019年年末增加24.58万公里，占公路总里程比重为95.1%，提高1.4个百分点。二级及以上等级公路里程70.24万公里，增加3.04万公里，占公路总里程比重为13.5%，提高0.1个百分点。高速公路里程16.10万公里，增加1.14万公里；高速公路车道里程72.31万公里，增加5.36万公里。国家高速公路里程11.30万公里，增加0.44万公里。

2020全年完成公路固定资产投资24312亿元，比2019年增长11.0%。其中：高速公路完成13479亿元，增长17.2%；普通国省道完成5298亿元，增长7.6%；农村公路完成4703亿元，增长0.8%。2021年前三季度，完成交通固定资产投资25632亿元，同比增长2.0%，两年平均增长5.9%，其中三季度两年平均增长3.9%、增速较上半年放缓3.2个百分点。完成公路投资18657亿元，同比增长4.9%。

第五章　沥青路面施工

沥青路面施工是一个工艺要求高、工序繁杂的施工过程。我国的公路路面大都是沥青混凝土路面，所以提升公路施工中沥青路面的技术是提升我国公路质量的重要部分。本节针对公路沥青路面施工技术进行阐述，以供参考。

第一节　多级嵌挤密级配沥青混合料路面施工

沥青混合料，按公称最大粒径分类可分为砂粒式、细粒式、中粒式、粗粒式、特粗式；按空隙率分为密级配（3%~6%）、半开级配（6%~12%）、开级配（18%以上，也称排水式沥青路面）；按施工方式可分为热拌沥青混合料、冷拌沥青混合料、再生沥青混合料。影响沥青混合料强度的主要因素有两个：一是矿料之间的嵌挤力和内摩擦阻力；二是沥青和矿料之间相互作用形成的黏结力和沥青材料本身的黏聚力。

一、材料技术要求

组成沥青混合料的材料有：沥青、集料、填料和添加剂等。沥青可分为道路石油沥青、乳化沥青、液体石油沥青、煤沥青和改性沥青等，集料可分为粗集料和细集料。多级嵌挤密级配热拌沥青混合料一般选用道路石油沥青。

1. 粗集料的质量技术要求

多级嵌挤密级配沥青混合料用粗集料包括碎石、破碎砾石、筛选砾石、钢渣和矿渣等，但高速公路和一级公路不得使用筛选砾石和矿渣。

2. 细集料的质量技术要求

多级嵌挤密级配沥青混合料的细集料包括天然砂、机制砂和石屑等，细集料应洁净、干燥、无风化、无杂质，并有适当的颗粒级配。

3. 填料

多级嵌挤密级配沥青混合料的矿粉，必须采用石灰岩或岩浆岩中的强基性岩石等憎水性石粉经磨细得到的矿粉，拌和机回收粉尘禁止使用，矿粉混合后的塑性指数应小于 4。

二、目标配合比设计

沥青混合料配合比设计的主要任务是选择合格的材料，确定各种粒径矿料和沥青的掺配比例，使之满足路用性能。热拌沥青混合料的配合比设计包括目标配合比设计、生产配合比设计及生产配合比验证三个阶段，最终的成果是通过一系列试验，确定沥青混合料的材料品种及配合比、矿料级配和最佳沥青用量。

1. 确定工程设计的级配范围

沥青路面工程的混合料设计级配范围由工程设计文件或招标文件规定，并根据公路等级、工程性质、气候条件、交通条件、材料品质等因素，进行充分的调查研究后确定。选定和调整工程设计级配宜遵循下列原则：

（1）夏季温度高，高温持续时间长，重载交通多的路段，宜选用粗型密级配沥青混合料（ACC 型），并取较高的设计空隙率。冬季气温低，低温持续时间长，重载交通较少的路段，宜选用细型密级配沥青混合料（AC-F 型），并取较低设计空隙率。

（2）确保高温抗车辙能力，兼顾低温抗裂性能的需要。

（3）确定各层的工程设计级配时考虑不同层位的功能需要，组合后的沥青路面，满足耐久、稳定、抗滑等要求。

（4）沥青混合料有良好的施工性能，易摊铺和压实，避免严重的离析。

2. 材料选择与取样

配合比设计使用的材料应和施工拟采用的材料一致。

3. 矿料配合比设计

对使用的每一种矿料进行筛分，传统上采取数解法、图解法、近似数解法等，常用图解法进行试配。现行施工规范要求，借助电子计算机的电子表格进行试配。绘制级配曲线和最大密度线，在工程设计级配范围内计算 1~3 组粗细不同的配合比，然后进行比选。

4. 制备马歇尔试件

选择适宜的沥青用量，分别制作马歇尔试件，测定矿料间 VMA。初选一组接近设计要求的矿料配合比作为设计级配，试件的制作温度应和施工温度一致。

5. 确定试件毛体积相对密度和理论最大相对密度

采用表干法测定试件的毛体积相对密度，对吸水率大于 2% 的试件宜用蜡封法。用真空法实测各组沥青混合料的最大理论相对密度 Y_u。

6. 确定最优级配

进行马歇尔试验，测定马歇尔稳定度和流值，计算沥青混合料试件的空隙率、矿料间隙率 VMA、有效的沥青饱和度 FVA 等体积指标，进行体积组成分析。

7. 选定沥青用量

以油石比和沥青用量为横坐标，以马歇尔试验的各项指标为纵坐标，将试验结果绘入图中，并连成圆滑的曲线。取密度最大值、稳定度最大值、空隙率目标值、沥青饱和度范围中值（或目标值）对应的沥青用量为 a1、a2，并根据工程的具体情况，如公路等级、气候状况、交通组成等调整确定最佳沥青用量。

8. 配合比设计检验

高速公路和一级公路的密级配沥青混合料，需在配合比设计的基础上进行各种使用性能的检验，包括：高温稳定性检验，动稳定度应合格；水稳定性检验、残留稳定度和残留强度比符合规定；低温抗裂性能检验，进行低温弯曲试验，破坏应变宜符合要求；渗水系数检验，对轮碾机成型的车辙试件进行渗水试验；必要时对钢渣进行活性检验等。

如上述试验中的一项或几项不合格，应重新进行矿料配比设计或沥青含量调整，使之满足要求。

三、生产配合比设计

采用间歇式拌和机施工时，烘干的热料经过二次筛分重新分成3~5个不同粒级的集料，需要重新进行配合比计算，确定各热料仓集料进入拌和仓的比例，并检验确定最佳沥青用量。流程各步骤的主要工作如下：

1. 料场集料级配组成的校核

对料场各种粗细集料重新取样筛分，如筛分结果发现集料的颗粒组成与进行目标配合比设计的集料颗粒组成有明显的差别，则应重新进行矿料配合比计算，重新确定各冷料仓的比例。

2. 热料仓集料筛分试验

对各个热料仓矿料取样做筛分试验，得出各热料仓矿料的颗粒组成，用于进行热料仓矿料配合比设计。

3. 热料仓矿料配合比设计

根据各热料仓集料的颗粒组成，计算出拌和时从各个热料仓的取料比例，得出混合后的矿料级配，即生产配合比。

4. 马歇尔试验检验

采用生产配合比颗粒组成和目标配合比确定的最佳沥青用量，以及最佳沥青用量的 ±0.3% 等三种沥青用量进行马歇尔试验，确定生产配合比的最佳沥青用量。

四、生产配合比验证

生产配合比验证阶段也是路段试验的一项重要内容,本节就沥青混合料生产配合比验证的内容进行阐述。

施工单位组织进行试拌试铺。拌和机按照生产配合比进行试拌,得到的混合料在试验路段上试铺,在场技术人员、监理人员和试验室工作人员对混合料级配、油石比、摊铺、碾压和成型混合料的表面状况进行观察和判断,同时,试验人员采集沥青混合料试样,进行马歇尔试验。具备条件的还可同时进行车辙试验和浸水马歇尔试验,以检验混合料的高温稳定性和水稳定性。试验人员还应现场取样进行抽提试验,抽提余下的矿料进行筛分试验,检验实际铺筑的沥青混合料矿料颗粒组成和沥青用量是否在目标配合比确定的范围内。

试验路段碾压完成并冷却后,试验人员还应钻芯取样,计算芯样试件的空隙率、矿料间隙率和饱和度等,还可以进行芯样马歇尔试验。芯样马歇尔试验结果由于受芯样厚度、芯样尺寸和外形等因素的影响,易产生应力集中问题,其稳定度和流值结果,仅作为参考,不能直接作为评价配合比优劣和是否合格的指标。

五、多级嵌挤密级配沥青混合料路面施工工艺

下面对各工序的施工要求予以分别叙述。

1. 准备下承层

沥青面层施工前应对下承层(或称下卧层)进行质量检查,不符合质量标准的不得铺筑沥青面层。下承层如已被污染,必须首先清洗,或经铣刨处理,下承层的坑槽碎裂等得到妥善处理。如下承层是基层时,必须喷洒透层油、透层油完全渗透入基层后方可铺筑面层;如下承层是旧沥青路面或沥青稳定碎石基层或中面层、下面层时,应喷洒黏层油。

2. 施工放样

施工前,应恢复中线,直线段每15~20m设一桩,曲线段每10~15m设一桩,并在路两侧边缘外设指示桩或用粉笔等示出两侧沥青路面边缘线。沥青中下面层施工时,可在两侧布设引导钢丝用以引导高程,钢杆间距不宜大于10m,防止钢丝下垂,表面层多采用雪橇式摊铺厚度控制方式或平衡梁控制方式。

3. 三阶段配合比设计和路段试验

三阶段配合比设计的具体步骤方法和注意事项,前文已做叙述。沥青面层路段试验的方法步骤前文也有论述,对于沥青面层来讲,路段试验还应解决以下几个方面的问题:

(1)确定合适的摊铺温度、摊铺速度和自动找平控制方式;

(2)确定运料车的数量及吨位大小;

(3)确定碾压温度、碾压组合方式、碾压遍数等;

(4) 确定松铺系数；

(5) 确定钻孔法实测计算密实度和用核子密度仪法检测密实度的对比关系。

4. 沥青混合料的拌制

拌制沥青混合料使用间歇强制式或连续式拌和机。当工程材料来源不稳定时，不得采用连续式拌和机。

沥青混合料的拌制时间应以混合料均匀、所有矿料颗粒全部裹覆沥青为度，并经试拌确定，间歇式拌和机每锅时间宜不少于45s，连续式拌和机的拌和时间由上料温度及拌和温度调节，改性沥青和SMA混合料的拌和时间应适当延长。

高速公路和一级公路施工用的间歇式拌和机必须配备计算机设备，拌和过程中逐盘采集并打印各个传感器测定的材料用量和沥青混合料的拌和量、拌和温度等各种参数。间歇式拌和机的振动筛规格应与矿料规格相匹配，最大筛孔宜略大于混合料的最大粒径，不同级配的混合料必须配置不同的筛孔组合，拌和机必须有二级除尘装置。

生产添加纤维的沥青混合料时，纤维必须在混合料中充分分散、拌和均匀。沥青混合料出厂时，应逐车检测沥青混合料的重量和温度，签发运料单。

5. 沥青混合料的运输

热拌沥青混合料宜采取较大吨位的自卸汽车运输，自卸车厢板上应涂一层防止沥青黏结的隔离剂（如喷洒少量植物油与肥皂水混合液等）。从拌和机装料时，应多次前后移动受料位置，减少混合料离析，运料车应采用苫布覆盖，以保温和防雨。

运料车进入现场前，应清除轮胎上的污染物。运料车辆在下承层行驶时，不准急转弯和急刹车，避免对透层、黏层或封层造成损伤。

运料车应在摊铺机前10~30 cm停住，不得撞击摊铺机，卸料过程中运料车应挂空挡，靠摊铺机推动前进。下坡摊铺时，自卸车应轻踩刹车，防止自卸车滑溜，必要时，应使用混合料转运车，以使混合料均匀连续地输送到摊铺机。

6. 沥青混合料的摊铺

热拌沥青混合料应使用沥青混合料摊铺机摊铺。一台摊铺机的摊铺宽度不宜大于6~7.5m。较宽的路面宜采用两台或多台摊铺机错开梯队的方式同步摊铺。

摊铺机必须缓慢、均匀、连续不间断地摊铺，不得随意变换速度或中间停顿，螺旋布料器在混合料内保持2/3的埋深，以提高平整度，减少混合料离析。

摊铺机应采用自动找平的方式，柔性基层和下面层宜采用钢丝引导的方式，上面层宜采用平衡梁控制厚度的方式，中面层可根据情况选用。

开始摊铺前应对熨平板进行预热，预热温度不低于100℃，用摊铺机摊铺的混合料，不应用人工反复修整。但出现局部缺料和明显离析等情况时，可使用人工局部找补或更换新混合料。

路面狭窄部分、加宽部分及半径过小的匝道等部位，摊铺机确实无法施工时，可采取人工摊铺的方法施工。人工摊铺时，注意以下事项：扣锹摊铺，不得远甩，边铺边用刮板整平，往返刮 2~3 次即可，不得反复刮料，避免矿料离析，铁锹等工具可涂油、肥皂水混合液和轻柴油，防止黏结，但不得频繁涂油，以免影响混合料质量。摊铺完成及时碾压，以有利于成型。

7. 热拌沥青混合料的碾压

沥青混合料的碾压分初压、复压、终压三个阶段进行。

初压宜采用钢轮压路机静压 1~2 遍，应将驱动轮面向摊铺机，初压应紧跟在摊铺机后，尽快使表面压实，减少热量散失。

复压应紧跟在初压后进行，密级配沥青混凝土的复压宜采用重型轮胎压路机，大粒径沥青碎石基层宜优先采用振动压路机复压，厚度小于 30 mm 的薄沥青层不宜采用振动压路机。碾压遍数经试验确定，对于构造物接头、拐弯死角等压路机无法碾压的部位，应使用振动夯板压实。在当天碾压的尚未冷却的路面上，不得停放任何机械设备，防止影响路面的平整度，为防止粘轮而采用向钢轮喷水的方法时，必须严格控制喷水量，且应成雾状。

SMA 路面不宜采用轮胎压路机，宜使用振动压路机碾压，并遵循"紧跟、慢压、高频、低幅"的原则；应防止出现过度碾压造成玛蹄脂上浮，出现构造深度减少的问题。OGFC 宜采用小于 12t 的钢筒式压路机碾压。

终压应紧跟复压进行，可选用双轮钢筒式压路机或关闭振动的振动压路机碾压，不少于 2 遍，到无明显轨迹为止。如经复压已无轨迹时，亦可免去终压。

8. 接缝处理

沥青路面的施工必须接缝紧密、连接平顺，不产生明显的接缝离析。

（1）纵向接缝

纵向接缝应尽可能采用梯队作业和热接缝，热接缝可预留 10~20cm 宽暂不碾压，作为后续路面的基准面，然后跨缝碾压，以消除缝迹。

当半幅施工或特殊原因而产生冷接缝时，宜加设挡板或加设切刀切齐，不宜冷却后用切割机做纵向切缝。摊铺时可重叠已铺冷却层 5~10 cm，铲走冷却层顶面上的混合料，跨缝碾压。跨缝碾压时，压路机在压实路面上行走，碾压新铺层 15 cm 左右，逐渐错轮进入新铺路面。

（2）横向接缝

高速公路和一级公路的表面层应采用垂直的平接缝，以下各层和其他等级道路各层均可采用斜接缝，搭接处应洒少量沥青。混合料中的粗集料应予剔除，并补上细料，搭接平整、充分压实。平接缝宜趁路面未冷透时，用凿岩机或人工刨除端部厚度不足部分，使工作缝与道路中线垂直。采用切割机制作平接缝时，留下的泥水应冲洗干净，干燥后应涂黏层油。铺筑新混合料后，先进行横向碾压，再纵向碾压成为一体。

9. 成品保护和开放交通

热拌沥青混合料路面应待铺层完全自然冷却至混合料表面温度低于 50℃后，方可开放交通。

铺好的沥青层，尤其是中下层应严格控制交通，保持路面的整洁，严禁在沥青层上堆放土和其他杂物，防止设备漏油等问题，禁止后续工程在沥青路面各层上拌制水泥砂浆。摊铺机每天摊铺结束后清理出的混合料残余物应运回料场或弃掉，清洗摊铺机熨平板等部位时，应采取措施防止污染路面。

第二节　SMA沥青路面施工

一、SMA 施工的特点

SMA 路面在国内外重交通道路中得到迅速发展，其原因除了这种路面在抵抗高温车辙、疲劳开裂、低温开裂的能力，抗水损害、抗滑以及耐久性等方面具有比传统密级配沥青混凝土无可比拟的优越性以外，在施工方面无须特殊机械设备，混合料生产装置，运料车辆和摊铺机均与传统密级配沥青混合料几乎完全相同，所用压实机具均相同。施工的方便也是促进其发展的重要原因之一。但 SMA 混合料的施工特性与施工工艺，具有其自身的显著特点，主要表现在以下几个方面。

1. 在 SMA 生产方面要求比较精细，对集料供给的控制要求严格

国外 SMA 混合料生产既采用间歇式拌和装置，也采用连续式滚筒拌和装置。我国由于集料生产没有专业化或专业化程度较低，集料规格往往不够稳定，如采用连续式拌和装置则难以保证沥青混合料的生产质量，故我国高速公路沥青路面施工均规定采用间歇式拌和装置。

由于 SMA 的特定性能是由坚固的间断级配集料构成的，构成集料骨架结构的粗集料与只起填充作用的细集料之间的比例变化，对压实混合料的空隙率具有线性的影响。因此，要求对通过断口上下侧筛孔的材料数量进行比较严格的控制。实际上意味着 SMA 混合料的体积特性随着 4.75mm 筛孔与 2.36mm 筛孔的通过率的变化而变化，而传统密级配沥青混凝土的体积特性受以上筛孔材料通过率的影响则很有限。所以，在 SMA 混合料生产上必须对集料级配进行比较严格的控制。为此，必须采用级配与规格稳定一致的组分集料（料堆集料）。如果 SMA 混合料的粗集料骨架结构被玛蹄脂过度填充，将形成不稳定的路面。一旦形成这样的过度填充，则将由玛蹄脂直接承受荷载，而玛蹄脂几乎没有抗变形的能力，因而将引起集料结构的破坏，导致路面早期出现车辙；相反，如果玛蹄脂对粗集料骨架结构的空隙填充不足，使压实 SMA 混合料的空隙率过大，路面将渗水，从而影响到 SMA 路面的耐久性，并可能导致路面出现早期水损害。因此，SMA 混合料生产必须对集料级

配和沥青用量进行严格的控制，尤其是 4.75 mm、2.36 mm 与 0.075 mm 三个关键筛孔的材料通过率，一定要与混合料设计配合比高度一致。

2. 与传统密级配沥青混合料相比，SMA 混合料不易发生粗细集料离析

与传统密级配沥青混合料不同，SMA 混合料在储存、运输和摊铺过程中，不会发生密级配沥青混合料经常出现的粗细集料离析的现象。因此，SMA 混合料的摊铺宽度可适当增大。

3. SMA 混合料中的玛蹄脂易从集料中析漏

由于 SMA 混合料中玛蹄脂含量较大而集料表面积相对较小，在结合料黏度较低时玛蹄脂容易从集料表面析漏出来。在混合料温度很高时，析漏现象容易发生在储存、运输和摊铺过程中。为了防止发生析漏，通常 SMA 需要采用纤维防漏剂，在南欧国家喜欢用改性沥青代替纤维。若同时使用纤维和改性沥青，不仅可以在施工过程中防止析漏现象，而且将进一步提高 SMA 的路面性能。

SMA 混合料的析漏问题，除在混合料设计时考虑外，在 SMA 混合料生产中，纤维必须正确添加、充分拌和、均匀地分散，防止纤维在混合料中集中。同时，在施工过程中对混合料的析漏实行监控。

4. 压实工艺与沥青混凝土不同

SMA 混合料的可压缩性很小，其压实特性与压实工艺与传统沥青混凝土有很大不同。

5. 必须按设计要求进行施工

SMA 混合料设计要求是施工的依据，施工必须满足设计要求，因此，只有在完成 SMA 混合料设计后，才能进行施工。

二、施工准备工作

施工前一定要做好原材料与施工机具的准备工作，原材料与施工机具必须满足设计和施工的要求。

1. 材料

（1）集料

SMA 混合料一般是 2~4 种集料（组分）混合而成的。为了形成粗集料的骨架结构，粗集料含量一般达 70%~80%，因此，粗集料的级配对生产的混合料质量具有重大影响。要重视各料堆集料规格（粒径、形状、棱角性）的一致性，超尺寸与欠尺寸的集料数量应控制在规范规定的范围内。不同粒径集料必须分别堆放，不得相混，且应堆放在硬质地面（用水泥加固的地面）上。堆放场地应有一定的坡度，以便排水，不得堆放在低洼积水处。细集料一般要求采用机制砂，也可部分采用洁净的硬质天然砂。而石屑为筛余下脚料，粉料与针片状颗粒很多，质量较差，尽量少用。必须使用时，就将小于 0.075 mm 的部分控制在 10% 以下。细集料尤其是石屑料堆必须搭棚覆盖，以免受潮后，冷料斗送料发生困难。

由于混合料中粗集料数量很大，一般需要一个以上的冷料斗送料，这样还可以减少料堆粗集料的变异性。

（2）填料（矿粉）

SMA混合料填料所占的份额较大，按SMA的级配规定通常要求通过0.075mm筛的百分率约为10%，这是与常规沥青混合料不同之处。SMA混合料对填料含量非常敏感，因此，填料的管理、储存与加入混合料都至关重要。填料必须存放在室内，保持干燥，能自由流动而不结块。由于填料需要量大，投放填料的设备能力应足够，所以，在拌和站现场设立填料筒仓是必要的。这些筒仓与填料储存系统连接，具有密封系统与螺旋推进器的喂料设备，应设有计量装置，填料从安装在底部的吹送器吹入间歇式拌和机或称料仓中。

我国《SMA技术指南》中规定回收粉用量不得超过填料总量的25%。回收粉实际上是冷集料进入干燥鼓后被热气流带入集尘室的粉料部分，理论上是可以使用的，因为它来自冷集料。但应取样试验其粒度分布与塑性指数以确定其如何使用。由于冷集料进入干燥鼓后失去部分粉料，故在根据热料仓集料进行生产配合比设计时，应相应补充矿粉数量，使生产配合比与设计配合比相一致。为了减少粉料损失的数量，首先要控制细集料中的粉料含量。

为了增加集料与结合料的黏附性，增强混合料抗剥落能力，最通用的方法是在矿粉中掺加一定数量的生石灰粉，生石灰粉占矿粉总量的20%左右。混合填料可在矿粉厂预先按比例混合好，以方便现场使用。

（3）沥青结合料

SMA生产中沥青结合料的加热与储存方法与常规沥青混合料的情况相类似。当使用改性沥青时，通常储存温度应比基质沥青稍有提高。由于改性高温储存时间较长，不仅聚合物可能发生离析，而且可能引起聚合物的降解，都将对改性沥青的性能造成损害。因此，承包商在运输和储存改性沥青方面，应遵从制造商的建议。沥青结合料加入混合料时必须精确进行计量。

（4）纤维

纤维的作用在于使SMA混合料在运输摊铺过程中将胶泥保持在粗集料上，防止其从混合料中离析。

通常采用木质素纤维，也可采用矿物纤维。木质素纤维的典型用量为混合料总质量的0.3%，矿物纤维的典型用量为0.4%。纤维通常有疏松纤维与颗粒纤维两种产品。两种产品均可采用人工添加或机械添加。

在人工添加纤维时，疏松纤维可以袋装方式添加。包装袋采用在拌和温度时易于熔化的材料制成，工人在每一干拌循环的适当时间将正确数量的纤维袋加进拌和锅。颗粒纤维也可按类似方法添加。人工添加的方法虽然可行，但工人操作紧张、劳动强度大，难免发生少加或漏加的情况，造成不良后果。故在大规模施工时，疏松纤维与颗粒纤维应尽可能采用机械添加的方式。纤维制造商设计并开发了专用的纤维添加设备，将干燥的疏松纤维置于设备的料斗中，用大叶片将疏松的纤维依次输入螺旋推进系统。该系统将材料调节到已知密度，然后纤维被机械计量并在相应时间吹入拌和机或称料仓。如国创公司根据美国专利开发的纤维投料机，计量精度可达 ±1%，使用效果良好。

颗粒纤维常含有给定数量的沥青结合料。如德国 JRS 出厂的 VLATOP 纤维，纤维中的沥青结合料必须计入混合料的沥青用量中。无论疏松纤维或颗粒纤维的添加机械都要进行标定，以保证混合料中纤维含量正确无误，避免在路面表面发生油斑；纤维的储存、管理与加入混合料的方法，应向纤维制造商咨询。如 JRS 公司根据含沥青的颗粒纤维 VLATOP 的特性，提出无须增加干拌时间，只要求在投入集料与填料的时段同时投入 VLATOP，每盘只需延长 5~10s 湿拌时间，即可达到混合料中纤维分散均匀的结果。

对各种原材料均要求供应商按批次提供质量检测报告，对集料、填料、沥青结合料（含改性沥青）、乳化沥青均需抽取代表性试样在现场试验室或中心试验室完成检测工作；对每批集料的颗粒粒径分布，均应抽取代表性试样进行检测，并须符合规范要求。

2. 主要机械设备

（1）间歇式沥青拌和装置 1 套，生产量 160~500 t/h。由于生产 SMA 混合料拌和时间加长等，生产率将降低，实际生产量将降至 100~200 t/h，可满足铺筑宽度 10~16 m、铺筑厚度 4~5cm 的 SMA 路面工程的需要。拌和装置应具有精确的计量设备和自动化装置，并具有每盘混合料配合比电脑打印记录，具有添加大量矿粉的足够能力，在拌和仓具有添加纤维的独立入口。

（2）如采用现场改性沥青，则应有一套与沥青拌和装置匹配的改性沥青现场加工研磨设备或高速剪切设备。该设备应能加工符合工程要求的改性沥青，生产能力至少 7 t/h，并配备 2~3 个立式改性沥青保温储存罐，每个储存罐容量不低于 10 t，并附搅拌设备，保持改性沥青在待用时处于均匀状态而不离析，并保证改性沥青在输入混合料拌和装置前有一定的发育时间，发育时间一般不少于 30 min。

如采用工厂成品改性沥青，则现场应备有容量为 20~30 t 的保温储罐，从该储罐向拌和机输送改性沥青。成品改性沥青的储存与使用应遵从改性沥青制造商的建议。

（3）如采用桶装沥青产品，则现场应配备脱桶设备。

（4）纤维添加机 1 台，与纤维产品的类型相适应。纤维添加量应满足间歇式拌和装置生产率的需要。

（5）摊铺机两台。每台摊铺宽度可达 12 m，能控制摊铺厚度并自动调平。建议采用 ABG 型或类似功能的摊铺机。

（6）10~12 t 双钢轮振动压路机 3~4 台，两个钢轮均为驱动轮与振动轮。

（7）手扶式小型振动压路机或人工机动夯具 2~3 台。

（8）手持式沥青洒布车 2 台，乳化改性沥青粘层用。

（9）载重 20t 自卸运料车 8~12 台。

（10）装载机 2~3 台。

（11）供水车及其他相关机具。

要求在 SMA 工程（含试验段）开工前，所有机械设备保持良好的工作状态，对其中的计量设备都应逐台进行检验标定。

三、施工环境条件

影响冷却时间或可压实有效时段的因素主要有以下几个方面：

1. 层厚：铺设厚度增加 25%，压实时间可延长 50%；
2. 摊铺温度：摊铺温度从 140℃提高到 160℃，压实时间可延长 40%；
3. 最低压实温度：从 90℃增加到 100℃，压实时间缩短 30%；
4. 风速：从 0 增至 20 km/h，压实时间可延长 19%。

由于 SMA 面层铺筑厚度薄，一般为 30~40mm，摊铺后散热很快，而且所用沥青比较黏稠，不少情况下还使用改性沥青，要求压实终结温度较高，故可压实的时间较短。因此，对施工环境条件的要求比常规沥青路面严格，而且需要相应地提高施工温度，以适当地延长有效压实时间。

在普通沥青 SMA 施工时，气温（荫处）及路床温度应高于 10℃，对于改性沥青 SMA 施工则应高于 15 ℃，且处于气温上升的情况下，并应在干燥、清洁、经整平的下卧层上铺筑。禁止在雨天施工，也应禁止在晚间施工。在大风天气与寒潮降温天气，混合料摊铺后，温度下降很快，来不及压实，是否进行施工应慎重考虑，即使施工也应采取特殊的质量保证措施。

四、施工温度

SMA 混合料所用沥青结合料比常规沥青混合料的针入度小、黏度高，因此，施工温度也较高。SMA 与普通沥青混合料相比，施工难度要大一些，尤其是同时使用改性沥青时，施工时应特别注意施工温度。因为 SMA 需要加入较多数量的冷矿粉、纤维，有的改性剂也是冷态直接投入的，所以集料的加热温度需要更高一些。当使用改性沥青时，温度低了有可能拌和不均匀，应该视改性剂及纤维稳定剂的品种和剂量的不同，确定施工温度。科学的方法是根据沥青结合料的黏温曲线决定，按《SMA 技术指南》中规定的等黏温度确定施工温度。但由于改性沥青的黏度很大，在有些时候，由黏温曲线得到的施工温度会太高，有可能使沥青老化，所以同时规定了沥青结合料加热和加工的最高温度。一般情况下，SMA 的施工温度可在普通沥青混合料施工温度的基础上提高 10℃~20℃以上。要注意《SMA 技术指南》规定的温度不是一成不变的，应根据施工的气候条件（温度和风），材料、压实层厚度的具体实际情况确定。因此，合理的施工温度应从保证沥青与混合料的质量与施工和易性两个方面进行确定。

SMA路面宜在较高的温度条件下施工，当气温或下卧层表面温度低于10℃时不得铺筑SMA路面。施工温度应根据沥青标号、黏度、改性剂的品种及剂量、气候条件及铺装层的厚度确定。

沥青混合料的温度应采用具有金属探测针的插入式数显温度计测量，不得采用玻璃温度计测量。在运料车上测量时宜在车厢侧板下方打一个小孔插入不少于15 cm量取。碾压温度可借助于金属改锥在路面上打洞后迅速插入温度计测量得到（必要时应移动位置）。施工温度在气温较低、风速较高、厚度较薄、运输较远时，采用较高值；反之用低值。

五、混合料拌和

生产符合设计要求的混合料是获得沥青路面优良质量的根本保证。SMA混合料设计结果包括混合料的级配组成、沥青用量、各组成材料的用量比例，以及混合料的体积特性与性能特性。SMA路面性能与混合料体积特性对级配组成非常敏感，尤其是对三个关键筛孔（4.75 mm、2.36 mm、0.075 mm）的通过率容许偏差的要求，比常规沥青混凝土更为严格。因此，SMA混合料生产，必须对级配组成进行比较精确的质量控制。

1. 混合料生产前的准备

生产SMA应采用间歇式沥青拌和机拌和，且必须配备有材料配比和施工温度的自动检测和记录设备，逐盘打印各传感器的数据。每个台班做出统计，计算矿料级配、油石比、施工温度，铺装层厚度的平均值、标准差和变异系数，进行总量检验，并作为施工质量检测的依据。

沥青混合料的质量是沥青路面好坏的先决条件。现在拌和厂生产的混合料的最大问题是级配变异性比较大，虽然油石比的变化已经相当小，但级配变化大，仍然不能说都是最佳油石比。级配变化大的主要原因当然是集料本身的变异性大，但有些拌和厂随意更改配比也是问题。根据国内外经验，对间歇式拌和机强制要求每一盘都要打印沥青混合料的拌和数量，各个热料仓、沥青、矿粉的用量、拌和温度，并由此统计一个台班的总数，再由各热料仓的二次筛分结果计算矿料级配，油石比、拌和温度的平均值、标准差及变异系数，还可以计算出一天铺筑的平均厚度，这要比一天取样1~2 kg抽提筛分的结果准确得多。同时，可以对拌和机的性能、施工操作人员的技术素质做出客观评价。因此，必须强制要求进行总量检验，这是提高沥青路面质量的重要步骤。

使用于SMA的改性沥青可以采用成品改性沥青或在现场制作改性沥青。当使用成品改性沥青时，应经常检验改性沥青的离析情况，各项指标应符合（SMA技术指南）中规定的技术要求。

当为现场制作时，加工工艺根据改性剂的品种和基质沥青确定。改性剂必须存放在室内，不得受潮或老化变色。拌和厂的电力条件应满足现场制作改性沥青的生产需要。基质沥青的导热油加热炉应具有足够的功率。改性沥青生产后宜进入贮存罐，经过不少于半小时的继续搅拌发育后使用，贮存和运输过程中不得发生离析。

各种原材料都必须堆放在硬质地面上，在多雨潮湿地区，细集料（含石屑）和矿粉应堆放在有棚盖的干燥地面上，当细集料潮湿使冷料仓供料困难时，应采取措施。

2. 混合料试拌与检验

按所确定的生产配合比与确定的施工温度进行混合料试拌，数量以 4~5 盘为宜。由于 SMA 混合料中添加纤维、填料数量多，而且结合料黏度较大，使拌和难度增大，故较常规沥青混合料而言，干拌与湿拌时间都需要加长，一般要求增加干拌和湿拌时间 5~15s。当采用机械添加纤维时，可不与集料干拌，因为与集料干拌反而会导致纤维上浮。如采用压缩空气将纤维吹入拌和机，沥青亦同步喷入与集料进行拌和。

适合的拌和时间与方式可以用目测混合料进行估计。对试拌混合料进行外观检查，逐盘查看混合料是否拌和均匀，是否出现花料、纤维团或纤维原状颗粒，或集料颗粒未被充分涂覆等。如存在上述问题，应找出原因加以解决，增加拌和时间或做出改变，务求获得均匀一致的混合料。可从第四、五盘混合料中采取 2 个试样，在室内进行抽提与筛分，并进行马歇尔试验，检验混合料级配组成、沥青含量与马歇尔体积特性同设计的一致性。

3. 混合料的拌和与储存

完成生产配合比设计与试拌后，可正式向拌和站下达生产指令。生产指令如下：

（1）冷集料送料比例、沥青用量、纤维用量。

（2）每盘混合料中各热料仓集料、填料、沥青结合料与纤维的精确数量。

（3）沥青结合料、集料加热温度；混合料出料温度。

（4）拌和方式、干拌与湿拌时间。

拌和机应配备专用的纤维稳定剂投料装置，直接将纤维自动加入拌和机的拌和锅或称量斗中。根据纤维的品种和形状的不同，可采取不同的添加方式。添加纤维应与拌和机的拌和周期同步进行。松散的絮状纤维应采用风送设备自动打散上料，并在矿料投入后干拌及喷入沥青的同时一次性喷入拌和机内。颗粒纤维宜在集料投入后立即加入，经 5~8 s 的干拌，再投入矿粉，总干拌时间应比普通沥青混合料增加 5~10s。

喷入沥青后的湿拌时间，应根据拌和情况适当增加，通常不得少于 5s，保证纤维能充分均匀地分散在混合料中。由于增加拌和时间、投放矿粉时间加长、废弃回收粉尘等原因而降低拌和机生产率，应在计算拌和能力时充分考虑到，以保证不影响摊铺速度，造成停顿。对逸出及废弃的粉尘，应添加矿粉补足，使 0.075 mm 通过率达到配合比设计要求，拌和的 SMA 混合料应立即使用，需在储料仓中存放时，以不发生沥青析漏为度，且不得储存至第二天使用。

当采用直接投入法制作改性沥青混合料时，改性剂必须计量准确，拌和均匀分散。胶乳类改性剂必须采用专用的计量投料装置按使用比例在喷入沥青后 10 s 内投入拌和锅中，供应胶乳的泵和管道、喷嘴必须经常检查，保持畅通。颗粒状改性剂可在投放矿料后直接投入拌和锅中。

沥青拌和厂设置专用的取样台，供在运料车上对混合料取样、测量温度、盖苫布使用，与普通热拌沥青混合料生产最大不同是各个料仓之间可能不平衡。因为 SMA 为间断级配，粗集料粒径单一量多、细集料很少、矿粉用量多，为此应该在筛孔、料斗、料仓的安排上合理调配。

SMA 的矿粉需要量大，一个螺旋升送器往往来不及供料，要在矿粉设备及人力安排上特别注意。为了减少损失，首先应减少粗细集料的含粉量和含泥量。SMA 使用的纤维，最好采用机械投入，利用风送式上料设备将纤维分散并送入拌和锅中，效果更好。

SMA 对集料要求较高，经常需要采取抗剥离措施，掺加生石灰粉是最好的办法。消石灰的添加方法可以是在添加矿粉的同时按比例混合后上粉，也可以由两个料仓分别按比例上石粉和消石灰。有的地方是在生产矿粉的过程中将石灰一起加入球磨机磨细，这样实际上是添加的生石灰，不是消石灰，效果会差一点。由于 SMA 混合料的沥青用量较大，所以拌和以后不宜长时间存放，要求必须当天使用完。

六、混合料运输

混合料运输是将拌和站生产的合格 SMA 混合料按规定温度及时运输到铺筑现场。

所需的运料车数量是拌和装置混合料生产率，生产总吨数、载重车循环时间与每车载荷量的函数。运料车循环由拌和站到铺筑现场的行程、装料、卸料及返程等环节组成。为提高运输效率，SMA 宜采用大吨位运料车运输，一般选择载重量大于 20 t 的自卸车做运料车。

由于 SMA 混合料胶泥黏稠，通常比常规沥青混合料更容易黏附在车厢上，当使用改性沥青结合料时，这种情况尤甚。因此，运料车在开始运输前，应在车厢及底板上涂刷一层植物油与肥皂水混合物，使混合料不与车厢黏结。但禁止使用纯燃料油作为隔离剂，这容易对沥青混合料造成不利影响。

在运料车装载时，应采用多次卸料，以减少较大集料滚落至卸料堆边部而引起的离析。采用一次卸料粗大颗粒将滚落至车厢周边，在车厢周边形成集料的离析。这种离析在车厢端部更为显著，并将在摊铺机后铺设的路面上明显地表现出来，离析面积可遍及整个摊铺面。采用多次卸料，则在车厢中形成的离析程度将大为减轻，而且可以完全不表现在道路上。

虽然 SMA 混合料因粗集料数量很大，粗细集料的离析现象并不如常规沥青混凝土那样明显。但较粗的 SMA 混合料如 SMA-16 也可能发生某种程度的离析，故对运料车的装载方法应重视。

由于 SMA 混合料尤其是改性沥青 SMA 混合料的黏度大，如果在运输过程中被风吹、间隙时间长，混合料势必结成硬壳，造成铺筑困难或路面不均匀，影响质量。所以在任何情况下，运料车在运输过程中都应加盖布，以防表面混合料降温结成硬壳。

运料车在运输途中，不得随意停歇，必须按指定路线进入现场。进入现场前应将底盘及车轮清洗干净，防止将泥土杂物带入施工现场。运料车卸料必须倒净，如发现有剩余的残留物，应及时清除。已冷却的残留物不容许倒在下卧层上。

运料车到达现场后，应逐车严格检查 SMA 混合料的温度，不得低于摊铺温度的要求。

七、混合料摊铺

混合料摊铺是保证 SMA 路面平整度与厚度的关键工序，必须认真做好。

1. 摊铺机的标定

在铺筑 SMA 混合料之前，应对摊铺机进行标定，包括料门、条式传送器和螺旋布料器的标定。重要的是适当设置料门高度，要将充足的混合料经条式传送器输送到螺旋布料器。在摊铺机向前移动时，使混合料高度等于或大于螺旋高度的 1/2，但不超过 2/3 的高度，并使螺旋布料器经常保持运转。

2. 下承层的处理

在铺筑 SMA 之前应对下承层表面用硬扫帚或电动工具清扫，有泥土等不洁物沾污时，应一边清扫一边用高压水冲洗干净，并待进入路面中水分蒸发后铺筑。若旧路面表面不平整，应铣刨或用热拌沥青混合料铺筑整平层，恢复横断面。

注意，必须喷洒符合要求的黏层油，用量宜为 0.3~0.4 L/m²。

3. 按梯队形式摊铺

SMA 可采用常规的沥青混合料摊铺方法进行摊铺，一台摊铺机的摊铺宽度不宜超过 6m，最大不得超过 8m。高速公路的沥青面层应采用两台以上相同型号的摊铺机成梯队形式摊铺，相邻两台摊铺机应具有相同的压实能力，摊铺间距不超过 20m，保证纵向接缝为热接缝。改性沥青 SMA 混合料宜使用履带式摊铺机铺筑。

4. 熨平板预热

在摊铺作业前一天，摊铺机与压路机应在现场就位，放置于摊铺起点附近。应对摊铺机进行运行前维护检查。在摊铺工作开始前 1 h 左右，必须将熨平板预热到接近混合料摊铺温度，熨平板预热温度应不低于 150℃，以保证摊铺起始端混合料不被熨平板扯坏，造成质量缺陷。在摊铺短距离后，由于热混合料已保持熨平板温度，可关闭加热器。

5. 摊铺机的自动调平系统

由于摊铺作业的表面不平整，摊铺机制造商已开发坡度控制机构或自动调平系统，通过修正熨平板牵引点的高度以调节与均衡摊铺机驶过的坡度和高程，摊铺出平整均匀的面层。

自动调平系统类型主要有挂线法与移动式参照系。移动式参照系包括机械接触式平衡梁与非接触式平衡梁两类。非接触式平衡梁自动调平系统采用的传感器主要有超声波传感器、激光传感器及光学传感器。

挂线法适用于大面积铺面工程，如机场跑道工程或基底不平整的情况。移动式参照系即平衡梁适用于基底基本平整的情况，此时摊铺机按等厚度原理进行铺筑。接触式平衡梁包括带滑靴或雪橇的各式浮动平衡梁。

SMA 层一般都是用于表面层，铺筑采用控制厚度的方法，通常是通过横跨摊铺机前后的浮动式平衡梁或拖挂的雪橇实现的。近年来平衡梁的长度越来越长（有的已经超过 16m），基准面的轮子也越来越多，这对于提高平整度是有好处的。但平衡梁越来越重也有其副作用，尤其是铺筑改性沥青 SMA 路面时，它会使轮子黏结沥青混合料，形成压痕和凹陷，甚至局部凹凸不平，在起步和终点及变坡路段、小转弯半径处尤感困难。因此，近年来国外出现了一种非接触式的平衡梁，并已经在我国不少高速公路和桥面铺装施工过程中得到了应用。这种非接触式的平衡梁是利用声呐系统，即用摊铺机前后两组高频的超声波传感器分别测量与摊铺层表面的距离，通过若干个声呐追踪器非接触式地检测已铺路面及铺筑面的高程，调整摊铺层厚度的一种非接触式设备，有助于提高摊铺层的平整度。例如丹麦的超声波测量系统，发射频率为 200Hz，5min 时间所对应的距离变化仅 0.825mm，具有很高的精度，由于它没有轮子直接接触摊铺层，与沥青混合料黏结少（尤其是黏度大的改性沥青），便于压路机紧跟摊铺机碾压，铺筑面的平整度能够得到更进一步的提高。施工结束后平衡梁可以折叠，搬运很方便，尤其适合于一些特殊的路段，如转弯半径小、起步、终点、匝道。据我国高速公路使用的实测结果，平衡梁伸展长度仅需 7.3 m，采用 4 个声呐，平整度能比接触式的平衡梁提高 5% 以上。对这种非接触式的平衡梁，值得在高速公路工程中推广应用。

6. 混合料摊铺数量控制

混合料摊铺数量通常按三种方法控制：按压实面的设计厚度；按单位面积混合料的平均数量；按竣工路面表面的设计标高。

为达到设计厚度要求，承包商必须铺筑平均厚度与设计厚度相等的面层。面层厚度的变异性取决于已有路面的不平整度，不够平整的已有路面较难满足设计厚度要求。SMA 混合料摊铺机松铺系数为 1.10~1.15，应由试铺最终确定。

当铺筑厚度较薄，或进行上面层铺筑时（如铺筑 SMA 路面），为了铺筑足够数量的路面，只进行厚度控制是不够的，应进行厚度与单位面积混合料质量（kg/m^2）的双重控制。如德国规范明确规定 SMA 混合料按铺筑厚度与铺筑质量进行双重控制，并作为两项重要的验收指标。

当要求修建的 SMA 路面达到预定的设计标高时，则应采用挂线法或其他方法控制标高。

7. 摊铺机作业

摊铺机开始铺筑前应将熨平板预热至 100℃以上，铺筑过程中应开动熨平板的振动或锤击等夯实装置。

SMA 混合料的摊铺速度应调整到与供料速度平衡，必须缓慢、均匀、连续不间断地摊铺。摊铺过程中不得随意变换速度或中途停顿。由于改性沥青或 SMA 生产影响拌和机生产率，摊铺机的摊铺速度应放慢，通常不超过3~4 m/min，容许放慢到1~2 m/min，当供料不足时宜采用运料车集中等候、集中摊铺的方式，尽量减少摊铺机的停顿次数，此时摊铺机每次均应将剩余的混合料铺完，做好临时接头。如等料时间过长，混合料温度降低，表面结硬成硬壳，影响继续摊铺时，必须将硬壳去除。

当SMA混合料同时使用改性沥青时，黏度高，摊铺阻力大。当下层洒布黏层油时，一般的轮胎式摊铺机将会顶不动运料车，产生打滑现象，所以需用履带式摊铺机摊铺，而且摊铺机的摊铺宽度也不能伸长太多。由于生产效率下降，SMA供料不足的问题比较突出，为使摊铺机不间断均匀地摊铺，摊铺速度要慢一些，宁可运料车等候摊铺，也不能摊铺机等候运料车。

SMA混合料的松铺系数应通过试铺确定。

改性沥青SMA混合料的摊铺温度应比普通沥青混合料的摊铺温度高10℃~20℃，混合料温度在卸料到摊铺机上时测量。当气温低于15℃时，不得摊铺改性沥青SMA混合料。

SMA表面层铺筑时宜采用平衡梁自动找平方式，平衡梁的橡胶轮应适当涂刷废机油等防黏结材料，在每次铺筑结束后必须清理干净。当同时使用改性沥青时宜采用非接触式平衡梁。

不得在雨天或下层潮湿的情况下铺筑SMA路面。

8. 人工找补

人工在新铺面层上补料，应在摊铺作业继续进行、碾压开始前施作，且仅用于局部整平。

9. 防止发生结合料析漏

SMA混合料在运输、等候及铺筑过程中，应注意观察，如发现有沥青析漏情况，应停止卸料，分析原因，采取降低施工温度、减少沥青用量或增加纤维用量等措施。

施工现场控制析漏，通常有以下几种方法：

（1）适当降低混合料生产温度。如发生析漏，摊铺面层发生油斑，主要原因为混合料温度过高，故首先要做也是最容易做的是降低混合料温度，可至少降低5℃。如仍不能解决问题，还可再次降低相同幅度的温度。

（2）适当降低结合料含量。如降低温度后仍不能完全制止析漏，则下一步需要改变的是适当降低结合料含量，降低值一般不超过0.3%。

（3）如果是因为纤维加入不正常，纤维量过少而发生析漏，则应设法加入足量纤维。如因纤维在混合料中分散不均匀，则应从混合料拌和工艺和时间上加以解决。

10. 防止发生混合料离析

混合料全幅摊铺的弊端很大，首先是粗集料容易产生离析，而离析和不均匀是造成路面早期损坏的主要原因。SMA属于间断级配，与一般的间断级配混合料都有一个缺点，就是施工容易离析，即施工的敏感性比较大，所以应该特别注意。

尤其对SMA-16，全幅摊铺时的离析无法避免，各个部位的温度也不均匀，这就相当于压实度不均匀。所以我们必须下功夫解决沥青混合料的离析和提高均匀性，这是当前提高沥青路面质量的关键。

我国目前使用的摊铺宽度达 12~15 m 的全幅摊铺的摊铺机，实际上在欧美国家是不允许使用的。在美国，摊铺宽度通常只有一个车道宽，由于宽度小，摊铺过程中的压实作用大，摊铺后的压实度能够达到 80%~85% 以上，相当于已经经过初压的效果，这样再进行压实的平整度会更好。所以应该对摊铺宽度予以限制，不宜超过 8 m。高速公路应采用梯队作业。有一些建设单位和施工单位认为全幅摊铺能够提高平整度，实际上是一种误解。实践证明，两台摊铺机摊铺不仅提高了压实度，而且对平整度的提高也很明显。

八、混合料压实

混合料压实是保证 SMA 路面具有优良抗车辙、抗水损害性能与耐久性的关键工序。没有充分地压实，再好的结合料、集料与混合料都无法使路面产生应有的力学强度与耐久性。由于在压实过程中不能检测压实度，混合料的压实度只能靠在压实过程中不折不扣地实施预先拟订的压实工艺（包括压实机具、压实温度、压实遍数）来保证。如果压实工艺打了折扣，在压实过程中很难发现，竣工后检验压实度不足，已无法挽回。在沥青路面的施工中，拌和和压实是两个最重要的工序。SMA 路面的压实工艺关系到 SMA 路面的成败。一般来说，SMA 的压实既特别讲究，又特别简单。之所以说特别讲究，是压实工艺与普通沥青混合料不同，压实机械、方法都不一样；之所以说特别简单，是只要掌握了要领，保持 SMA 混合料在高温时碾压，它不会像普通沥青混合料那样容易发生推塑、变形。

1. 压路机数量应与铺筑速度匹配

SMA 施工时必须有足够数量的压路机，压路机的最少数量根据与铺筑速度匹配的原则，由压路机的碾压宽度、碾压速度要求的碾压遍数计算配置。铺筑双车道高速公路沥青路面时，用初压、复压和终压的各种压路机数量不得少于 5 台。

混合料摊铺后，必须紧跟着在尽可能高的温度状态下开始碾压，不得等候。除必要的加水等短暂歇息外，压路机在各阶段的碾压过程中应连续不间断地进行；也不得在低温状态下反复碾压 SMA，以防止磨掉石料棱角或压碎石料，破坏集料嵌挤。碾压温度应符合规范的要求。

SMA 路面的初压宜采用刚性碾静压，每次碾压应直至摊铺机跟前。初压区的长度通过计算确定以便与摊铺机的速度匹配，一般不宜大于 20m。高速公路宜采用两台压路机同时进行，初压遍数一般 1 遍，以保证尽快进入复压。

摊铺机的铺筑宽度越宽，摊铺机自身的碾压效果越差，初压的要求也越高。

SMA 路面的复压应紧跟在初压后进行。试验证明，直接使用振动压路机初碾不会造成推壅。也可直接用振动压路机初压，如发现初压有明显推壅，应检查混合料的矿料级配及油石比是否合适。压路机的吨位以不压碎集料，又能达到压实度为度。复压宜采用重型的振动压路机进行，碾压遍数不少于 4 遍；也可用刚性碾静压，复压遍数不少于 6 遍。

终压采用刚性碾紧接在复压后进行,以消除轨迹,终压遍数通常为 1 遍。若复压后已无明显轨迹或终压看不出明显效果时可不再终压。即允许采用振动压路机同时进行初压、复压、终压一气呵成。

压路机的碾压遍数,在施工过程中实际上是很难统计的,很难准确确定究竟压了几遍,即使是压路机驾驶员也只能有个大概数。实际上,压路机的遍数是由摊铺机的摊铺速度、压路机的台数决定的。例如高速公路一侧铺筑宽度 10.5 m,摊铺速度为 4 m/min,每小时铺筑面积为 2 520 m^2,采用碾压宽度为 1.9 m 的压路机碾压,每次碾压搭接宽度 20cm,实际碾压宽度 1.7m,压路机速度为 4km/h,每小时碾压面积为 6800m^2,一台压路机可以碾压 2~7 遍。如果需要碾压 6 遍,再考虑压路机的加水、停歇等因素,压路机的台数不宜少于 4 台。另外需要初压和终压的压路机,总台数 4~5 台,所以要求压路机台数为 4~6 台。如果压实得好,SMA 层的压实度均可达 98%~100%,即使以双面 75 次击实次数成型的马歇尔设计密度为标准密度,也可以达到 98% 以上。

2. 不宜采用轮胎压路机

通常情况下 SMA 不宜采用轮胎压路机碾压,以防搓揉过度造成沥青玛蹄脂挤到表面而达不到压实效果。在极易造成车辙变形的路段等特殊情况下,由于减少沥青用量必须使用轮胎压路机碾压时,应通过试验论证,确定压实工艺,但不得发生沥青玛蹄脂上浮或挤出等现象。

振动压路机碾压 SMA 应遵循"紧跟、慢压、高频、低幅"的原则,即压路机必须紧跟在摊铺机后面碾压,碾压速度要慢,要匀速,并采取高频率、低振幅的方式碾压。

实践证明,由于 SMA 结构组成的特点,石料有很强的相互嵌挤作用,初压时前轮不会发生明显的推壅,SMA 的碾压比普通沥青混合料更方便,施工平整度更好。在施工过程中,"能否在高温状态下用振动压路机碾压面不产生推壅"以及"表面既有较大的构造深度又基本上不透水"是鉴别是不是真正的 SMA 的两个重要标志,应时刻进行检验。如果产生推壅现象,说明粗集料没有充分嵌挤,就不是真正的 SMA;如果路面渗水严重,也不是真正的 SMA。

3. 紧跟摊铺机进行碾压

压路机应该紧跟摊铺机向前推进碾压,碾压段长度大体相同,每次碾压到摊铺机跟前后折返碾压。SMA 的碾压速度不得超过 5 km/h。

4. 防止过度碾压

由于 SMA 的重要机理是粗集料相互嵌挤的作用,所以碾压时必须密切注意压实度的变化,防止过度碾压,过度碾压会使粗集料的棱角破碎、断裂。在压实度达到 98% 以上或者现场取样的空隙率不大于 6.5% 后,宜中止,终止请明确碾压。如碾压过程中发现有沥青玛蹄脂部分上浮或石料压碎、棱角明显磨损等过度碾压的现象时,碾压即应停止,并分析原因。

5. 防止混合料黏附轮子

为了防止混合料黏附在轮子上,应适当洒水使轮子保持湿润。水中可掺加少量的清洗剂。但应该严格控制水量以不粘轮为度，且喷水必须是雾状的，不得采用自流洒水的压路机。

6. 压路机的停留

压路机碾压过程中不得在当天铺筑的路面上长时间停留或过夜。

7. 压路机的转向

在压路机倒转方向时，在反向行驶前必须停驶。停驶必须缓慢实现，且压路机应轻轻地转向，机轮停止时不要与行驶方向呈直角。如果压路机轮与行驶方向呈直角停驶，将发生难以消除的压路机印迹。在压路机改变方向时，应尽量减少对混合料的推移。

8. 局部人工补压

在靠近路缘、罩盖等压路机不能有效碾压的部位的沥青混合料，应用人工操作的小型振动压路机或机动夯进行压实。

第三节　SMA施工质量管理和验收

对施工过程中的集料、沥青结合料与SMA混合料以及施工的各个工序进行严格的质量管理与检测，其目的在于保证SMA路面产品的各项指标，如集料级配、沥青含量、体积特性、析漏特性、压实度等与混合料设计结果即最终现场配合比最大限度地一致，误差在容许限度以内。只有这样才能使工程质量得到有效保证，并防止发生各种质量事故。在SMA混合料的生产与铺筑过程中应完成的试验，包括集料级配、沥青特性与含量、温度、室内试样混合料特性理论最大相对密度、路面原位密度、构造深度平整度、厚度与外观检查等。

一、材料质量检验

1. 集料级配

施工单位应定期检测用于SMA混合料生产的料堆集料。虽然集料特性非常重要，但在料源与加工方法不变的情况下，施工中的常规试验只限于料堆集料的级配。如果在混合料生产过程中，料堆中增加另外的集料，则料堆补充的新材料必须具备与原集料的级配相同的料源与级配，并位于容许偏差的范围内，否则料堆集料的级配可能改变。即使在混合料生产过程中料堆没有接受另外的集料，其级配也可因堆料或卸料方法而改变。因而保持料堆集料规格的稳定，以及选取具有代表性的试样进行筛分是至关重要的，这有利于对SMA混合料进行严格的级配控制。当料堆级配发生较大变化时，应对料堆集料的上料比例进行必要的调整，还应定期对间歇式装置的热料仓集料级配进行分析，作为对混合料级配的进一步校核。对 SMA 混合料的集料级配控制应比常规沥青混合料更加严格。

2. 沥青结合料

在施工过程中，用于 SMA 的沥青结合料的常规指标应每日抽样进行试验。普通沥青包括 25℃针入度、软化点与 15℃延度。改性沥青包括 25℃针入度、软化点、5℃延度、弹性恢复和 PI 值。这些指标不仅应符合我国沥青路面施工规范与改性沥青路面施工规范的要求，而且应符合所设计的 PG 性能分级相应的常规指标的要求。

但胶泥试验评价只用于混合料设计阶段，而不用于现场施工质量控制。在通常情况下，只要沥青结合料性能符合要求，则胶泥性能相应会满足要求。

二、试验段铺筑

SMA 施工难度较大，施工工艺不当会带来一定风险，所以在没有取得铺筑 SMA 成功的经验和成熟的施工工艺前，不宜大面积铺筑 SMA 面层。初次铺筑 SMA 路面时，应取得有经验的技术依托单位的指导。另外，在路基尚未沉降稳定的软土路段上也不宜铺筑 SMA 路面。

在确定铺筑 SMA 面层的工程正式铺筑前，必须针对当地的气候、交通特点和材料情况，铺筑试验段。试验段应位于施工现场，其铺筑条件应与大面积施工相同。长度宜为 200~500m，应能反映拌和装置的生产能力，使装置各组成部分运转到能生产出组成稳定一致的混合料，并检验混合料是否符合配合比设计的沥青结合料用量、矿料级配及混合料马歇尔特性，检查 SMA 表面的均匀性、构造深度和渗水情况。同时，通过试验路还要确定合理的碾压模式与施工工艺。为正式施工配合比及施工工艺做出适当调整，将大面积施工过程中可能出现的质量问题通过试验段的铺筑及时发现并加以解决。

铺筑试验段后，应该提出配合比设计及试验段铺筑报告，确定标准配合比及最佳油石比，经主管部门批准，下达开工令后才能正式铺筑。

三、混合料的取样与试验

1. 混合料取样

混合料取样地点和取样方法与频率必须做出明确的规定。SMA 混合料应按认可的方法进行取样。试验可取自装载时的载重车，也可取自摊铺机后，一般多在储料仓放料至载重车的过程中进行混合料取样。取样时应防止玛蹄脂黏附在工具上，导致量测的沥青含量偏少。取样和试验的频率应从混合料质量控制的需要确定，一般每工作日至少进行 2 组试验（级配、沥青含量、体积特性、析漏和原位密度）。为了保持良好的质量控制，每日应进行 2~3 组试验，取样应用随机方式进行，以便不偏离结果。

2. 混合料试验

在施工过程中，必须将确定的试验数据及时地集中起来，使施工单位能对SMA混合料的质量与压实度进行控制，并使业主具有接受或拒绝混合料的判断能力。

（1）沥青含量和级配试验

沥青含量和级配是SMA混合料质量与性能的根本保证，普遍采用离心抽提法和燃烧法进行试验。离心抽提试验法为我国试验规程规定的标准方法。用离心法抽提的沥青溶液中，不可避免地会混入少量通过滤纸的细矿粉成分，这些混入的细矿粉可按规程用压力过滤器回收，或用燃烧法测量。对漏入抽提液中矿粉数量的标定工作很重要，否则将使沥青含量的试验结果偏大；用燃烧法确定沥青含量的方法，对确定SMA结合料含量效果也很好，但应考虑纤维燃烧的影响。可以通过在室内进行试验标定确定，也可在燃烧残留物中计入纤维灰分的方法确定沥青含量，否则得出的沥青含量也将偏大。经抽提或燃烧后，混合料的集料级配应用水洗法筛分确定。用上述方法确定的级配与沥青含量应与建立的混合料现场配合比（JMF）相符合，偏差在容许限度以内。

（2）压实试件体积特性试验

将拌和装置生产的混合料抽取的试样，用四分法减少到适当数量，在规定的压实温度下，按双面各锤击50次，压实制备马歇尔试件。每次3~4个试件，并测定试件的毛体积相对密度，同时，用真空饱水法测定混合料的理论最大密度。然后确定试件的空隙率VV、VMA与VFA等体积参数。试验结果与设计配合比的容许偏差如下：VV一般为±60.5%，个别试样可为±1.0%；VMA ≤ 17%；VFA则应满足70%~80%的要求；马歇尔稳定度仍要求不小于6 kN。

（3）原位密度检测

原位密度是指SMA路面竣工后，钻孔取得的毛体积密度。在路面施工过程中应对混合料的原位密度进行不断检测，以保证密度达到要求。通常要求压实SMA混合料的最小密度为理论最大密度的94%，即最大空隙率为6%。目标密度应为最大理论密度的95%，目标空隙率为5%。原位密度的测定以钻取芯样的毛体积相对密度pluse为准。由于SMA在较低空隙率时仍有较高的渗水性，故量测芯样密度时应仔细操作。由于SMA路面表面构造粗糙，用核子密度仪的检测结果应用芯样法进行校正。

对于原位密度的容许偏差值要如下：按理论最大密度，目标值为95%，最小为94%；按马歇尔试件密度，目标值为99%，最小值为98%。

（4）析漏试验

由于SMA混合料必须具有稳定添加剂，以防止胶泥从粗集料析漏，故应定期对混合料进行析漏试验，使其满足最大析漏损失的要求。拌和装置生产的SMA混合料，在厂拌温度下进行析漏试验。

四、SMA 路面构造深度

　　SMA 路面的构造深度是抗滑性能的重要标志。如果结合料太软、结合料含量过高或设计空隙率过小都会使 SMA 路面构造深度变浅，甚至失去抗滑性；如果结合料含量过少、设计空隙率过大或施工过程中压实不足，则构造深度虽然很大，但因空隙率太大，不仅会降低混合料物理力学性能而且路面将渗水，必将影响其耐久性。SMA 路面在正确设计与正常施工的条件下，保持一定的构造深度与良好的抗滑性能，正是 SMA 路面特性的标志。

　　一般情况下，SMA 表面构造深度与 SMA 公称集料最大尺寸基本成正比。在正常情况下，SMA 路面的构造深度范围 SMA-10 应为 0.6~1.0 mm，SMA-13 应为 0.85~1.5 mm。

五、路面厚度与平整度

　　SMA 路面厚度与平整度的要求与常规沥青混合料相同，应按我国沥青路面施工规范的规定执行。但路面厚度与平整度是两项非常重要的质量指标，也是沥青路面施工验收指标，必须给予足够重视。路面厚度与平整度的质量主要应在混合料摊铺与压实过程中进行严格地控制。

　　SMA 路面厚度的容许误差，一般规定最多不得低于设计厚度的 10%。由于 SMA 路面一般较薄，为了保证足够的厚度，除在摊铺过程中进行厚度控制外，还应按单位面积的铺筑质量进行控制。

　　关于沥青路面平整度的要求，我国规范规定按 3 m 平整度仪检测，高速公路平整度（标准差）不超过 1.8 mm。但许多情况下，检测值都在 1.0 mm 以下，故应把 SMA 路面平整度提高到不超过 1.2 mm。对桥面隧道路面由于长度有限，平整度可用 3 m 直尺检测，最大间隙不应超过 3 mm。

六、施工过程质量控制要点

1. 重视施工前的质量管理

　　首先要加强对材料如集料、沥青结合料、填料、纤维的质量检查与管理。尤其是料堆集料的品质、粒径、形状及棱角性，必须符合规格要求。不合格的材料不得进入施工现场。

　　重要交通道路沥青和成品改性沥青应具有产品质量检验单。产品到场后，应按照规定取样检验，不得以样品的质检报告代替。检验不符合要求的成品改性沥青不得使用。

　　现场制作的改性沥青，应随机取样，检查改性沥青质量，确认是否符合聚合物改性沥青质量技术要求。主要有以下几点：

（1）改性沥青试样制作必须在改性沥青制备现场进行，不得二次加热，以防改性剂离析。

（2）当采用聚合物胶乳做改性剂时，应检测固体物含量，按要求剂量用预混法制作改性沥青试样并检查质量。

（3）改性剂在基质沥青中应分散均匀，细度达到制作要求（通常为 1~10μm）。采用放大 100 倍以上的显微镜观察后宜制作照片留存备查。

拌和装置、摊铺机、压路机的规格与性能应满足施工要求，所有机械的计量部分均应完成标定工作，并处于正常工作状态。

2. 严格进行施工过程中的质量管理

在施工过程中除对材料、混合料进行质量检测，并验证其是否达到相应质量要求外，最为重要的是对各施工工序的工艺进行严格的管理。只有对各工序的施工工艺过程进行严格的控制，才有可能获得满意的检测结果。其中 SMA 混合料生产、摊铺与压实三道工序的质量控制更为关键。

（1）对 SMA 面层，应特别重视材料质量、施工温度和压实工序的管理，使混合料形成充分嵌挤并达到稳定的状态，切忌片面追求平整度而降低压实度。

（2）SMA 路面如出现"油斑"，应分析原因，仔细检查纤维添加的方式、数量、时间，是否漏放及拌和是否均匀等，严重的应予铲除。

（3）对 SMs 混合料的质量控制重点是检测混合料试件的密度和 VV、VMA、VCA、VFA 等四大体积指标。

（4）在 SMA 混合料的生产过程中的质量控制，主要是拌和温度、矿料级配、沥青用量，它首先应该利用拌和楼打印机的数据进行总量检验，同时，进行抽提筛分校核。这些指标都采用表干法测定的毛体积相对密度计算。检测马歇尔稳定度和流值的主要目的是看试件质量是否能稳定在一个基本不变的水平上，并不是混合料质量合格与否的依据。

（5）沥青混合料拌和厂的质量管理和检查按下列规定进行：

随时检查沥青、集料的加热温度，逐车检查并记录 SMA 混合料的出厂温度。

路面钻孔取样或用核子密度仪检查压实度和空隙率。但当使用改性沥青，在钻孔取样过程中发生下列情况时，可减少钻孔次数至每千米 1 个孔，甚至不予钻孔。减少钻孔次数或不钻孔时，必须增加核子密度仪的检测次数。核子密度仪检测时应先用沙子将表面铺平并经过标定。

随时在碾压成型的路面上倒少量水，观察水的渗透情况，应基本上不透水（看不出水或者透水很慢）。

用铺沙法检测路表构造深度。良好的 SMA 结构在碾压成型后，应该是基本上不透水或者渗水很慢的，表面具有足够的构造深度。这是鉴别是不是真正的 SMA 的重要标志。

按规定随机取样，检查工地混合料的矿料级配和油石比。在对改性沥青混合料进行抽提试验时，应注意对某些不溶于溶剂的改性剂（如 PE）的数量做计算修正。

拌和厂逐盘打印的打印结果必须保存备查，每天进行总量检验，并作为施工质量管理的依据。

按要求进行马歇尔试验，计算空隙率等体积指标。

（6）现在一些工程存在片面追求平整度，不重视压实度的错误倾向，如降低温度碾压、不敢采用振动压路机等，导致开放交通后平整度迅速降低，对路面的危害极大。为提高 SMA 路面的平整度，应采取以下措施：

首先要保证基层及中、下面层的平整度达到要求。根据经验，通常情况下每铺筑一层最多只能提高平整度（标准差）0.2~0.4 mm。

应采用比较长的浮动基准梁（或滑靴、拖杠、各种平衡梁）控制方式的自动找平装置，尤其是非接触式平衡梁的效果最好。

应采用两台以上摊铺机呈梯队方式全幅摊铺，并充分保证供料，连续摊铺不停顿。为此必须有足够的配套的拌和能力，用大吨位运料车供料，且车的数量有富余。

碾压要保持均衡，速度要慢，折返时关闭振动，方向要渐渐地改变，碾压时保持直线方向行走，压路机的折返点不得在同一个断面上。

对桥涵、通道等构造物的接头处，要进行特殊处理；对软土地基路段，要采取预压等防止不均匀沉降的措施；对匝道及港湾式紧急停车带等摊铺机和压路机难以按正常施工工艺操作的部位，要辅以小型机械或人工仔细操作，以免各种原因造成的跳车。实际上沉降不稳定的路段是不宜铺筑 SMA 路面的，否则会造成不必要的经济损失。

除迫不得已的情况外，所有工序都必须由机械连续稳定地施工，避免人工修整。

所有机械不能在未冷却结硬的路面上停留。原则上所有机械，尤其是压路机从开始碾压进入角色后便不能停机休息，直至一天的施工结束后开出现场。

3. 施工前场与后场统一管理

前场（铺筑现场）与后场（拌和现场）应保持密切联系，发现质量问题应及时沟通，以便协调前后场工作，及时解决存在的质量问题。

4. 试验检测人员必须合格

试验检测人员应具有高的素质与熟练试验技术，必须经过培训，并取得合格证书，这是保证检测结果质量的关键。取样与试验误差可能占到试验结果总偏差很高的比例，因此，只有依靠试验检测人员的高素质，才能将取样与试验误差减至最小。

科学的施工组织计划是指导工程施工，取得良好经济效益和社会效益的前提。如果施工前没有周密的计划，没有进行合理组织和科学管理，必将产生各分部分项工程间、各工序间相互矛盾，机械劳动力及材料调配紊乱，导致各种资源的浪费，甚至出现一些重复的无效劳动，难以保证施工质量及安全，拖延工期，直接影响建设项目的投资效果。

1. 公路养护施工计划的任务

公路养护施工要多快好省地完成施工生产任务，必须有科学的施工组织计划，合理地解决好一系列问题。其具体任务如下：

（1）确定开工前必须完成的各项准备工作；

（2）计算工程数量、合理部署施工力量，确定劳动力、机械台班、各种材料、构件等的需要量和供应方案；

（3）确定施工方案，选择施工机具；

（4）安排施工顺序，编制施工进度计划；

（5）确定工地上的设备停放场、料场、仓库、办公室、预制场地等的平面布置；

（6）制定确保工程质量及安全生产的有效技术措施。

另外，公路养护工程的施工方案可以是多种多样的。应依据公路养护工程具体任务的特点、工期要求、劳动力数量及技术水平、机械装备能力、材料供应及构件生产、运输能力、气候等自然条件及技术经济条件进行综合分析，从几个方案中反复比较，选择最理想的方案。

2.公路养护施工计划的分类

（1）维修养护计划。其编制程序一般是按照自下而上、上下结合的原则进行，公路基层养护管理部门每年年初根据公路养护设施量、公路养护标准、养护里程、实际调查的养护情况、公路路面五项指标的测试结果及公路养护规定等，合理编制公路维修保养年度作业计划，并上报公路主管部门。经审查批准后，基层养护管理部门按上级主管部门最后核定投资额编制年度养护作业计划，并按每季、每月的养护工作量编制季、月养护计划和旬作业计划。

（2）大修和专项工程计划。基层养护管理单位应根据养护段各项设施的服务情况和状况，在年终向上级主管部门报送下一年度的单项工程计划及概算。经主管部门审查汇总后，根据养护资金的使用情况，编制年度专项工程计划。合理编制施工计划和施工方案及预算，并报上级主管部门，经审核同意后，基层单位即可安排施工。

公路养护施工组织计划的编制，要根据公路养护工程的特点，按照客观的施工规律和当时当地的具体施工条件和工期要求等，统筹考虑施工活动中的人工、材料、机械、资金和施工方法等各主要因素，对整个工程的施工进度和相应的资源分配、消耗等做出科学而合理的安排。同时，施工组织设计要体现国家的方针、政策，要确保工程质量和施工安全，做到增产节约、降低工程成本。在编制过程中一般参考下列规定和要求进行编制：

1.公路养护管理办法

养护管理办法是公路管理部门依据《公路法》及国家有关政策，结合本地养护工作实际而制定的养护管理规定，用于明确养护工作的管理、设计、监理、施工等工作职责和权限，使养护工作有章可循、有法可依。养护管理办法规定公路管理机构或公路经营公司应当安排足够的养护资金，按照《公路养护质量检查评定标准》，根据公路养护技术规范和操作规程对公路进行养护，使公路及其附属设施经常处于良好的技术状态。养护部门要制订好施工组织计划，选择切实可行的施工方案和效果最好的施工组织方法组织公路养护工作。

2. 公路养护技术规范

公路养护技术规范是用以指导公路养护技术管理的行业标准，主要内容为公路养护的一般规定、基本要求、养护技术措施及相应的对策等。由于公路养护涉及的内容较多，为了保证工作质量，要正确选择技术措施。编制施工组织设计时，要对工程情况进行分析，确定施工方案和资源情况。收集相关的定额、规范和技术标准，作为编制施工组织计划和质量管理措施的依据。

3. 公路养护质量检查评定标准

公路养护质量是指公路工程设施竣工验收交付使用后所保持的质量状况和服务水平，它包含公路设计、施工所形成的内在质量状况和公路养护所保持、提高现有技术状况的程度。

4. 计划文件和合同文件

编制施工组织设计主要有计划文件和合同文件，其中计划文件是指由公路业主编制的年度养护工作安排，包括工程内容、维修位置、数量、计划资金、施工期限要求、养护管理部门对养护维修设计、施工的指标等；合同文件是指公路业主与养护施工单位签订的合同，包括工程简述、工程计划开、竣工日期、工程数量、质量标准、工程单价、总造价、结算方式，缺陷责任，双方的权利和义务等。施工组织设计中使用的工程数量和工程内容等均应来源于计划文件或合同。

5. 工程设计文件

工程设计文件的内容，包括设计方案说明、设计图纸、施工组织计划及预算等，是编制施工组织设计的主要依据。编制施工组织设计时，查阅设计文件应了解施工方案，各项工程的结构形式和结构特点，工程数量的分布情况，个别工程对施工的特殊要求，采用新技术、新工艺、新结构、新材料的情况等。设计文件中的施工组织计划包括施工的总说明、工程进度图、主要材料计划表、主要施工机具、设备计划表等资料，为编制下一步的施工组织设计提供了较为详细的数据依据。

6. 养护安全作业规程、环保要求

养护安全作业规程要求公路管理部门和交通安全管理部门采取有效措施，防止因作业发生事故：加强安全教育和培训，严格按照标准和规定布设作业场区的标志和设施，并精心照管、保持正确。上路作业的人员要着作业服饰，依法作业，努力营造好的作业环境和通行环境。因此，施工组织设计中要考虑安全作业的因素，编制养护作业计划时，要增加安全作业措施（方案）内容，做好作业组织、作业方式、施工现场交通控制等设计。

随着人们生态意识、环保观念的增强，要求养护维修保持不破坏和污染环境。因此，施工组织设计中要考虑并做好保护环境的设计和制定保护环境需要采取的措施，如拌和场地布置要合理利用土地；维修的废料不能随意丢弃，运回基地集中堆放，重新开发回收利用的途径；拌和站应有除尘等措施，保证排放不污染环境等。

7. 路况调查资料

路况调查是公路日常养护的一项基础工作，是养护维修立项的依据，不应间断和遗漏。

调查内容包括路基、路面、桥涵构造物等，检查方法包括综合调查、专项调查、检测和特殊检查等。由于养护专项工程是通过路况普查和检测，经过技术可行性、方案可行性论证、计算和评价而确定的，因此，施工组织设计时应依据立项时路况普查的结果而进行。在调查中，对病害情况进行统计，分出轻、中、重等级，作为施工进度及排列作业顺序和流水方向的依据。

8. 拟投入设备的有关技术资料

设备的技术资料是指设备的型号、功率、容积、长度等主要能力方面的指标数据。通过调查合理选择，使设备的各种性能达到施工方案的要求，如铣刨机最大铣刨深度、每小时铣刨数量，摊铺机的幅宽、自重、摊铺效率等，以便在编制施工组织设计时合理排出工期，配置相应的运输车辆和其他辅助设备，并依此编制主要施工机具、设备计划表。表中应列出机具、设备名称、规格、数量（台班、台数）、使用期限，以及按年、季的计划用量等。

9. 拟采用材料的调查资料

材料的调查资料是指对维修所需材料储量、产地、规格、运输距离等资源情况的调查资料，使所需材料满足施工要求，也是计算运输量和运输工具数量的可靠性资料，可参考设计文件提供的资料。外购材料如沥青、水泥等要调查供应及发货地点、规格、单价、可供应数量、运输方式及运输费用；地方材料如砂子等要调查产地、质量、单价、运输方式、运输距离及运输费用；自采加工材料如碎石等要调查料场、加工场位置、可开采数量、运距等情况。调查后编制主要材料计划表，表中列出材料的名称、规格、单位、数量、来源、运输方式，按年、季的计划用量等。

10. 养护材料运输调查

材料运输调查主要是对材料运输方式的调查，因公路的封闭性，材料的运输调查较为重要，它不仅直接影响工程进度，而且在很大程度上也影响工程造价。因此，要调查清楚：沿线及附近地区的铁路、公路、河流的位置，车站、码头到工地的距离和卸货与存储能力；装卸运输标准；公路桥梁的最大承载力，航道的封冻、洪水及枯水期；当地汽车修理厂的情况及能力；民间运输能力；公路的上路地点、运输距离（包括因封闭而延长的距离）等，应根据调查结果，制订好运输方案，使设计运距与实际运距相符并经济合理。

11. 劳动力的市场价格

劳动力市场价格调查主要是对当地可动用的劳动力数量、技术水平及类别、施工能力、劳动力工资水平等情况进行调查。调查满足公路施工需求的可能性和数量，作为编制劳动力需要量计划的依据。不同的工作可选择不同水平的工人来完成，如公路养护的一些小型维修，就可以在社会上联系固定的合作伙伴来完成，专项维修则必须配备熟练的技术工人。

12. 沿线气候、水文、地质资料

沿线气候、水文、地质资料包括地形、地貌、地质、地下水、地面水、气温、降雨、风力及风向等其他（滑坡、地震、泥石流等）情况。了解沿线气候、水文、地质资料，在施工组织设计中可以合理安排工程的施工方法、工期及施工时间，以及制定在不良气候和

地质条件下，养护维修应采取的对策和措施。如根据地质条件选择不同的路基土石方施工方法，根据气温和降雨时间安排好水泥混凝土工程、路面工程及砌筑工程的施工工期，根据风力确定高空作业及吊装的方案和安全设施等。

公路养护工程施工组织设计文件由以下部分组成：

1. 总说明。总说明是主要工程的基本情况，包括养护维修编制依据、工程概况、气候环境条件、工期、主要工程内容、施工布局和计划安排、施工重点和对策、质量和安全规定，降低工程成本的技术组织措施以及施工单位的一般情况等。

2. 施工组织机构。包括施工组织机构施工组织机构框图、成本核算体系框图、施工指挥系统框图、人员进场计划表、主要岗位职责。

3. 施工工艺方法。包括施工工艺方法路面施工方法、桥面铺装施工方法、沥青混凝土面层施工工艺流程图等。

4. 质量保证措施。包括质量保证措施质量保证措施说明、质量保证体系框图。

5. 工程进度计划。包括工程进度计划总体工程进度计划表，沥青混凝土面层工程进度计划图等。总体工程施工进度计划是在确保工期和工程质量的前提下对各单项施工顺序进行安排，主要内容包括工作量和开、竣工时间，资金安排计划，施工技术措施，方案和施工方法等。其目的是在宏观上控制工程的进度。在施工总体安排时要考虑季节和气候的影响因素，如春季可安排绿化植树工程、夏季安排路面和桥梁等砌筑工程施工，秋季安排排水设施整修、冬季安排除雪等。

6. 施工安全与防护。包括施工安全与防护施工安全与防护措施、安全领导小组框图。

7. 文明施工要求。

8. 材料、设备、资金。材料、设备、资金包括设备进场计划表、材料供应计划表、资金使用计划表。

9. 现场布置图。现场布置图包括路线平面图和场地平面布置图。

（1）路线平面图。路线平面图是以整个工程为对象的施工平面布置总方案图，一般应包括以下内容：

标明拟维修的主要工程施工项目的位置，如路基、路面等重点工程的位置、路线里程、收费站、服务区等。

为工程施工服务的设施及位置，如料场、仓库、沥青拌和站、生活用房等。

施工管理机构，如现场管理单位、监理机构、工程施工队等。

重要地形地物、建筑设施，与施工有关的已有公路、车站、码头、河流、不良地质路段等。

（2）场地平面布置图。在施工技术复杂或施工条件困难的重点工程地段，由于施工环节多，需要动用较多的机械、设备和人力，要做好施工现场的施工布置，采用较大比例尺（一般为1：500~1：100）在等高线地形图上按比例绘制。图上应详细绘出施工作业现场、辅助生产设施、办公和生活等区域的布置情况，对原有地物也应适当描绘。

布置施工场地应遵循有利生产、方便生活、保护环境、安全可靠的原则，具体安排时，应注意以下几点：

在满足施工要求的条件下，尽可能布置紧凑，充分利用每寸土地，保护环境。

在施工区、辅助生产区、生活区应合理划分和布局，既要有利施工、便于管理，又要避免相互干扰，保障职工生活。

施工作业场地的布置应符合工艺流程，最大限度地缩短工地内的运输距离，在确保施工顺利进行的情况下尽量减少临时工程。

必须符合劳动保护、安全生产的要求，要有防洪、防火、防盗的设施。

总工期和分项工期计划表，是在施工方案的基础上，根据合同工期的主要项目、施工布置，对各项工程的施工时间和施工顺序做出的具体安排。主要包括工程的数量及其分布情况、各施工项目的施工期限、施工顺序与衔接情况、各专业队之间的相互配合、调动安排等内容。力求以最少的人工、机械和技术物质消耗，保证在规定工期内完成质量合格的单位工程施工任务。

施工组织机构图是施工单位为完成公路施工任务而组建的负责现场指挥、管理工作的组织机构，一般有以下两种形式：

自养项目施工组织机构。自养项目一般由养护中心（公司）承担。

专业养护单位的组织机构。专业养护单位通过招标方式确定，其施工组织机构可按照项目实施的要求来组建。项目管理组织成员来自公司内部、不同部门和单位，首先，聘任项目经理，从有关部门抽调管理人员组成项目机构；然后，抽调队伍归其指挥，建立一个项目工程队，组织新的项目管理实体。项目完成后，工程队成员仍回原单位。

其中各部门的管理内容如下：

项目经理部：一般设项目经理、项目副经理、总工程师、总会计师，对项目总体负责，以确保项目施工计划的实施。

工程技术质量科：负责质量管理、技术管理、计划、统计管理、预算合同管理。

材料设备科：料场调查、材料采购供应、机械设备管理、能源管理、维修保养。

综合行政办公室：负责本工程的财务、人事、劳资管理和后勤服务。

资金使用计划，包括资金使用时间、资金数目、资金使用的用途等，是工程顺利实施的保证。应根据项目工期进度计划安排资金使用计划表，便于每月或按项目规定时间申请资金及资金筹措。

人员进场计划是施工过程中所需人员（包括项目指挥人员、施工管理及技术人员、主要技工及操作手、后勤人员等）根据施工安排进入施工现场的时间和数量安排计划。在编制过程中要合理制订符合施工规律的人员进场计划，避免人员数量频繁波动。

主要材料进场计划是施工中材料进场时间和数量的计划，包括材料名称、规格、使用数量计划，可反映出不同时期材料的储备数量，用以合理确定仓库的面积、保障施工供给。

检测仪器进场计划是指为配合路基、路面等施工，对工地所用试验仪器的进场安排计划，内容包括检测仪器名称、规格、数量、使用用途、进场时间等。在工前准备阶段，应组织好检测仪器的进场，以便对各种原材料、加工材料及结构性材料的物理力学性能，以及施工结构体的几何尺寸等技术参数进行检测。

施工技术设计主要是对施工过程中的技术问题的设计，包括工程结构设计、材料配合比设计、施工中的关键工序的设计、施工技术措施等。具体参阅有关设计和施工规范。

质量控制标准是指在施工过程中对产生质量问题的因素和环节，依据施工技术规范的要求制定的质量控制标准，以及为达到此标准而采取的措施和方法，以确保工程质量既符合规定要求，又满足用户期望。

施工过程是各种工艺密切配合的生产活动，工艺越复杂，需控制的环节越多。如路面施工过程中，路面是用各种材料，如沙、碎石、沥青等经过制备、运输、摊铺和压实铺筑而成，因此，路面施工的质量在很大程度上取决于路面材料的制备、摊铺和压实工艺各环节的综合体现和密切配合，缺一不可。

主要工艺流程是指对施工难度大、耗用资源多，或施工技术较为复杂的工程项目分成若干步骤（工序），排列出工艺流程。工艺流程图使工程的各个环节一目了然，便于操作和管理，在施工技术规范和养护规范中列有各种工序的工艺流程，可以参照执行。

养护维修工程动用较多的工、料、机且为不间断交通作业，危险因素多。为保证施工作业的顺利实施和人民生命财产的安全，一般采取下列安全措施：

成立以主要负责人为领导的安全责任小组。施工工地设立安全工程师，班组设立安全检查员，层层落实安全检查责任，共同督促和检查操作人员操作规程和各项安全施工制度；每年开工前要进行养护施工安全教育和培训，讲解安全作业事项，做好安全培训工作；作业期间组织安全检查，由交警、路政及养护管理人员组成检查小组，进行作业期间的安全检查，发现安全隐患及时提出，并采取措施。

第四节　透层、黏层和封层施工

透层是指在半刚性基层上部为了增强半刚性基层与沥青层的黏结而洒布的乳化沥青，透层油要求能够透入基层表面一定深度；下封层的目的是防止渗透入路面的水分继续下渗进入半刚性基层，采用单层热沥青表处；黏层油设置于沥青层与沥青层之间以增强沥青层间的黏结，采用乳化沥青。

透层油、下封层与黏层油的喷洒统一使用智能沥青洒布车，应根据所洒布材料选择合适的喷嘴，确保喷洒的沥青成均匀雾状，沥青洒布车喷洒时应保持稳定的速度和喷洒量，同时应当调整喷油管的高度使同一地点接受 2~3 个喷油嘴喷洒的沥青。喷洒的沥青应当均匀，不得有洒花漏空或成条状，也不得有堆积，喷洒不足的要补洒，过量的应当清除。沥青喷洒过程中严禁一切车辆和行人通过。

喷洒区附近的结构物或其他已施工部位应当加以保护，以免溅上沥青受到污染。洒布车喷洒完一个车道停车后，应当用油槽接住排油管滴下的沥青，以防局部沥青过多。

一、透层油

透层油宜在无机结合料稳定粒料基层施工完毕后表面稍干但未硬化状态下立即喷洒，透层油应采用沥青含量不低于50%的慢裂阴离子PA-2或非离子乳化沥青PN-2，洒布量控制在（1.2±0.2）kg/m²（乳化沥青总量），可以通过试洒确定。喷洒后应通过钻孔或挖掘确认透层油透入基层的深度不小于5 mm，并能与基层成为一体。

透层油的洒布应当在上基层铺筑完成以后表面稍干但尚未硬化的状态下进行，在第一次喷洒时应当对喷洒量进行标定以满足要求，同时，进行开挖检验以观察其渗透深度。

透层油洒布以前应当用扫帚将基层表面的所有杂物和浮土扫出基层以外，同时，对路缘石及构造物等进行遮挡。透层油洒布后的养生时间应根据沥青品种及气候条件确定，在养生结束前禁止行人与车辆通行。

当气温低于10℃或大风天气，即将降雨或正在下雨时都不得喷洒透层油。

二、下封层

为了更好地防止水分下渗及与沥青层更好地黏结，要求无机结合料稳定碎石基层与沥青层之间设置下封层，下封层应于沥青层铺筑前一天施工，下封层采用单层热沥青表处。

采用与面层基质沥青相同的70-A级热沥青，洒布量为1.2 kg/m²，同步撒布采用0.4%沥青用量进行预拌的5~10 mm碎石，撒布量为6~8 kg/m²（具体应通过试验确定）。对透层油与下封层的沥青总量应控制在1.6~1.8 kg/m²。

下封层应当进行试洒，以确定热沥青与预拌碎石的撒布量。下封层沥青洒布以后，紧接着用碎石撒布车撒布预拌碎石，碎石撒布应当均匀，撒布不匀的地方采用扫帚及时扫匀，达到全面覆盖、厚度一致、集料不重叠。预拌碎石撒布后用6~8 t轻型钢轮压路机或胶轮压路机静压一遍，压路机应当行驶平稳并不得刹车或调头。

下封层施工完毕以后应当封闭交通，必须行驶的施工车辆最少应在12h后方可上路，并保证行驶过程中不得急刹车和调头。

下封层应选择干燥和较热的季节施工，并在最高气温低于15℃时期前半个月完成，即将降雨时也不得施工。

三、黏层油

沥青层之间应当喷洒黏层油，黏层油应采用沥青含量不低于50%的快裂阳离子乳化沥青，其洒布量为 0.4 kg/m2（乳液总量）。

黏层油应在沥青层铺筑的当天进行洒布，待乳化沥青破乳、水分蒸发完成以后，紧跟着铺筑沥青面层，确保黏层不受污染。黏层油的洒布量应当通过试洒布进行确定。

当气温低于 10℃时不得喷洒黏层油，路面潮湿时也不得喷洒黏层油，用水洗刷后或雨后应待表面干燥后喷洒。

第五节　沥青路面基层冷再生施工新技术

一、乳化沥青冷再生混合料级配设计

1. 拌和顺序及拌和时间

研究发现，由于乳化沥青在拌和过程中容易破乳，如果过长时间的拌和或者拌和压实中所需的用水量少于最佳用水量，乳化沥青会提前破乳，从而造成不易压实和强度降低。所以拌和顺序应如下：铣刨料、新料和水泥；外加水；乳化沥青，在每一次添加后都要进行拌和，前两次拌和可以适当延长拌和时间，使得集料之间均匀分散，并且得到一定的润滑，在最后添加乳化沥青时，为避免过早破乳，拌和时间为 45s。

2. 确定合成级配

由于在长期的气候环境和车辆荷载等因素的作用下，路面上的集料会出现细化的现象，在铣刨机器的铣刨过程中会使集料进一步的细化。同时，有关研究发现铣刨机在路面的铣刨速度也会影响铣刨料的粒径大小，铣刨机铣刨速度越快，铣刨料的粒径越大；铣刨速度越慢，铣刨料的粒径越小。但是研究发现，在冷再生配合比设计中，由于随着再生混合料中沥青旧料掺量的增加，其力学性能均逐渐变差，所以冷再生配合比设计过程中，不仅要考虑其经济性，而且也要兼顾其力学性能。掺入高棱角性的粗集料能提高路面的稳定度、抗车辙能力和摩擦系数，掺入干净的细集料能提高混合料的空隙率性能，如 VA、VMA 和 VFA。所以在保证混合料具有良好的路用性能的同时应尽可能地提高沥青铣刨料的回收比例，从而达到充分利用沥青铣刨料的目的。以回收沥青路面铣刨料为基础，掺入一定量的新集料，从而使其合成级配满足工程设计级配的要求。

（1）沥青铣刨料

为了完善结构上的不足，通过振动筛分机把铣刨料分成 3 档，分别为 0~5 mm、5~10mm 和 10~20 mm。

（2）新集料

新集料分别采用0~3mm和10~20mm的石灰岩，主要起到改善级配和提高相关的路用性能。

（3）矿粉

由于乳化沥青通过细料才能得到分散，因此，乳化沥青冷再生混合料的路用性能对于矿料中0.075 mm的通过率比较敏感，要求有足够的细料。矿粉主要为石灰岩矿粉，主要是作为填料，减少再生混合料的空隙。

3. 合成级配设计

关于冷再生混合料设计规范并没有统一的标准，只是在一些国家（如美国、加拿大和德国等西方国家）有相关的技术指南和级配范围，而且在同一个国家里不同地区部门之间都有自己的施工经验和室内试验结果，其中以美国的沥青协会（AI）、沥青再生协会（ARRA）和ASTM的冷再生混合料级配设计为主。

对比美国三个协会的冷再生混合料集料合成级配发现，ARRA与ASTM推荐的再生混合料集料合成级配范围相差不大。而AI推荐的冷再生混合料集料合成级配较其他两个协会所推荐的合成级配范围要小，且偏细。总体来说，美国在冷再生混合料设计方面具有一定的试验和施工经验。

根据各档旧料和新料的筛分结果进行掺配。冷再生层只能用于公路等级较低或者所处层位较低的层位，如高速公路和一、二级公路沥青面层的下面层及基层或者底基层，三、四级公路沥青路面的面层。为了使级配更加规范严谨，在再生混合料合成级配范围中增加了两个限定范围：控制点和限制区。控制点主要是控制级配必须通过的范围，分别为最大公称粒径、中等粒径（2.36 mm）和最小尺寸（0.075 mm）；限制点是在中等尺寸（4.75 mm或2.36 mm）和0.3 mm尺寸进行限制，为不可以通过的区域，当级配曲线通过此限制区时，表示该混合料中有过多的细料，会导致在施工过程中很难得到压实，并且不利于抵抗永久变形。

再生混合料的最佳含水量主要包括铣刨料本身含水量、外加水用量和乳化沥青中的含水量。乳化沥青和水一样在混合料压实过程中会提供润滑作用，这和泡沫沥青在再生混合料中的作用有所不同。水在再生混合料中不仅仅提供润滑作用，使混合料得到很好的压实，而且能稀释乳化沥青，从而使乳化沥青能够均匀地分散在矿料之间，水在乳化沥青和矿质集料中发挥一种媒介的作用。当再生混合料含水量小于最佳的总液体含量时，容易使乳化沥青不能均匀地分散在集料之间；外加水用量和乳化沥青中的含水量总和起不到再生混合料在拌和和压实过程中所需的润滑作用时，使得乳化沥青加快破乳，不利于施工的现场控制；当再生混合料含水量大于其最佳总液体含量时，会使混合料在压实过程中出现弹簧现象，从而无法对混合料进行压实，造成混合料的密度降低，最终使早期强度达不到预期的效果，也会延长其养生时间。

最佳含水量大部分通过重型击实试验确定，而我国《公路沥青路面再生技术规范》建议是根据控制乳化沥青用量在4%以下添加不同用量的水进行重型击实试验来确定。由于在实际现场压实过程中，主要是通过压路机对路面施加碾压、搓揉的作用，而重型击实类似于马歇尔成型方法对路面施加垂直的冲击和垂直荷载，每击实一次施加一次量化的击实功。而且在重型击实过程中由于只是围绕着筒边进行击实，往往很难满足所需的最大击实功。旋转压实成型方法是通过对混合料施加固定的压力和角度，在均匀的转速下进行成型，旋转压实成型方法与压路机在路面上进行压实较吻合，所以通过重型击实的方法来确定最佳总液体用量是否就是现场压实所需的最佳含水量值得研究。鉴于此，本节通过用重型击实和旋转压实成型的方法，分别来确定同一级配相同掺量的乳化沥青冷再生混合料的最佳含水量，研究在以上两种不同的成型方法下确定的最佳含水量的差别，研究主要通过下面三个步骤进行分析，其中水泥作为填料进行外掺，掺量为1.5%。

在沥青路面冷再生中，水泥往往作为一种常用的外掺辅助结合料，添加一定量的水泥有利于提高冷再生混合料的早期强度和抗水损害能力。有关研究表明，掺加1%的水泥后经过48h乳化沥青完全破乳，随着水泥用量的不断增加，乳化沥青破乳速度会加快。破乳速度的加快可能是由于在混合料里乳化沥青和集料电荷之间的相互吸引，以及水的吸收流失使得乳化沥青不稳定。通过对添加水泥后的乳化沥青在25℃水里进行针入度试验，并和未添加水泥的乳化沥青进行对比发现，添加水泥后的乳化沥青相对于未添加水泥的乳化沥青的25℃针入度要小，这说明水泥的添加使得乳化沥青变脆，不利于冷再生混合料的低温稳定性和抗疲劳性能。水泥的添加虽然提高了冷再生混合料的早期强度和抗水害性能，但也会降低乳化沥青的稳定性和冷再生混合料的低温性能等，正因为水泥在冷再生混合料中扮演着双重角色，所以水泥作为外掺剂，掺量一般不超过2%。我国的《公路沥青路面再生技术规范》中建议水泥等活性填料一般不超过1.5%。

4. 最佳乳化沥青用量的确定

虽然冷再生技术已经得到广泛的应用，但是关于最佳乳化沥青用量的确定还没有一个统一的方法。由于冷再生沥青路面材料主要由破碎的旧沥青混合料铣刨料、少量的新集料、乳化沥青和少量的水泥组成，并且是破碎的旧沥青路面面层材料加乳化沥青在常温下拌制的混合料，正是组成材料的多样性，使得冷再生混合料区别于一般的热拌混合料和水泥稳定类基层材料，具有复杂性，使确定冷再生乳化沥青最佳用量的方法多样化。

二、冷再生施工工艺及质量控制技术

1. 旧路面铣刨

路面铣刨根据再生方案采用传统铣刨方式进行，尽量使大部分路面铣刨料粒径控制在冷再生混合料的最大公称粒径范围内。当铣刨速度过快时，铣刨料的粒径过大，不能满足级配设计的粒径要求，造成浪费；当铣刨的速度过慢时，同理也会造成铣刨料的粒径过小，也不利于在配合比设计过程中充分利用铣刨料。铣刨时严格控制铣刨用水量，用水要均匀，铣刨料分类运输至拌和站统一存放。

2. 铣刨料的分档及存放

对路面铣刨下来的回收沥青路面材料经卡车运输到拌和厂的运输带上，通过运输带传输到筛分机对收回的铣刨料进行分档，筛分为 0~5 mm、5~10 mm、10~20 mm 三档，分开堆放存储，根据生产配比利用旧料，生产前测其含水量。

3. 新料和旧料添加

设备配用六个冷料仓和水泥、矿粉罐各一个，根据生产配比细分添加，并通过精密计量仪器严格控制各档料的掺量，从而确保混合料级配良好。

4. 混合料运输及摊铺压实

运输车应该保证其车厢内干净，并在装料过程中前后移动，尽量避免混合料发生离析现象。根据试验路的摊铺长短，拌和站和摊铺现场的距离来控制运输车的车次和发车时间的间隔，并在运输过程中在混合料顶面用篷布覆盖，以免运输时间过长和温度过高造成乳化沥青的提早破乳，从而影响施工质量。

摊铺机的熨平板应该根据冷再生混合料试验路的宽度进行调节。由于冷再生为冷铺，所以在摊铺过程中熨平板不用加热，且应保证连续、均匀、不间断地摊铺，随时检查混合料摊铺的松铺厚度，尽可能地减少裂缝的出现。

冷再生混合料的压实是冷再生质量保证的重要环节，所以选择合适的压实方式至关重要。

第六节　废旧橡胶沥青路面施工技术

将废胎胶粉应用于道路工程，不仅节约资源、保护环境，而且能降低路面噪声，改善沥青路面的使用性能。我国近年来通过一系列的研究和推广，橡胶沥青技术取得长足进步，铺筑大量实体工程，实现废旧轮胎资源化利用，保护环境，改善路面的使用性能，延长道路的使用寿命。

一、材料

1. 废旧胶粉的种类和规格

胶粉根据细度分为三种规格：

（1）粗胶粉：40 目以下（0.425 mm 以上）；

（2）细胶粉：40~80 目之间（0.425~0.180 mm 之间）；

（3）微细胶粉：80~200 目之间（0.180~0.075 mm 之间）。

2. 橡胶沥青

（1）橡胶沥青可用于沥青混合料、碎石封层、应力吸收层、防水黏结层或其他路面结构层。

（2）加工橡胶沥青的基质沥青宜选用 70#（A/B 级）道路石油沥青。

3. 粗集料料源特性

（1）粗集料应采用石质坚硬、耐磨、洁净、干燥、不含风化颗粒、表面粗糙、近立方颗粒的碎石或破碎砾石。对受热易变质的集料，宜采用经拌和机烘干后的集料进行检验。

（2）当粗集料与沥青黏附性不满足要求时，可掺加消石灰粉或生石灰粉等无机抗剥落剂，也可在沥青中掺加耐热、耐水、长期性能好的有机抗剥落剂，如聚酰胺类有机抗剥落剂。无机抗剥落剂可替代部分填料，推荐用量为矿料总质量的 1%~2%；聚酰胺类有机抗剥落剂的推荐用量为橡胶沥青质量的 0.3%~0.4%，具体掺加量应通过试验确定。

4. 粗集料规格

粗集料应按一定的粒径规格加工，应加强粗集料生产、储存、运输与使用各环节的管理，保证粗集料的颗粒级配稳定性。

二、配合比设计

1. 一般规定

（1）橡胶沥青混合料的配合比设计，宜在对同类公路配合比设计和使用情况充分调查研究的基础上进行充分借鉴成功经验，选用符合要求的材料，进行配合比设计。

（2）按照马歇尔体积法进行配合比设计时，要根据混合料设计空隙率的要求，并结合其他体积参数，确定混合料的最佳油石比。

（3）橡胶沥青混合料的矿料级配均应采用间断级配。根据矿料情况以间断级配骨架结构为原则，优化设计矿料级配。

2. 矿料级配

常用的橡胶沥青混合料按生产工艺分为湿法和干法。橡胶沥青混合料的矿料级配为间断级配，公称最大粒径一般不大于 19 mm。

3. 混合料设计标准

橡胶沥青混合料设计采用马歇尔试验配合比设计方法。当采用其他方法设计橡胶沥青混合料时，应按规范规定进行马歇尔试验及各项配合比设计检验，并报告不同设计方法各自的试验结果。

4. 橡胶沥青混合料配合比设计

优选矿料级配，确定最佳沥青用量，符合配合比设计技术标准和配合比设计检验要求。以此作为目标配比，供拌和机确定各冷料仓的供料比例、进料速度及试拌使用。

橡胶沥青混合料的生产宜采用间歇式拌和机，应按规定方法取样测试各热料仓的材料级配，确定各热料仓的配合比，供拌和机控制室使用。同时，选择适宜的筛孔尺寸和安装角度，尽量使各热料仓的供料大体平衡。通过室内试验及从拌和机取样综合确定橡胶沥青混合料生产时的最佳沥青用量。由此确定的最佳沥青用量与目标配比设计结果的差值不宜大于±的0.2%。

（1）拌和机按生产配合比结果进行试拌。铺筑试验段，并取样进行马歇尔试验，同时，从路上钻取芯样检测空隙率的大小，由此确定生产用的标准配合比。

（2）确定施工级配允许波动范围。根据标准配合比及施工质量管理要求中各筛孔的允许波动范围，制定施工用的级配控制范围，用以检查沥青混合料的生产质量。

（3）经设计确定的标准配合比在施工过程中不得随意变更。生产过程中应加强跟踪检测，严格控制进场材料的质量，如遇材料发生变化并经检测沥青混合料的矿料级配、马歇尔技术指标不符合要求时，应及时调整配合比，使混合料的质量符合要求并保持相对稳定，必要时重新进行配合比设计。

三、橡胶沥青及混合料施工

1. 一般规定

（1）橡胶沥青混合料（ARHM）适用于各等级公路的沥青面层。

（2）橡胶沥青混合料路面的适宜层厚为30~80mm。

（3）橡胶沥青路面各面层集料的最大粒径宜从上至下逐渐增大，并应与压实层厚度相匹配。单层的压实厚度不宜小于集料公称最大粒径的2.0~3.0倍。

2. 橡胶沥青的生产

橡胶沥青宜采用现场加工方式，加工厂的设置必须符合国家有关环境保护、消防安全等规定。

（1）为防止橡胶粉颗粒结团，橡胶粉中宜掺入占其总重2%~4%的碳酸钙或滑石粉。

（2）橡胶粉应存储在通风、干燥的仓库中，并采取有效的防淋、防潮和防火措施。

（3）橡胶粉现场存储时间一般不宜超过180 d。

3. 橡胶沥青的加工

（1）橡胶沥青宜采用低速剪切或强力搅拌法加工；

（2）橡胶沥青生产分为连续式和间歇式，宜采用专用设备间歇式生产橡胶沥青；

（3）橡胶沥青的加工温度宜控制在180℃~200℃，当橡胶粉掺量较大或天然橡胶含量较高时，加工温度可适当提高，但不应高于210℃；

（4）橡胶沥青在反应罐内加工搅拌的时间，即反应时间，一般为45~60min；

（5）在生产过程中，应及时检测橡胶沥青的技术指标，当采用连续式生产时，应每隔45~60min抽样检测橡胶沥青的技术指标。

4. 橡胶沥青的使用与储存

橡胶沥青原则上应在10h内使用完毕。当由于不可抗力,如需临时存储时,应将橡胶沥青的温度降到145℃~155℃范围内存储,存储时间一般不超过3d。当经过较长时间存储,再次使用前,应检测橡胶沥青的指标是否满足技术要求。如果不满足要求,则应重新加工或掺加一定剂量(掺量一般小于10%)的废胎胶粉,重新预混反应直至满足技术要求。

5. 橡胶沥青混合料的拌和

(1)拌和厂的准备。

橡胶沥青混合料宜采用间歇式拌和机拌制;

拌和厂的设置必须符合国家有关安全、环境保护等方面的规定;

拌和厂位置的选择应充分考虑运距和路况的影响及交通堵塞的可能,确保混合料的温度下降不超过规定要求,且不致因颠簸造成混合料离析;

拌和厂应具有完备的排水设施,料场及场内道路应做硬化处理,各种集料必须分隔贮存,细集料场应设防雨顶棚,防止材料污染和相互混杂。

(2)橡胶沥青混合料拌和设备的各种传感器必须定期检定,频率不少于每年一次。冷料供料装置需经标定得出集料供料曲线。

(3)间歇式拌和机应符合下列要求:

总拌和能力满足施工进度要求。拌和机除尘设备良好,能达到环保要求。

冷料仓的数量满足配合比需要,通常不宜少于5~6个。

(4)拌和机的矿粉仓应配备振动装置,以防止矿粉起拱。添加消石灰、生石灰等外掺剂时,宜增加粉料仓,也可由专用管线和螺旋升送器直接加入拌和锅,若与矿粉混合使用时应避免二者因密度不同发生离析。

(5)拌和机必须有二级除尘装置,回收矿粉不允许再次使用。

(6)橡胶沥青混合料的拌和时间应根据具体情况经试拌确定,以沥青均匀裹覆集料为标准。采用湿法工艺时,一般间歇式拌和机每盘的生产周期不宜少于45~50 s,其中干拌时间不少于3~5s;采用干法工艺时,拌和机应配备同步添加橡胶粉的投料和称重计量装置,橡胶粉宜在集料投入的同时自动加入,经10~15 s的干拌,使废胎胶粉在集料中充分分散,拌和均匀后,再同时喷入沥青、投入矿粉,每盘的生产周期不宜少于55~65 s。

(7)当橡胶沥青黏度大于2.5 Pas时,橡胶沥青的加热温度应提高5℃~10℃。

(8)拌和机宜备有保温性能良好的成品储料仓,贮存过程中混合料温降不得大于10℃,且不能有沥青滴漏。橡胶沥青混合料宜随拌随用,贮存时间不宜超过10h。

(9)拌和机在生产过程中应打印每盘料的生产数据,包括每盘料各个热料仓的矿料、填料、沥青用量和拌和的时间(精确到秒)、温度。每天应用拌和总量检验各种材料的配比和油石比的误差。定期对拌和机的计量和测温装置进行校核。

6. 橡胶沥青混合料的运输

(1)橡胶沥青混合料宜使用较大吨位的运料车运输,但不得超载运输,不得急刹车、急弯掉头，以免损伤透层或封层。运料车的运力应稍有富余，施工过程中摊铺机前方应有运料车等候。对高等级道路，待等候的运料车宜多于5辆后开始摊铺。

（2）运料车每次使用前后必须清扫干净，在车厢板上涂一薄层防止沥青黏结的隔离剂或防黏剂，但不得有余液积聚在车厢底部。从拌和机向运料车上装料时，应多次前后挪动汽车位置，平衡装料，以减少混合料离析。运料车厢四周外壁和顶部需用厚棉被或其他保温材料裹覆，以减少混合料在运输过程中的温度损失，并防雨、防污染。

（3）现场应设专人指挥运料车就位，配合摊铺机卸料。运料车进入摊铺现场时，轮胎上不得沾有泥土等可能污染路面的脏物，否则应清洗干净。宜采用数显插入式热电偶温度计（必须经常标定）检测橡胶沥青混合料的出厂温度和运到现场温度，若混合料不符合施工温度要求，或已经结成团块已遭雨淋的不得铺筑。

（4）摊铺过程中运料车应在摊铺机前10~30cm处停住，空挡等候，由摊铺机推动运料车前进开始缓缓卸料，应避免料车撞击摊铺机，影响摊铺层的平整度。卸料过程应尽量保持连续均衡，减少混合料离析，并避免撒落到下承层上。运料车每次卸料必须倒净，如有剩余，应及时清除，防止硬结。

7. 橡胶沥青混合料的摊铺

（1）铺筑高速公路、一级公路橡胶沥青混合料时，一台摊铺机的铺筑宽度不宜超过6.0m（双车道）或7.5 m（3车道以上），通常宜采用两台或更多台数的摊铺机前后错开10~20 m成梯队同步摊铺，两幅之间应有30~60 mm宽度搭接，并躲开车道轨迹带，上下层的搭接位置宜错开200 mm以上。

（2）橡胶沥青混合料宜采用履带式沥青摊铺机摊铺。应提前调整摊铺机的工作状态，在摊铺前0.5~1 h将熨平板预热至不低于100℃，摊铺时熨平板应采用中强夯等级，使铺面的初始压实度不小于85%。摊铺机熨平板必须拼接紧密，不应存有缝隙，防止卡入粒料将铺面拉出条痕。

（3）摊铺机应缓慢、均匀、连续不间断地摊铺，不得随意变换速度或中途停顿。摊铺速度宜控制在1~3m/min。摊铺过程中应随时观察粗细料是否均匀，松铺厚度是否符合规定，当发现异常或混合料出现明显的离析、波浪、裂缝、拖痕时，应及时分析原因，予以消除。

（4）摊铺机应采用自动找平方式，下面层宜采用钢丝绳引导的高程控制方式，中、上面层宜采用非接触式平衡梁摊铺厚度控制方式。

（5）摊铺机的螺旋布料器应根据摊铺速度调整并保持一个速度均衡的转动，两侧应保持有不少于送料器2/3高度的混合料，以减少在摊铺过程中混合料的离析。

（6）用机械摊铺的混合料未压实前，施工人员不得进入踩踏，不宜人工反复修整。特殊情况下，不得不由人工做局部找补或更换混合料时，需仔细进行，特别严重的缺陷应整层铲除。

（7）橡胶沥青路面施工的最低气温应不低于15℃，寒冷季节遇大风降温，不能保证迅速压实时不得铺筑橡胶沥青混合料。橡胶沥青混合料的最低摊铺温度根据铺筑层厚度、气温、风速及下卧层表面温度确定。每天施工开始阶段宜采用较高温度的混合料，但拌和机出料温度不应超出废弃温度。

（8）对高等级道路，橡胶沥青混合料的松铺系数应通过试验路段的试铺、试压确定。对于低等级道路松铺系数可通过试验路确定，也可按照经验确定，一般为1.18~1.20。

8. 橡胶沥青混合料的压实

（1）橡胶沥青路面施工应配备足够数量的压路机，根据初压、复压、终压（包括成型）的碾压步骤，选择合理的压路机组合方式，以达到最佳碾压效果。高速公路铺筑双车道橡胶沥青路面的压路机数量不宜少于5台。施工气温低、风大、碾压层较薄时，压路机数量应适当增加。

（2）压路机钢轮上的淋水喷头，应疏通、调试好，能有效控制喷水量。在碾压过程中，根据情况应随时调整喷水的大小，不得过度喷水碾压。

（3）在整个碾压过程中，应有专人指挥，负责碾压各个阶段的衔接。

（4）压路机应以慢而均匀的速度碾压；压路机的碾压路线及碾压方向不应突然改变而导致混合料推移；碾压区的长度应大体稳定，两端的折返位置应随摊铺机前进而推进，横向不得在相同的断面上。

（5）压路机的碾压温度应根据混合料种类、压路机、气温层厚等情况经试压确定。在不产生严重推移和裂缝的前提下，初压、复压、终压都应在尽可能高的温度下进行。同时不得在低温状态下反复碾压，使石料棱角磨损、压碎、破坏集料嵌挤。橡胶沥青混合料的初压温度不宜低于155℃，复压温度不宜低于135℃，终压结束温度不宜低于105℃。

（6）初压应紧跟摊铺机后面，并保持较短的初压区长度，以尽快使表面压实，减少热量散失。采用振动压路机初压时，可直接采用"高频、低幅"的模式碾压1~2遍。碾压时应将压路机的驱动轮面向摊铺机，从外侧向中心碾压。在超高路段应从低处向高处碾压，在坡道上应将驱动轮从低处向高处碾压。在整个碾压过程中应控制钢轮上的洒水量，以刚好不粘轮的洒水量为宜。

（7）复压应紧跟在初压后进行，且不得随意停顿。碾压段的总长度应尽量缩短，通常不超过50m。采用不同型号的压路机组合碾压时宜安排每台压路机做全幅碾压，以保证不同部位压实度的均匀性。宜优先采用振动压路机复压，碾压2~4遍。钢轮压路机的静压力应不低于12.5 t。振动压路机的振动频率宜为35~50 Hz，振幅宜为0.3~0.8 mm。层厚较薄时采用高频率、低振幅，以防集料破碎。相邻碾压带重叠宽度为10~20 cm。振动压路机折返前应先停止振动。

（8）在复压结束后，应用3 m直尺检测路面的纵横向平整度，结合终压及时修补，以保证良好的平整度水平。终压可选用双轮钢筒式压路机或关闭振动的振动压路机碾压，宜不少于2遍，至无明显轨迹为止。

四、橡胶沥青路面施工质量管理和检查验收

1. 橡胶粉进场前应提供全套物理、化学指标的合格检测报告；进场后应按不少于1次/10 t的频率抽检物理指标。

2. 湿法和干法工艺橡胶粉的掺量应严格按设计确定，误差应控制在设计掺量值的2%，不允许出现负误差。

3. 橡胶沥青的质量控制：

为确保橡胶沥青的质量，需进行黏度、针入度、软化点、延度、弹性恢复等指标的检测，其中黏度是关键指标，需经常性检测。

黏度检测分为橡胶沥青生产检测和混合料生产检测两部分。对于橡胶沥青生产检测，如采用连续式生产，每隔1 h从生产罐中抽取样品进行检测；如采用间歇式生产，每罐抽检一次。每次检测平行试验应不少于3个样本。对混合料生产进行检测是在生产混合料前和生产过程中从储油罐中提取样品进行检测，每隔4 h抽取一个样本。当橡胶沥青的生产和混合料生产同步进行时，可只进行橡胶沥青的生产检测。

现场黏度检测时，其试验温度为175℃，从取样到试验结束应在1 h内完成，试验过程应记录试验的时间范围。

以上各试验指标的数据应满足相应工程设计文件的要求。

4. 橡胶沥青混合料技术指标控制。

橡胶沥青混合料拌和厂应按以下步骤对其混合料的生产过程进行控制。单点检查评价方法应符合相关试验规程的要求。

从料堆和皮带运输机随时目测各种材料的质量和均匀性，检查有无泥块、冷料仓有无窜仓。目测混合料拌和是否均匀、有无花白料、油石比是否合理等。

检查控制室拌和机各项参数的设定值。控制屏的显示值，核对计算机采集和打印记录的数据与显示值是否一致。

检测混合料的材料加热温度、混合料出厂温度，取样用燃烧炉法检测混合料的矿料级配、油石比。筛分应至少检查0.075mm、2.360mm、4.750mm、9.500mm，公称最大粒径等5个筛孔的通过率。

取样成型马歇尔试件，测定其空隙率、稳定度流值，计算 VMA、VFA。

应严格控制混合料生产过程中的拌和温度和拌和时间，特别是橡胶沥青的温度和干法施工时混合料干拌时间。

以上各试验数据应满足相应工程设计文件的要求。如发现问题应及时调整，必要时需要停工，待问题解决后方可开工。

第六章 流水施工（流水作业）组织

流水作业法是公路工程施工组织的科学方法，它建立在合理分工、紧密协作和大批量生产的基础上，施工中将产品生产的各道工序分配给不同的专业队依次去完成，每个专业队沿着一定的方向，在不同的时间相继对各种施工项目进行相同的施工。基于此，本章将对流水施工组织展开分析。

第一节 施工组织方法与流水施工的概念

1. 施工过程

施工过程就是生产工程产品的过程，它是由一系列的施工活动组成的。施工过程的基本内容包括劳动过程和自然过程。一般情况下主要是劳动过程，在某些情况下还要包含自然过程，如水泥混凝土的自然养生等。水泥混凝土施工过程就是劳动过程和自然过程的结合。为了便于施工过程的时间组织，需要对施工过程进行分类。

2. 施工过程的分类

根据施工过程所需的劳动资料及其对产品所起的作用，施工过程做如下分类。

（1）施工准备过程

施工准备过程是指产品在进行生产前所进行的全部技术和现场的准备过程，如施工放样测量、实验室的标准击实试验及各种施工准备等。施工准备过程在时间组织中可能要占用工程项目总体时间，也可能不占用工程项目总体时间（需要考虑是否影响工程的工期）。

（2）基本施工过程

基本施工过程是指为了直接完成工程产品而进行的施工活动，如开挖基础、砌筑基础、回填土等。一般要估用工程项目总体时间，因此，一定要反映在进度计划中。

（3）辅助施工过程

辅助施工过程是指为保证基本施工过程的正常进行所必需的各种辅助施工活动，如动力（电、压缩空气）的供应、设备维护或维修、钢材的下料、机制砂的加工等。施工准备过程在时间组织中一般不占用工程项目总体时间，但可能某些情况下要占用工程项目总体时间。

（4）服务施工过程

服务施工过程是指为基本施工过程和辅助施工过程服务的各种服务活动，如原材料、半成品、燃料的供应与运输。服务施工过程在时间组织时一般不占用工程项目总体时间。

基本施工过程是施工过程中最主要的组成，一般所说的施工过程就是指基本施工过程。施工过程所包括的范围可大可小，既可以指分部分项工程及工序，也可以指单位工程或单项工程。基本施工过程可以由大到小依次逐层分解为单项工程、单位工程、分部工程、分项工程、工序、操作、动作。

（5）单项工程

具有独立设计文件，建成竣工后能独立发挥设计规定的生产能力或效益的工程。例如：独立的桥梁工程或隧道工程。这些工程一般包括与已有公路的连接线，建成后可以独立发挥交通功能。但是一条路线中的桥梁或隧道，在整个路线未修通前，并不能发挥交通功能，也就不能作为一个单项工程。一般情况下，一个合同段可作为一个单项工程，一个单项工程又可以由多个单位工程组成。

（6）单位工程

单位工程是单项工程的组成部分。它具有独立设计文件，可独立组织施工，并可单独作为成本计算对象的工程。单位工程建成竣工后一般不能独立发挥设计规定的生产能力或效益。例如，一个合同段内的路基工程、路面工程、桥梁（每座）、隧道（每座）、立交工程、交通安全设施、环保工程、机电工程。

（7）分部工程

分部工程是单位工程的组成部分。一般是按照单位工程中的结构部位、路段长度（一般3km）、施工特点或施工任务进行划分。例如，路基土石方、路基排水、大挡土墙、桥梁下部、基础与上部、隧道明洞、洞口、洞身开挖、隧道路面等。

（8）分项工程

分项工程是分部工程的组成部分。它按照不同的施工方法、施工部位材料、工序路段长度等进行划分。分项工程是概预算定额的基本计量单位，是工程量清单的分项细目。例如，路基土石方分部工程划分为土方路基、石方路基、软土地基等分项工程。

（9）工序

工序是指一个人或多个人，在工作地利用工具或机械对同一劳动对象连续的施工。工作地就是工人的施工场所，即工地或现场。劳动对象就是具体的工程产品或其部件。工序的主要特征是劳动者、劳动工具（机械）、劳动对象均不发生变化——如果其中一个发生变化，就意味着从一个工序转入另一个工序。

工程施工中，大部分是固定性产品施工，一般情况下劳动对象的工作地不变，施工人员或工具（机械）按顺序经过工地对劳动对象进行加工活动。因此，施工中一般将每一个工人或班组所进行的技术上相同、组织上不可分开的施工活动称为一道工序。例如，"钢筋混凝土预制"这个分项工程（也有称之为操作过程）就由这几道工序组成：安底模—绑扎钢筋—安侧模—浇筑混凝土—拆除模板—养生。

施工过程至少能分解到工序。工序可以进一步分解为操作和动作，可是并非所有的分项工程都可以分解到操作和动作，但是至少可以分解到工序。所以，工序是施工组织的基本单元，也是施工过程时间组织计算所考虑的基本单元。

（10）操作

操作是指工人为完成工序产品的组成部分所进行的施工活动。例如"模板安装"工序是由取运模板、拼装模板等操作组成。操作是由一系列相关联的动作组成。

（11）动作

动作是指工人施工时一次能完成的最基本的施工活动。如"拼装模板"这个操作由一块模板与另一块模板的拼接和固定这两个动作组成。

必须指出，就具体的施工对象而言，由于产品或项目的复杂程度不同，各种工程产品形成所经历的过程（施工过程）并不完全相同，有些分项工程就是工程产品，如底基层、基层；有些分部工程才是工程产品，如桥梁上部构造现场浇筑才是产品，而钢筋加工及安装只是半成品；作为单位工程的桥梁工程，其最终产品至少需要经过桥梁基础及下部构造、上部构造现场浇筑、桥面系及附属工程这三个分部工程产品的综合施工组成。一般来说，分项工程（操作过程）得到半成品，分部工程（也有称之为综合过程）得到产品。对于一些复杂工程，则需要将几个分部工程组成单位工程形成最终的产品。

划分和研究施工过程的基本目的在于：正确划分工序，以便合理组织施工；正确编制施工进度计划和资源供应计划及工程费用计划；科学地制定定额等。编制进度计划时（时间计划）分部工程的施工时间绝不是其各分项工程施工时间的和；同理，分项工程的施工时间也不是各工序时间的简单和；在施工过程时间组织时应考虑施工的组织方法造成的不同（见本章第二节）。而资源供应计划和费用计划，分部工程的资源数量与费用是其各分项工程资源数量的汇总和与其各分项工程费用的汇总和，以此类推。

3. 施工过程的组织原则

影响施工过程组织的因素很多，如施工性质、施工类型、机械设备条件、施工规模、自然条件等，使施工过程的组织难度加大，因此，科学合理地组织施工过程尤为重要。其原则归纳如下：

（1）施工过程的连续性

施工过程的连续性是指施工各阶段、各工序的进行，在时间上是紧密衔接的，不发生各种不合理的中断（或停顿）现象。即施工中，劳动对象（施工对象）始终处于被加工或被检验状态；或者施工过程处于自然过程中，其劳动者不出现停顿的窝工现象。保持和提高施工过程的连续性，可以避免不必要的等待和窝工，提高劳动生产率；缩短建设周期，节省流动资金，非常具有经济意义。施工过程的连续性同施工技术水平有关，机械化和自动化水平高就容易实现施工的连续性。

（2）施工过程的协调性

施工过程的协调性，也称比例性。它是指施工各阶段、各工序之间在施工能力上要保持一定的比例，各施工环节的劳动力生产效率、设备数量等都要互相协调，不发生脱节和比例失调的现象。协调性是保证施工顺利进行的前提，使施工过程中人力和设备得到充分利用，避免了施工中的停顿和等待，从而缩短施工周期。从这一点来看，施工过程协调性是施工过程连续性的保证，没有协调性就可能没有连续性，如在流水施工中施工能力配置不当就会造成窝工或间歇。

（3）施工过程的均衡性

施工过程的均衡性，也称节奏性。它是指施工过程的各个环节，都要按照施工计划的要求，在一定时间内完成相等数量的产品（工作量），或产品（工作量）数量的变化率相同。即单位时间的产量趋于相同或产量递增（减）量趋于相同。均衡施工，使各施工班组或设备的施工负荷保持相对稳定，不发生时紧时松或前紧后松现象。施工产量的均衡自然带来资源（工、料、机）消耗的均衡；能充分利用设备和工时，避免赶工造成费用增加，降低施工成本，保证施工质量；有利于资源的调配，使资源的使用也趋于均衡。

（4）施工过程的经济性

施工过程的经济性是指施工过程组织除应满足技术要求外，还必须追求经济效益，要用最小的施工投入得到尽可能大的施工产出。施工组织的根本目的就是在不影响工程质量和进度的条件下，尽可能降低工程造价。所以，连续性、协调性、均衡性这三项原则最终都要通过经济性来反映，以是否经济可靠作为衡量标准。

上述施工过程组织的四原则，是相互制约、互为条件的。在进行施工组织时，必须保证全面符合这四原则，不可偏废，但其中经济性是目的性原则。

4. 施工过程的组织

施工过程的组织可以分为空间组织和时间组织及资源组织。时间组织直接影响资源组织。

（1）空间组织

施工过程的空间组织有两方面问题。第一，是施工项目各种生产、生活、运输、行政办公等设施的空间布置问题，即施工平面图设计（将在第五章中论述）；第二，是施工作业队伍在空间（主要是具体工程施工平面空间）的布置问题。施工作业队伍的设置也是施工组织机构的设置的内容，既要考虑技术因素，也要考虑组织因素。施工作业队伍的设置可以按照以下原则进行。

工艺原则，又称工艺专业化原则。它要按照施工工艺性质的不同来设置施工作业队伍。在同一作业队伍里，配置着同工种的工人和同工种所需的机械设备，进行着同类工艺的施工。这种形式的特点是能够充分发挥设备能力，便于进行专业化的技术管理，在一定程度上能适应多种规格施工的要求。但是，由于每道工艺不能独立地产出产品，所以作业队伍之间的协作关系增加，管理比较复杂。

对象原则，又称产品专业化原则。它是按照产品（构件、分部工程等）的不同而分别设置的施工作业队伍。在产品专业化作业队伍里，集中了为制造某种产品所需要的各种设备和工种。对相同的产品进行不同工艺的施工，其工艺过程基本上是封闭的，能独立地产出产品（半成品）。这种形式简化了协作关系，便于管理；但是，这种形式需要较多的设备投资，技术工人和机械设备由于分散使用，不能充分发挥工人和设备的生产能力，对于产品品种变化适应能力较差。

混合原则。通常在一个施工项目的施工过程组织中，上述两种作业都可能会存在，这样的施工作业组织即构成了施工过程组织中的混合原则。

（2）时间组织

进行施工过程时间组织的目的，就是要求在时间上使各施工作业队伍之间，按设计的施工顺序紧密衔接，在符合工艺要求、充分利用工时和设备的条件下，尽量缩短生产周期。施工过程的组织要考虑每个具体施工过程所花费的时间及对工程施工项目总体时间（工期）的影响。时间组织的方法与施工组织方法（或者施工作业法）密不可分。施工组织方法的不同决定着时间和资源的不同；时间组织的基本作业法与施工组织的基本方法相同。

根据施工作业队伍在各施工段间的施工先后顺序，施工组织方法可以分为顺序作业法、平行作业法、流水作业法三种基本施工组织方法（作业法），以及将其进行一定组合的方法。可根据施工组织方法进行施工过程的时间组织，即编制施工进度计划。

（3）资源组织

施工资源需要量计划的编制可根据施工进度计划进行，当然如果资源供应不能满足进度计划所需要的资源，那只有两种调整途径：一是调整资源供应计划以适应进度要求；二是反过来调整进度计划以符合资源供应情况。

顺序作业法指当有若干个施工任务时，在完成一个任务后，接着再去完成另一个任务，依次按顺序进行，直至完成全部任务的作业组织方法。

这种施工组织方法（作业法）具有如下特点：没有充分利用工作面进行施工，工期较长；每天投入施工的劳动力材料和机具的种类比较少，有利于资源供应的组织工作；施工现场的组织、管理比较简单；不需要专业分工协作。使用该方法时，若由一个施工队完成全部施工任务，该施工队的人员是多面手，而设备尤其不能实现专业化生产，不利于提高劳动生产率；若按工艺专业化原则成立专业工作队（班组），各专业工作队不能连续作业，劳动力和材料的使用可能不均衡，无法发挥专业优势，所以在专业分工条件下一定不要采用顺序作业法。

平行作业法指当有若干个施工任务时，各个施工任务同时开工、平行生产的一种作业组织方法。

平行作业法有以下特点：充分利用了工作面进行施工，工期较短；每天同时投入施工的劳动力、材料和机具数量较大，影响资源供应的组织工作；如果各工作面之间需共用某种资源时施工现场的组织管理比较复杂、协调工作量大；与顺序作业法相同，不需要专业分工协作。

这种方法的实质是用增加资源的方法来达到缩短工期的目的，一般适用于需要突击性施工时的施工作业组织。

流水作业法指当有若干个施工任务时，各个施工任务相隔一定时间依次进行施工生产，相同的工序依次进行，不同的工序平行进行的一种作业组织方法。土木工程流水施工是借用工业流水生产的概念，首先劳动力必须专业分工，每个人或班组（专业队）只完成一道工序，在一个面加工完成该道工序，流动到另一个工作面施工相同的工序。与工业流水的最大不同是加工的工件不动（土木构造物固定于地面），人员（加工者）流动。

流水作业法具有以下特点：前提是必须分工，即必须按工艺专业化原则成立专业工作队（专业班组、工班），实现了专业化生产，有利于提高劳动生产率，保证工程质量；专业工作队能够连续作业，相邻工作队的开工时间能最大限度地搭接；尽可能地利用了工作面进行施工，工期比较短；每天投入的资源量较为均衡，有利于资源供应的组织工作，批量化生产优势最明显；需要较强的组织管理能力，满足施工过程的组织原则。

这种方法可以充分利用工作面，有效地缩短工期，一般适用于工序繁多、工程量大面又集中的大型构筑物的施工，如大型桥梁工程、立交桥、隧道工程等施工的组织。

$$总工日 = \sum（人工数量 \times 日）$$

不论是顺序作业法、平行作业法还是流水作业法，三个柱状图的面积都相同。将分项或分部工程的总工日数除以总人数来获得其施工持续时间（生产周期）的准确度较低、偏差较大，而且施工进度偏快。工序是施工组织的基本单元，最好是在工序这一级进行时间计算较准确，详见第五章的相关内容。

当空间上可以划分工作面且没有工艺关系制约时，可以采用立体交叉平行流水；如果有工艺制约关系时，则可进行空间流水施工。

1. 有节拍（有节奏）流水

（1）等节拍（节奏）流水

等节拍（节奏）流水也叫等步距等节拍（节奏）流水、稳定流水，是指每道工序的施工时间相同，在各施工段上的施工时间也相同，即流水节拍值全部相等。顺其自然所安排的流水施工就是既无窝工又无间歇的形式。

（2）异节拍（节奏）流水

以五座通道流水施工为例，假设每座通道的工艺顺序和工序时间相同，具体如下：挖基2天+清基2天+浇基4天+台身8天+盖板4天+回填6天。异节拍流水是指同一工序在各施工段上所花费的施工时间（流水节拍）相同，而各个工序之间的施工时间却不相同。异节拍（节奏）流水可以有以下两种流水组织形式。

异节拍成倍节拍流水是一种将流水施工组织成理想流水施工的形式，也就是既无窝工又无间歇的流水施工。为了使流水施工的效果更好，最好各道工序流水节拍之间还能成为倍数关系。

分别流水实质上是将有节拍的异节拍流水，按无节拍流水形式进行组织。

2. 无节拍（无节奏）流水

同一工序在各施工段上流水节拍不完全相同，各工序间流水节拍也不相同。无节拍流水也是常见的流水施工形式，它有三种流水的表现形式：有窝工有间歇、不窝工有间歇、有窝工无间歇。施工组织设计既要考虑技术又要考虑经济，一般更偏向经济，所以在组织无节拍流水施工时，一般是选择不窝工有间歇形式的流水施工。

流水参数共有三大类：工艺参数、空间参数、时间参数。

1. 工艺参数

（1）施工过程

在施工项目中，施工过程的范围可大可小。由大到小可分为单项工程、单位工程、分部工程、分项工程以及工序。在流水施工组织中为了简便和直观一般称之为"工序"。施工过程数目（工序个数、工序道数）用 n 表示。

（2）流水强度（V）指施工过程在单位时间内（多人）完成的工程数量 V（施工过程或工序每日的产量）= 人数（台数）× 产量定额。

2. 空间参数

（1）工作面（个数 A）

专业工种的工人从事施工所具备的活动空间（作业空间数目）。

（2）施工段（段数 m）

施工的内容（细目）在平面上划分成若干劳动量大致相等的段落。一般情况下无特别约定或说明时，以 1 个施工段就只有 1 个工作面来处理。

施工段的划分应注意：划分界限应与结构物的界限相一致，如伸缩缝沉降缝处；流水施工段的大小应保证施工有足够的作业空间，还应考虑施工机械的效率长度；各流水施工段上所消耗的资源量应尽可能相近，使流水施工的效果更理想；流水施工段的多少应与主导施工过程相协调，尤其在空间流水时特别重要。

流水作业法对批量化生产最有利，因而对施工对象的标准化程度要求高。施工中在不考虑施工工期限定条件时，同类型的施工段数量越多，流水作业法的优势越明显；但是，这绝非可以作为平面流水施工应满足 m ≥ n 的理由。

（3）施工层（r）

在组织流水施工时，为了满足专业工种对操作高度和施工工艺的要求，可将拟建工程在竖向上划分为若干个操作层。施工层可以是房屋的楼层，也可以不是（例如，框架结构一个楼层内的砌墙可以分为两个施工层：无脚手架层和有脚手架层）。在公路施工中，路基工程的高填方或深挖方地段、高桥墩等施工项目也可以竖向划分为施工层。

施工层的划分要根据施工对象的具体情况和施工方法而定。例如，挖掘机施工土质路堑，施工层就由挖掘机的臂长决定；而石质路堑的施工层，取决于每次爆破作业的深度。

技术间歇是施工技术要求所必需的间歇时间，如油漆的干燥时间、水泥混凝土的凝固时间等。技术间歇有两种情况，一种是至少需要的间歇时间，即最小间歇时间（有些教科书简称为MI）。例如，管涵施工中水泥混凝土垫层浇筑完成后至少3天才能吊装涵管，少于3天不行，多于3天则可以；另一种是最多不能超过的间歇时间，即最大间歇时间（有些教科书简称为MA）。房屋的水磨石地面，对地面打磨要求就是既有最小间歇时间（假设要3天后），又有最大间歇时间（假设要在5天前完成，否则水泥混凝土太硬不易打磨）。一般情况下，人们不做约定或说明的技术间歇都是指最小间歇时间，最小间歇时间是施工中最常见的技术间歇。

组织间歇是施工组织所需要的间歇，如基底的检验时间、人员转移等。

搭接时间是表示前一道工序还未全部完成，后道工序可以提前开始施工。实际上，搭接关系是从宏观上的施工段来看工序之间的关系，而从微观上工作面来看依然是衔接。例如，基坑开挖与砌筑基础两工序之间，当一个施工段的基坑足够大可以分成两个以上工作面时，只有一个开挖班组（专业队），只要第一个工作面的基坑先开挖完成就可以进行第一个工作面的砌筑基础，同时，开挖的人员和设备转入第二工作面进行开挖基坑，这就形成了一施工段内开挖和砌筑基础之间的搭接关系。搭接时间与间歇时间的含义相反，计算符号也相反。

施工进度计划是项目施工组织设计的重要组成部分，对工程履约起着主导作用。编制施工总进度计划的基本要求：保证工程施工在合同规定的期限内完成；迅速发挥投资效益；保证施工的连续性和均衡性；节约费用、实现成本目标。

1. 顺序作业法（也称依次作业法）的主要特点

（1）没有充分利用工作面进行施工。（总）工期较长。

（2）每天投入施工的劳动力、材料和机具的种类比较少，有利于资源供应的组织工作。

（3）施工现场的组织、管理比较简单。

（4）不强调分工协作，若由一个作业队完成全部施工任务，不能实现专业化生产，不利于提高劳动生产率；若按工艺专业化原则成立专业作业队（班组），各专业队是间歇作业，不能连续作业，材料供应也是间歇供应，劳动力和材料的使用可能不均衡。

2. 平行作业法的主要特点

（1）充分利用工作面进行施工，（总）工期较短；

（2）每天同时投入施工的劳动力、材料和机具数量较大，材料供应特别集中，所需作业班组很多，影响资源供应的组织工作；

（3）如果各工作面之间需共用某种资源时，施工现场的组织管理比较复杂、协调工作量大；

（4）不强调分工协作，各作业单位都是间歇作业，此点与顺序作业法相同。

这种方法的实质是用增加资源的方法来达到缩短（总）工期的目的，一般适用于需要突击性施工时施工作业的组织。

3. 流水作业法的主要特点

（1）必须按工艺专业化原则成立专业作业队（班组），实现专业化生产，有利于提高劳动生产率，保证工程质量；

（2）专业化作业队能够连续作业，相邻作业队的施工时间能最大限度地搭接；

（3）尽可能利用工作面进行施工。工期比较短；

（4）每天投入的资源量较为均衡，有利于资源供应的组织工作；

（5）需要较强的组织管理能力。

这种方法可以充分利用工作面，有效地缩短工期，一般适用于工序繁多、工程量大且集中的大型构筑物的施工，如大型桥梁工程、立交桥、隧道工程、路面等施工的组织。

4. 公路工程常用的流水施工组织

（1）公路工程常用的流水参数。

工艺参数：施工过程数（工序个数），流水强度 V。

空间参数：工作面 A、施工段 m、施工层。

时间参数：流水节拍 t、流水步距 k、技术性间歇时间、组织性间歇时间、搭接时间等。

（2）公路工程流水施工分类。

按节拍的流水施工可以分为两类。

一是有节拍（有节奏）流水：等节拍（等节奏）流水、异节拍（异节奏）流水。

二是无节拍（非节奏）流水。

按施工段在空间分布形式的流水施工可以分为流水段法流水施工、流水线法流水施工。

（3）路面工程的线性流水施工组织。一般路面各结构层施工的速度不同，从而持续时间往往不同。组织路面流水施工时应注意的要点如下：

各结构层的施工速度和持续时间。要考虑影响每个施工段的因素，水泥稳定碎石的延迟时间、沥青拌合能力、温度要求、摊铺速度、养护时间、最小工作面的要求等。

相邻结构层之间的速度决定了相邻结构层之间的搭接类型，前道工序的速度快于后道工序时选用开始到开始搭接类型；否则选用完成到完成搭接类型。

相邻结构层工序之间的搭接时距的计算如下：

$$时距 = 最小工作面长度 / 两者中快的速度$$

首先，要落实施工组织；其次，为实现进度目标，应注意分析影响工程进度的风险，并在分析的基础上采取风险管理的措施；最后，采取必要的技术措施，对各种施工方案进行论证，选择既经济又能节省工期的施工方案。

施工进度计划应准确、全面地表示施工项目中各个单位工程或各分项、分部工程的施工顺序、施工时间及相互衔接关系。施工进度计划的编制应根据各施工阶段的工作内容、工作程序、持续时间和衔接关系，以及进度总目标，按资源优化配置的原则进行。在计划实施过程中应严格检查各工程环节的实际进度，及时纠正偏差或调整计划，跟踪实施，如此循环、推进，直至工程竣工验收。

施工总进度计划是以工程项目群体为对象，对整个工地的所有工程施工活动提出时间安排表。其作用是确定分部、分项工程及关键工序准备、实施期限，开工和完工的日期；确定人力资源、材料、成品、半成品、施工机具的需要量和调配方案，为项目经理确定现场临时设施、水、电、交通的需要数量和需要时间提供依据。因此，正确编制施工总进度计划是保证工程施工按合同期交付使用、充分发挥投资效益、降低工程成本的重要基础。

规定各工程的施工顺序和开、竣工时间，以此为依据确定各项施工作业所必需的劳动力、机具（械）设备和各种物资的供应计划。

常用的表达工程进度的计划方法有网络计划图和横道图两种形式。

采用网络图的形式表达单位工程施工进度计划，能充分揭示各项工作之间相互制约和相互依赖的关系，并能明确反映出进度计划中的主要矛盾；可采用计算软件进行计算、优化和调整，使施工进度计划更加科学，也使进度计划的编制更能满足进度控制工作的要求。

采用横道图的形式表达单位工程施工进度计划，可以比较直观地反映出施工资源的需求及工程持续时间。

1. 流水施工的基本参数

在组织流水施工时，用以表达流水施工在工艺流程、空间布置和时间排列等方面的特征和各种数量关系的参数，称为流水施工参数，它主要包括工艺参数、空间参数和时间参数三类。

（1）工艺参数。工艺参数是指在组织流水施工时，用以表达流水施工在施工工艺上开展的顺序及其特征的参数，包括施工过程数和流水强度两个参数。

施工过程数（n: $n=1$, …, i, …, n）。组织流水施工时，通常把施工对象划分为若干个施工过程，根据每个施工过程组织一个或几个专业化的施工队进行施工，这样可以提高工人的操作熟练程度，进而提高劳动效率。

流水强度（V）。流水强度是指某一个施工过程在单位时间内能够完成的工程量，也称为流水能力或生产能力。流水强度又分为机械施工过程流水强度和人工操作过程流水强度。

（2）空间参数。空间参数是指用以表达流水施工在空间布置上所处状态的参数，包括工作面、施工段数和施工层。

工作面（A）。工作面是指施工人员或施工机械进行施工所需的活动空间。工作面的大小，表明可以安排施工人数或机械台数的多少。每个施工人员的工作场地或每台施工机械所需工作面的大小，取决于施工过程的性质和安全施工的要求。工作面确定得合理与否，直接影响专业工作队的施工效率。

施工段数（m: $m=1$, …, j, …, m）。施工段数是指为了组织流水施工，将施工对象在平面或空间上划分成若干个劳动量大致相等的施工段落，称为施工段或流水段。一个施工段根据需要可以包括若干个工作面，它是流水施工的主要参数之一。

施工层。施工层是指在施工对象的竖向上划分的操作层数。其目的是满足操作高度和施工工艺的要求。

（3）时间参数。时间参数是指用来表达组织流水施工的各施工过程在时间排列上所处状态的参数，包括流水节拍、流水步距、间歇时间、搭接时间、施工过程持续时间和流水施工工期。

流水节拍（t_{ij}：$i=1$，…，n；$j=1$，…，m）。当某一施工过程在所有施工段上持续时间均相等时，此施工段上的持续时间称为流水节拍。

此时，该施工过程的施工是有节奏的。流水节拍通常以 t_{ij} 表示，它是组织流水施工的基本参数之一。

流水节拍的大小可以反映施工速度的快慢、节奏感的强弱和资源消耗量的多少。影响流水节拍数值大小的因素主要有：项目施工时所采取的施工方案，各施工段投入的劳动力人数或施工机械台数、工作班次，以及该施工段工程量的多少；为避免工作队转移时浪费工时，流水节拍在数值上最好是半个班的整倍数。

流水步距（k_i, $i+1$：$i=1$，2，…，$n-1$）。流水步距是指相邻两个施工过程（或专业工作队）相继投入同一施工段开始施工的时间间隔。流水步距一般用 ki, $i+1$ 来表示，其中 i（$i=1$，2，…，$n-1$）为施工过程的编号，它是流水施工的主要参数之一。

流水步距的数目取决于参加流水的施工过程数。如果施工过程数为 n 个，则流水步距的总数为 $n-1$ 个。

流水步距的大小取决于相邻两个施工过程（或专业工作队）在各个施工段上的流水节拍及流水施工的组织方式。确定流水步距时，一般应满足以下基本要求：

各施工过程按各自流水速度施工，始终保持工艺先后顺序；

各施工过程的专业工作队投入施工后应尽可能保持连续作业；

相邻两个施工过程（或专业工作队）在满足连续施工的条件下，能最大限度地实现合理搭接。

间歇时间（Z_j, $j+1$：$j=1$，…，m）。间歇时间包括技术性间歇时间和组织性间歇时间两类。间歇时间的产生会造成施工过程的中断，会使流水步距增加而使工期延长，但有时是必要的。因此，在组织施工时还是应尽量减少或避免其发生。间歇时间通常是按照工艺要求和实际工作需要的时间确定的，特别是组织性间歇时间的产生与施工条件和验收情况联系紧密，要根据实际情况确定。

技术性间歇时间。技术性间歇时间是指由于施工工艺和质量的要求，在相邻两个施工过程之间必须留有的时间间隔。如在混凝土施工过程中，根据建筑材料或现浇构件等的工艺性质，以及在考虑合理的工艺等待时间后留有的必要的养护时间等。

组织性间歇时间。组织性间歇时间是指由于组织方面的因素，在相邻两个施工过程之间必须留有的时间间隔。如对已结束的施工过程进行检查、验收和对将要进行的施工过程进行必要的准备工作所需的时间。

2.非节奏流水施工

非节奏流水施工方式是建设工程流水施工的普遍方式。

（1）非节奏流水施工的特点。

各施工过程在各施工段的流水节拍不全相等；

相邻施工过程的流水步距不尽相等；

专业工作队数等于施工过程数；

各专业工作队能够在施工段上连续作业，但有的工作面可能有闲置的时间。

（2）流水步距的确定。

在非节奏流水施工中，通常采用"累加数列、错位相减、取大差法"计算流水步距。累加数列、错位相减、取大差法的基本步骤如下：

对每一个施工过程在各施工段上的流水节拍依次累加，求得各施工过程流水节拍的累加数列；

将相邻施工过程流水节拍累加数列中的后者错后一位，相减得一个差数列；

在差数列中最大值，即为这两个相邻施工过程的流水步距。

第二节 平面流水施工组织

对于无节拍流水施工的组织，可能会发生窝工和间歇。为了组织不窝工的流水施工，最简单的方法是引入流水步距概念，其目的是通过计算的方法来消除流水施工组织中的窝工。

上述各项计算内容确定之后，即可编制施工进度计划的初步方案。编制时，首先应选择施工进度计划的表达形式，即横道图或网络图。

横道图比较简单、直观，多年来人们已习惯采用。其编制方法如下：

1.根据施工经验直接安排的方法

这种方法是根据经验资料及有关计算，直接在进度表上画出进度线，比较简单实用。其一般步骤是：先安排主导分部工程的施工进度，再安排其余分部工程并尽可能配合主导分部工程，最大限度地合理搭接起来，使其相互联系，形成施工进度计划的初步方案。

在主导分部工程中，应先安排主导施工项目（分项工程）的施工进度，力求其施工班组能连续施工，而其余施工项目应尽可能与它配合、搭接或平行施工。

2.按工艺组合组织流水施工的方法

这种方法是将某些在工艺上有关系的施工过程归并为一个工艺组合，组织各工艺组合内部的流水施工，然后将各工艺组合最大限度地搭接起来，组织分别流水。

上述采用横道图编制施工进度计划有一定的局限性。当单位工程项目中包含的施工过程较多且其互相之间的关系比较复杂时,横道图就难以充分暴露矛盾。尤其是在计划的执行过程中,当某些施工过程进度由于某种原因提前或拖后时,对其他施工过程及总工期产生的影响难以分析,因而不利于施工人员抓住主要矛盾控制施工。

采用网络图的形式表达单位工程施工进度计划,可以弥补横道图的不足。它能充分揭示工程项目中各施工过程间的互相制约和依赖关系,明确反映出进度计划中的主要矛盾;能利用计算机进行计算、优化和调整,不仅减轻工作量,而且使进度计划更科学、更便于控制。

施工进度计划初步方案编好后,应根据业主和有关部门要求、合同规定、经济效益及施工条件等,从下述几个方面进行检查与调整,以使其满足要求且更加合理。

1. 施工顺序的检查和调整

施工进度计划安排的施工顺序应符合建筑施工的客观规律。应从技术、工艺、组织上检查各个施工项目的安排是否正确合理,如屋面工程中的第一个施工项目应在主体结构屋面板安装与灌缝完成之后开始。应从质量、安全方面检查平行搭接施工是否合理、技术组织间歇时间是否满足,如主体砌墙一般应从第一个施工段填土完成后开始,检查在混凝土浇筑以后的拆模时间是否满足技术要求。总之,所有不当或错误之处,应予以修改或调整。

2. 施工工期的检查和调整

初始施工进度计划编制后,不可避免会存在一些不足之处,必须进行调整。检查与调整的目的在于使初始方案满足规定的目标,确定相对理想的施工进度计划。一般应从以下几个方面进行检查与调整:

(1) 各施工过程的施工顺序、互相搭接、平行作业和技术间歇是否合理。

(2) 施工进度计划的初始方案中工期是否满足要求。

(3) 在劳动力方面,主要工种工人是否满足连续、均衡施工的要求。

(4) 在物资方面,主要机械、设备、材料等的使用是否基本均衡,施工机械是否充分利用。

(5) 进度计划在绘制过程中是否有错误。

经过检查,对于不符合要求的部分需进行调整。对施工进度计划调整的方法一般有:增加或缩短某些分项工程的施工时间;在施工顺序允许的情况下,将某些分项工程的施工时间向前或向后移动;必要时,还可以改变施工方法或施工组织措施。

应当指出,上述编制施工进度计划的步骤不是孤立的,而是互相依赖、互相联系的,有的还交叉同时进行。由于施工过程是一个复杂的生产过程,其影响因素很多,制订的施工进度计划也是不断变化的,所以应随时掌握施工动态,不断进行调整。

流水施工有工艺、时间和空间三个基本参数。工艺参数是用来表达流水施工时开展施工工艺的顺序及特征的参数,该参数包括施工过程数和流水强度两种参数。施工过程数可以根据工程对象或施工方法来划分,如以分项工程或分部工程、单位工程作为一个施工过程。流水强度是指一个施工过程在单位时间内完成的工程量,如浇筑混凝土时一个作业班浇筑的混凝土立方量；时间参数是用来表达流水施工时有关时间安排的参数，包括流水节拍、流水步距、流水工期、间歇时间、搭接时间等参数，其中最常用的是前面3个参数。流水节拍是指施工队完成一个施工过程所需要的时间，流水步距是指相邻两个施工过程进入流水施工的时间间隔，流水工期是指完成一个流水施工所需的全部时间；空间参数是用来表达流水施工时与空间状态相关的参数，包括工作面、施工段和施工层3个参数。工作面是指安排专业工种或施工机械所需的活动空间，施工段是将施工对象在平面上或空间上划分为劳动量大致相当的施工段落，施工层是多、高层建筑在竖向划分的区段。

流水施工组织方法可按照施工范围划分或按照施工工程分解程度划分、按照流水施工节奏特征划分。按照施工范围划分，分为分项工程流水施工、分部工程流水施工、单位工程流水施工、群体工程流水施工等不同组织方式；按照施工工程分解程度划分，分为彻底分解流水施工和局部分解流水施工；按照流水施工节奏特征划分，分为有节奏流水施工和无节奏流水施工两大类，其中有节奏流水施工又分为等节奏流水施工（也称为全等节拍流水施工）和异节奏流水施工两小类，而异节奏流水施工还可再细分为等步距异节奏流水施工（也称为分别流水施工）和异步距异节奏流水施工（也称为成倍节拍流水施工）两种。流水施工的组织程序为：确定施工顺序，划分施工过程，确定施工过程数→划分施工段、施工层，确定施工段数和施工层数→计算流水节拍→确定流水施工组织方式和专业施工队数→计算流水步距→计算流水工期→绘制流水施工进度计划表。

下面结合一个案例分析流水施工在建筑工程中的应用。该工程为4层全框架混凝土结构，主体结构采用流水施工。

首先，根据定额手册和当地实际用工生产率计算的主体结构劳动量为：搭设脚手架96工日，立柱筋48工日，安装柱、梁、板（含梯）模板360工日，浇筑柱混凝土80工日，绑扎梁、板（含梯）筋160工日，浇筑梁、板（含梯）混凝土240工日，拆模120工日，砌筑砌块墙240工日。

其次，划分施工过程。该工程施工顺序为：搭设脚手架→立柱筋→安装柱、梁、板模板→浇筑柱混凝土→绑扎梁、板（含梯）筋→浇筑梁、板（含梯）混凝土→拆模→砌筑砌块墙。脚手架搭设与钢筋绑扎、模板安装并行操作，不列入流水施工。主导该工程施工过程的是柱、梁、板模板安装，为了保证主导施工过程连续作业，要将其他施工过程合并考虑，在平面上划分2个施工段，因有层间关系，所以决定组织无节奏流水施工。施工段数 $m=2 \times r=2 \times 4=8 \geq n=8$（$m$、$n$、$r$ 分别为施工段数、施工过程数和施工层数）。

公路养护质量的基本要求是：保持路面整洁、横坡适度、行车舒适，路肩整齐、边坡稳定、排水畅通，桥梁、隧道、涵洞等构造物维护完好，安全设施鲜明，沿线设施完善，绿化协调美观。要使公路的养护质量水平达到一定的高度，必须建立和完善与之相适应的养护质量管理体系和制度，采用先进的管理方法和手段，也只有这样，才能使养护质量有高的标准。

公路养护质量管理，是通过对公路养护维修施工单位、工程监理单位和监督管理部门的科学管理实施的。应当按照"质量第一"的方针和全面质量管理要求，采取有效的技术管理措施，不断提高养护质量管理水平，建立和健全"政府监督、社会监理、企业自检"的质量管理体系，严格执行质量审核制度。

施工单位的质量管理是工程质量的基础和保证。因此，施工单位必须按照公路工程建设法律、法规、规章、技术标准和规范的规定，结合公路工程质量管理的特点，按照设计文件、施工合同和施工工艺的要求组织施工。

施工单位应制定和完善相应的岗位规范、质量责任考核办法，加强施工的自检、自查和交接验收工作，建立有效的质量自检体系，推行全面质量管理，落实质量责任制，做好工程质量的全过程控制，确保工程养护质量。

养护工程施工质量控制，应包括所用材料的质量检验、修筑试验段、施工过程中的质量控制和工序之间的检查验收。

施工前，应对沥青材料按照规定的技术标准进行各项技术指标的测试。在施工过程中，也要抽样检查，根据实际情况做针入度、软化点、延度的试验，对石料、沙、石屑以及矿粉也应进行质检。

石料的测试项目有：抗压强度、磨耗率、磨光值、压碎值等。

沙、石屑则要测定其相对密度、级配组成、含水量、含土量等。

矿粉则要测定其相对密度和含水量并要进行筛析试验。

在施工过程中，应对沥青混凝土性能进行抽样调查，其项目有马歇尔稳定度、流值、空隙率、饱和度、沥青抽提试验、抽提后的矿料级配组成等。

为了确保工程质量，避免返工现象，施工单位应指定专人进行下列工作：

量测并记录沥青混凝土到达工地、摊铺、初压、复压和终压时的温度和摊铺层厚度。

加强测量工作，确保基准线的准确，并利用允许误差调整横坡度，以保证各结构层厚度，满足设计要求。

初压后及时检查平整度、路拱，进行必要的修整，坚决消除沥青混凝土摊铺时的离析现象，保证结构层的稳定度和密实度这两项重要指标达到设计要求。

在完成沥青混凝土面层施工后，施工单位应及时提供自检资料，并会同其他基础资料提交驻地监理工程师，作为面层验收的依据。

公路养护质量应进行有效的社会监理制度。质量监理是监理工程师受业主的委托，在委托权限的范围内，按照合同条件、设计条件及技术规范的规定和要求，对工程施工全过程实施的全面的质量控制和管理。质量监理不同于政府部门的质量监督，也不同于施工单位的质量自检，它是监理工程师以合同条款、设计条件和技术规范为依据，建立相应的组织系统，执行规定的工作程序，运用各种有效的手段和方法，对影响工程质量的各环节、各部位进行全方位、全天候、全过程的监督和管理。

监理工程师的质量检查工作主要如下：

1. 检查施工单位的施工工艺是否符合技术规范的规定，是否按开工前监理工程师批准的施工方案进行施工。

2. 检查施工中所使用的原材料、混合料是否符合经批准的原材料质量标准和混合料配比要求。

3. 对每一道工序完工后进行严格的质量验收，合格后才能允许施工单位进行下一道施工工序。

4. 对施工过程中产生的工程缺陷或质量事故进行调查、处理，达到设计要求后才允许施工单位继续施工。

监理工程师应尽可能地增加检查时间，加密检查点，使检查工作达到足够的深度和广度，从而尽可能早地发现问题，做到防患于未然。对已发生的质量问题，应及时责令其进行处理。

公路工程质量监督管理部门，是对公路工程质量进行监督管理审核的专职机构，它依据国家的有关法规和交通运输部颁布的技术规范、规程和质量检验评定标准，对公路工程质量进行强制性的监督管理。因而，建设、设计、监理和施工单位在工程实施阶段必须自觉接受政府质量监督部门的监督。对于公路的各项工程，应按此要求接受公路管理部门的工程质量审核，以保证高速公路的养护质量。

公路养护质量工作实行统一管理、统一规划、统一制度、统一标准、分级负责、分类实施的质量管理体系。高速公路养护质量管理体系一般采用以下模式：高速公路公司负责编制养护中、长期发展规划；制定各项管理制度和办法；制订下达年度养护计划；负责检查、监督养护工程建设市场管理情况；审批大修工程或个别技术难度很大的专项工程的技术方案、预算、决算和招标、评标方案，并组织交工验收和竣工验收工作；定期检查、评定、考核养护质量和养护管理情况，并做出奖惩决定。

分公司依据公司的养护发展规划、年度计划，负责编制本公司的养护发展规划和年度计划，并制订季度计划；根据公司各项管理办法，制定具体的实施细则并认真抓好落实；负责组织管理大修工程项目或个别技术难度很大的专项工程项目；审批专项工程的技术方案、预算、决算和招标评标方案，并组织交工验收和竣工验收工作；按季进行养护质量和养护管理的检查、评定、考核和奖惩。

管理处（管理中心）作为公司的业主代表对所辖路段的养护工作负全责。它根据分公司、子公司的养护发展规划和计划，负责编制本单位的发展规划和年、季度计划，并应制订月度计划加以组织实施；负责管理经常性的保养维修工作和组织管理专项工程项目；按照分公司、子公司的各项管理实施细则，落实各项养护措施；按月进行养护质量和养护管理的检查、评定、考核和奖惩。养护经费的使用应建立分级、分类、分项支出的核算制，维修保养经费，公司按月全额拨付，由管理处（管理中心）管理使用，按季办理决算报分公司审查，分公司每半年汇总1次报公司备查；养护专项、大修工程经费，公司依据工程预算按工程进度拨付，管理处（管理中心）、分公司按监理工程师的计量进行支付，工程完工后编制决算，分级审批，已完专项工程分公司按季汇总决算上报公司备查。

控股子公司的养护发展规划和年度计划，大修工程的预、决算、技术方案以及招标、评标方案的审批工作，考核养护质量的奖惩办法，养护经费的拨付使用等按本公司的章程规定执行。但发展规划应符合公司发展规划的总体要求，大修工程的技术方案须征得公司同意，年度计划、预算、决算和招标、评标工作接受公司的指导、监督，并报公司备案。

第三节　空间流水施工组织

有节奏流水是指同一施工过程在每一个施工段上的流水节拍都相等的流水施工组织方式。按不同施工过程中每个施工段的流水节拍相互关系又可以分为如下两类：

全等节奏流水。各施工过程流水节拍在每一个施工段上的流水节拍都相等；

异节奏流水。同一施工过程在每一个施工段上的流水节拍相等，不同施工过程之间，每个施工段的流水节拍不完全相等。通常也可将其细分为一般异节奏流水和成倍异节奏流水。

全等节奏流水施工是指在组织流水施工时，各施工过程在每一个施工段上的流水节拍相等，且不同施工过程的每一个施工段上的流水节拍互相相等的流水施工组织方式；即在组织流水施工时，如果所有的施工过程在各个施工段上的流水节拍都彼此相等，这种流水施工组织方式称为全等节奏流水施工，又称为全等节拍流水施工或固定节拍流水施工。它是一种最理想的流水施工组织方式。

1. 基本特点

（1）所有流水节拍都彼此相等；

（2）所有流水步距都彼此相等，而且等于流水节拍；

（3）每个专业工作队都能够连续作业，施工段没有间歇时间（工作面没有闲置）；

（4）专业工作队数目等于施工过程数目。

2. 组织步骤

（1）确定项目施工起点流向，分解施工过程；

（2）确定施工顺序，划分施工段；划分施工段时，一般可取 $m=N$；

（3）根据等节拍专业流水要求，确定流水节拍 1 的数值；

（4）确定流水步距 K。

各施工过程在各施工段上的流水节拍相等，但相互之间不等，且无倍数关系。根据组织方式可以组织按工作面连续组织施工或按时间连续组织施工。通过上述两种方式组织施工可以发现一般异节奏流水施工具有以下特点：

（1）若时间连续，则空间不连续；

（2）若空间连续，则时间不连续；

（3）不可能时间、空间都连续。

成倍节拍流水施工，指同一施工过程在各个施工段上的流水节拍相等，不同施工过程之间的流水节拍不完全相等，但符合各个施工过程的流水节拍均为其中最小流水节拍的整数倍的条件。根据组织方式可以组织按工作面连续组织施工或按时间连续组织施工。通过上述两种方式组织施工可以发现它具有一般异节奏流水具有的特点。

在组织流水施工时，同一施工过程在各个施工段上的流水节拍相等，不同施工过程如果在每个施工段上的流水节拍均为其中最小流水节拍的整数倍。为了加快流水施工的速度，在资源供应满足的前提下，对流水节拍长的施工过程，组织几个同工种的专业工作队来完成同一施工过程在不同施工段上的任务，专业施工队数目的确定根据流水节拍的倍数关系而定，从而就形成了一个工期短、类似于等节拍专业流水的等步距的异节拍专业流水施工方案。

1. 基本特点

（1）同一施工过程在各施工段上的流水节拍彼此相等，不同施工过程在同一施工段上的流水节拍彼此不等，但均为某一常数的整数倍。

（2）流水步距彼此相等，且等于流水节拍的最大公约数。

（3）各专业工作队（时间）能够保证连续施工，施工段（空间）没有空闲。

（4）专业工作队数目大于施工过程数目。

2. 组织步骤

（1）确定施工起点流向，分解施工过程。

（2）确定施工顺序，划分施工段；划分施工段、不分施工层时，可按划分施工段原则确定施工段数 m。

（3）按异节拍专业流水确定流水节拍。

在加快成倍节拍流水施工进度计划图中，除表明施工过程的编号或名称外，还应表明专业工作队的编号。在表明各施工段的编号时，一定要注意有多个专业工作队的施工过程。各专业工作队连续作业的施工段编号不应该是连续的，否则无法组织合理的流水施工。从上例可以看出，加快成倍节拍流水施工具有以下特点：

（1）时间连续，空间连续。

（2）流水步距 K 为各施工过程流水节拍最大公约数。

在建筑工程施工管理的过程中，流水施工技术的应用，可以实现对当前项目工期的有效缩短，以实现对项目施工效率的整体提升。在传统的情况下，建筑工程项目的施工流程通常都是基于原始的施工计划顺序来依次展开施工的。这导致在此种模式下进行施工的过程中，容易出现导致施工时间被损耗的问题，令施工活动的展开以及施工效率受到影响。而通过对流水施工技术的运用，能够使各个部门在展开工作的过程中，更加顺畅的实施相应的工作管理内容，以对自身的职责进行更好的履行，并实现对总体项目施工效率的有效提升。而后防止在施工的过程中，由于施工形式之间不适应的问题，导致施工的时间被浪费，而在应用流水施工技术的过程中，其运用可以实现对施工环节的进一步优化，并更加高效与合理地对现有的各类资源以及能源进行运用，而后以此为基础，对流水施工技术的使用价值进行彰显。并且在施工的过程中，各个环节之间的连接关系是非常紧密的，各个环节中需要履行的责任与义务也有着一定的差异，这使得需要基于流水施工技术来对施工对位的团队合作意识进行培养，令建设施工项目的展开得到保障。此外，基于对流水施工技术的应用，可以实现当前项目施工活动成本的优化，并基于对施工技术人员的严格筛选以及专业知识技能培训，来实现对施工人员技术水平的提升。

流水施工技术中的全节拍施工所针对的是当前项目的总体施工队伍。这也使得其在具体实施的过程中，需要根据当前施工项目的具体要求来展开统合分析，从而实现对施工原材料的一次性划分与分配，以实现对各类资源与能源的高效合理利用。同时，运用全节拍施工技术，能够使节拍与步距保持高度的一致性，使其可以通过对施工过程中一致性要求进行把握，以通过对相关施工技术的布置，使施工作业的连续进行得到保障，并使施工项目的综合效率得以提升。

对于流水施工技术而言，其可以通过采取成倍节拍流水来实现对相关建筑施工内容的拓展。从而能够针对非统一的施工方式来实现对施工项目整体效果的提升，并从当前的整体建设施工内容出发，来针对日常施工的具体内容，采取相应的措施进行建设。而在进行项目施工前，需要注意的是不同的施工环节，在施工时间上也有着明显的差异。这就使得在进行整体建设的过程中，需要针对不同的施工环节内容以及施工时间进行研究与把握，并对相关施工环节内部人员的情况进行熟悉，以针对具体的相关施工人员，通过更加贴近与符合项目实际情况的方式来进行人员的添加，从而实现对整体施工时间的节约，以使项目的展开能够最大限度地满足施工项目的具体要求，令流水施工技术在应用后便能够实现对整体工作时间的有效缩减。

建立完善的养护质量管理制度，对于确保工程质量是至关重要的。

1. 对于公路管理部门而言，需要做好以下工作：

（1）制定养护质量管理实施细则，健全规章制度，依靠科学养护，实行规范化管理。

（2）建立技术管理体系，养护技术管理主要包括交通情况调查、公路路况登记、养护检查与质量评定、工程检查与验收、路面管理系统和桥梁数据库开发与应用、计划统计与科研、档案管理等工作。按实际需要配合养护工程技术人员，加强业务培训，提高养护人员的管理水平。

（3）建立三级路桥检测机构，对所属公路进行检测。各级检测机构配备必要的技术人员和检测设备，取得相应资质。

（4）积极采用现代化管理手段和先进养护技术，大力推广应用新技术、新材料、新工艺、新设备，吸取和借鉴国内外高速公路养护的先进经验和技术成果，不断提高养护管理水平。

2. 对于施工单位而言，养护质量管理制度的建设主要有以下工作：

（1）建立由项目经理负责、技术负责人主持的工程质量组织体系。工程质量组织体系包括质检室、工地实验室、技术室及各单位工程中的质检组。其职责是组织、实施工程项目，对进场材料进行质量检验和试验，提出技术方案措施。

（2）加强全员质量思想意识，树立正确的质量观。坚持预防为主的方针，强化质量意识，落实质量责任。

（3）认真编制施工组织设计，严格、科学地组织施工；经常检查施工的组织设计与施工方案的落实情况。

（4）建立健全工程材料进场检查验收和取样送检制度，保证工程材料按质、按量、按时的供应。

（5）在项目负责人和技术负责人的领导下，质检室设立专职工程师负责日常质量管理工作，定期组织质量检查。如出现问题，质检人员有权制止，必要时可向主管领导提出暂停施工进行整改的建议。

（6）加强施工人员的技术培训，提高工种岗位的实践技能，提高人员素质。

（7）施工中坚持自检、互检、交接检制度，所有工序坚持标准化操作。

（8）建立质量责任制，明确落实施工人员的质量责任，提高施工人员自我控制施工质量的意识。

（9）坚持工前有交底、工中有检查、工后有验收的操作管理制度，做到施工操作程序化、标准化、规范化。

（10）处理好质量与进度的关系，摆正"进度服从质量"的思想，坚持好中求快、好中求省，严格按照标准、规范和设计要求组织、指导施工。

环境保护是我国一项长期的基本国策。在社会主义经济建设过程中，为了正确处理环境保护与经济发展的关系，坚持环境与经济协调发展的思想，国家制定了"经济建设、城乡建设、环境建设同步规划、同步实施、同步发展，实现经济效益、社会效益、环境效益统一"的指导方针，相继颁布《环境保护法》等各项有关环境保护方面的专门法律，发布了20多项环保法规和360项环保标准，以指导各行各业在经济建设活动中的环境保护工作。就公路工程环保而言，国家体现的是公路建设与环境保护并举的原则，同时提出"保护优先，防护为主，防治结合"的方针，为公路工程建设过程中的环境问题，指出明确的方向。

通过环境影响评价，对项目存在的环境影响问题进行分析、预测，并针对不利环境的影响提出防治措施，要求项目在规划设计阶段和建成运营阶段严格落实执行。涉及亚行和世行贷款的项目对环境保护问题尤为重视，要求在环境影响评价报告的基础上编制环境保护行动计划，以指导项目的整个实施过程。因此，在公路施工过程中实行环境保护，是对项目全过程环境保护管理不可缺少的重要环节，也完全符合国家关于环境保护必须与工程主体"同时设计、同时实施、同时交付使用"的三同时原则。

公路工程施工环境保护监理工作制度具体如下：

1. 例会制度

建立施工环境保护监理例会制度，定期召开环保会议。在例会期间，施工单位对近一段时间的环境保护工作进行回顾性总结，监理工程师对该月单位工程的环境保护工作进行全面评议，肯定工作中的成绩，提出存在的问题及整改要求。每次会议都应形成会议纪要。

2. 报告制度

监理单位在定期编报的月报或年报中，应包括环保监理工作情况，主要内容有：当前阶段环保工作的重点和取得的成果、现存的主要环境保护问题、建议解决的方案、随后的工作计划。

3. 函件来往制度

监理工程师在现场检查过程中发现的环境保护问题，应通过书面监理通知单形式，通知施工单位需要采取的纠正或处理措施。情况紧急需口头通知时，随后必须以书面函件形式予以确认。同样，施工单位对环境问题处理结果的答复以及其他方面的问题，也应致函监理工程师。

4. 人员培训制度

对监理工程师必须进行培训，持证上岗，并协助建设单位组织工程施工人员的环境保护培训。

5. 工作记录制度

施工环境保护监理记录是信息汇总的重要渠道，是监理工程师做出决定的重要基础资料。其内容主要有：会议记录、监理日记、环保监理月报、气象及灾害记录、质量记录、交工与竣工文件等。

第四节 无节拍流水施工段次（顺）序的优化

在实际施工中，通常每个施工过程在各个施工段上的工程量彼此不相等，或者各个专业工作队的生产效率相差悬殊，造成多数流水节拍彼此不相等，不能组织等节拍专业流水或异节拍专业流水。在这种情况下，往往利用流水施工的基本原理，在保证施工工艺、满足施工顺序要求和按照专业工作队连续的前提下，按照一定的计算方法，确定相邻专业工作队之间的流水步距，使其在开工时间上最大限度地、合理地搭接起来，形成每个专业工作队都能连续作业的流水施工方式。这种施工方式称为无节奏流水，也叫作分别流水，它是流水施工的普遍形式。

无节奏流水施工是指各施工过程在各施工段上的流水节拍彼此不等，相互之间无规律可循的流水施工组织形式。

必须保证每一个施工段上的工艺顺序是合理的，且每一个施工过程的施工是连续的，即专业工作队一旦投入施工是连续不间断的，同时，各个施工过程施工时间的最大搭接也能满足流水施工的要求。但必须指出，这一施工组织在各施工段（工作面）上允许出现暂时的空闲，即暂时没有工作队投入施工的现象。

1. 基本特点

（1）各个施工过程在各个施工段上的流水节拍通常不相等。

（2）在多数情况下，流水步距彼此不相等，而且流水步距与流水节拍之间存在着某种函数关系。

（3）每个专业工作队都能连续作业（时间连续），施工段可能有空闲（空间可能有空闲）。

（4）专业工作队数目等于施工过程数目。

2. 组织步骤

（1）确定施工起点流向，分解施工过程；

（2）确定施工顺序，划分施工段；

（3）按相应的公式计算各施工过程在各施工段上的流水节拍；

（4）按照最大差法确定相邻两个专业工作队之间的流水步距；

（5）绘制流水施工进度计划表。

组织无节奏流水的关键就是正确计算流水步距。计算流水步距可用取大差法，由于该方法是由苏联专家潘特考夫斯基提出的，所以又称为潘氏方法。这种方法简捷、准确，便于掌握。其具体方法如下：

1）对每一个施工过程在各施工段上的流水节拍依次累加，求得各施工过程流水节拍的累加数列；

2）将相邻施工过程流水节拍累加数列中的后者错后一位，相减后求得一个差数列；

3）在差数列中的最大值，即为这两个相邻施工过程的流水步距。

施工项目是包括一定工作内容的施工过程，是进度计划的基本组成单元。施工项目划分的一般要求和方法如下。

1. 明确施工项目划分的内容

应根据施工图纸和施工方案，确定拟建工程可划分成哪些分部分项工程，明确其划分的范围和内容。如单层厂房的设备基础是否包括在厂房基础的施工项目之内、室内回填土是否包括在基础回填土的施工项目之内等。

2. 掌握施工项目详细程度

编制控制性施工进度计划时，施工项目可以划分得粗一些，一般只明确到分部工程。如一般多层砌体结构建筑控制性进度计划中，只列出土方工程、基础工程、主体结构工程、装修工程等各分部工程项目。编制实施性施工进度计划时，施工项目应当划分得细一些，特别是其中的主导施工过程均应详细列出分项工程或更具体的内容，以便于掌握施工进度，起到指导施工的作用。如在多层砌体结构建筑实施性施工进度计划中，应将基础工程进一步划分为基坑开挖、地基处理、基础砌筑和回填土等分项工程。

3. 某些施工项目应单独列项

对于工程量大、用工多、工期长、施工复杂的项目，均应单独列项，如结构吊装等。凡影响下一道工序施工的项目（如回填土）和穿插配合施工的项目（如框架结构的支模、绑扎钢筋等），也应单独列项。

4. 将施工项目适当合并

为了使计划简洁清晰、重点突出，根据实际情况，可将一些在施工顺序上和时间安排上互相穿插配合的施工项目或由同一专业队完成的施工项目适当合并。主要有以下几种情况：对于一些次要的施工过程，可将它们合并到主要施工过程中去，如基础防潮层可合并到基础砌筑项目内；对于一些虽然重要但工程量不大的施工过程，可与相邻施工过程合并，如基础挖土可与垫层合并为一项，组织混合班组施工；同一时间由同一工种施工的可合并在一起，如各种油漆施工，包括门窗、栏杆等可并为一项；对于一些关系比较密切、不容易分出先后的施工过程也可合并，如玻璃和油漆，散水、勒脚和明沟等均可合并为一项。

5. 根据施工组织和工艺特点列项

如一般钢筋混凝土工程划分为支模、绑扎钢筋、浇筑混凝土等施工项目，而现浇框架结构分项可细一些，分为绑扎柱钢筋、安装柱模板、浇筑柱混凝土、安装梁板模板、绑扎梁板钢筋、浇筑梁板混凝土、养护、拆模等施工项目。但在混合结构工程中，现浇工程量不大的钢筋混凝土工程一般不再分细，可合并为一项，组织混合班组施工。

抹灰工程一般分室内、外抹灰。外墙抹灰只列一项，如有其他块材饰面等装饰，可分别列项。室内的各种抹灰应分别列项，如地面抹灰、顶棚及墙面抹灰、楼梯间及踏步抹灰等，以便组织施工和安排进度。

6. 设备安装应单独列项

土建施工进度计划列出的水暖电气卫和工艺设备安装等施工项目，只要表明其与土建施工的配合关系，一般不必细分，可由安装单位单独编制施工进度计划。

7. 项目划分应考虑施工方案

施工项目的划分，应考虑采用的施工方案。如厂房基础采用敞开式施工方案时，柱基础和设备基础可划分为一个施工项目；而采用封闭式施工方案时，则必须分别列出柱基础、设备基础这两个施工项目；结构吊装工程采用分件吊装法时，应列出柱吊装、梁吊装、屋架扶直就位、屋盖吊装等施工项目；而采用综合吊装法时，则只要列出结构吊装一项即可。

8. 项目划分应考虑流水施工安排

如组织楼层结构流水施工时，相应施工项目数量应小于或等于每层施工段数量。混合结构房屋如果每层划分为2个施工段，施工项目可分为砌墙（包括脚手架、门窗过梁、楼梯施工等）与安装预应力混凝土楼板（包括现浇圈梁等）2项；如果划分为3个施工段，则可分为砌墙、现浇圈梁，安装预应力混凝土楼板 3 项。

9. 区分直接施工与间接施工

直接在拟建工程的工作面上施工的项目，经过适当合并后均应列出。不在现场施工而在拟建工程工作面之外完成的项目，如各种构件在场外预制及其运输过程，一般可不必列项，只要在使用前运入施工现场即可。

施工项目划分和确定之后，应大体按施工顺序排列，依次填入施工进度计划表的"施工项目"一栏内。

工程量应根据施工图纸、有关计算规则及相应的施工方法进行计算。计算时应注意以下几个问题。

1. 注意工程量的计量单位

工程量的计量单位应与现行定额中所规定的计量单位一致，以便计算劳动量、材料需要量时直接套用定额，而不必进行换算。

2. 注意所采用的施工方法

计算工程量时应注意与所采用的施工方法一致，使计算所得工程量与施工实际情况相符合。如计算柱基土方工程量时，开挖方式是单独开挖、条形开挖还是整片开挖，基坑是否放坡，是否加工作面，坡度和工作面尺寸是多少等，都直接影响着工程量。

3. 注意结合施工组织的要求

组织流水施工时的项目应按施工层、施工段划分，列出分层、分段的工程量。如每层、每段的工程量相等或出入不大时，可计算一层、一段的工程量，再分别乘层数、段数，即得该项目的总工程量，或根据总工程量分别除以层数、段数，可得每层、每段的工程量。

4. 正确套用预算文件中的工程量

如已编制预算文件，且施工项目的划分与施工进度计划一致时，可直接套用施工预算的工程量，不必重新计算。当某些施工项目与预算项目不同或有出入时（如计量单位、计算规则和采用定额不同等），则应根据施工实际情况加以修改、调整或重新计算。

在流水施工展开无节拍施工的过程中，需要能够基于对施工项目的特性进行深入的分析，从而结合项目在具体化要求标准上的体现，基于对相关施工条件的把握，实现对施工项目节奏的良好控制。而且在施工的过程中，不应当单一地运用同一种节奏来进行施工活动的展开。这是由于流水施工技术的应用优势往往都比较的显著，并且可以完成对不同类型施工环境的整合，以实现对施工项目的统筹兼顾，令总体施工的效率得以提升，同时，维持在一个良好且独立的运行状态下，使各个施工流程的良好衔接状态可以得到保障，实现对间隔时间的良好控制。此外，需要注意的是流水施工技术的运用在一定程度上也会对施工状态产生影响。例如，在某施工项目进行施工的过程中，采取相应的针对性措施来实现对施工时间的有效控制，以结合项目的实际施工项目，编制出一个较为合理的管控方案，以对项目中施工技术的应用要点有一个良好的把握；并以此为基础设计出一个严苛的执行标准与要求，实现对专业工作人员知识境内培训工作的定期展开，从而对工作人员自身的综合素养进行强化。

为了使流水施工技术在应用后能够实现对建筑工程施工管理周期的有效缩短,并降低施工过程中的成本投入,就要在利用该项施工工艺的过程中,实现对各类施工环节的妥善划分,以对各个环节内容进行精准的定位与分析,从而令施工环节的展开与运作更加秩序化;并基于在施工人员、设备、材料、场地等方面管理内容的强化,来实现对建筑工程行业内容的深度管控。对于流水施工技术在建筑工程管理中,其自身在应用过程中有着十分重要的作用。而且为了能够基于对流水施工技术对施工成本损耗的降低,以及提高施工效率等作用的发挥,来实现对建筑工程市场竞争能力的提升,就要对管理方面的内容进行强化。例如,在某企业投入使用流水施工技术之前,通过站在一个宏观的角度,来对各项管理细节进行深度优化,以此实现对项目资源的全方位分析,并通过对施工进度的把握,实现对流水施工模式的完善。

1. 公路施工对生态环境的影响

(1) 道路的廊道与分割效应

对于生物来说,尤其是对地面的动物,公路的建设导致自然生态环境的人为分割,使生态环境岛屿化,不利于生物多样性的保护。为避免生态环境岛屿化造成的生物多样性受损,许多自然保护区需要建立与其他自然保护区域、自然地域的通道,这就是我们经常所说的"生物走廊"。

(2) 水文影响

公路建设会改变地表径流的固有态势,从而造成冲、淤、涝、渍等局部影响。

(3) 对土地利用的影响

公路建设对土地利用的影响较为显著,将改变沿线被征用土地的利用现状,其中对耕地的占用较为突出。

(4) 生态敏感地区的影响

交通运输线路长,会穿越各种生态系统,其中不可避免地会涉及一些特殊、敏感的生态能区,如湿地、荒地、自然保护区、天然森林、森林公园、水源保护区、风景名胜区、特殊地质地貌区以及生态脆弱区、自然灾害多发区等。

2. 防治措施

(1) 充分考虑公路环保措施,严格控制公路占地面积和临时用地规模,减少对耕地和植被的破坏;避开环境敏感性区域,如学校、工厂、医院、名胜古迹、自然保护区、精密食品基地等。

(2) 重视水土资源,减少水土流失。工程设计应充分考虑水土流失预防措施。一是注意填挖平衡,减少土石方量,减少借土弃土;二是做好边坡防护设计工作,确保边坡稳定,以减少将来使用过程中的不良病害发生,并应根据地质情况多采用种草植树的绿化护坡方法;三是做好沿线排水设计;四是合理取土、规范弃土、保护耕地、少占良田,应尽量在荒地或低产耕地集中取土,取土后对取土坑进行后期利用;弃方应集中堆弃,不占农田，堆弃后应上覆表土，播种绿化。

（3）注意保持原有的灌溉系统和自然水网体系。桥梁布置应尽量避免影响河流水文、水流特征，做到顺应地形和原水体流向；避免改称或堵塞大型河沟；对小型排灌系统，如遭破坏应予以恢复或加以调整，合理设置小桥涵位置，必要时对原有排灌体系进行优化合并或改移；做好项目自身的排水系统，增加必要构造设施以防止路基路面排水对农田水利的冲击。

（4）做好公路沿线景观设计工作，首先路线要尽量与地形地貌相吻合，减少土石方量，减少对自然风景的破坏，避开受保护的景观空间；还要加强道路沿线绿化，以补充和改善沿线景观，如边坡尽量采用种草植树的护坡方式。

公路施工过程中对水环境的影响主要来自施工作业中的生产废水和施工人员生活污水两方面。施工作业的生产废水主要指工程中各大、中、小桥梁建设过程中钻孔桩污水和施工机械所产生的含油污水等。

桥梁施工中对水体的影响主要是桥桩建设时采用钻孔灌注桩，其对河道水体的影响主要是钻孔扰动河水使底泥浮起，局部悬浮物（SS）增加，河水变得较为混浊。

公路建设由于建筑材料堆放、管理不当，特别是易流失的物资如黄沙、土方等露天堆放，遇暴雨时将可能被冲刷进入水体；建材在运输过程中的散落也会随雨水进入附近的水体；而施工中，如水泥拌和后没有及时使用造成的废弃，部分建材等也会随雨水进入附近的水体。

公路建设中的汽车维修站及施工设备维修站的污水，常含有泥沙和油类物质，若不经过处理直接排入周围水体，必将造成水域的油类污染。

公路施工时施工人员集中生活，在特大桥、大桥、互通等大型施工场地，施工人员可达数百人。如果施工营地生活污水直接排放，对附近河道会产生一定的污染。

根据我国的水土流失发展状况，确定了"预防为主、全面规划、综合防治、因地制宜、加强管理、注重效益"的水土保持工作方针，把预防保护工作摆到了首位。

防治公路建设造成水土流失的总原则是"谁开发谁保护,谁造成水土流失谁负责治理"。根据水土保持法规规定的"谁开发谁保护，谁造成水土流失谁治理"的原则，公路建设水土流失防治责任范围包括项目建设区（一般指公路建设主体工程区取土场、弃土弃渣场以及临时工程占地等）和直接影响区（一般指由于公路建设行为而造成水土流失危害的直接产生影响区域，如项目区外的拆迁安置区、排水承纳区等）。

要求县级以上人民政府根据当地水土流失的具体情况，划定水土流失重点防治区，即重点预防保护区、重点监督区、重点治理区，进行分类指导、分区防治。

建设项目中的水土保持设施，必须与主体工程同时设计、同时施工、同时投产使用。建设项目设计中要同时编制水土保持方案；并经水行政主管部门批准，施工时要同时按水土保持方案的要求建设水土保持设施，主体工程与相关水土保持设施要同时建成竣工投入使用。

凡从事可能引起水土流失的生产建设活动的单位和个人,必须首先编报水土保持方案,经水行政主管部门批准后方可审批环境影响报告,才能申请计划部门立项。

县级以上地方人民政府水行政主管部门及其水土保持监督管理机构,地方政府设立的水土保持机构,对水土流失的防治实施监督检查,这是贯彻实施水土保持法的重点保证。

1. 水土保持的原则

公路建设水土保持必须按照经济规律和生态规律进行,以保护生态环境为基点来建立水土保持目标,促进经济的发展。公路建设水土保持应当遵守水土保持法规、水土保持技术标准和环境保护总体要求的共同原则。同时,还要根据主体工程设计及施工的特点,遵守以下基本原则:

(1) 坚持"预防为主、防治结合"的水土保持方针;

(2) 水土保持与公路建设相结合;

(3) 因地制宜、因害设防,重点治理与一般防护相结合;

(4) 公路水土保持管理与地方水土保持管理相结合。

2. 水土保持的预期目标

公路施工及运营过程中,通过布设水土保持工程的生物措施,使新增水土流失得到有效缓解,项目区原有的水土流失得到有效措施,减少水土流失造成的危害。恢复和保护公路沿线水土保持设施,加大公路绿化工程,改善生态环境。具体目标如下:

(1) 通过采用有效的水土保持措施,使边坡稳定,岩石、表土不裸露,为公路安全运行服务,避免水土流失对工程本身的危害;

(2) 取土场全部做防护处理,使开挖坡不裸露,并覆土加以利用;

(3) 通过对弃土(渣)场进行综合治理,使在工程施工过程中产生的弃土、石渣得到有效拦挡或利用;

(4) 工程与植物措施相结合,使泥沙不进入下游河道,不影响河流正常行洪;

(5) 做好公路绿化工程的养护,使生态环境明显改善。

第五节 公路工程流水施工的特点

一、线性工程(路面)的搭接施工(流水线法)

公路流水施工有流水段法和流水线法。流水段法主要用于涵洞、桥梁的墩台等的施工;流水线法适合于线形工程,如公路、铁路管线等。

二、公路线性流水组织的注意事项

1. 施工段划分：主要注意机械使用效率和结构物的整体性要求，稳定类路面的延迟时间（水泥稳定类宜控制在 3~4h 内，作业长度以 200m 为宜）；沥青路面关注温度的要求，同时考虑设备能力之间的匹配。

2. 划分施工细目：要考虑工艺关系和组织关系，以及单位工程、分部分项工程、工序的划分要求。

3. 建立施工专业队（或班组）：注意工种的划分，数量的计算。

4. 确定线性流水方向：考虑工程量的分布，材料供应和运输条件、通车要求等，如果是路面面层摊铺还应根据拌和站的位置来决定流水的方向。

三、流水作业法的经济效果

流水作业法的经济效果，主要表现为提高劳动生产率、缩短工期、降低成本、提高质量、有利于资源供应工作等。

四、公路流水作业组织的分级

根据流水作业组织范围的大小，公路流水作业组织通常可划分为以下四个等级。

1. 分项工程流水作业

分项工程流水作业也被称为细部流水作业。它是在一个分项工程（专业工种）内部按照工序组织起来的流水作业。如土方路基（挖方段）施工的挖土、运土、卸土、空回等，路拌法稳定类底基层施工的下承层准备施工测量、备料、摊铺、拌和、整型、碾压、养生，这些都属于细部流水作业的组织。

2. 分部工程流水作业

分部工程流水作业也称为专业流水作业，它是在一个分部工程内部的各分项工程之间组织起来的流水作业。如大型挡土墙的基础、墙身、墙背填土等，路面工程路段的垫层、基层、面层、路缘石、路面边缘排水系统、人行道等。

3. 单位工程流水作业

单位工程流水作业也称为综合流水作业，它是在一个单位工程内部的各分部工程之间组织起来的流水作业。如路基工程的路基土石方工程、排水工程、挡土墙、防护工程等，桥梁工程的基础、下部构造、上部构造现场浇筑、桥面系和附属工程等。

4. 工程项目流水作业

工程项目流水作业也称为大流水作业或群体工程流水作业。它是在若干相互关联的单位工程之间组织起来的流水作业,最终是要完成一个工程项目的施工任务。如果将路基工程路面工程、桥梁工程、隧道工程、环保工程、安全设施等组成流水作业,该流水作业完成公路项目施工即告结束。

施工环境保护监理,是指监理单位受建设单位的委托,依法对施工单位在施工过程中影响环境的活动进行监督管理,确保各项环保措施满足公路施工环境保护的要求。

1. 监理任务

公路施工环境保护监理是针对施工过程环境保护的全方位、全环节、全过程的监理,其主要任务为:

(1)根据相关法律法规、监理合同的有关条款、公路项目环境评价的内容及相关批复对工程建设过程中污染环境、生态破坏防治及恢复的措施进行监督管理,如噪声、废气、污水等污染物的排放应达标,减少水土流失和生态环境破坏,也称为"环保达标监理";

(2)对建设项目配套的环保工程进行施工监理,确保"三同时"的实施,如对水处理设计、噪声屏障、绿化工程、自然保护区、水源保护区以及风景名胜保护区的保护等进行监理,也称为"环保工程监理"。

2. 监理依据

公路工程施工环境保护监理的主要依据包括:国家有关的法律、法规、条例、办法和规定,地方性法规和文件;国家标准,主要有噪声标准、空气标准、水质标准和振动标准等;项目的环境影响评价和水土保持报告及批复;项目的环境行动计划;工程设计文件;监理合同;施工合同以及有关补充协议;施工工程中的会议纪要和文件。

3. 监理工作程序

公路工程施工环境保护监理一般应按照下列工作程序进行:

(1)依据监理合同,设计文件,环评报告,水土保持方案以及施工合同、施工组织设计等编制施工环境保护监理规划;

(2)按照施工环境保护监理规划、工程进度、各项环保对策措施等编制施工环境保护监理实施细则;

(3)依据编制的施工环境保护监理规划和实施细则,开展施工期环境保护监理;

(4)工程竣工后,编写施工环境保护监理总结报告,整理监理档案资料,提交建设单位;

(5)参与工程竣工环保验收。

4. 监理工作方式

监理工程师一般应常驻工地,对施工活动的环保工作进行动态管理。工作方式以巡视为主,根据施工区污染源分布情况,监理工程师定期进行巡视。对特别关心的节点可以进行旁站监理,必要时还可以进行环境监测。巡视和旁站监理的情况,均应予以详细记录。监理过程中如发现环境污染和生态破坏等情况,监理工程师应立即通知施工单位限期整改。一般性或操作性的问题,可以采取口头通知形式;口头通知无效或有污染隐患时,应发布书面的监理通知,要求施工单位整改,并根据施工单位的书面回复检查整改结果;严重的环境问题，还应同时向建设单位汇报。如整改情况不理想，可以发布停工指令。

5. 事故处理

当工程施工过程中出现重大环境污染和生态破坏事故时，按如下程序处理：

（1）施工单位在发生事故后，除在规定时间口头报告监理工程师外，应尽快提出书面报告事故初步调查结果，报告应初步反映该工程名称、部位污染事故原因、应急环保措施等；

（2）立即汇报建设单位，及时向当地汇报，同时书面通知施工单位暂停该工程的施工，并根据环保主管部门有关意见，采取有效的环保措施；

（3）监理工程师和施工单位对污染事故继续深入调查，并和有关方面商讨后，提出事故处理的初步方案后报建设单位、交环保主管部门研究处理；

（4）督促施工单位做好善后工作。

公路工程施工准备阶段的环境保护监理要点如下。

1. 施工临时用地

（1）为避免因选地址不慎造成的生态影响，基本上应采取避让的措施。通过实地踏勘，避开各种生态敏感点，对于公路施工区域附近可能存在的生态敏感点，应加强管理，防止产生人为干扰；

（2）施工区域临近城镇或农村的居民点时，应尽可能租用当地的民居作为施工生活区。若无现成的房屋可以租用，应尽可能避开农林等生产用地。

2. 生活、办公区及试验室

（1）妥善处理生活垃圾；

（2）修建临时性污水处理设施；

（3）厨房应设置排风系统。

3. 临时施工道路的潜在环境影响

（1）应规划好临时施工道路的路线走向，以减少植被破坏为首要原则，尽量利用现有道路；若无现成道路可利用，则应严格控制施工道路修筑边界，路线走向必须绕开各种生态敏感点（区）；

（2）对于施工道路边界上可能出现的土质裸露边坡，应有临时防护设施；

（3）施工便道属临时性质，载重汽车来往频繁容易损坏，应随时保持运行状态良好，减少扬尘污染；

（4）运输车辆行驶产生的扬尘影响植物（作物）正常的繁殖和发育过程，应通过路面硬化处理以及定期清扫、洒水以抑制扬尘的发生，路面应始终保持湿润；

（5）施工噪声应当符合国家规定的施工场界排放标准（该阶段施工场界噪声的限值为昼间75dB，夜间55dB）；

（6）在施工前，对现场初始的地形地貌、地表植被等自然特征应有客观的文字描述和完整的影像记录，以作为将来进行恢复的依据和参考。施工结束后，必须恢复临时占用土地原有的土地利用功能。

4. 监理准备工作

在施工准备阶段，监理工程师应做好以下准备工作。

（1）熟悉工程资料，掌握工程整体情况（包括工程环境影响区域）；

（2）编制施工环境保护监理规划；

（3）根据施工环境保护规划，编制各单位工程环境保护监理实施细则；

（4）根据工程情况，配置必需的环境监测设备和仪器；

（5）建立环保工作网络，要求施工单位建立环境保护管理体系；

（6）审查施工单位编制的《施工组织设计》，对不符合工程环保要求的环节和内容提出改正要求，对中间遗漏的环节和内容要求增补；

（7）审查取（弃）土场、采石场的选址，对生态敏感点和取（弃）土场、采石场进行必要的实地踏勘；

（8）审查施工单位的临时用地方案，所有便道、便桥、便隧必须经监理工程师审批同意后才能使用；

（9）参加第一次工地会议，对施工单位进行环境保护监理交底；

（10）对现场试验室放射源的处置，监理工程师应全过程旁站监理，保证放射源得到妥善处置；

（11）施工场地和便道附近有敏感保护对象时，对施工车辆做出限速行驶的规定，并对执行情况进行巡检；

（12）对营地、办公区、试验室、材料堆场、拌和场、预制场以及取（弃）土场的环保措施执行情况、环保设施运行维护情况进行巡检。

路基施工应做好临时排水，并与永久性排水系统相结合，避免积水及冲刷边坡，取土场、弃土场应做好水土保持措施，施工产生的振动、噪声、扬尘应减少到最低限度。

场地清理及结构物拆除环保要点。开挖施工中表层土保护是一个重点环境保护问题，表层土流失除引起水土流失外，也可能引发一系列生态平衡失调，如植被丢失、景观破坏等。

路面拌和场应远离自然村落，并在其常年主导风向下风处，场地应硬化处理。沥青路面拌和设备配料除尘装置应保持良好的除尘效果，施工过程中剩余的废弃物必须及时收集到弃料场集中处理，不得随意抛弃。路面施工应与路基、桥梁施工有合理的安排，减少交叉施工引起的环境污染。

在路面工程开工前，监理工程师应审批施工方案的环保措施，尤其是对沥青拌和场选址方案的审批；监理工程师根据现场施工情况，确定本阶段环保监理的巡视、旁站计划，对施工单位环保措施的执行效果进行复核；监理工程师应特别注意沥青拌合料废料的处置方法，并随时对执行情况进行巡检；监理工程师应特别注意沥青烟气的污染防治，在靠近水源地区施工时，还应注意水源保护问题；对施工过程中不符合环保要求的行为，监理工程师可以发出监理指令，责令改正。

在路基开工前，监理工程师应审批施工单位编制的施工方案，对其环保措施提出审查意见；监理工程师应根据工程情况，确定本阶段环保监理的巡视旁站计划，对施工单位环保措施的执行效果进行检查；挖除地表土，并将表土搬运到经监理工程师同意的贮料堆；地表清理遇到古树名木或珍稀植物采取移植等就地保护措施时，监理工程师应审查其移植方案，并对移植过程全程旁站监理；监理工程师应严格控制路基开挖在用地范围内分段进行，同时配合挡土墙、边坡防护的修筑；弃土弃渣的堆放地点应事先经监理工程师同意；对施工过程中不符合环保要求的行为，监理工程师可以发出监理指令，责令改正；施工过程中，监理工程师应关注扬尘、噪声、废水、石油类等环境监测指标，必要时可根据需要进行现场监测。

第七章 公路工程质量管理

对于公路工程而言，施工质量管理工作尤为关键，不仅能够确保公路工程现场施工的顺利进行，而且能提高公路工程的整体质量。因此，在公路工程施工质量管理过程中，管理人员必须要加强对其管理工作的重视，并为工程施工提供制度依据，提升公路工程施工水平。本章将对公路工程的质量控制、检验、评定等方面展开分析。

第一节 公路工程质量控制的常用方法

一、进行工程质量管理策划

在对设计文件审核与分析后，项目经理应负总责，协调相关部门进行项目质量管理策划，包括：

1. 质量目标和要求；
2. 质量管理组织和职责；
3. 施工管理依据的文件；
4. 人员、技术、施工机具等资源的需求和配置；
5. 场地、道路、水电、消防、临时设施规划；
6. 质量控制关键点分析及设置；
7. 进度控制措施；
8. 施工质量检查、验收及相关标准；
9. 突发事件的应急措施；
10. 对违规事件的报告和处理；
11. 应收集的信息及其传递要求；
12. 与工程建设有关方的沟通方式；

13. 施工管理应形成的记录；

14. 质量管理和技术措施；

15. 施工企业质量管理的其他要求。

二、现场质量检查控制

现场工程质量检查分开工前检查、施工过程中检查和分项工程完成后的检查。现场质量检查控制的方法主要有：测量、试验、观察、分析、记录、监督、总结改进。

1. 开工前检查：其目的是检查是否具备开工条件，施工工艺与施工组织设计对照是否正确无误，开工后能否连续正常施工，能否保证工程质量。

2. 工序交接检查与工序检查：工序交接检查应建立制度化控制，并坚持实施。对于关键工序或对工程质量有重大影响的工序，在自检、互检的基础上，还要组织专职人员进行工序交接检查，以确保工序合格，使下道工序能顺利展开。

3. 隐蔽工程检查：凡是隐蔽工程均应经检查认证后方可覆盖。

4. 停工后复工前的检查：因处理质量问题或某种原因停工后再复工时，均应检查认可后方可复工。

5. 分项、分部工程完工后的检查：应按规定的程序和要求，经检查认可并签署验收记录后，才允许进行下一工程项目施工。

6. 成品、材料、机械设备等的检查：主要检查成品、材料等有无可靠的保护措施及其落实是否有效，以控制不发生损坏、变质等问题；检查机械设备的技术状态，以确保其处于完好的可控制状态。

7. 巡视检查：对施工操作质量应进行巡视检查，必要时还应进行跟踪检查。

三、工程质量控制的关键点

1. 质量控制关键点的设置

应根据不同管理层次和职能，按以下原则分级设置。

（1）施工过程中的重要项目、薄弱环节和关键部位；

（2）影响工期、质量、成本、安全、材料消耗等重要因素的环节；

（3）新材料、新技术、新工艺的施工环节；

（4）质量信息反馈中缺陷频数较多的项目。

关键点应随着施工进度和影响因素的变化而调整。

2. 质量控制关键点的控制

（1）制定质量控制关键点的管理办法。

（2）落实质量控制关键点的质量责任。

（3）开展质量控制关键点 QC 小组活动；

（4）在质量控制关键点上开展一次抽检合格的活动；

（5）认真填写质量控制关键点的质量记录；

（6）落实与经济责任相结合的检查考核制度。

3. 质量控制关键点的文件

（1）质量控制关键点业务流程图；

（2）质量控制关键点明细表；

（3）质量控制关键点（岗位）质量因素分析表；

（4）质量控制关键点作业指导书；

（5）自检、交接检、专业检查记录以及控制图表；

（6）工序质量统计与分析；

（7）质量保证与质量改进的措施与实施记录。

（8）工序质量信息。

4. 质量控制关键点实际效果的考察

质量控制关键点的实际效果表现在施工质量管理水平和各项指标的实现情况上。要运用数理统计方法绘制工程项目总体质量情况分析图表，该图表要反映动态控制过程与施工项目实际质量情况。各阶段质量分析要纳入施工项目方针目标管理。

5. 公路工程质量控制关键点

（1）土方路基工程施工中常见的质量控制关键点：

1）施工放样与断面测量；

2）路基原地面处理，按施工技术合同或规范规定要求处理，并认真整平压实；

3）使用适宜材料，必须采用设计和规范规定的适用材料，保证原材料合格，正确确定土的最大干密度和最佳含水量。

4）压实设备及压实方案；

5）路基纵、横向排水系统设置；

6）每层的松铺厚度、横坡及填筑速率；

7）分层压实，控制填土的含水量，确保压实度达到设计要求。

土的最佳含水量是土基施工的一个重要控制参数，是土基达到最大干密度所对应的含水量。根据不同的土的性质，测定最佳含水量的试验方法通常有：

①轻型、重型击实试验；

②振动台法；

③表面振动击实仪法。

压实度是路基质量控制的重要指标之一，是现场干密度和室内最大干密度的比值。压实度越高、路基密实度越大，材料整体性能越好。现场压实度的测定方法有：

①灌砂法；

②环刀法；

③核子密度湿度仪法。

（2）路面基层（底基层）施工中常见的质量控制关键点：

1）基层施工所采用设备组合及拌和设备计量装置校验；

2）路面基层（底基层）所用结合料（如水泥、石灰）的剂量；

3）路面基层（底基层）材料的含水量、拌和均匀性、配合比；

4）路面基层（底基层）的压实度、弯沉值、平整度及横坡等；

5）如采用级配碎（砾）石还需要注意集料的级配和石料的压碎值；

6）及时有效的养护。

（3）水泥混凝土路面施工中常见的质量控制关键点：

1）基层强度、平整度、高程的检查与控制；

2）混凝土材料的检查与试验，水泥品种及用量确定；

3）混凝土拌和、摊铺设备及计量装置校验；

4）混凝土配合比设计和试件的试验。混凝土的水灰比、外加剂掺加量、坍落度应控制；

5）混凝土的摊铺、振捣、成型及避免离析；

6）切缝时间和养护技术的采用。

水泥混凝土抗折强度与抗压强度的测定是混凝土材料质量检验的两个重要试验。

水泥混凝土抗折（抗弯拉）强度试验是以150mm×150mm×550mm的梁形试件在标准养护条件下达到规定龄期后，在净跨径450mm的双支点荷载作用下进行弯拉破坏，并按规定的计算方法得到强度值。水泥混凝土抗折强度是混凝土的主要力学指标之一，通过试验取得的检测结果是路面混凝土组成设计的重要参数。

水泥混凝土抗压强度试验是以边长为150mm的正立方体标准试件，标准养护到28d，再在万能试验机上按规定方法进行破坏试验测得抗压强度。当混凝土抗压强度采用非标准试件时应进行换算得到抗压强度值。通过水泥混凝土抗压强度试验，可以确定混凝土的强度等级，其是评定混凝土品质的重要指标。

（4）沥青混凝土路面施工中常见的质量控制关键点：

1）基层强度、平整度、高程的检查与控制；

2）沥青材料的检查与试验。沥青混凝土配合比设计和试验；

3）沥青混凝土拌和设备及计量装置校验；

4）路面施工机械设备配置与压实方案；

5）沥青混凝土的拌和、运输及摊铺温度控制；

6）沥青混凝土摊铺厚度的控制和摊铺中的离析控制；

7）沥青混凝土的碾压与接缝施工。

沥青混凝土配合比设计采用马歇尔试验配合比设计法。该法首先按配合比设计拌制沥青混合料，再制成规定尺寸试件，12h之后测定其物理指标（包括表观密度、空隙率、沥青饱和度、矿料间隙率等），然后测定稳定度和流值。热拌沥青混合料配合比设计应通过目标配合比设计、生产配合比设计及生产配合比验证三个阶段，确定沥青混合料的材料品种及配合比、矿料级配、最佳沥青用量。

马歇尔稳定度试验是对标准击实的试件在规定的温度和速度等条件下受压，测定沥青混合料的稳定度和流值等指示所进行的试验，这种方法适用于马歇尔稳定度试验和浸水马歇尔稳定度试验。马歇尔稳定度试验主要用于沥青混合料的配合比设计及沥青路面施工质量检验。浸水马歇尔稳定度试验主要是检验沥青混合料受水损害时抵抗剥落的能力，通过测试其水稳定性检验配合比设计的可行性。

（5）桥梁基础工程施工中常见的质量控制关键点：

1）扩大基础

①基底地基承载力的检测确认，满足设计要求。

②基底表面松散层的清理。

③及时浇筑垫层混凝土，减少基底暴露时间。

④大体积混凝土施工裂缝控制。

2）钻孔桩

①桩位坐标与垂直度控制。

②护筒埋深。

③泥浆指标控制。

④护筒内水头高度。

⑤孔径的控制，防止缩径。

⑥桩顶、桩底标高的控制。

⑦清孔质量（嵌岩桩与摩擦桩要求不同）。

⑧钢筋笼接头质量。

⑨导管接头质量检查与水下混凝土的灌注质量。

3）沉井

①初始平面位置的控制。

②刃脚质量。

③下沉过程中沉井倾斜度与偏位的动态控制。

④封底混凝土的浇筑工艺确保封底混凝土的质量。

（6）水中承台施工中常见的质量控制关键点：

水中承台施工一般可采用筑岛围堰、钢板桩围堰、钢吊箱围堰、钢套箱围堰等。

1）钢围堰施工中常见的质量控制关键点

①钢围堰的设计与加工制造质量控制。

②钢围堰入水、落床及入土下沉过程中平面位置、高程等的控制。

③钢围堰下沉到位后的清底及整平。

④封底混凝土浇筑时的导管布设与封底混凝土厚度控制。

⑤承台混凝土配合比设计。
⑥抽水后封底混凝土基底的调平。
⑦承台混凝土浇筑导管布设及混凝土振捣。
⑧大体积混凝土温控设施的设计、施工及大体积混凝土养护。
⑨各类预埋件的施工质量控制。

2）钢套箱施工的质量控制关键点
①钢套箱的设计与加工制造质量控制。
②钢套箱水平及竖向限位装置的施工质量控制。
③封底混凝土浇筑时的导管布设与封底混凝土厚度控制。
④承台混凝土的配合比设计。
⑤抽水后封底混凝土的调平。
⑥承台混凝土浇筑导管布设及混凝土振捣。
⑦大体积混凝土温控设施的设计、施工及大体积混凝土养护。
⑧各类预埋件的施工质量控制。

（7）桥梁下部结构施工中常见的质量控制关键点：

1）实心墩
①墩身锚固钢筋预埋质量控制。
②墩身平面位置控制。
③墩身垂直度控制。
④模板接缝错台控制。
⑤墩顶支座预埋件位置、数量控制。

2）薄壁墩
①墩身锚固钢筋预埋质量控制。
②墩身平面位置控制。
③墩身垂直度控制。
④模板接缝错台控制。
⑤墩顶支座预埋件位置、数量控制。
⑥墩身与承台联结处混凝土裂缝控制。
⑦墩顶实心段混凝土裂缝控制。

（8）桥梁上部结构施工中常见的质量控制关键点：

1）简支梁桥
①简支梁混凝土的强度控制。
②预拱度的控制。
③支座预埋件的位置控制。
④大梁安装时梁与梁之间高差的控制。
⑤支座安装型号、方向的控制。

⑥梁板之间现浇带混凝土质量控制。

⑦伸缩缝安装质量控制。

2）连续梁桥

①支架施工：支架沉降量的控制。

②先简支后连续：后浇段工艺控制、体系转换工艺控制、后浇段收缩控制、临时支座安装与拆除控制。

③挂篮悬臂施工：浇筑过程中的线形控制、边跨及跨中合龙段混凝土的裂缝控制。

④预应力梁：张拉力及预应力钢筋伸长量控制。

3）拱桥

①预制拼装：拱肋拱轴线的控制。

②支架施工：支架基础承载力控制、支架沉降控制、拱架加载控制、卸架工艺控制。

③钢管拱：钢管混凝土压注质量控制。

4）斜拉桥（斜拉索为专业制索厂制造）

①主塔空间位置的控制。

②斜拉索锚固管或锚箱空间定位控制。

③斜拉桥线形控制。

④牵索挂篮悬臂施工：斜拉索索力控制、索力调整。

⑤悬臂吊装：梁段外形尺寸控制、斜拉索索力控制、索力调整。

⑥合龙段的控制。

5）悬索桥

①猫道线形控制。

②主缆架设线形控制。

③索股安装：基准索股的定位控制、索股锚固力的控制。

④索股架设中塔顶位移及索鞍位置的调整。

⑤紧缆：空隙率的控制。

⑥索夹定位控制。

⑦缠丝拉力控制。

⑧吊索长度的确定。

⑨加劲梁的焊接质量控制。

（9）公路隧道施工中常见的质量控制关键点：

1）正确判断围岩级别，及时调整施工方案；

2）认真测量、检查和修正开挖断面，减少超挖；

3）制订切实可行的开挖方案，包括新奥法、矿山法的选择，炮孔布置、装药量、每一循环的掘进深度；

4）喷锚支护，控制在开挖后围岩自稳定时间的 1/2 以内完成；

5）认真观测，收集资料，做好施工质量的信息反馈。

第二节 公路工程质量缺陷处理方法

一、质量缺陷性质的确定

质量缺陷性质的确定，是最终确定缺陷问题处理办法的首要工作和根本依据。一般通过下列方法来确定缺陷的性质：

1. 观察现场情况和查阅记录资料。其指对有缺陷的工程进行现场情况、施工过程、施工设备和施工操作情况等进行现场观察和检查。主要包括查阅试验检测报告、施工技术资料、施工过程记录、施工日志、施工工艺流程、施工方案、施工机械运转记录等相关记录，同时，在特殊季节关注天气情况等。

2. 检验与试验。通过检查和了解可以发现一些表面的问题，得出初步结论，但往往需要进一步的检验与试验来加以验证。

检验与试验，主要是通过检查、测量与该缺陷工程有关技术的指标，以便准确找出产生缺陷的原因。例如，若发现石灰土的强度不足，则在检验强度指标的同时，还应检验石灰剂量、石灰与土的物理化学性质，以便发现石灰土强度不足是因为材料不合格、配比不合格或养护不好，还是因为其他如气候之类的原因造成的，检测和试验的结果将作为确定缺陷性质和制定随后的处理措施的主要依据。

3. 专题调研。有些质量问题，仅仅通过以上两种方法仍不能确定。如某大桥在交工后不到一年的时间里出现了超过规范要求的裂缝，仅通过简单的观察和查阅现有资料很难确定产生裂缝的根本原因，找不到原因也就无从确定进一步的处理措施。在这种情况下就需要采用专项调研，通过对勘测、设计、施工各个环节的调查、分析研究，辅之以辅助的检测手段，确定质量问题的性质和为随后采取的措施提供依据

在这种情况下，为了查明产生问题的根本原因，有必要组织有关方面的专家或专题调查组提出检测方案，对所得到的一系列参考依据和指标进行综合分析研究，找出产生缺陷的原因，确定缺陷的性质。这种专题研究，对缺陷问题的妥善解决作用重大，因此，经常被采用。

二、质量缺陷的处理方法

1. 整修与返工。缺陷的整修，主要是针对局部性的、轻微的且不会给整体工程质量带来严重影响的缺陷。如水泥混凝土结构的局部蜂窝、麻面，道路结构层的局部压实度不足

等。这类缺陷一般可以通过比较简单地修整得到处理,不会影响工程总体的关键性技术指标。由于这类缺陷很容易出现,因而修补处理方法最为常用。

返工的决定应建立在认真调查研究的基础上。是否返工,应视缺陷经过补救后能否达到规范标准而定,对于补救后不能满足标准的工程必须返工。如某承包人为赶工期,曾在雨中铺筑沥青混凝土,监理工程师只得责令承包人将已经铺完的沥青面层全部清除重铺,一些无法补救的低质涵洞也被炸掉重建,温度过低或过高的沥青混合料在现场被监理工程师责令报废等。

2. 综合处理办法。综合处理办法主要是针对较大的质量事故而言的。这种处理办法不像返工和整修那样简单具体,它是一种综合的缺陷(事故)补救措施,能够使得工程缺陷(事故)以最小的经济代价和工期损失重新满足规范要求。处理的办法因工程缺陷(事故)的性质而异,性质的确定则以大量的调查及丰富的施工经验和技术理论为基础。具体做法可组织联合调查组、召开专家论证会等方式。实践证明,这是一条合理解决这类问题的有效途径。例如,某桥梁上部为4孔20m预制空心板结构,下部为桩基础形式。0号桥台施工放样时发生错误,导致第一孔跨径增加了50cm,发现时桩基础、承台、台身已全部完成,空心板预制了二分之一。经综合论证,采用下部不变、改变上部的方式,第一孔空心板跨径增加了50cm,增加费用约2万元。而采用返工方式,需要大约8万元和2个月工期。

第三节 路基工程质量检验

一、土方路基工程质量检验

1. 基本要求

(1)在路基用地和取土坑范围内,应清除地表植被、杂物、积水、淤泥和表土,处理坑塘,并按规范和设计要求对基底进行压实;

(2)路基填料应符合规范和设计的规定,经认真调查、试验后合理选用;

(3)填方路基须分层填筑压实,每层表面平整,路拱合适,排水良好;

(4)施工临时排水系统应与设计排水系统结合,避免冲刷边坡,勿使路基附近积水;

(5)在设定取土区内合理取土,不得滥开滥挖。完工后应按要求对取土坑和弃土场进行修整,保持合理的几何外形。

2. 实测项目

土方路基实测项目有:压实度、弯沉值、纵断高程、中线偏位、宽度、平整度、横坡、边坡。

二、石方路基工程质量检验

1. 基本要求

（1）石方路堑的开挖宜采用光面爆破法。爆破后应及时清理险石、松石，确保边坡安全、稳定。

（2）修筑填石路堤时应进行地表清理，逐层水平填筑石块，摆放平稳，码砌边部。填筑层厚度及石块尺寸应符合设计和施工规范规定，填石空隙用石碴、石屑嵌压稳定。上、下路床填料和石料最大尺寸应符合规范规定。采用振动压路机分层碾压，压至填筑层顶面石块稳定，18t以上压路机振压两遍无明显标高差异。

（3）路基表面应整修平整。

2. 实测项目

石方路基实测项目有：压实、纵断高程、中线偏位、宽度、平整度、横坡、边坡坡度和平顺度。

三、砌体挡土墙质量检验

1. 基本要求

（1）石料或混凝土预制块的强度、规格和质量应符合有关规范和设计要求。

（2）砂浆所用的水泥、沙、水的质量应符合有关规范的要求，按规定的配合比施工。

（3）地基承载力必须满足设计要求，基础埋置深度应满足施工规范要求。

（4）砌筑应分层错缝。浆砌时坐浆挤紧，嵌填饱满密实，不得有空洞；干砌时不得松动、叠砌和浮塞。

（5）沉降缝、泄水孔、反滤层的设置位置、质量和数量应符合设计要求。

2. 实测项目

砌体挡土墙实测项目有：砂浆强度、平面位置、顶面高程、竖直度或坡度、断面尺寸、底面高程、表面平整度；

干砌挡土墙实测项目有：平面位置、顶面高程、竖直度或坡度、断面尺寸、底面高程、表面平整度。

四、路基填筑方面的质检

1. 清表和特殊地段处理。路线根据要求在实地测设好之后，路基首先要做的工作便是清理表面，路基质检员的工作是在现场指导或察看情况。在路基底层宽度范围内的植被、树木等应先清理掉，清理彻底后，如果土质较好，则压路机压实，反之则进行换填，换填的限度是 80 厘米，应根据实地土质情况确定换填深度，换填时应换填当地好的料种，换填结束进行压实。若在路基底层出现特殊地段，如淤泥等，应先彻底清除淤泥再进行换填，此时清除时没有深度要求。换填结束后，路基质检员自带仪器进行自检。此时由于是路基底层，要检测的主要是压实度、宽度和中线偏差，这三项必须保证。自检通过后，和旁站监理一块质检。待通过且可以转序后进行下层工序。

2. 路基工程层层质检项目。路基底层结束后，接下来的是分层填筑，分层填方时需层层检测，此时要注意路槽的作用，路槽有防止料外泄、控制厚度的作用。所以说，一层结束后，如果没有做好路槽，质检员不予质检，目的是防止施工员不做路槽直接上料，从而浪费料，控制不好厚度，而且边坡还不平顺。

（一）挖方路基的质检

一条线路应填挖结合，挖方经实验室试验后，可用；用于填方，不可用，则为弃方。挖方的利用是施工单位节省资金的一个重要来源。挖方路基不同于填方路基的要求和外观评定。挖方路基在距路基顶面 80 厘米处进行分层换填，换填当地最好的料种。

（二）基坑回填

基坑回填是路基与桥台之间的基坑进行回填，回填从桥基础开始填至原地面或路基现层面。路基填筑需要分层填筑，质检人员应在台背按照要求画出红线，红线间距为 20 厘米，来指导施工，促使施工员按红线进行分层施工。基坑回填一般机械不能入内，须用小夯进行夯实，小夯振压至填筑层面不松散。填筑材料必须为石渣等透水性材料，否则视为不合格，不予质检。基坑回填时应注意石块粒径，大粒径石块必须捡出或砸碎，否则会对质量造成不良影响。基坑填筑完后，不能直接在盖板涵和涵洞顶面跑车，应垫至少 20 厘米再跑车，防止车辆压裂盖板涵和涵洞。

（三）台背回填

大多数台背回填的首要任务是基坑回填，待填至与圆地面相平后，为台背回填。台背回填也要分层回填，质检员按要求在台背画出红线，20 厘米一层指导施工。台背回填的宽度为台身高加 2 米，其中填筑必须用透水性材料分层填筑。填筑完后用机械振压。机械压不到的地方须用小夯夯实。桥梁施工时，若台背后填筑了非透水性材料，必须清除干净，再进行回填，台背回填应慢于路基填筑，正确程序是路基填筑一层，压实可以转序后，台背回填一层，直到顶面，全部如此。另外，填筑材料的粒径也应加以控制。

第四节 路面工程质量检验

一、水泥稳定粒料（碎石、沙砾或矿渣等）路面基层、底基层的检验

1. 基本要求

（1）粒料应符合设计和施工规范要求，并应根据当地料源选择质坚、干净的粒料，矿渣应分解稳定，未分解渣块应予剔除；

（2）水泥用量和矿料级配按设计控制准确；

（3）路拌深度要达到层底；

（4）摊铺时要注意消除离析现象；

（5）混合料处于最佳含水量状况下，用重型压路机碾压至要求的压实度从加水拌和到碾压终了的时间不应超过 3h，并应短于水泥的终凝时间；

（6）碾压检查合格后立即覆盖或洒水养护，养护期要符合规范要求。

2. 实测项目

（1）水泥稳定粒料（碎石、沙砾或矿渣等）基层和底基层主要检验内容包括：压实度、平整度、纵断高程、宽度、厚度、横坡、强度；

（2）级配碎（砾）石或填隙碎石（矿渣）基层和底基层实测项目有：压实度、弯沉值、平整度、纵断高程、宽度、厚度、横坡。

二、水泥混凝土面层的检验

1. 基本要求

（1）基层质量必须符合规定要求，并应进行弯沉测定，验算的基层整体模量应满足设计要求；

（2）水泥强度、物理性能和化学成分应符合国家标准及有关规范的规定；

（3）粗细集料、水、外加剂及接缝填缝料应符合设计和施工规范要求；

（4）施工配合比应根据现场测定水泥的实际强度进行计算，并经试验，选择采用最佳配合比；

（5）接缝的位置、规格、尺寸及传力杆、拉力杆的设置应符合设计要求；

（6）路面拉毛或机具压槽等抗滑措施，其构造深度应符合施工规范要求；

（7）面层与其他构造物相接应平顺，检查井井盖顶面高程应高于周边路面 1~3 mm。

雨水口标高按设计比路面低 5~8 mm，路面边缘无积水现象；

（8）混凝土路面铺筑后按施工规范要求养护。

2. 实测项目

水泥混凝土面层实测项目有：水泥混凝土面板的弯拉强度、平整度、板厚度、水泥混凝土路面的抗滑构造深度、相邻板间的高差、纵横缝顺直度、水泥混凝土路面中线平面偏位、路面宽度、纵断高程和路面横坡。

三、沥青混凝土面层和沥青碎（砾）石面层的检验

1. 基本要求

（1）沥青混合料的矿料质量及矿料级配应符合设计要求和施工规范的规定；

（2）严格控制各种矿料和沥青用量及各种材料和沥青混合料的加热温度，沥青材料及混合料的各项指标应符合设计和施工规范要求。沥青混合料的生产，每日应做抽提试验、马歇尔稳定度试验。矿料级配、沥青含量、马歇尔稳定度等结果的合格率应不小于90%；

（3）拌和后的沥青混合料应均匀一致，无花白、无粗细料分离和结团成块现象；

（4）基层必须碾压密实，表面干燥、清洁、无浮土，其平整度和路拱度应符合要求；

（5）摊铺时应严格控制摊铺厚度和平整度，避免离析，注意控制摊铺和碾压温度，碾压至要求的密实度。

2. 实测项目

沥青混凝土面层和沥青碎（砾）石面层的实测项目有：厚度、平整度、压实度、弯沉值、渗水系数、抗滑（含摩擦系数和构造深度）、中线平面偏位、纵断高程、路面宽度及路面横坡。

第五节　桥梁工程质量检验

一、桥梁总体

1. 基本要求

（1）桥梁施工应严格按照设计图纸、施工技术规范和有关技术操作规程要求进行；

（2）桥下净空不得小于设计要求；

（3）特大跨径桥梁或结构复杂的桥梁，必要时应进行荷载试验。

2. 实测项目

桥梁总体的实测项目有：桥面中线偏位、桥宽（含车行道和人行道）、桥长、引道中心线与桥梁中心线的衔接以及桥头高程衔接。

二、钻孔灌注桩施工质量检验

1. 基本要求

（1）桩身混凝土所用的水泥、沙、石、水、外加剂及混合材料的质量和规格必须符合有关规范的要求，按规定的配合比施工；

（2）成孔后必须清孔，测量孔径、孔深、孔位和沉淀层厚度，确认满足设计或施工技术规范要求后，方可灌注水下混凝土；

（3）水下混凝土应连续灌注，严禁有夹层和断桩；

（4）嵌入承台的锚固钢筋长度不得低于设计规范规定的最小锚固长度要求；

（5）应选择有代表性的桩用无破损法进行检测，重要工程或重要部位的桩宜逐根进行检测。设计有规定或对桩的质量有怀疑时，应采取钻取芯样法对桩进行检测；

（6）凿除桩头预留混凝土后，桩顶应无残余的松散混凝土。

2. 实测项目

钻孔灌注桩实测项目有：混凝土强度、桩位、孔深、孔径、钻孔倾斜度、沉淀厚度、钢筋骨架底面高程。

三、沉井施工质量检验

1. 基本要求

（1）混凝土桩所用的水泥、沙、石、水、外加剂及混合材料的质量和规格必须符合有关规范的要求，按规定的配合比施工；

（2）沉井下沉应在井壁混凝土达到规定强度后进行。浮式沉井在下水、浮运前，应进行水密性试验；

（3）沉井接高时，各节的竖向中轴线应与第一节竖向中轴线相重合。接高前应纠正沉井的倾斜；

（4）沉井下沉到设计高程时，应检查基底，确认符合设计要求后方可封底；

（5）沉井下沉中出现开裂，必须查明原因，进行处理后才可继续下沉；

（6）下沉应有完整、准确的施工记录。

2. 实测项目

沉井实测面目有：各节沉井混凝土强度、沉井平面尺寸、井壁厚度、沉井刃脚高程、中心偏位（纵、横向）、沉井最大倾斜度（纵、横方向）、平面扭转角。

四、扩大基础质量检验

1. 基本要求

（1）所用的水泥、沙、石、水、外加剂及混合材料的质量和规格必须符合有关规范的要求，按规定的配合比施工；

（2）不得出现露筋和空洞现象；

（3）基础的地基承载力必须满足设计要求；

（4）严禁超挖回填虚土。

2. 实测项目

扩大基础的主要实测项目有：混凝土强度、平面尺寸、基础底面高程、基础顶面高程、轴线偏位。

五、钢筋加工及安装施工质量检验

1. 基本要求

（1）钢筋、机械连接器、焊条等的品种、规格和技术性能应符合国家现行标准规定和设计要求；

（2）冷拉钢筋的机械性能必须符合规范要求，钢筋平直，表面不应有裂皮和油污；

（3）受力钢筋同一截面的接头数量、搭接长度、焊接和机械接头质量应符合施工技术规范要求；

（4）钢筋安装时，必须保证设计要求的钢筋根数；

（5）受力钢筋应平直，表面不得有裂纹及其他损伤。

2. 实测项目

钢筋加工及安装施工的实测项目有：受力钢筋间距，箍筋、横向水平钢筋、螺旋筋间距，钢筋骨架尺寸，弯起钢筋位置、保护层厚度。

六、预应力筋的加工和张拉质量检验

1. 基本要求

（1）预应力筋的各项技术性能必须符合国家现行标准规定和设计要求；

（2）预应力束中的钢丝、钢绞线应梳理顺直，不得有缠绞、扭麻花现象，表面不应有损伤；

（3）单根钢绞线不允许断丝，单根钢筋不允许断筋或滑移；

（4）同一截面预应力筋接头面积不超过预应力筋总面积的25%，接头质量应满足施工技术规范的要求；

（5）预应力筋张拉或放张时混凝土强度和龄期必须符合设计要求，严格按照设计规定的张拉顺序进行操作；

（6）预应力钢丝采用镦头锚时，镦头应头形圆整，不得有斜歪或破裂现象；

（7）制孔管道应安装牢固，接头密合、弯曲圆顺。锚垫板平面应与孔道轴线垂直；

（8）千斤顶、油表、钢尺等器具应经检验校正；

（9）锚具、夹具和连接器应符合设计要求，按施工技术规范的要求经检验合格后方可使用；

（10）压浆工作在5℃以下进行时，应采取防冻或保温措施；

（11）孔道压浆的水泥浆性能和强度应符合施工技术规范要求，压浆时排气、排水孔应有水泥原浆溢出后方可封闭；

（12）按设计要求浇筑封锚混凝土。

2. 实测项目

预应力筋的加工和张拉的实测项目有：管道坐标（包含梁长方向和梁高方向）、管道间距（包含同排和上下层）、张拉应力值、张拉伸长率、断丝滑丝数。

七、承台质量检验

1. 基本要求

（1）所用的水泥、沙、石、水、外加剂及混合材料的质量和规格必须符合有关规范的要求，按规定的配合比施工；

（2）必须采取措施控制水化热引起的混凝土内最高温度及内外温差在允许范围内，防止出现温度裂缝；

（3）不得出现露筋和空洞现象。

2. 实测项目

承台实测项目有：混凝土强度、尺寸、顶面高程和轴线偏位。

八、混凝土墩、台身浇筑质量检验

1. 基本要求

（1）混凝土所用的水泥、沙、石、水、外加剂及混合材料的质量和规格，必须符合有关技术规范的要求，按规定的配合比施工；

（2）不得出现空洞和露筋现象。

2. 实测项目

混泥土墩、台身浇筑的实测项目有：混凝土强度、断面尺寸、竖直度或斜度、顶面高程、轴线偏位、节段间错台、大面积平整度、预埋件位置。

九、墩、台帽或盖梁混凝土浇筑质量检验

1. 基本要求

（1）混凝土所用的水泥、沙、石、水、外加剂及混合材料的质量和规格必须符合有关技术规范的要求，按规定的配合比施工；

（2）不得出现露筋和空洞现象。

2. 实测项目

墩、台帽或盖梁混凝土浇筑实测项目有：混凝土强度、断面尺寸、轴线偏位、顶面高程、支座垫石预留位置。

十、预制和安装梁（板）质量检验

1. 基本要求

（1）所用的水泥、沙、石、水、外加剂及混合材料的质量和规格必须符合有关规范的要求，按规定的配合比施工。

（2）梁（板）不得出现露筋和空洞现象。

（3）空心板采用胶囊施工时，应采取有效措施防止胶囊上浮。

（4）梁（板）在吊移出预制底座时，混凝土的强度不得低于设计所要求的吊装强度；梁（板）在安装时，支承结构（墩台、盖梁、垫石）的强度应符合设计要求。

（5）梁（板）安装前，墩、台支座垫板必须稳固。

（6）梁(板)就位后，梁两端支座应对位，梁(板)底与支座以及支座底与垫石顶须密贴，否则应重新安装。

（7）两梁（板）之间接缝填充材料的规格和强度应符合设计要求。

2. 实测项目

梁（板）预制实测项目有：混凝土强度、梁（板）长度、宽度、高度、断面尺寸、平整度和横系梁及预埋件位置；

梁（板）安装实测项目有：支座中心偏位、倾斜度、梁（板）顶面纵向高程、相邻梁（板）顶面高差。

十一、就地浇筑梁（板）质量检验

1. 基本要求

（1）所用的水泥、沙、石、水、外加剂及混合材料的质量和规格必须符合有关规范的要求，按规定的配合比施工；

（2）支架和模板的强度、刚度、稳定性应满足施工技术规范的要求；

（3）预计的支架变形及地基的下沉量应满足施工后梁体设计标高的要求，必要时应采取对支架预压的措施；

（4）梁（板）不得出现露筋和空洞现象；

（5）预埋件的设置和固定应满足设计和施工技术规范的规定。

2. 实测项目

就地浇筑梁（板）的实测项目有混凝土强度、轴线偏位、梁（板）顶面高程、断面尺寸、长度、横坡、平整度。

十二、悬臂梁施工质量检验

1. 基本要求

（1）悬臂梁浇筑或合龙段浇筑所用的水泥、砂、石、水、外加剂及混合材料的质量和规格必须符合有关规范的要求，按规定的配合比施工；

（2）悬拼或悬浇块件前，必须对桥墩根部（0号块件）的高程、桥轴线做详细复核，符合设计要求后，方可进行悬拼或悬浇；

（3）悬臂梁施工必须对称进行，应对轴线和高程进行施工控制；

（4）在施工过程中，梁体不得出现宽度超过设计和规范规定的受力裂缝。一旦出现，必须查明原因，经过处理后方可继续施工；

（5）必须确保悬浇或悬拼的梁接头质量，梁段间胶结材料的性能、质量必须符合设计要求，接缝填充密实；

（6）悬臂梁合龙时，两侧梁体的高差应在设计允许范围内。

2. 实测项目

悬臂梁浇筑的实测项目有混凝土强度、轴线偏位、顶面高程、断面尺寸、合龙后同跨对称点高程差、横坡、平整度。

悬臂梁拼装的实测项目有合龙段混凝土强度、轴线偏位、顶面高程、合龙后同跨对称点高程差。

十三、拱的安装施工质量检验

1. 基本要求

（1）拱桥安装必须严格按设计规定的程序进行施工；

（2）拱段接头采用现浇混凝土时，必须确保其强度和质量，在达到设计规定强度时，方可进行拱上建筑的施工；

（3）安装过程中，如杆件或节点出现开裂，应查明原因，采取措施后，方可继续进行；

（4）合龙段两侧高差必须在设计规定的允许范围内。

2. 实测项目

主拱圈安装的实测项目有轴线偏位、拱圈高程、对称接头点相对高差、同跨各拱肋相对高差、同跨各拱肋间距。

十四、斜拉桥混凝土索塔质量检验

1. 基本要求

（1）混凝土所用的水泥、砂、石、水、外加剂及混合材料的质量和规格必须符合有关规范的要求，按规定的配合比施工；

（2）索塔的索道孔、锚箱位置及锚箱锚固面与水平面的交角均应控制准确，锚垫板与孔道必须互相垂直；

（3）分段浇筑时，段与段间不得有错台；

（4）不得出现漏筋和空洞现象。

（5）横梁施工中，不得因支架变形、温度或预应力而出现裂缝，横梁与塔柱紧密连成整体。

2. 实测项目

塔柱的实测项目有混凝土强度、塔柱底偏位、倾斜度、外轮廓尺寸、壁厚、锚固点高程、孔道位置、预埋件位置。

十五、悬索桥索鞍安装质量检验

1. 基本要求

（1）索鞍成品必须按设计和有关技术规范要求验收合格，并有产品合格证，方可安装；

（2）必须按要求放置底板或格栅，并与底座混凝土连成整体。底座混凝土应振捣密实，强度符合设计要求；

（3）安装前应进行全面检查，如有损伤，必须做处理。索槽内部应清洁，不应沾上减少缆索和索鞍之间摩擦的油或油漆等材料；

（4）索鞍就位后应锁定牢靠。

2. 实测项目

主索鞍安装的实测项目有最终偏位、高程、四角高差。

散索鞍安装的实测项目有底板轴线纵、横向偏位、底板中心高程、底板扭转、安装基线扭转、散索鞍竖向倾斜角。

十六、悬索桥主缆架设质量检验

1. 基本要求

（1）索股成品应有合格证，必须按设计和有关技术规范要求验收合格方可架设；

（2）索股入鞍、入锚位置必须符合设计要求，架设时严禁索股弯折、扭转和散开；

（3）索股锚固应与锚板正交，锚头锁定装置应牢固。

2. 实测项目

主缆架设的实测项目有索股高程、锚跨索股力偏差、主缆空隙率、主缆直径不圆度。

十七、桥面铺装施工质量检验

1. 基本要求

（1）水泥混凝土桥面的基本要求同水泥混凝土路面、沥青混凝土桥面的基本要求同沥青混凝土路面；

（2）桥面泄水孔进水口的布置应有利于桥面和渗入水的排除，其数量不得少于设计要求，出水口不得使水直接冲刷桥体。

2. 实测项目

桥面铺装实测项目有强度或压实度、厚度、平整度、横坡及抗滑构造深度。

第六节　隧道工程质量检验

一、隧道总体质量检验

1. 基本要求

（1）洞口设置应符合设计要求；

（2）必须按设计设置洞内外的排水系统，不淤积、不堵塞；

（3）隧道防排水施工质量必须符合相关规定。

2. 实测项目

隧道总体实测项目有车行道、净总宽、隧道净高、隧道偏位、路线中心线与隧道中心线的衔接、边坡、仰坡。

二、（钢纤维）喷射混凝土支护质量检验

1. 基本要求

（1）材料必须满足规范或设计要求；

（2）喷射前要检查开挖断面的质量，处理好超前挖；

（3）喷射前岩面必须清洁；

（4）喷射混凝土与围岩紧密接合，喷层厚度应符合要求，不能有空洞，喷层内不容许添加片石和木板等杂物，必要时应进行黏结力测试。喷射混凝土严禁挂模喷射。受喷面必须是原岩面；

（5）支护前应做好排水措施，对渗漏水孔洞、缝隙应采取引棒、堵水措施，保证喷射混凝土质量；

（6）采用钢纤维喷射混凝土时，钢纤维抗拉强度不得低于380MPa，且不得有油渍及明显的锈蚀。钢纤维直径宜为0.3~0.5mm，长度为20~25mm，且不得大于25mm。钢纤维含量宜为混合料质量的1%~3%。

2. 实测项目

（钢纤维）喷射混凝土支护实测项目有喷射混凝土强度、喷层厚度、空洞检测。

三、隧道工程检测的必要性

（一）加强公路工程试验检测工作的必要性和重要性

1. 通过试验检测，能充分利用当地出产的材料，便于就地取材。譬如建设地点的砂石、填料等等，可借助试验检测这种有效手段，通过对砂石进行密度、级配、含泥量、压碎值、轴心抗压强度、最大干容重、液塑性指标试验等等，来判定原材料是否满足施工技术规范的要求，便于就地取材，以便选择质优、量大，便于开采和运输的材料，组织、安排施工计划，可加快工程进度、降低工程造价。

2. 通过试验检测，有利于推广新技术、新工艺和材料的应用。及时有效地对某一新材料、新技术、新工艺进行试验检测，以鉴别其可行性、适用性、有效性、先进性，从而为完善工程设计理论和施工工艺积累实践经验，采集相关资料、数据。这对于推动施工技术进步，提高工程进度、质量等将起到积极的作用。

3. 通过必要的试验检测，可科学地评定所用各种原材料及其成品、半成品材料的质量好坏。有了这套有效科学的测试手段，对于任何一种材料均可通过对其规定性能的相关检验，从而评定其产品是否合格。这对于合理地应用材料、提高工程质量是非常重要的。

综上所述，可见试验检测对于提高工程质量、加快工程进度、降低造价、推动施工技术进步，将起到非常重要的作用。因此，加强试验检测工作，势在必行，应当引起高度重视。

（二）试验工作的主要范围

1. 路基土石方填筑开工前必须进行的试验：含水量、密度、颗粒分析、液塑限、土的有机质含量、土的强度试验（CBR）。

2. 桥涵构造物等工程开工前必须进行的试验：

（1）砂石（砾、碎）料试验：表观密度、堆积密度、筛分、含泥量试验、石料针片状含量试验、含水量测定、压碎值、磨耗值、软弱颗粒含量试验。

（2）水泥材料试验：力学试验、细度、标准稠度、凝结时间、胶砂强度试验。

（3）水泥砂浆试验：水泥砂浆的密度、稠度、抗压强度试验、配合比设计标准试验。

（4）水泥混凝土试验：水泥砼的密度、坍落度、抗压、抗冻强度、劈裂抗拉强度试验、配合比设计标准试验。

（5）钢材的检验与试验：标准代号、表面形状、钢筋级别、公称直径、屈服点抗拉强度、伸长率、冷弯试验，以及搭接筋长度和焊接质量的检测、试验。

（6）水质分析：氯离子含量、硫酸根含量、pH值（酸碱度）试验。

3. 路面开工前必须进行的试验：

（1）无机结合料稳定材料试验：含水量、标准击实、抗压强度、抗拉强度、内抗压回弹模量、稳定土配合比设计、稳定土中水泥或石灰剂量的测定、石灰的化学分析。

（2）矿料试验

1）碎石的压碎值、磨耗值、视密度、磨光值、细长扁平颗粒含量及颗粒组成等各项指标的试验检测，砂的视密度、坚固性、砂含量等指标的试验检测。

2）矿粉的视密度、含水量、粒度范围等指标的试验检测。

（3）沥青混合料试验

1）沥青原材料试验：相对密度、软化点针入度粘度、闪点溶解度、含蜡量及加热损失试验。

2）沥青混合料试验：密度、空隙率、马歇尔稳定度和流值、残留稳定度、沥青含量、筛分试验、配合比设计标准试验。

（三）加强试验检测工作，提高工程质量的措施及途径

1. 试验检测人员素质，技术水平有待提高

我省各地施工单位技术水平不一，试验检测人员缺乏，且素质低，甚至用非所学，缺乏一支业务素质较高的质检人员队伍。因此，针对我省当前存在的这种情况，有必要充实试验检测队伍，提高其整体素质和业务水平。在此方面，我省交通主管部已引起重视并开始落实。连续几年来省厅质监站已组织全省公路系统试验检测技术人员分期到省相关部门进行系统培训，这就是一个良好的开端。

2. 健全法制，完善质检机构和工程质量治理制度，是提高我省公路工程质量的一个重

要保障。这对推动我省的公路建设的健康发展将起到积极作用，但随着形势的发展，现有的法规制度已不能适应公路建设的高速发展需要。因此，对于上述法规制度还有必要进一步完善发展，以便使公路建设单位做到有章可循、有法可依。另外，对于试验检测机构，还有待进一步完善，加强治理，严格治理，制定一套可行的治理措施，使质检机构逐渐规范化、专业化。

3. 进一步建立完善公路工程质量保证体系，增强工程质量意识

实行"政府监督、社会监理、企业自检"三级质量保证体系。各级质量治理部门应各司其职，按质量第一的方针和全面质量治理要求，采取切实有效的措施，不断提高质量治理水平。在实际工作中，应严格实行质量自检，加强质量治理和质量监督，逐步建立完善三级质量保证体系。其次，有提高建设各方面质量的意识，分工负责，责任到人，真正落实质量岗位责任制。

（四）公路工程隧道施工检测要点

公路隧道施工检测主要包括两个方面的内容：一是对公路隧道施工质量进行检测；二是对公路隧道施工进行监控量测。

1. 公路隧道施工质量检测

第一，从公路隧道工程中经常出现的各种质量问题来看，其中绝大部分质量隐患的原因，都是因为在施工时管理不当而埋下的，因此，必须加强对施工过程的质量检测。超前支护的强度不够、预加固不符合施工要求等，都有可能造成隧道坍塌的重大事故，或出现冒顶等问题，严重影响施工质量，使施工进度受到严重的影响，造成工程材料的极大浪费。开挖隧道前和过程中，为了确保围岩的稳定性，必须采取必要的辅助方法。例如，可以采用一边用学子面掘进的办法完成加固，一边换拱的方式进行施工。

第二，后续工序主要受爆破成形结果的直接影响。我们应认真落实特长隧道的有关施工的特殊要求，充分认识到工程风险，特别是复杂的隧道水文地质存在着不可预估的风险，应充分利用隧道断面仪，对爆破质量及时进行检测，特别是应重点检查爆破之后的隧道断面，将其与设计的断面进行比较，从中掌握隧道超挖和欠挖的情况；并对隧道围岩进行检查，尤其是应重点检查围岩的变形状况，应坚决杜绝盲目施工、随意施工，确保隧道结构稳定、牢固和施工过程的安全。

第三，着重搞好支护质量，特别是应搞好锚杆的安装质量，严格控制喷射砼的质量，切实注意钢构件的质量。工程质检部门必须对锚杆的间距和方向进行检测，注意检测注浆锚杆的抗拔力等性能情况。认真检测喷射砼的厚度、平整度等情况是否符合施工要求。检测钢构件的规格大小是否符合要求，锚杆连接、节间连接情况是否稳固，钢架间距长度是否得当，各个构件和围岩之间的接触情况。同时，加强探测支护后边的施工情况，特别是重点探测其回填的密实度。严格检测各项支护质量，确保隧道施工操作过程做好相应的检测工作。

第四，衬砌砼质量检测包括衬砌的几何尺寸、衬砌砼强度、砼完整性、砼裂缝、衬砌背后回填密实度和衬砌内部钢架、钢筋分布等的检测。外观尺寸用直尺量测，砼强度及其完整性则用无损技术探测检测，砼裂缝用塞尺或裂缝观测仪检测，衬砌背后的回填密实度用钻孔法或地质雷达法检测。

2. 公路隧道施工监控量测

施工监控量测是新奥法施工的一项重要内容，它既是施工安全的保障措施，又是优化结构受力、降低材料消耗的重要手段。量测的基本内容有隧道围岩变形、支护受力和衬砌受力。隧道周边位移采用收敛计和全站仪量测。隧道拱部沉降采用精密水准仪和全站仪量测。围岩内部的位移，采用机械式多点位移计量测。锚杆轴力用测力锚杆量测。

3. 公路隧道环境监测

环境监测主要分施工环境监测和运营环境检测。施工环境检测的主要任务是检测施工过程中的粉尘和有害气体。这里的有害气体主要是 CH_4，若 CH_4 达到一定浓度且施工中防治措施不当，则可能引发爆炸，造成人员伤亡或经济损失。

四、隧道工程质量检测的目的和意义

1. 隧道质量监控的目的

（1）通过围岩地质状况和支护状况描述，对围岩进行合理的分类及对稳定性进行合理的评价；

（2）对隧道拱顶下沉周边收敛位移进行监测，根据量测数据确认围岩的稳定性，判断支护效果，指导施工工序预防坍塌，保证施工安全；

（3）对周边收敛位移进行监测，根据变形的速率及量值判断围岩的稳定程度，选择适当的二衬支护时机，指导现场施工；

（4）地表下沉。对隧道埋深较浅段进行地表沉降监测，判定隧道开挖对地表的影响，与拱顶下沉数据相互印证；

（5）通过测定锚杆长度和注浆饱满度，检测锚杆长度和注浆效果；

（6）选测组合。通过对围岩压力、钢支撑应力、衬砌应力等选测项目的监测判断围岩稳定性及支护效果，反馈设计，指导现场施工。

2. 隧道质量监控的意义

隧道监控量测作为新奥法的三大核心之一，对评价隧道施工方法的可行性、设计参数的合理性、了解隧道施工实际围岩级别及其变形特性等能够提供准确、及时的依据，对隧道二次衬砌的施作时间具有决定性意义，是保障隧道建设成功的重要手段。隧道监控量测的主要任务应做到提高安全性、修正设计、指导施工、积累建设经验，并通过对实测数据的现场分析、处理，及时向施工方、监理方、设计方和业主提供分析资料。

第七节 质量检验评定

一、单位工程、分部工程和分项工程的划分

1. 单位工程
单位工程是指在建设项目中,根据签订的合同,具有独立施工条件的工程。
2. 分部工程
在单位工程中,应按结构部位、路段长度及施工特点或施工任务划分为若干个分部工程。
3. 分项工程
在分部工程中,应按不同的施工方法、材料、工序及路段长度等划分为若干个分项工程。

二、工程质量评分依据

1. 工程质量检验评分以分项工程为单元,采用百分制进行。在分项工程评分的基础上,逐级计算各相应分部工程、单位工程、合同段和建设项目评分值。
2. 工程质量评定等级分为合格与不合格,应按分项、分部、单位工程、合同段和建设项目逐级评定。
3. 施工单位应对各分项工程按《公路工程质量检验评定标准第一册土建工程》所列基本要求、实测项目和外观鉴定进行自检,按"工程质量检验评定用表"及相关施工技术规范提交真实、完整的自检资料,对工程质量进行自我评定。
4. 工程监理单位应按规定要求对工程质量进行独立抽检,对施工单位检评资料进行签认,对工程质量进行评定。
5. 建设单位根据对工程质量的检查及平时掌握的情况,对工程监理单位所做的工程质量评分及等级进行审定。
6. 质量监督部门、质量检测机构依据《公路工程质量检验评定标准第一册土建工程》对公路工程质量进行检测评定。

三、工程质量评分方法

1. 分项工程质量评分
分项工程质量检验内容包括基本要求、实测项目、外观鉴定和质量保证资料四个部分。

只有在其使用的原材料、半成品、成品及施工工艺符合基本要求的规定，且无严重外观缺陷和质量问题，保证资料真实并基本齐全时，才能对分项工程质量进行检验评定。

涉及结构安全和使用功能的重要实测项目为关键项目，其合格率不得低于90%（属于工厂加工制造的交通工程安全设施及桥梁金属构件不低于95%，机电工程为100%），且检测值不得超过规定极值，否则必须进行返工处理。实测项目的规定极值是指任一单个检测值都不能突破的极限值，不符合要求时该实测项目为不合格。

分项工程的评分值满分为100分，按实测项目采用加权平均法计算。存在外观缺陷或资料不全时，需减分。

$$分项工程得分 = \frac{\sum[检查项目得分 \times 权值]}{\sum 检查项目权值}$$

分项工程评分值 = 分项工程得分 - 外观缺陷减分 - 资料不全减分项

（1）基本要求检查。

分项工程所列基本要求，对施工质量优劣具有关键作用，应按基本要求对工程进行认真检查。经检查不符合基本要求规定时，不得进行工程质量的检验和评定。

（2）实测项目计分。

对规定检查项目采用现场抽样方法，按照规定频率和下列计分方法对分项工程的施工质量直接进行检测计分。

检查项目除按数理统计方法评定的项目以外，均应按单点（组）测定值是否符合标准要求进行评定，并按合格率计分

检查项目合格率（%）= 检查合格的点（组）数 / 该检查项目的全部检查点（组）数

检查项目得分 = 检查项目合格率 × 100%

（3）外观缺陷减分。

对工程外表状况应逐项进行全面检查，如发现外观缺陷，应进行减分。对于较严重的外观缺陷，施工单位必须采取措施进行整修处理。

（4）资料不全减分。

分项工程的施工资料和图表残缺，缺乏最基本的数据，或有伪造涂改者，不予检验和评定。

2. 分部工程和单位工程质量评分

分项工程和分部工程区分为一般工程和主要（主体）工程，分别给予1和2的权值。进行分部工程和单位工程评分时，采用加权平均值计算法确定相应的评分值。

$$分部（单位）工程评分值 = \frac{\sum 分项（分部）工程评分值 \times 相应权值}{\sum 分项（分部）工程权值}$$

3. 合同段和建设项目工程质量评分中，施工合同段工程质量评分采用所含各单位工程质量评分的加权平均值，即

$$施工合同段工程质量评分值 = \frac{\sum(单位工程评分值 \times 该单位工程投资额)}{合同段总投资额}$$

整个工程项目工程质量评分采用加权平均法进行,即

$$工程质量评分值 = \frac{\sum(合同段工程质量评分值 \times 该合同段投资额)}{\sum 施工合同段投资额}$$

四、质量保证资料

施工单位应有完整的施工原始记录、试验数据、分项工程自查数据等质量保证资料,并进行整理分析,负责提交齐全、真实和系统的施工资料和图表。工程监理单位负责提交齐全、真实和系统的监理资料。质量保证资料应包括以下六个方面:

1. 所用原材料、半成品和成品质量检验结果;
2. 材料配比、拌和加工控制检验和试验数据;
3. 地基处理、隐蔽工程施工记录和大桥、隧道施工监控资料;
4. 各项质量控制指标的试验记录和质量检验汇总图表;
5. 施工过程中遇到的非正常情况记录及其对工程质量影响分析;
6. 施工过程中如发生质量事故,经处理补救后达到设计要求的认可证明文件等。

五、工程质量等级评定

1. 分项工程质量等级评定

分项工程评分值不小于 75 分者为合格、小于 75 分者为不合格;机电工程、属于工厂加工制造的桥梁金属构件不小于 90 分者为合格,小于 90 分者为不合格。

评定为不合格的分项工程,经加固、补强或返工、调测,满足设计要求后,可以重新评定其质量等级,但计算分部工程评分值时按其复评分值的 90% 计算。

2. 分部工程质量等级评定

所属各分项工程全部合格,则该分部工程评为合格;所属任一分项工程不合格,则该分部工程为不合格。

3. 单位工程质量等级评定

所属各分部工程全部合格,则该单位工程评为合格;所属任一分部工程不合格,则该单位工程为不合格。

4. 合同段和建设项目质量等级评定

合同段和建设项目所含单位工程全部合格,其工程质量等级为合格;所属任一单位工程不合格,则合同段和建设项目为不合格。

六、公路工程质量检测的意义

（一）工程试验检测环节的重要性

以公路工程建设为例，随着公路等级的不断提升，对于公路工程的建设要求也不断提高，各级交通管理部门、施工单位虽然已经对公路质量检测及施工质量提高重视，但是在现存的许多工作之中，仍旧有一些施工单位"上有政策、下有对策"，原材料的质量未能达到施工技术要求；有些单位虽然具备足够的试验检测设备，建立试验基地，也组织相关的工程试验检测人员进行检测，但由于各种原因，已有资源不能充分发挥功能。大量的工程实践经验都表明：如果不重视现场的施工监测和质量管理工作，不注意实际检测，仅仅依靠以往的经验去评估工程的好坏，就容易导致在建设初期，工程质量就出现破坏迹象。因此，必须在施工开始时就配备足量且有丰富经验的试验检测人员，建立健全的工程质量检测管理体系，这样才可以达到缩短工期、提高质量、降低成本的目的。另外，工程试验检测人员必须努力抓好施工过程之中的每一个环节，力图降低人为的误差，提高试验检测的准确度，保证检测结果的可靠性。只有如此，工程试验检测环节才能在工程质量检测中发挥其应有的作用。

（二）开工阶段和施工阶段工程试验检测对工作质量的控制

1. 施工前的各项原料检测

对于每一个工程项目而言，在项目开工之前，都要对工程项目的各个部分配以详尽的工程质量控制指标，如所使用的水泥及砂石的型号品质、集料规格、不同型号混凝土之间的掺配，这些数据是施工中的重要参数，亦是竣工后相关质量检测的重要依据。所以，及时提供科学精准的试验数据对工程技术人员来说是十分重要的。在项目开工之前，负责工程的工程试验检测人员会依据项目的设计要求与给定的工程质量技术标准，结合施工地点的实际情况来确定所要使用的施工材料。例如，混凝土、水泥、砂石等的相关配合比，为工程的顺利施工打下良好基础。

对于路基填土而言，最重要的两个因素是干密度和含水量，施工中应尽量达到最大干密度与最佳含水量，这就需要进行击实试验；对于沥青混合料，一般采用马歇尔试验测量稳定度和流值等指标，而且在施工过程中，为保证路面质量，应严格控制沥青用量、摊铺温度、压实方法等因素。诸如此类的做法，既能够为工程的施工提供经济可行的配料方案，也能够为日后的施工积累大量的数据资料，更能够保证工程质量、降低工程成本。所以说，工程试验检测是项目开工前必不可少的准备工作。

2. 项目施工中的工程试验检测

对于一个安全性能达标、工程质量好的工程而言，每道工序都需要严加把关，不仅要注重施工工艺，更要狠抓施工质量，做好施工过程之中的工程试验检测。例如，在公路路基的施工建设中，每一层材料的选取、摊铺的厚度、配备何种碾压的机器以及所采用材料的含水量都对路基压实质量有直接的影响。在路基建设成型之后，对路面铺装的质量也有很大的影响，虽然经过多年的车辆碾压，也可以使路面发生破损。

但是现场所测得压实度数据却可以直接体现出路基的强度与质量的好坏。在施工建设完成一部分之后，应该按照一定的标准对其进行检验。检测的内容主要涵盖建筑物的中线偏移量、相对于检测轴线的实际位置、压实度、偏移量等等。例如，对于压实度的检测，一般选用灌砂法、路面取芯法；为反映路面各结构层及土基的整体强度和刚度，一般使用弯沉仪进行测量；在进行水泥混凝土抗压抗折程度检测时，应注意控制仪器荷载，避免由于荷载过快或过慢造成试验误差，或者是仪器的损坏。

（三）竣工阶段工程试验检测对工作质量的控制

在项目的施工进程中，合理有效地进行工程试验检测，可以做到对材料性能更好了解，从而更加合理、更加经济地进行施工。在项目竣工之后，无论项目规模的大小还是工期长短都需要进行一次整体的交工验收，在所组织的验收技术人员中，试验检测人员也是必不可少的，他们要完成很多的项目现场检测工作，如路基压实度、平整度、路面强度、隧道抗渗等各种检测。尤其是项目交工验收时施工单位所上交的工程质量自检报告中，对于试验检测数据资料，也要专门整理成册，以方便竣工时工程试验检测人员查阅。这些资料既反映了在工程施工之中施工方对于工作质量的控制情况，也体现了施工单位对工程质量试验检测的手段是否完善合理，为验收人员评定工程质量提供重要依据，也是该工程日后养护维修的重要依据。

在项目完成之后，对于整个工程进行试验检测，也是一项任务量巨大的工程。不仅需要对该工程的整体进行试验检测，也需要对各个环节、各道工序分别进行检测，这样做的目的不仅是为了保证整个工程的工作质量，也为检测提供具体依据。众所周知，一个完整的工程需要很多道不同的工序，在对各道工序的试验检测中，要保证各个工序的质量合格及上下级工序之间的衔接恰当合理。在对工程整体质量进行评估时，必须依据各个环节之中所测得工程相关数据，以及竣工后整个工程的整体质量，给予该工程一个综合性的评定。工程试验检测工作人员要依据相关数据，评定该工程是否达到预期效果，是否符合国家的或者有关部门的相关标准。唯有如此，才能起到工程试验检测工作在竣工验收中的作用。

七、公路工程质量检测工作的现状分析及措施

（一）公路工程试验检测工作的现状分析

1. 公路工程试验检测工作未能得到重视

试验室建设需要大量的资金投入及满足相应资质等级数量要求的检测工程师、检测员。试验检测不能直接为企业创造价值，这对有些施工企业来说，试验检测工作似乎只有投入

而没有产出，从而对试验检测工作没有足够的重视。因此，普遍存在试验人员，在待遇方面或多或少都比其他技术和管理岗位要低的现象。加之试验检测工作是一项十分繁重、枯燥的工作，并且由于公路工程施工环境较差，其试验检测工作环境也相对较差，导致试验检测人员积极性不高，从事这一行业的意愿不强，人员挂靠现象时有发生，造成从事试验检测行业的试验人员无论从数量和质量上都不能满足工程建设需要。

2. 公路工程试验检测机制受到阻碍

随着科学技术水平的不断创新，公路工程试验检测技术也有所提升，但其运行机制阻碍了试验检测行业的发展。在目前的公路工程管理当中，真正完全独立法人的第三方检测机构所占比例不多，大多公路工程试验检测机构都隶属于施工或监理单位，试验检测人员的作用与投入经费的多少都会受到所属单位的制约，使得公路工程试验检测工作独立开展业务受到很多客观条件的约束和干扰，造成公路工程试验检测工作无法发挥对工程质量的控制作用。

3. 公路工程试验检测数据信息存在虚假现象

随着国家的不断发展、公路工程建设规模的不断扩大，公路工程施工企业承揽工程也不断扩张，在建项目数量也随之增加。而试验检测人才库的建设往往跟不上工程扩张的速度，加剧了公路工程试验检测业务需求量与试验检测人力资源的短缺出现相互矛盾的现象。能否按照所规定的检测频率进行检测成了一个普遍的问题。施工企业管理水平有高有低，难免有施工项目管理水平低下的，难以做到按计划有条不紊地进行施工，从而施工企业补假资料是一个普遍现象。再者，施工企业良莠不齐，为偷工减料对检测数据造假也并不罕见，以上种种，使所建立起来的试验室沦为了造假资料、应付检查的工具，试验检测结果编造或者修改调整数据的现象时有发生，导致试验检测工作与施工过程中的质量控制作用没有真正发挥出来，试验检测结果的数据不具有真实性与可靠性。

（二）加强试验检测工作，提高工程质量的措施及途径

1. 充分意识到加强试验检测的重要性

试验检测是为了更好地确保工程质量得到有效的提升。因而作为施工企业，必须利用试验检测得出各项技术参数，从而更好地开展施工，为工程质量奠定坚实基础的同时减少工程的投资，实现施工企业经济效益的最大化。对于施工企业管理者而言，只有意识到加强试验检测的重要性，才能从根本上意识到试验检测在公路工程建设中的作用，进而为试验检测工作的高效开展奠定坚实的基础。

2. 致力于试验检测技术、设备的更新

随着公路建设的高速发展，传统的公路检测技术和设备存在多项问题的弊病日益凸显，同时，也反映出我国相关机构的研究工作人员对无损检测技术应用更新没有高度重视的现状。运输业的高度发展及国家整体经济的发展离不开道路网络的通畅，对现代化道路的要求也越来越高，使得传统的一般公路检测技术已经无法满足现代公路高性能、高精确度的

检测要求。因此,需要引进并掌握新的检测技术与设备,提高检测的水平,才能充分地保证现代公路工程保质保量地建成,也达到对公路工程建设质量的监督作用。这就需要施工企业加强对试验方面的投资,加强对试验检测技术人员的培训,不断强化其专业技术水平和责任意识,从而更加主动积极地参与到试验检测工作中来,并切实做好检测设备的维护和保养工作。尤其是加强试验检测新技术、新方法、新设备的更新,这样才能更好地确保检测结果的精准性。

3. 切实做好施工过程中的各项检测工作

一是施工企业应建立设施齐全的工地试验室,配备具有较高技术水平的试验检测人员,并建立一套完整的试验室质量管理体系,从而提高试验数据的精确性、可靠性;二是施工中的关键工序和重要施工部位进行严格监督,并详细认真地填写工程记录;三是及时对分项工程进行质量验收,验收不合格的项目,坚决返工处理;四是工程竣工后应严格检测验收,对检测中发现的质量隐患应及时提出,没通过验收的必须返工。

4. 进一步建立完善公路工程质量保证体系,增强工程质量意识

目前实行"政府监督、社会监理、企业自检"三级质量保证体系。各级质量管理部门应各司其职,按质量第一的方针和全面质量管理要求,采取切实有效的措施,不断提高质量管理水平。在实际工作中,应严格实行质量自检,加强质量管理和质量监督,逐步建立完善三级质量保证体系。其有增强建设各方面的质量意识,分工负责、责任到人,真正落实质量岗位责任制。

第八章 公路工程项目施工安全标准化管理

我国公路施工技术不断发展、日益完善，各类公路逐步普及。公路施工所跨地域的特点千差万别，现场状况相对复杂，所以加强对公路施工的管理显得十分重要。采用标准管理不仅能把整个公路施工项目进行得合理规范、有条不紊，还能保证项目进度，提高路建的质量和安全。本章围绕公路施工项目，针对其特点对公路施工标准化管理进行分析。

第一节 特殊工序作业安全作业要点

1. 土石方开挖安全技术

（1）基坑开挖时，两人操作间距应大于3.0m，不得对头挖土；挖土面积较大时，每人工作面不应小于6 m²。挖土应由上而下，分层分段按顺序进行，严禁先挖坡脚或逆坡挖土，或采用底部掏空塌土方法挖土。

（2）挖土方不得在危岩、孤石的下边或贴近未加固的危险建筑物的下面进行。

（3）基坑开挖应严格按要求放坡，操作时应随时注意土壁的变动情况，如发现有裂纹或部分坍塌现象，应及时进行支撑或放坡，并注意支撑的稳固和土壁的变化。当采取不放坡开挖时，应设置临时支护，各种支护应根据土质及基坑深度经计算确定。

（4）机械多台阶同时开挖，应验算边坡的稳定，挖土机离边坡应有一定的安全距离，以防塌方，造成翻机事故。

（5）在有支撑的基坑槽中使用机械挖土时，应防止破坏支撑。在坑槽边使用机械挖土时，应计算支撑强度，必要时应加强支撑。

（6）基坑槽和管沟回填土时，下方不得有人，对所使用的打夯机等要检查电气线路，以防止漏电、触电，停机时要关闭电闸。

（7）拆除护壁支撑时，应按照回填顺序，从下向上逐步拆除；更换支撑时，必须先安装新的，再拆除旧的。

（8）爆破施工前，应做好安全爆破的准备工作，画好安全距离，设置警戒哨。闪电鸣雷时，禁止装药、接线，施工操作时严格按安全操作规程办事。

（9）炮眼深度超过 4 m 时，需用两个雷管起爆；如深度超过 10 m，则不得用火花起爆，若爆破时发现拒爆，必须先查清原因后再进行处理。

2. 桩基础工程安全技术

（1）打（沉）桩。

打（沉）桩前，应对邻近施工范围内的原有建筑物、地下管线等进行检查，对有影响的工程，应采取有效的加固防护措施或隔振措施，施工时加强观测，以确保施工安全；

打桩机行走的道路必须平整、坚实，必要时铺设道砟，经压路机碾压密实；

打（沉）桩前应先全面检查机械各个部件及润滑情况及钢丝绳是否完好，发现问题应及时解决；检查后要进行试运转，严禁带病工作；

打（沉）桩机架安设应铺垫平稳、牢固。吊桩就位时，桩必须达到 100% 强度，起吊点必须符合设计要求；

打桩时桩头垫料严禁用手拨正，不得在桩锤未打到桩顶就起锤或过早刹车，以免损坏桩机设备；

在夜间施工时，必须有足够的照明设施。

（2）灌注桩。

施工前，应认真查清邻近建筑物的情况，采取有效的防振措施；

灌注桩成孔机械操作时应保持垂直平稳，防止成孔时突然倾倒或冲（桩）锤突然下落，造成人员伤亡或设备损坏；

冲击锤（落锤）操作时，距锤 6 m 范围内不得有人员行走或进行其他作业，非工作人员不得进入施工区域内；

灌注桩在已成孔尚未灌注混凝土前，应用盖板封严或设置护栏，以防掉土或人员坠入孔内，造成重大人身安全事故；

进行高空作业时，应系好安全带，灌注混凝土时，装、拆导管人员必须戴安全帽。

（3）人工挖孔桩。

井口应有专人操作垂直运输设备，井内照明、通风、通信设备应齐全；

要随时与井底人员联系，不得随意离开岗位；

挖孔施工人员下入桩孔内需戴安全帽，连续工作不宜超过 4 h；

挖出的弃土应及时运至堆土场堆放。

3. 地基处理安全技术

（1）在灰土垫层、灰土桩等施工中，粉化石灰和石灰过筛时，必须戴口罩、风镜、手套、套袖等防护用品，并站在上风头；向坑槽、孔内夯填灰土前，应先检查电线绝缘是否良好，接地线、开关应符合要求，夯打时严禁夯击电线。

（2）夯实地基时，起重机应支垫平稳，遇软弱地基，需用长枕木或路基板支垫。提升夯锤前应卡牢回转刹车，以防夯锤起吊后吊机转动失稳，发生倾翻事故。

(3)夯实地基时,现场操作人员要戴安全帽;夯锤起吊后,吊臂和夯锤下15 m内不得站人,非工作人员应远离夯击点30 m以外,以防夯击时飞石伤人。

(4)在用深层搅拌机进行入土切削和提升搅拌时,一旦发生卡钻或停钻现象,应切断电源,将搅拌机强制提起之后,才能启动电动机。

(5)已成的孔尚未夯填填料之前,应加盖板,以免人员或物件掉入孔内。

(6)当使用交流电源时应特别注意各用电设施的接地防护装置;施工现场附近有高压线通过时,必须根据机具的高度、线路的电压,详细测定其安全距离,防止高压放电发生触电事故;夜班作业时,应有足够的照明及备用安全电源。

4.地下建筑防水安全技术

(1)防水混凝土施工。现场施工负责人和施工员必须十分重视安全生产,牢固树立安全促进生产、生产必须安全的思想,切实做好预防工作。所有施工人员必须经过安全培训,考核合格后方可上岗。

施工员在下达施工计划的同时,应下达具体的安全措施,每天出工前,施工员要针对当天的施工情况,布置施工安全工作,并讲明安全注意事项。

落实安全施工责任制度、安全施工教育制度、安全施工交底制度、施工机具设备安全管理制度等,并落实到岗位、责任到人。

防水混凝土施工期间应以漏电保护、防机械事故和保护为安全工作重点,切实做好防护措施。

遵章守纪,杜绝违章指挥和违章作业,现场应设立安全措施及有针对性的安全宣传牌、标语和安全警示标志。

进入施工现场必须佩戴安全帽,作业人员衣着灵活紧身,禁止穿硬底鞋、高跟鞋作业,高空作业人员应系好安全带,禁止酒后操作、吸烟和打架斗殴。

(2)水泥砂浆防水层施工。

现场施工负责人和施工员必须十分重视安全生产,牢固树立安全促进生产、生产必须安全的思想,切实做好预防工作。

施工员在下达施工计划的同时,应下达具体的安全措施,每天出工前,施工员要针对当天的施工情况,布置施工安全工作,并讲明安全注意事项。

落实安全施工责任制度、安全施工教育制度、安全施工交底制度、施工机具设备安全管理制度等。

特殊工种必须持证上岗。

遵章守纪,杜绝违章指挥和违章作业,现场设立安全措施及有针对性的安全宣传牌、标语和安全警示标志。

进入施工现场必须佩戴安全帽,作业人员衣着灵活紧身,禁止穿硬底鞋、高跟鞋作业,高空作业人员应系好安全带,禁止酒后操作、吸烟和打架斗殴。

（3）卷材防水工程施工。

1）由于卷材中某些组成材料和胶粘剂具有一定的毒性和易燃性，因此，在材料保管、运输、施工过程中，要注意防火和预防职业中毒、烫伤事故发生。

2）在施工过程中做好基坑和地下结构的临边防护，防止出现坠落事故。

3）高温天气施工，要有防暑降温措施。

4）施工中的废弃物要及时清理，外运至指定地点，避免污染环境。

（4）涂料防水工程施工。

1）配料在施工现场应有安全及防火措施，所有施工人员都必须严格遵守操作要求。

2）着重强调临边安全，防止抛物和滑坡。

3）在高温天气施工需做好防暑降温措施。

4）涂料在储存、使用的过程中应注意防火。

5）在清扫及砂浆拌和过程中要避免灰尘飞扬。

6）施工中生成的建筑垃圾要及时清理、清运。

（5）金属板防水层工程施工。

1）施工人员作业时，必须戴安全帽、系安全带并配备工具袋。

2）现场焊接时，在焊接下方应设防火斗。

3）在高温天气施工需做好防暑降温措施。

4）施工中产生的建筑垃圾应及时清理干净。

第二节 临时用电安全技术要求

1.公路工程施工现场临时用电的基本原则

（1）施工现场的电工、电焊工属于特种作业工种，必须按国家有关规定经专门安全作业培训，取得特种作业操作资格证书，方可上岗作业。其他人员不得从事电气设备及电气线路的安装、维修和拆除。

（2）施工现场的临时用电必须采用TN-S接地、接零保护系统,即具有专用保护零线(PE线)、电源中性点直接接地的220/380V三相五线制系统。

（3）施工现场的临时用电必须按照"三级配电二级保护"设置。

（4）施工现场的用电设备必须实行"一机、一闸、一漏、一箱"制，即每台用电设备必须有自己专用的开关箱，专用开关箱内必须设置独立的隔离开关和漏电保护器。

（5）正确识别"小心有电、靠近危险"等标志或标牌，不得随意靠近、随意损坏和挪动标牌。

2. 配电室的安全技术要点

（1）施工现场配电室位置应靠近电源，周边道路畅通，进、出线方便，周围环境灰尘少、潮气少、振动小，无腐蚀介质、无易燃易爆物品；不要设在容易积水的场所或其正下方，并避开污染源的下风侧。尽量靠近负荷中心，以减少线路的长度和导线的截面积，提高配电质量，便于维护。

（2）配电室和控制室应能自然通风，并应采取措施防止雨雪和小动物出入；成列的配电屏（盘）和控制屏（台）两端应与重复接地及保护零线做电气连接。

（3）配电屏（盘）正面的操作通道宽度单列布置不小于1.5 m，双列布置不小于2 m，配电屏（盘）后的维护通道宽度不小于0.8 m，侧面的维护通道不小于1 m；配电室的顶棚距地面不低于3 m；配电室内设值班或检修室时，该室外距配电屏（盘）的水平距离应大于1 m，并应有屏障隔离；配电室内的裸母线与地面垂直距离小于2.5 m时，应采取遮拦隔离，遮拦下面通行道的高度不小于1.9 m；配电装置的上端距顶棚不小于0.5 m。

（4）配电屏（盘）应装设有功和无功电度表，并应分路装设电流、电压表；电流表与计费电度表不许共用一组电流互感器，配电屏（盘）应装设短路、过负荷保护装置和漏电保护器；配电屏（盘）上的各配电线路应编号，并标明用途标记，配电屏（盘）或配电线路维修时，应悬挂停电标志牌，停、送电必须由专人负责。

（5）配电室的建筑物和构筑物的耐火等级应不低于3级，室内应配置沙箱和绝缘灭火器；母线均应涂刷有色油漆；配电室的门向外开，并配锁，专人保管。

3. 施工现场配电线路的安全技术要点

施工现场的配电线路包括室外线路和室内线路。室内线路通常有绝缘导线和电缆的明敷设和暗敷设，室外线路主要有绝缘导线架空敷设和绝缘电缆埋地敷设两种，也有电缆线架空明敷设的。

（1）室外线路的安全技术要点

室外架空线路由导线、绝缘子、横担及电杆等组成。室外架空线路必须采用绝缘铜线或绝缘铝线，铝线的截面积大于$1 mm^2$，铜线的截面积大于$10 mm^2$。

架空线路严禁架设在树木、脚手架及其他非专用电杆上，且严禁成束架设；在临近输电线路的建筑物上作业时，不能随便往下扔金属类杂物，更不能触摸、拉动电线或电线接触钢丝和电杆的拉线。

严禁在高压线下方搭设临建、堆放材料和进行施工作业；在高压线一侧作业时，架空线与施工现场地面最小距离一般为4 m，与机动车道一般为6 m，与铁路轨道一般为7.5 m。

电杆埋设深度宜为杆长的1/10加0.6 m。但在松软地质处应加大埋设深度或采用卡盘等加固。跨越机动车道的成杆应采取单横担双绝缘子；15°~45°的转角杆应采用双横担双绝缘子；45°以上的转角杆应采用十字横担；直线杆采用针式绝缘子，耐张杆采用蝶式绝缘子。

敷设电缆的方式和地点，应以方便、安全、经济、可靠为依据，电缆直埋方式，施工简单、投资省、散热好，应首先考虑；敷设地点应保证电缆不受机械损伤或其他热辐射，同时应尽量避开建筑物和交通设施。

电缆直接埋地的深度不小于 0.6 m，并在电缆上下均匀铺设不小于 50 mm 厚的细沙，再覆盖砖等硬质保护层，并插上标志牌；电缆穿过建筑物、构筑物时需设置套管。

室外电缆线架空敷设时，应沿墙壁或电杆设置，严禁用金属裸线作绑线，电缆的最大弧垂距地面不小于 2.5 m。

（2）室内线路的安全技术要点

在宿舍工棚、仓库、办公室内严禁使用电饭煲、电水壶、电炉、电热杯等较大功率电器。如需使用，应由项目部安排专业电工在指定地点安装可使用较高功率电器的电气线路和控制器；严禁使用不符合安全的电炉、电热棒等。

严禁在宿舍内乱拉乱接电源，非专职电工不准乱接或更换熔丝，不准以其他金属丝代替熔丝（保险丝）；严禁在电线上晾衣服和挂其他东西等。

室内线路必须采用绝缘导线，距地面高度不得小于 2.5 m；接户线在挡距内不得有接头，进线处离地高度不得小于 2.5 m，过墙应穿管保护，并采取防雨措施，室外端应采用绝缘子固定。室内导线的线路应减少弯曲，采用瓷夹固定导线时，导线间距应不小于 35 mm，瓷夹间距应不大于 800 mm；采用瓷瓶固定导线时，导成间距应不小于 100 mm，瓷瓶间距应不大于 1.5 m，钢索配线的吊、架间距不宜大于 12 m；采用护套绝缘导线时，允许直接敷设于钢索上。

导线的额定电压应符合线路的工作电压；导线的截面积要满足供电容量要求和机械强度要求，但铝线截面应不小于 2.5 mm²，铜线的截面应不小于 1.5 mm²，导线应尽量减少分支，不受机械作用；室内线路布置尽可能避开热源，应便于线路检查。

4. 施工现场配电箱与开关箱设置的安全技术要点

（1）施工现场临时用电一般采用三级配电方式，即总配电箱（或配电室），总配电箱以下设分配电箱，再以下设开关箱，开关箱以下就是用电设备。

（2）总配电箱应设在靠近电源的地区；分配电箱应装设在用电设备或负荷相对集中的地区；分配电箱与开关箱的距离不得超过 30 m；开关箱应由末级分配电箱配电，开关箱与其控制的固定式用电设备的水平距离不宜超过 3m。

（3）配电箱与开关箱应装设在通风、干燥及常温场所。严禁装设在有严重损伤作用的瓦斯、烟气、蒸气、液体及其他有害介质中，不得装设在易受撞击、振动、液体浸溅及热源烘烤的场所；配电箱与开关箱周围应有足够两人同时工作的空间和通道，不得堆放任何妨碍操作、维修的物品，不得有杂草、灌木等。

（4）配电箱、开关箱应采用铁板或优质绝缘材料制作，铁板厚度应大于 1.5mm；配电箱内的电器应首先安装在金属或非木质的绝缘电器安装板上，然后整体紧固在配电箱箱体内；金属板与配电箱箱体应做电气连接。

（5）配电箱、开关箱内的连接线采用绝缘导线，接头不松动，不得有外露带电部分；

配电箱、开关箱内的工作零线应通过接线端子板连接，与保护零线接线端子板分设；配电箱、开关箱的金属箱体、金属电器安装板及箱内电器不应带电金属底座、外壳等必须做保护接零，保护零线应通过接线端子板连接。

（6）动力配电箱与照明配电箱宜分别设置，如合置在同一配电箱内，动力和照明线应分路设置。

（7）配电箱、开关箱中的导线进线口和出线口应设在箱体的下底面，严禁设在箱体的上顶面、侧面、后面箱门处；进线和出线应加护套分路成束并做防水弯；导线束不得与箱体进、出口直接接触；进入开关箱的电源线，严禁用插销连接；移动式配电箱、开关箱的进口线、出口线必须采用橡胶绝缘电缆。

（8）配电箱、开关箱应装设牢固、端正，移动式配电箱、开关箱应装设在坚固的支架上，固定式配电箱、开关箱的下底面与地面的垂直距离应大于 1.3 m、小于 1.5 m；移动式分配电箱、开关箱的下底与地面的垂直距离宜大于 0.6 m、小于 1.5 m；所有的配电箱、开关箱必须防雨、防尘。

5. 配电箱、开关箱内的电器装置安全技术要点

（1）配电箱、开关箱内的电器装置必须可靠完好，严禁使用破损、不合格电器，各种开关电器的额定值应与其所控制的用电设备的额定值相适应。

（2）每台用电设备应有各自专用的开关箱，必须实行"一机一闸一漏"制，严禁用同一个开关电器直接控制两台及两台以上的用电设备（含插座）。

（3）在停、送电时，配电箱、开关箱之间应遵守合理的操作顺序。送电操作顺序：总配电箱—分配电箱—开关箱；断电操作顺序：开关箱—分配电箱—总配电箱。

正常情况下，停电时首先分断自动开关，然后分断隔离开关；送电时先合隔离开关，后合自动开关（出现电气故障时的紧急情况除外）。

（4）使用配电箱、开关箱时，操作者应接受岗前培训，熟悉所使用设备的电气性能和掌握有关开关的正确操作方法。

（5）总配电箱、分配电箱应装设总隔离开关和分路隔离开关、总熔断器和分路熔断器（或总自动开关和分路自动开关）。总开关电器的额定值，动作整定值应与分路开关电器的额定值、动作整定值相适应。

（6）总配电箱还必须安装漏电保护器、总电流表、总电度表和其他仪器。开关箱内的开关电器必须在任何情况下都可以使用电设备实行电源分离。

（7）开关箱内也必须安装漏电保护器，使用于潮湿和有腐蚀介质场所的漏电保护器应采用防溅型产品。总配电箱和开关箱中的漏电保护器应合理选用，使之具有分级分段保护的功能，漏电保护器至少每月检查一次，确保完好有效。

6. 配电箱、开关箱使用与维护的安全技术要点

（1）施工现场所有配电箱、开关箱都要由专人负责（专业电工），所有配电箱、开关箱应配锁，并标明其名称、用途，做出分路标记。

（2）开关箱操作人员应熟悉开关电器的正确操作方法，施工现场停业作业1 h以上时，应将动力开关箱断电上锁。

（3）配电箱、开关箱内不得放置任何杂物，不得挂接其他临时用电设备。使用和更换熔断器时，要符合规格要求，严禁用铜丝等代替保险丝。

（4）所有配电箱和开关箱每月必须由专业电工检查、维修一次，电工必须穿戴绝缘防护用品，使用电工绝缘工具，非电工人员不许私自乱接电器和动用施工现场的用电设备。

7. 自备发电机组的安全技术要点

（1）大型桥梁施工现场、隧道和预制场地，应有自备电源，以免因电网停电造成工程损失和出现事故。

（2）施工现场临时用自备发电机组的供配电系统应采用三相五线制中性点直接接地系统，并必须独立设置，与外电线路隔离，不得有电气连接；自备发电机组电源应与外电线路电源连锁，严禁并列运行；发电机组应设置短路保护和过负荷保护。

（3）发电机控制屏宜装设交流电压表、交流电流表、有功功率表、电度表、功率因素表、频率表和直流电流表。

（4）发电机组的排烟管道必须伸出室外；发电机组及其控制配电室内严禁存放储油桶。

（5）在非三相五线制供电系统中，电气设备的金属外壳应做接地保护，其接地电阻不大于4Ω，且不得在同一供电系统上有的接地、有的接零。

8. 电动机械设备的安全技术要点

（1）塔式起重机、拌和设备、室外电梯、滑升模板、物料提升机等需要设置避雷装置的井字架等。除应做好保护接零外，电动机械的金属外壳必须有可靠的接地措施或临时接地装置，防止电动机械的金属外壳带电，否则电流就会通过地线流入地下，发生人身触电事故。

（2）电动机械的供电线路必须按照用电规则安装，不可乱拉乱接。

（3）电动施工机械的负荷线，必须按其容量选用无接头的多股铜芯橡胶护套软电缆，其中绿/黄色线在任何情况下只能用作保护零线或重复接地。

（4）每一台电动机械的开关箱内，除应装设过负荷、短路、漏电保护装置外，还必须装设隔离开关，以便在发生事故时，迅速切断电源。

（5）大型桥梁外用电梯，属于载人、载物的客货两用电梯，要设置单独的开关箱，特别要有可靠的极限控制及通信联络。

（6）塔式起重机运行时，要注意与外电架空线路或其他防护设施保持安全距离。

（7）移动电动机械必须事先关掉电源，不可带电移动电动机械。

（8）电动机械发生故障需停电检修。同时，必须悬挂"禁止合闸"等警告牌，或者派专人看守，以防有人误将闸刀合上。

（9）电动机械操作人员要增强安全观念，严格执行机电设备安全操作规程。在操作时，应穿工作服、绝缘鞋等个人安全防护用品，严禁用手和湿布擦电动机械设备或在电线上悬挂衣物。

9. 电动工具使用的安全技术要点

（1）施工现场使用的电动工具一般都是手持式的，如电钻、冲击钻、电锤、射钉枪、电刨、切割机、砂轮、手持式电锯等。按其绝缘和防触电性能可分为三类，即Ⅰ类工具、Ⅱ类工具、Ⅲ类工具。

（2）一般场所（空气湿度小于75%）可选用Ⅰ类或Ⅱ类手持式电动工具，其金属外壳与PE线的连接点不应少于两处。装设的额定漏电动作电流不大于15mA，额定漏电动作时间小于0.1s的漏电保护器。

（3）在潮湿场所或金属构架上操作时，必须选用Ⅱ类或由安全隔离变压器供电的Ⅰ类手持式电动工具，严禁使用Ⅰ类手持式电动工具。使用金属外壳Ⅱ类手持式电动工具时，其金属外壳可与PE线相连接，并设漏电保护。

（4）在狭窄场所（锅炉内、金属容器、地沟、管道内等）作业时，必须选用由安全隔离变压器供电的1类手持式电动工具。

（5）手持电动工具应配备装有专用的电源开关和漏电保护器的开关箱，严禁一台开关接两台以上设备，其电源开关应采用双刀控制；使用手持电动工具前，必须检查外壳、手柄、负荷线、插头等是否完好无损，接线是否正确（防止相线与零线错接）。

（6）手持电动工具开关箱内应采用插座连接，其插头、插座应无损坏、无裂纹，且绝缘良好；发现手持电动工具外壳、手柄破裂，应立即停止使用并进行更换。

（7）手持式电动工具的负荷线应采用耐气候型橡胶护套铜芯软电缆，并且不得有接头。在使用前必须进行空载检查，运转正常后方可使用。

（8）作业人员使用手持电动工具时，握其手柄，不得利用电缆提拉，且应穿绝缘鞋、戴绝缘手套。

（9）长期搁置不用或受潮的工具在使用前应由电工测量绝缘阻值是否符合要求。

10. 施工现场照明电器的安全技术要点

（1）一般场所选用额定电压为220V的照明器，特殊场所必须使用安全电压照明器，如隧道工程、有高温、导电灰尘或灯具距地高度低于2.4 m等场所，电源电压应不大于36 V；在潮湿和易触及带电体场所的照明电源电压不得大于24 V；特别潮湿场所，导电良好地面、锅炉或金属容器、管道内工作的照明电源电压不得大于12 V。

（2）临时照明线路必须使用绝缘导线。临时照明线路必须使用绝缘导线，户内（工棚）临时线路的导线必须安装在离地2 m以上支架上；户外临时线路必须安装在离地2.5 m以上支架上，零星照明线不允许使用花线，一般应使用软电缆线。

（3）在坑洞内作业，夜间施工或作业工棚、料具堆放场、仓库、办公室、食堂、宿舍及自然采光差等场所，应设一般照明、局部照明或混合照明。在一个工作场所内，不得只设局部照明。

（4）停电后作业人员需及时撤离现场的特殊工程，如夜间高处作业工程、隧道工程等，还必须装设由独立自备电源供电的应急照明。

（5）对于夜间可能影响飞机及其他飞行器安全通行的主塔及高大机械设备或设施，如塔式起重机外用电梯等，应在其顶端设置醒目的红色警戒照明。

（6）正常湿度（≤75%）的一般场所，可选用普通开启式照明器。

（7）潮湿或特别潮湿（相对湿度大于75%）的场所，属于触电危险场所，必须选用密闭性防水照明器或配有防水灯头的开启式照明器。

（8）含有大量尘埃但无爆炸和火灾危险的场所，属于触电一般场所，必须选用防尘型照明器，以防灰尘影响照明器安全发光。

（9）有爆炸和火灾危险的场所，亦属触电危险场所，应按危险场所等级选用防爆型照明器。

（10）存在较强振动的场所，必须选用防振型照明器。

（11）有酸碱等强腐蚀介质场所，必须选用耐酸碱型照明器。

（12）一般220 V灯具室外高度不低于3 m，室内不低于2.4 m；碘钨灯及其他金属卤化物灯安装高度宜在3 m以上。

（13）任何灯具必须经照明开关箱配电与控制，应配置完整的电源隔离、过载与短路保护及漏电保护电器；路灯还应逐灯另设熔断器保护；灯具的相线开关必须经开关控制，不得直接引入灯具。

（14）进入开关箱的电源线，严禁用插销连接。

（15）暂设工程的照明灯具宜用拉线开关控制，其安装高度为距地面2~3 m，职工宿舍区禁止设置床头开关。

11. 施工现场安全用电技术档案的八个要点

（1）施工现场用电组织设计的全部资料；

（2）修改施工现场用电组织设计资料；

（3）用电技术交底资料；

（4）施工现场用电工程检查验收表；

（5）电气设备试、检验凭单和调试记录；

（6）接地电阻，绝缘电阻，漏电保护器漏电动作参数测定记录表；

（7）定期检（复）查表。

12. 触电事故的原因分析

（1）缺乏电气安全知识，自我保护意识淡薄

电气设施安装或接线由非专业电工操作，而不是由自己安装。安装人无基本的电气安全知识，装设不符合电气基本要求，容易造成意外触电事故。发生这种触电事故的原因都是缺乏电气安全知识，无自我保护意识。

（2）违反安全操作规程

施工现场中，不得图方便，不用插头，在电箱乱拉乱接电线；在宿舍私自拉接电线照

明，在床上接音响设备、电风扇，有的甚至烧水、做饭等，极易造成触电事故；还存在凭经验用手去试探电器是否带电或不采取安全措施带电作业，或怀着侥幸心理在带电体（如高压线）周围作业，不采取任何安全措施违章作业等行为，造成触电事故等。

（3）不使用TN-S接零保护系统

有的工地未使用TN-S接零保护系统，或者未按要求连接专用保护零，无有效的安全保护系统。不按"三级配电二级保护""一机、一闸、一漏、一箱"设置，造成工地用电使用混乱，易造成误操作，并且在触电时，安全保护系统未起可靠的安全保护效果。

（4）电气设备安装不合格

电气设备安装必须遵守安全技术规定，否则由于安装错误，当人身接触带电部分时，就会造成触电事故。如电线高度不符合安全要求，修建过低，架空线乱拉、乱扯，有的还将电线拴在脚手架上，导线的接头只用老化的绝缘布包上，以及电气设备没有做保护接地、保护接零等，一旦漏电就会发生严重的触电事故。

（5）电气设备缺乏正常检修和维护

由于电气设备长期使用，易出现电气绝缘老化、导线裸露、胶盖刀闸胶木破损、插座盖子损坏等。如不及时检修，一旦漏电，将造成严重后果。

（6）偶然因素

电力线被风刮断，导线接触地面引起跨步电压，当人走近该地区时就会发生触电事故。

第三节 机械设备安全操作要点

1. 机械设备的概念及安全管理的必要性

机械设备主要包括锅炉、压力容器（含气瓶，下同）、压力管道、电梯、起重机械、客运索道、大型游乐设施和场（厂）内专用机动车辆。这些机械设备数量多、分布广，涉及生产、生活诸方面，是人们日常工作、生活中广泛接触且不可缺少的设备设施。国家对各类机械设备的安全管理十分重视，相继制定了有关方面的法规、标准，有效地降低了机械设备事故的发生。但是，由于近年来各类机械设备的数量急剧增长，在生产制造和使用运营过程中安全问题仍十分严峻，重大安全生产事故隐患依然存在。因此，必须采取强有力的措施，加强对机械设备的安全监管，杜绝各类设备事故，减少人员伤亡和财产损失。

2. 机械设备安全控制要求

（1）机械设备生产、使用单位的主要负责人应当对本单位机械设备的安全和节能全面负责。

（2）以公路建设、铁路建设、电站建设、船舶修造等行业（领域）为重点，逐步在新造和在用大型起重机械上安装安全监控管理系统,强化大型起重机械技术安全管理和控制,促进现场操作标准化和规范化,实现大型机械安全形势的根本好转。

(3)机械设备安全管理制度。

机械设备安全责任制:包括各职能部门安全责任制和各岗位安全责任制。

机械设备安全规章制度:包括机械设备安装使用、维护保养、监督检查管理制度,机械设备隐患排查和整改制度,机械设备报检制度,机械设备安全培训制度,机械设备安全技术交底制度,机械设备事故应急救援制度等。

机械设备安全操作规程:根据机械设备种类及相关的法规、安全技术规范的要求,编制机械设备各岗位安全操作规程。

机械设备应急救援预案:根据本单位机械设备使用情况,制订重大事故应急救援预案和防范突发事故的应急措施,以便在发生事故时,能果断、准确、迅速地将影响范围缩小到最低程度;配备相应的抢险装备和救援物资;每年至少组织一次救援演练。

(4)机械设备的行政许可。

机械设备使用单位应当在设备投入使用前或者投入使用后30d内,到设备所在地市以上的机械设备安全监督管理部门办理机械设备使用登记。登记标志应当置于或者附着于该机械设备的显著位置。

机械设备行政许可变更。机械设备停用、注销、过户、迁移、重新启用应到机械设备安全监督管理部门办理相关手续。

机械设备作业人员必须持证上岗。机械设备作业人员必须经有关主管部门考核合格,取得国家统一格式的证书方可上岗操作。作业人员必须与企业办理聘任手续并到有关部门备案。

(5)机械设备定期检验。

机械设备报检。机械设备使用单位应在机械设备检验合格有效期届满前1个月向机械设备检验检测机构提出定期检验要求(各机械设备的检验日期可从检验报告、合格标志上查看)。

机械设备报检要求。起重机械报检时,必须提供保养合同、有效的作业人员证件。

机械设备换证。机械设备检验合格后,携带使用证、检验合格标志、检验报告、保养合同、保养单位的保养资质到有关主管部门办理年审换证手续。

(6)机械设备安全培训。

发生机械设备事故的原因主要表现为人的不安全行为或者设备的不安全状态。按照《机械设备安全监察条例》要求,机械设备使用单位应当对机械设备作业人员进行机械设备安全、节能教育和培训,保证机械设备作业人员具备必要的机械设备安全、节能知识。因此,对人为因素,应通过培训教育来纠正。机械设备的作业人员包括设备的安装、维修保养、操作等人员。机械设备作业人员在持证上岗的基础上,应做到有安全培训计划、有培训记录、有培训考核。

安全生产是保护劳动者的安全和健康，是促进社会生产力发展的基本保证，也是保证社会主义经济发展、进一步实行改革开放的基本条件。为保障从事公路工程施工生产人员的安全，预防事故发生，促进公路事业的发展，必须实施安全生产管理。

安全是指建造"实物"的人在建造"实物"过程中的生命安全和身体健康。如果说质量是管物的，那么安全则是管人的。各类建筑构筑物、公路、桥梁等，是施工企业的产品，没有产品的质量，企业就无法生存和发展；不能保证施工人员的安全和健康，就难以生产合格的产品；没有合格的产品，企业也就不复存在，因此质量与安全是工程建设中永恒的主题。安全工作搞好，施工人员就能在安全舒适的环境中作业，顺利地生产出优质的产品。

安全生产是工程质量的前提条件，而工程质量的好坏，也是安全的保障。低劣的工程质量，如发生隧道坍塌、桥梁断裂、公路沉陷等事故的豆腐渣工程，直接威胁着人们的安全和健康。如果说质量是业主追求的最终目标，安全则是实现这一目标的最基本的环境条件。安全监理就是这一环境的基本保障。

在已经实施工程建设监理的建设项目中，一些监理单位只注重对施工质量、进度和投资的监控，况且以往工程建设监理工作的主要内容中，没有把安全监理作为一项重要内容加以规范，只是把安全监理作为质量控制工作内容的一部分，而且监理单位一般没有配备安全工程技术人员，只是由质量工程师代管。这样，施工安全监控的效果往往较差，施工现场因违章指挥、违章作业而发生的伤亡事故局面难以得到有效的控制。近几年来，建筑物倒塌、大桥垮塌时有发生，有的在建设过程中发生，有的在已经投入生产使用后发生。

要扭转工程建设项目事故多发的被动局面，只有提高认识、健全机构、加强监管、落实责任保障投入、严格执法、照章作业，加强安全监理工作，使安全监理成为工程建设监理的一项重要监理内容。而且要配备这方面的人才，加强这方面的工作。

安全监理是工程建设监理工作的重要组成部分，是对公路工程施工过程中安全生产状况所实施的监督管理。为了搞好安全监理工作，必须了解施工安全的意义，明确安全监理所包括的责任、内容、任务、程序。

（1）工程监理单位对本单位所承接的工程建设项目安全监理工作负责，督促承包人建立健全安全生产及安全技术措施并督促其实施；

（2）审查施工方案及安全技术措施并督促其实施；

（3）项目总监理工程师对该项目的安全监理工作全面负责；

（4）项目监理人员在总监理工程师的领导下，按照职责分工，履行现场安全监督检查的职责，并对各自承担的安全监理工作负责；

（5）监理工程师按照法律法规和工程建设强制性标准实施监理，并负责建设工程安全生产；

（6）定期组织施工现场安全生产专项检查，每月向工程安监站报告工地安全生产情况。

工程监理单位违反本条例的规定，有下列行为之一的，责令限期改正；逾期未改正的，责令停业整顿，并处10万元以上、30万元以下的罚款；情节严重的，降低资质等级，直至吊销资质证书；造成重大安全事故，构成犯罪的，对直接责任人，依照刑法有关规定追究刑事责任；造成损失的，依法承担赔偿责任。

（1）未对施工组织设计中的安全技术措施或者专项施工方案进行审查的；

（2）发现安全事故隐患未及时要求施工单位整改或者暂时停止施工的；

（3）施工单位拒不整改或者不停止施工，未及时向有关主管部门报告的；

（4）未按照法律、法规和工程建设强制性标准实施监理的。

工程项目总监理工程师主持编制的项目监理计划中应包括安全监理内容，根据工程项目特点明确安全监理的范围，制定安全监理工作程序和制度，确定监理人员的安全监理职责。

各专业监理工程师编写的监理细则应确定安全监理的具体内容及重点、监控的方法和措施。

对新材料、新技术、新工艺及危险性较大的分项（或分部）工程设置特殊监控点，编制安全监理岗位守则，明确监控措施和方法。

第四节　安全专项方案编制

1. 编制安全专项方案的法律依据

施工单位应当在施工组织设计中编制安全技术措施和施工现场临时用电方案，对下列达到一定规模的危险性较大的分部分项工程编制专项施工方案，并附具安全验算结果，经施工单位技术负责人、总监理工程师签字后实施，由专职安全生产管理人员进行现场监督：

（1）基坑支护与降水工程；

（2）土方开挖工程；

（3）模板工程；

（4）起重吊装工程；

（5）脚手架工程；

（6）拆除、爆破工程；

（7）对工程中涉及深基坑、地下暗挖工程、高大模板工程的专项施工方案，施工单位还应当组织专家进行论证、审查。

2. 安全专项方案编制的主要内容

（1）工程概况：危险性较大的分部分项工程基本概况、水文地质条件、施工平面布置、施工要求和技术保证条件；

（2）编制依据：相关法律、法规、规范性文件、标准、规范及图纸（国标图集）、施工组织设计等；

（3）分部分项工程影响质量、安全的风险源分析及相关预防措施；

（4）设计计算书和设计施工图等设计文件；

（5）施工准备：包括施工图进度计划、材料与设备计划；

（6）施工部署：包括技术参数、工艺流程、施工方法、施工技术要点；

（7）人员计划：专职安全生产管理人员、特种作业人员等资格要求；

（8）施工控制：检查验收、安全评价、预警观测措施；

（9）应急预案及处置措施。

3. 危险性较大的工程范围

危险性较大的分部分项工程和超过一定规模危险性较大的分部分项工程见表8-1。

表8-1 危险性较大的分部分项工程范围

序号	危险性较大的分部分项工程	超过一定规模危险性较大的分部分项工程
1	不良地质条件下有潜在危险性的土方、石方开挖	（1）深度大于或等于5 m的基坑（槽）的土（石）方开挖、支护降水工程； （2）开挖深度虽未超过5 m，但地质条件、周围环境和地下管线复杂，或影响毗邻建筑（构筑）物的安全，或存在有毒有害气体分布的基坑（槽）的土方开挖、支护、降水工程
2	滑坡和高边坡处理	（1）滑坡量大于100000m²的中型以上滑坡体； （2）高度大于或等于20 m的土质边坡，或高度大于或等于30 m的岩质边坡
3	桩基础、挡墙基础、深水基础及围堰工程	（1）深度大于或等于15 m的人工挖孔桩或开挖深度不超过15 m，但地质条件复杂或存在有毒有害气体分布的人工挖孔桩工程； （2）深度大于或等于5 m的挡墙基础； （3）水深大于或等于20 m的深水基础、水深大于或等于10 m的围堰工程
4	桥梁工程中的梁、拱、柱等构件施工	（1）长度大于或等于40 m的预制梁的运输与安装，钢箱梁吊装； （2）长度大于或等于150 m的钢管拱安装施工； （3）高度大于或等于40 m的墩柱、高度大于或等于100 m的索塔等的施工

续表

序号	危险性较大的分部分项工程	超过一定规模危险性较大的分部分项工程
5	隧道工程中的不良地质隧道、高瓦斯隧道、水底或海底隧道等	（1）隧道穿越高地应力区、岩溶发育区、区域地质构造、煤系地层、采空区等工程地质或水文地质条件复杂的地质环境； （2）浅埋、偏压、连拱、小净距、大跨度、变化断面等结构受力复杂的隧道工程； （3）VI、V级围岩连续长度占总隧道长度10%以上且连续长度超过50 m； （4）高瓦斯隧道； （5）长度大于或等于1000 m的水底、海底隧道
6	水上工程中的打桩船作业、施工船作业、外海孤岛作业、边通航边施工作业等	（1）离岸无掩护条件下的桩基施工； （2）开敞式水域大型预制构件的运输与吊装作业； （3）沉箱的浮运与安装作业； （4）深水防波堤施工； （5）在三级以上通航等级的航道上进行的水上水下施工
7	水下工程中的水下焊接、混凝土浇筑、爆破工程等	（1）水下爆破工程； （2）30 m水深以上的潜水作业（水下焊接、混凝土浇筑等）
8	爆破工程	爆破工程为C级及以上
9	大型临时工程中的大型支架、模板、便桥的架设与拆除；桥梁、码头的加固与拆除	（1）50 m及以上落地钢管脚手架工程，用于钢结构安装等满堂承重支撑体系，承受单点集中荷载7 kN以上； （2）混凝土模板支撑工程高度>8 m；跨度>18m，施工总荷载>15 kN/m²，集中荷载≥20 kN/m²； （3）挂篮、移动模架等模板施工工艺； （4）便桥搭设、中型桥梁、中型码头的加固与拆除
10	其他危险性较大的工程	上跨下穿或临近既有线路施工

注：对于超过一定规模、危险性较大的分部分项工程，各地可根据实际情况，进一步细化。

工程项目总监理工程师主持编制的项目监理计划中应包括安全监理内容，根据工程项目特点明确安全监理的范围，制定安全监理工作程序和制度，确定监理人员的安全监理职责。

各专业监理工程师编写的监理细则应确定安全监理的具体内容及重点、监控的方法和措施。

对新材料、新技术、新工艺及危险性较大的分项（或分部）工程设置特殊监控点，编制安全监理岗位守则，明确监控措施和方法。

安全生产贯穿于自开工到竣工的施工生产的全过程，因此，安全工作存在于每个分部分项工程、每道工序中。也就是说，哪里的安全防护措施不落实，哪里就可能发生伤亡事故。安全监理不仅要监督检查各部位安全防护措施的贯彻落实，还应该了解公路施工中的主要安全技术，才能采取有效的措施，预防各类伤亡事故的发生，确保安全生产。安全施工的内容包括以下三个方面。

1. 控制施工人员的不安全行为

人是施工生产中的主体，也是安全生产的关键，搞好安全生产，必须首先控制人的不安全行为。人的不安全行为分为生理上的、心理上的、行为上的三种。生理上的不安全行为，即身体上的缺陷，使其不能适应某些生产的速度、工作条件和环境；心理上的不安全行为，即受到了某些因素的刺激和影响，产生了思想和情绪上的波动，身心不支、注意力转移，发生了误操作和误判断；行为上的不安全行为，即为了某种目的和动机有意采取的错误行为。

必须根据人的生理和心理特点，合理安排和调配工作，预防不安全行为；通过培训教育，增强安全意识，做到不伤害自己、不伤害他人，也不被他人伤害。

2. 控制"物"的不安全状态

施工人员在公路施工过程中，要使用多种工具、机械、设备、材料等，也要接触各类的设施、设备等，这些材料、工具、设施、设备等统称为"物"。不仅要这些"物"保持良好的状态和技术性能，还应该使其操作简便、灵敏可靠，并且具有保证工作者免受伤害的各类防护和保险装置。

3. 作业环境的防护

在任何时间、季节和条件下施工，对于任何作业都必须给施工人员创造良好的、没有任何危险的环境和作业场所。

如果以上三个方面都齐备，安全生产就有了保障。缺少一个方面，就会留下安全隐患，给发生伤亡事故创造了条件和机会。

监理工作是受建设单位的委托，按照合同规定的要求，完成授权范围内的工作，安全监理也同样是受委托要完成的任务。因此，监理工程师应认真地研究安全施工所包括的范围，并依据相关的施工安全生产的法规和标准进行监督和管理。

安全生产涉及施工现场所有的人、物和环境。凡是与生产有关的人、单位、机械、设备、设施、工具等都与安全生产有关，安全工作贯穿于施工生产的全过程，所以实施安全监理工作时必须对施工全过程进行安全监理。如监理工程师在施工现场往往要对脚手架的搭设及模板的安装、拆除进行检查验收，这就是安全工作的内容。

安全监理的任务主要是贯彻落实国家安全生产的方针、政策，督促施工单位按照公路施工安全生产法规和标准组织施工，消除施工中的冒险性、盲目性和随意性，落实各项安全技术措施，有效地杜绝各类安全隐患，杜绝、控制和减少各类伤亡事故，实现安全生产。安全监理的具体任务主要有以下几个方面：

（1）贯彻执行"安全第一，预防为主"的方针，国家现行的安全生产的法律、法规，有关行政主管部门的安全生产的规章和标准；

（2）督促施工单位落实安全生产的组织保证体系，建立健全安全生产责任制；

（3）督促施工单位对工人进行安全生产教育及分部、分项工程的安全技术交底；

（4）审查施工方案及安全技术措施；

（5）检查并督促施工单位按照公路工程施工安全技术规程要求，落实分部、分项工程或各工序、关键部位的安全防护措施；

（6）监督检查施工生产的消防、冬季防寒、夏季防暑、文明施工、卫生防疫等项工作；

（7）不定期地组织安全综合检查；

（8）发现违章冒险作业的要责令其停止作业，发现隐患的要责令其停工整改。

4. 施工准备阶段安全监理的主要工作

工程开工前，监理工程师应严格审查承包人的各项安全保证方案，审查重点有以下方面：

（1）督促业主与承包人签订工程项目安全施工责任书，督促总包单位与分包单位签订工程项目安全施工责任书。

（2）审查总包、分包单位的安全生产许可证或专业主管部门颁发的安全生产资质。

（3）督促承包人建立健全施工现场安保体系。

（4）督促施工总承包单位对分包单位的安全生产工作统一领导、统一管理，提出明确的安全生产制度、管理措施，并认真实施监督检查。

（5）审查施工承包单位编制的施工组织设计中的安全技术措施或专项安全施工方案是否符合工程建设强制性标准。审核应包括以下内容：

1）安全管理、质量管理和安全保证体系的组织机构，包括项目经理、项目总工、专职安全管理人员、特种作业人员配备的数量及安全资格培训持证上岗情况；

2）施工安全生产责任制、安全管理规章制度、安全操作规程的制定情况；

3）起重机械设备、施工机具、电器设备及其他特种设备等的设置是否符合规范要求，各种保险、限位等安全装置是否齐全有效，并是否具备相应的生产（制造）许可证、产品合格证明及检定结果；

4）施工中采用新技术、新工艺、新设备、新材料的，是否都制定了相应的安全技术措施；

5）基坑支护、模板、脚手架工程、起重吊装工程和整体提升脚手架拆装等专项方案是否符合法律法规及强制性标准，是否按规定进行论证和办理批准手续；

6）施工现场临时用电方案的安全用电技术措施和电气防火措施；

7）施工企业安全事故应急救援预案的编制情况和项目针对重点部位、重点环节编制的监控措施和应急预案情况；

8）根据施工的不同阶段环境、季节、气候的变化制定安全措施的情况；

9）施工总平面图是否合理，办公、宿舍、食堂等临时设施的设置以及施工现场场地、道路、排污、排水、防火措施是否符合有关安全技术标准规范和文明施工的要求；

10）制定的安全管理目标。

（6）督促承包人做好逐级安全技术交底工作和开展经常性的安全教育培训活动。

（7）复查承包人的大型施工机械、安全设施验收手续，并签署意见。

5.施工阶段安全监理的主要工作

安全生产贯穿于工程施工的全过程，安全监理是对施工安全进行过程控制，应以预防为主。在工程施工过程中，监理工程师在巡视、旁站过程中应对施工生产安全情况、承包人安全保证体系运转情况进行检查，监督承包人按照工程建设强制性标准和专项安全施工方案组织施工，制止违规作业。具体应注意以下几个方面：

（1）监督承包人按照工程建设强制性标准和经审批的安全施工方案组织施工，制止违规施工作业。

（2）在施工阶段实施监理过程中，发现违规施工，责令其改正；存在安全事故隐患的，应当要求承包人整改并检查整改结果，签署复查意见；情况严重的，应当要求承包人停止施工，并及时报告业主；承包人拒不整改或不停止施工的，应及时向安全监督部门报告。

（3）督促承包人做好洞口、临边高处作业等危险部位的安全防护工作，并设置明确的安全警示标志，督促承包人有效控制现场的废水、扬尘、噪声、振动、坠落物等，营造良好的工作环境。

（4）督促承包人定期组织施工安全自查工作。

（5）在定期召开的工地例会上，评述安全生产管理现状及存在的薄弱环节和问题，并提出意见和建议，把安全作为工地例会的主要内容之一，使预防落到实处。

（6）对高危作业，将易发生安全事故的危险源和薄弱环节作为安全监控的重点，可采取旁站、巡视和平行检查等形式，加大检查监控力度。

（7）对危险性较大的分部、分项工程进行安全巡查检查，每天不少于一次，发现违规施工和存在安全事故隐患的，及时要求承包人整改，并检查整改结果，签署复查意见；承包人拒不整改或者不停止施工的，现场监理应及时向当地建设行政主管部门报告。

各级监理机构应建立施工安全监理资料及台账，每次对施工安全检查的情况、发现的问题、监理的指令及承包人处理的措施和结果均应记录在规定表格及台账中。

第五节 公路工程安全风险分级管控与隐患排查治理

一、安全生产事故隐患排查的基本概念

安全生产事故隐患（简称事故隐患），是指生产经营单位违反安全生产法律、法规、规章、标准、规程和有关安全生产管理制度的规定，或者因其他因素在生产经营活动中存

在可能导致事故发生的物的危险状态、人的不安全行为和管理上的缺陷。排查的依据是国家和有关部门的法律法规等。

排查的事故隐患分为一般事故隐患和重大事故隐患。一般事故隐患是指危害和整改难度较小,发现后能够立即整改排除的隐患;重大事故隐患是指危害和整改难度较大,应当全部或者局部停产停业,并经过一定时间整改治理方能排除的隐患,或者因外部因素影响致使生产经营单位自身难以排除的隐患。

二、安全生产事故隐患排查的目标及内容

公路工程施工安全生产隐患排查的目标:落实工程项目安全生产主体责任和相关单位的安全管理责任,深入排查治理交通基础设施建设过程中的安全隐患,从而实现"两项达标""四项严禁""五项制度"的总目标。

1. 两项达标

(1) 施工人员管理达标:一线人员用工登记、施工安全培训记录、安全技术交底记录、施工意外伤害责任保险等都要符合有关规定;

(2) 施工现场安全防护达标:施工现场安全防护设施和作业人员安全防护用品都要按照规定实行标准化管理。

2. 四项严禁

(1) 严禁在泥石流区、滑坡体、洪水区等危险区域设置施工驻地;

(2) 严禁违规进行挖孔桩作业,钻孔确有困难的不良地质区,设计单位要进行专项安全设计并按设计变更规定,经批准后实施;

(3) 严禁长大隧道无超前预报和监控量测措施施工;

(4) 严禁违规立体交叉作业。

3. 五项制度

(1) 施工现场危险告知制度。严格执行安全技术交底制度,施工单位负责项目管理的技术人员,应当如实向施工作业班组、作业人员详细告知作业场所和工作岗位存在的危险因素,并由双方签字确认。在上述场所应设置明显安全警示标志,在无法封闭施工的工地上,还应当悬挂当日施工现场危险告示,以告知路人和社会车辆。

(2) 施工安全监理制度。开展施工安全监理工作,加大现场安全监管力度。监理单位应当按照法律、法规和工程建设强制性标准进行监理,编制安全生产监理计划,明确监理人员的岗位职责、监理内容和方法,审查施工组织设计中的安全技术措施或专项施工方案,核验施工现场机械设备进场检查验收记录,对危险性较大的工程作业加强巡视检查,督促隐患整改。

(3) 专项施工方案审查制度。对下列危险性较大的分部分项工程应当编制专项施工方案,并附安全验算结果,经施工单位技术负责人、监理工程师审查签字确认后实施,由

专职安全员进行现场监督。必要时，施工单位对上述所列工程的专项施工方案，还应当组织专家进行论证、审查。

（4）设备进场验收登记制度。施工单位在工程中使用施工起重机械和整体提升式脚手架、滑模爬模、架桥机等自行式架设设施前，应当组织有关单位进行验收，或者委托具有相应资质的检验检测机构进行验收。使用承租的机械设备和施工机具及配件的，由承租单位和安装单位共同进行验收，验收合格的方可使用。验收合格后30天内，应当向当地交通主管部门登记。

（5）安全生产费用保障制度。将安全生产费用支取、使用情况纳入监理范畴。建设单位在施工招标文件中应当对安全生产保障措施提出明确要求。施工单位在工程投标报价中应当包含安全生产费用，一般不得低于工程造价的1.5%，且不得作为竞争性条件。安全生产费用应当用于施工安全防护用具及设施的采购和更新、安全施工措施的落实、安全生产条件的改善，不得挪作他用。

公路工程施工安全生产事故隐患排查治理涉及的单位主要有各项目建设、勘察、设计、施工、监理等单位。

第六节　公路工程施工应急管理

1. 应急救援预案编制的目的

应急救援预案是针对可能发生的事故，为迅速、有序地开展应急行动而预先制订的行动方案；是为了及时、有效地应对重大生产安全事故，保证职工生命安全与健康和公众生命，最大限度地减少财产损失、环境损害和社会影响而采取的重要措施。

安全生产事故应急救援的预案编制是应急救援体系建设工作的核心内容，是安全生产工作的重要组成部分。通过应急救援的预案编制，建立健全规范、科学、操作性强的应急预案体系，对于提高应对突发事（故）件的能力、保障人民群众的生命财产安全和企业健康发展具有十分重要的意义。

2. 应急救援预案的类型

应急救援预案有综合应急预案、专项应急预案、现场处置方案三种主要类型。

3. 应急救援预案编制的主要内容

（1）总则：编制的目的；适用范围；应急组织体系的确定、工作原则与职责分工；应急响应；信息发布；后期处置；人员物资等保障措施；培训与演练；奖励与处罚等。

（2）生产经营单位危险性分析：危险源与风险分析，主要阐述本单位存在的重点危险源及风险分析结果。

（3）应急组织机构及职责：明确应急组织形式，构成单位或人员，并尽可能以结构图的形式表示出来；指挥机构及职责，明确应急救援指挥机构总指挥、副总指挥、各成员单位及其相应职责。应急救援指挥机构根据事故类型和应急工作需要，可以设置相应的应急救援工作小组，并明确各小组的工作任务及职责。

（4）预防与预警措施：危险源监控、预警提示信息、信息报告与处置等。

（5）应急响应：

1）响应分级。针对事故危害程度、影响范围和单位控制事态的能力，将事故分为不同的等级。按照分级负责的原则，明确应急响应级别；

2）响应程序。根据事故的大小和发展态势，明确应急指挥、应急行动、资源调配、应急避险、扩大应急等响应程序；

3）应急结束。明确应急终止的条件，事故现场得以控制，环境符合有关标准，导致次生、衍生事故隐患消除后，经事故现场应急指挥机构批准后，现场应急结束。

（6）信息发布：明确事故信息发布的部门、发布原则，事故信息应由事故现场指挥部及时准确地向新闻媒体通报。

（7）后期处置：主要包括污染物处理、事故后果影响消除、生产秩序恢复、善后赔偿、抢险过程和应急救援能力评估及应急预案的修订等内容。

（8）保障措施：

1）通信与信息保障。明确与应急工作相关联的单位或人员通信联系方式和方法，并提供备用方案。建立信息通信系统及维护方案，确保应急期间信息通畅；

2）应急队伍保障。明确各类应急响应的人力资源，包括专业应急队伍、兼职应急队伍的组织与保障方案；

3）应急物资装备保障。明确应急救援需要使用的应急物资和装备的类型、数量、性能、存放位置、管理责任人及其联系方式等内容；

4）经费保障。明确应急专项经费来源、使用范围、数量和监督管理措施，保障应急状态时生产经营单位应急经费的及时到位；

5）其他保障。根据本单位应急工作需求确定的其他相关保障措施（如交通运输保障、治安保障、技术保障、医疗保障、后勤保障等）。

（9）培训与演练及奖励与处罚：要明确对本单位人员开展的应急培训计划、方式和要求，如果预案涉及社区和居民，要做好宣传教育和告知等工作；明确应急演练的规模、方式、频次、范围、内容、组织、评估、总结等；明确事故应急救援工作中奖励和处罚的有关内容。

结　语

　　公路工程的建设发展迅速。目前，整体的施工管理水平较以往有很大的提高。施工技术水平也在不断地进步当中。企业只有不断地提高自身的技术水平，加强自身管理，才能有效地保证自身的经济效益，保证公路工程项目的质量，从而为我国经济稳定发展做出贡献。

　　公路工程施工的技术管理是公路工程施工中的一项极其关键的工作，在施工管理中占有重要的地位。认真做好这项工作，不仅能够提高工程质量、节约成本，还能缩短工期、增长效益。加强公路施工技术管理，保证施工过程的顺利开展，对提高工作效率、降低工程施工成本、保障公路工程质量具有重要意义。因此，要重视技术管理的每一环节，通过科学合理的施工方案、切实可行的技术措施和周密细致的技术管理，确保工程施工质量，提高经济效益，提高施工企业的市场竞争能力。新形势的到来对公路技术管理提出了更高要求。而技术管理为适应这一要求，需要从所有组成部分入手，进行升级和改进，改变传统不合理的做法，提高技术管理整体水平，发挥应有的保证工程质量的作用。

　　总之，公路工程施工技术管理是公路工程施工中的一项极其关键的工作，在施工管理中占有重要的地位。施工技术管理是衡量一个项目质量好坏的重要因素，技术管理工作落实到位，就能对预期的施工目标起到保障作用；反之，就会影响整个工程的工程质量和经济效益。

参考文献

[1] 湖南省土木建筑学会，杨承想，陈浩主编.绿色建筑施工与管理2018版[M].北京：中国建材工业出版社，2018.

[2] 汪双杰，王佐，陈建兵编著.青藏高原工程走廊冻土环境与高速公路布局[M].上海：上海科学技术出版社，2018.

[3] 庄传义编著.公路工程施工新理念与新技术[M]徐州：中国矿业大学出版社，2014.

[4] 邱洪兴编著.土木工程概论[M].南京：东南大学出版社，2015.

[5] 王明慧编著.西南山区高速铁路建设技术与实践[M].成都：西南交通大学出版社，2017.

[6] 建造师执业资格考试命题研究中心编；彭磊，刘倩，陈烨，韩宁昌等编写委员会.建设工程经济[M].北京：北京理工大学出版社，2016.

[7] 刘磊著.土木工程概论[M].成都：电子科技大学出版社，2016.

[8] 朱浮声主编.工程勘察与岩土工程：2012年辽宁工程勘察与岩土工程学术会议文集[M].沈阳：东北大学出版社，2014.

[9] 李霞.浅析公路施工企业财务管理的现存状况及对策[J].中国产经，2022(04):90-92.

[10] 施秋生.公路施工企业财务管理研究[J].中国集体经济，2022(05):131-132.

[11] 王学武.公路施工中填石路基施工技术的应用刍议[J].居舍，2022(03):67-69.

[12] 许永庆.公路施工关键部位施工技术分析[J].居业，2022(01):31-32+35.

[13] 郭科峰.国有公路施工企业合并重组业务所得税处理[J].财会学习，2021(36):121-123.

[14] 于立波.公路施工的安全防控技术探究[J].城市建筑，2021,18(33):196-198.

[15] 陈慧.公路施工企业成本管理问题研究[J].企业改革与管理，2021(21):145-146.

[16] 顾鹏.公路施工软土地基处理技术及控制要点探究实践[J].工程建设与设计，2021(20):168-170.

[17] 叶建敏.探究如何加强公路施工企业内部控制与财务管理[J].中国产经,2021(20):106-107.

[18] 赵一亮.论高速公路施工项目材料设备管理[J].石油化工建设，2021,43(05):37-38.

[19] 宋鹏飞. 高速公路施工会计核算及成本管理办法 [J]. 工程技术研究，2021,6(19):161-162.

[20] 王毅. 公路施工中软土路基的施工技术处理分析 [J]. 四川水泥，2021(10):191-192.

[21] 蔡安刚. 公路施工新技术及新工艺的应用 [J]. 四川水泥，2021(10):283-284.

[22] 沈春燕. 公路施工企业财务管理存在的问题及对策 [J]. 中国管理信息化，2021,24(18):8-9.

[23] 任许存. 农村公路施工要点与维护管理探析 [J]. 黑龙江交通科技，2021,44(09):58-59.

[24] 王将，张乙彬. BIM技术在高速公路施工安全管理中的应用 [J]. 黑龙江交通科技，2021,44(09):212-213.

[25] 胡文霞. 公路项目施工招标投资控制分析 [J]. 黑龙江交通科技，2021,44(09):270-271.

[26] 张民侠. 公路施工企业预算管理问题及对策探究 [J]. 企业改革与管理，2021(16):208-209.

[27] 刘鹏，闵祥. 公路施工管理存在的问题及应对措施 [J]. 散装水泥，2021(04):90-92.

[28] 卫香娟. 研究公路施工中的土石混填路基施工技术 [J]. 黑龙江交通科技，2021,44(08):17-18.

[29] 李小杰，翟镇宇. 公路施工的安全管理研究 [J]. 智能城市，2021,7(15):79-80.

[30] 任立奇. 公路施工中软土路基的施工技术处理研究 [J]. 四川建材，2021,47(08):89-90+94.

[31] 闫志伟. 公路施工中混凝土裂缝的成因及对策 [J]. 江西建材，2021(07):152+154.

[32] 马伟. 浅谈农村公路建设项目中施工现场管理的要点和必要性 [J]. 科技视界，2021(21):183-184.

[33] 吴继卫. 试析公路施工企业如何加强财务共享中心建设 [J]. 财经界，2021(21):147-148.

[34] 李佳宁. 高速公路施工管理常见问题及对策 [J]. 居舍，2021(20):129-130.

[35] 余娟. 公路施工中软土地基处理分析 [J]. 四川建材，2021,47(07):72-73.

[36] 门志平. 资金预算视角下公路施工企业财务集中管理探析 [J]. 财会学习，2021(19):76-78.

[37] 王梅. 浅谈公路施工企业财务管理信息化的建设 [J]. 纳税，2021,15(18):73-74.

[38] 杨军红，陈宝光，陈国龙，杨旭. 基于BIM技术的高速公路施工进度管理实施框架研究 [J]. 施工技术，2021,50(12):25-28+46.

[39] 郑艳江. 基于层次分析法的公路施工风险影响量化研究 [J]. 山西交通科技，2021(03):7-9.

[40] 秦耕. 公路施工企业施工合同法律风险管理研究 [D]. 重庆交通大学，2021.

[41] 程淑薇. 江西萍乡至莲花高速公路工程项目施工现场安全评价研究 [D]. 华东交通大学，2021.

[42] 徐玉博. 基于数字化平台的公路施工物料进出场管控研究 [D]. 新疆农业大学，2021.

[43] 陈雪峰, 陈书雪. 微创新技术在绿色公路施工中的应用与实践 [C]. 第七届全国绿色公路技术交流会论文集，2021:9.

[44] 张生威. 公路施工中现场管理问题及其对策 [J]. 低碳世界，2021,11(05):239-240.

[45] 解斌, 林莉丽. 公路施工技术管理基础工作中存在的问题及对策 [J]. 工程技术研究，2021,6(10):182-183+241.

ON HUMAN BEING

Loving & Living Without Purpose

Written by: Carl Bozeman,
Elizabeth, Colorado

ON HUMAN BEING

Other books by Carl Bozeman:

On Being God – Beyond Your Life's Purpose

Are You Listening? Addressing the Divine Within

More information can be found at Carl's website:

www.spiritual-intuition.com

Email: *carl@spiritual-intuition.com*

ON HUMAN BEING

Copyright © 2012 by Carl Bozeman; Denver Colorado
All rights reserved

Printed in the United States of America

No part of this publication may be reproduced, stored in or introduced into a retrieval system, or transmitted, in any form, or by any means (electronic, mechanical, photocopying, recording, or otherwise), without the prior written permission of both the copyright owner and publisher of this book.

The scanning, uploading, and distribution of this book via the internet or via any other means without the permission of the publisher or copyright owner is illegal and punishable by law. Please purchase only authorized electronic editions, and do not participate in or encourage electronic piracy of copyrighted materials. Your support of author's right is appreciated.

Copyright owner website: http://www.spiritual-intuition.com

Table of Contents

CONTRIBUTORS TO THIS BOOK II
FORWARD III
INTRODUCTION V
COSMIC TRAIN 11
DISEMBARK; PLANET EARTH 23
COSMIC STORYTELLING 35
FAITH – OUR MYTHOLOGICAL PARTNER 47
EMOTIONS; TREES AND HUMAN BARK 55
COSMIC DECEPTION 73
WHAT'S HAPPENING? 81
DUALITY – MONITORING YOUR ILLUSION 93
SAVIORISM; CAN YOU REALLY BE SAVED? 109
CREATIVE RESPONSIBILITY 117
STREAM OF LIFE 125
AFTERWORD 136

Contributors to this Book

Contributors to this book are many. Literally everyone who has been a part of my life experience directly or indirectly has played a role in the creation of this book. I could not be where I am now nor could I have written these words had it not been for each and every one of you including those reading right now. I thank you for allowing me to be a part of your experience. These are not my words; they are yours.

Forward

I said to my soul, be still and wait without hope, for hope would be hope for the wrong thing; wait without love, for love would be love of the wrong thing; there is yet faith, but the faith and the love and the hope are all in the waiting. Wait without thought, for you are not ready for thought: So the darkness shall be the light, and the stillness the dancing. ~ T. S. Eliot

Introduction

As I look upon the layered blue waters separated by the uneven lines of foaming white waves breaking onto the California coastline I am moved at such beauty but saddened that this will be the last time I see it. The short flight from Santa Barbara to Los Angeles to visit three of my four children lets me reflect on my troubled life. This is the last time I will see them and that they will see me. Later I will travel to Seattle to see my fourth child to say goodbye to him as well. They won't know it is goodbye. All they will know is how much I love them, how much they have meant to me and how very proud I am of each of them. Their memory of me will be the pleasant time we spend together these next few days.

My marriage is over. I alone have wrecked it in every way and broken the woman I adored above all others. My infidelity, mental illness and erratic nature have ended what was once my greatest comfort and relationship with my best friend. I ponder my life as a child growing up in Tacoma, Washington with six sisters in a house too small to contain us. My father leaving abruptly at the age of seven and without any reason that I comprehended and, whom, I would not see or hear from for over fifty years. I consider the embarrassment of poverty and destitution that immediately befell us upon his leaving. How everything spun out of control and neighbors, relatives and my very own mother transformed into monsters who would abuse me physically, mentally and sexually. How my best friend, an older gentleman and neighbor would break the trust of innocence and sexually abuse me while crying and begging me to forgive him. A tear runs down my cheek as I recall those awful times. It is all I remember but not for long, I tell myself.

I reflect on my years as a father, husband and provider to my own family and all the activities I participated in with them so they could have what I could not. How I had protected them from the ugliness I had known when I was a child. I was dedicated to them and to my wife who stood with me as the demons of my past percolated into my awareness. I was a mess and I tried to protect my family from my own suffering and sadness but I could not. I would pour myself into over twenty five years of therapy and medication and an endless search to find that one moment in a cruel past that would set the demons free and free me from the depression, post-traumatic stress and multiple personalities I suffered from. It would never happen. The moment would not come and so I would bring it all to an end myself. As I sat aboard that airplane, looking down, I felt relief but not freedom. Freedom would come later. A sudden but quiet end to misery, suffering and the unanswered question: Why?

While visiting my three children in Los Angeles we had decided to go to a late night movie that would start a few hours later but were unsure how to pass time until then. We were gathered at my oldest son's apartment where we chose a DVD to watch, which, we all agreed would be a good means to kill time until it was time to go to the theatre. I was in an easy place and I was calm and relaxed. The struggle was soon to be over and knowing this gave me great peace. There was nothing else to do but have fun and enjoy this short time with my children. Then it happened.

Suddenly, I felt myself lifting out of my body in a most unsettling way. I hovered just above my children and myself and watched them, and me, watching the movie. I felt the lightness of this strange state and there was a purity to it that made me feel the cleanest I had ever felt. I was completely given over to what I was in that state and no longer felt any connection, whatsoever, to the person sitting in the chair as the physical me. In an instant I was swept up into an awareness that the human before me was not who I was. I was, clearly, not that body and despite all the suffering that that body had been through there was nothing that would alter this exhilarating new perception of who I was. I could see that I was not the experiences of my physical body rather I now knew I was the "experiencer" of my physical body.

This recognition completely washed away everything I held as significant and causal in making the decision to end my life. None of what I perceived myself to be when that decision was made existed anymore and I realized, in that moment I truly was free. This new sense of freedom opened me up and everything about my existence changed. Who I truly am was trapped in a human body whose only awareness was human experience and all the human could do to stop it was to end the physical life. All that went away. I now saw something far beyond the human identity I had become and all my perceptions of what used to be changed in a way that became grand and wonderful. As this "I" settled back into my physical body I knew I was not what I once believed myself to be and I saw life, intelligence oozing in everything and it took my breath away! The double sidedness of everything, I once experienced, physically, ended. There was nothing that was not magnificent and in that magnificence all things blended into each other.

Soon thereafter I left my marriage of thirty two years, stopped all anti-depressant medications, ended all therapy, quit my job and career and began to write, which is what I continue to do. I was saved in a moment of despair and complete release of all worldly things and literally freed from darkness.

The title of this book is "On Human Being – Loving & Living Without Purpose." It is a book about "tip toeing through humanity and walking lightly leaving most of what we find along the way intact and without our markings upon it. It is about finding the inner self that sojourns for a little while and returns to whatever cosmic reality we come from. It is about rethinking what we think! Actually, it is about replacing our thinking with spontaneous action that boils up from somewhere inside. It is about the discovery of our unique and innate natures as divine beings. This is a book that reinforces that our unique human experience already is the purpose!

Carl Bozeman

Chapter 1

Cosmic Train

Earth life is a vacation from the cosmic train we all ride on through our infinite existence. It is a unique experience all of us who choose to visit get to enjoy, if we accept that the only reason we are here is to enjoy. It may seem erroneous to consider that we are here to experience three dimensional reality as a vacation or as something we should enjoy when we see so much pain, suffering and sorrow in the world. The reality of existence here on earth is that it is nothing in comparison to our existence in eternity. We are no less infinite on earth than we are in eternity.

While aboard the cosmic train, a few of us have gotten off here at earth and as we pass through the gates of birth, we enter a new kind of awareness that overwhelms everything else we once knew. The old awareness gets tucked away but is always there. We sense that there is more to us, but in the new earthly awareness, it is difficult to hold onto and pull it into this reality. Some do and we see them as mysterious and unique, but never allow that, we too, are just as they are. Earthly awareness is so tactile and sensory. The stimuli we take in through our earthly senses overwhelms us in a sea of experience and richness that is difficult to separate from the reality of who we truly are. So we are driven to find answers in this reality to that mysterious knowing we have about ourselves that is bigger than our means of communication can express. We look for meaning and purpose in terms of what we see and in the expressions we communicate, but even with all of that, we are sometimes left empty. The search continues.

The purposes of life are explored and examined but the answers we seek lay hidden.

There really is no purpose in this life other than to experience reality as only humans can. Every aspect of life should be embraced and we should revel in every minute of it regardless of whether we judge the experience good or bad. Our purpose, if there is any purpose, is to live and live abundantly in the richness of sensory experiences our human existence allows. Our existence "is" the meaning of life! Living "it" is its only purpose. However, it is ours to choose how we let the sensory awareness of this life be measured. We can choose to embrace it and enjoy all its ups and downs, or we can be miserable as we slog our way through it to our death, or the entrance back on the cosmic train we disembarked from. We make it what it is and we can blame no one for our experience. Sure, our innate nature has been masked, but it is not unknowable. We live according to our awareness and that is as it should be. That is what we came here for; therefore, every minute of earthly awareness should be basked in for its wonderful and delicious sensory experience.

The search for a greater meaning or purpose to life is in some ways its own problem. It suggests that we cannot be here for any other reason than to embrace and enjoy everything about life. It leads us to question our lives and the experience we have as meaningful in ways that they are not meant to be. It adds seriousness to our existence that drives us to meanings that can only make sense in this reality but do not begin to address our own innate knowing that we are so much more than what we sense in this existence, or than what language will allow us to describe. That is a lot about what this existence is about - coming to grips with the limitations of awareness and communication we otherwise have as gods. There is no way we can describe our divine nature in the languages of humans, but we are not supposed to. Remember we are on vacation and compared to our divine nature, the pace here on earth is slowed down considerably. Our infinite state is a quickened state in which our awareness is of things incomprehensible in this life... earth life is seriously slowed down. In fact, our own human-ness slows us down even more.

For instance, it has been proven scientifically that our bodies, including what we call our physical senses, take in sensory input, several billion bits of information every second, and yet what we are capable of being conscious of is in the range of twenty to thirty bits per second. Something about this experience as humans filters out so much of what goes on that what we are conscious of is infinitesimal to what is really happening. When we consider our divine or spiritual natures, the information we receive is even greater than what we experience on the human level. In fact, our spiritual sensitivity is so finely tuned it is barely detectable and in most scientific circles, it is nonexistent simply because we do not have the three dimensional means to detect it. What is not detectable in this reality is usually left to speculation, theory or is just relegated as non-existent. Even though most of us at one time or another have felt something in ourselves that is more far-reaching than we can articulate, if we cannot define it, or measure it, it cannot be, or so says our science.

Human consciousness or sub consciousness is not the extent of our experience. We have built in conditions and filters that sift through the enormous amount of information, bombarding us every second, which screen out the majority of our experience. This is what I mean when I refer to life as an illusion in my book <u>On Being God</u>. What makes it into our conscious awareness is what we have been conditioned or programmed to know and accept. Most of us have heard that when the Spanish ships appeared on the horizon upon discovering the "New World", the inhabitants could not see them. There was nothing in their conditioning that could explain what they saw and yet intuitively they saw something. Their programming simply could not identify it and nothing in their experience, other than clouds, could the ships on the horizon be compared to.

We know it took the shamans of those native people several days to come up with a description they could then convey to the rest of the people. Only then could they identify this new phenomenon and only then could they put this new description into their own language and make it part of their experience. Consider how much is going by us if in every second of life, billions and billions of images, sounds, smells, tastes, touches and any number of sensory inputs we can't possibly remember get discarded by processes we barely understand. Life goes on around us at light speed but we only sense it at a snail's pace. And the civilizing of ourselves, as we refer to it, is only slowing it down even more. Think about what is passing us by.

In the early 1990's, I worked for a telecommunications company whose products helped optimize the available bandwidth of copper phone lines around the world. Cellular technology was in its infancy as was fiber optics, so maximizing the available telephone bandwidth was of major importance because there were only so many copper lines available to an ever increasing population of telephone users. The product we developed was a device that would convert an analog voice signal to a digital signal, remove any extraneous noise such as the static or ambient noise one often heard on a telephone land line, and then packetize the cleaned up digital signal into small packets that would be sent across the line to another device that would assemble the packets, convert the digital signal to an analog signal and, wonder of wonder, a voice was heard speaking just as on any phone call.

What was so unique about this product, for the time, was that in processing calls in such a way and by eliminating all the extraneous noise, we could put sixteen voice conversations across a telephone line that up to that time could only carry one, representing a huge savings to businesses who were paying for multiple lines at great cost as well as a serious improvement to the usage of the available bandwidth.

One of the interesting facets of developing this technology was the idea that the extraneous noise in normal telephone conversations carried no useful information and could be removed without any affect to those speaking and those listening. Little did our developers know that the noise did provide one very important piece of information.

All of us who have used the old land line telephones always had a sense that our call was viable because we could hear the noise of the connection during breaks in the conversation. The information carried by the noise was that the call was still connected. Even though the noise adds nothing to the words spoken or heard, it did add to the assurance that in between words spoken and words heard the line was still connected. When we removed that assurance, sure enough, people who used the new technology complained that during the breaks in a conversation, the line went so silent they couldn't tell if the connection was still intact. The familiar noise of land line conversations was a carrier of information that, like so much in our reality, is taken for granted but missed if it is gone.

We are missing more and more in our reality due to the stripping away of the noise of life that civilization, culture, and upbringing filters out, and the absence of it is causing us to be aware of less but to seek more. In other words, we are starving ourselves of the richness of life in all its forms and replacing it with the illusions of culture and civilization that have been drained of nutrients necessary to the soul. Our aloneness in the world stems not from the isolation we feel from our brothers and sisters. It stems from the filtering of life that has isolated us from our own god-ness and that of everyone else. That is what we seek in life – not human connection, but divine connection. Individually and societally, we are crying out more and more for something to fill our satiated souls, and more and more civilization devises empty stimulation to keep us in control – in check from venturing away from the illusion we know.

The illusion we live, like the processed foods we eat, have been stripped of those things that would enrich and nourish us and replaced with fillers and synthetic nutrients that satisfy temporarily but do not fill us. Our connections to nature have been replaced with television, radio, internet and other civilized forms of media that have been carefully engineered to play to an illusory beat we have all been taken in by. Like the packetizing of small pieces of digitized voice from a telephone call, information is carefully fed to us at a rate not to exceed our ability to pay attention. So much of the information is stripped away that we only get teased with what is really happening and before we have a chance to try to figure out what information has been stripped away, we are hit with another perfectly timed, perfectly sized packet of seriously reduced information.

The illusion is so complete that we, as participators in it, have accepted slogans such as "give them what they want" believing that what we want is what we are being given. Meanwhile, for those who search for greater awareness, getting outside of the illusion is extremely difficult and so they search in vain among the institutions of civilization for the soul nourishment they crave.

What was intended to be a stopping off point, a vacation from other awareness has now become a desperate struggle to somehow survive natural forces that, while once were so much a part of us, have now become the enemy. Our illusion of what this reality is has become so synthesized that we have replaced what was always intended – enjoyment, enrichment, tranquility and nourishment - with a struggle fraught with peril, tragedy and synthetic stimulation. Our cosmic vacation has become so empty, so stressful that we now look for ways to vacation from the vacation! And where do we go? To those places with as little civilization as possible. We go to those places where we can rest, soak up the sun, or be inspired by the beauty of a natural wonder such as a mountain, a river, the ocean or a canyon. We sometimes go to the civilized, manmade attractions but, while fun and stimulating; they often leave us empty and un-refreshed.

The oldest among us recall fondly the quieter and less hectic times they grew up in and the freedoms they enjoyed then that are so distant now. The youngest of us cannot even conceive of these things they describe. The sterilizing manner of civilization removes the adventure and connectedness to the world whose intention it was all along to enrich us and enliven us from an infinite "other world" reality. Our souls came here for enrichment, not our bodies, and yet it is our bodies that our civilized world caters to. The experience of life has become a race, a competition to find purpose and meaning by indulging the senses in every possible way, such that the soul is lost completely to the gratification of the physical or three dimensional aspect of our lives. We hear the statement that "we are spiritual beings having a physical experience". Yes, we are having a physical experience, but not to the extent that we completely overshadow our spiritual nature.

In the Old Testament, there is a story of the man Job whom most have heard of in some form or another. The story of Job is the story of a man who has everything this life can offer. He is a man of great wealth, influence and notable character. He is God-fearing and righteous and is blessed with a large family, creature comforts, as we call them and the respect of everyone in his country. Job's story takes a bizarre twist as Satan convinces God to let him break Job and show God that if he were to lose all the things in life he possesses, that Job would lose his faith and curse God. God allows Satan to literally take everything from Job including his family, wealth, and good fortune. Satan is even allowed to cause great scourges and illness to come upon Job, but Job, while physically broken in every way, never forsakes his faith, nor does he turn against God. Job does, however, question why one as righteous as he, is treated so poorly by the God he worships. He even asks God to take his life and end his misery. Job suffers all that is thrown at him, but never accepts that he is evil or that God is punishing him for some act he has committed. Job does seek for answers to his suffering and requests to speak to God face to face. God grants Job's request and appears to him as a whirlwind.

It is extremely interesting God's response to Job and very relevant to our experience here in this life. Instead of speaking in any way to Job about his suffering, God directs Job to look all around and take in all the beauty and wonder he is surrounded by. God covers every aspect of creation and life on this earth and not once addresses Job as a sinful man or in a way Job desires. All manner of creatures are mentioned as well as the wind, rain, water, snow, hail and frost. It can be taken that God rules over everything and is greater than all things but it is as if God is trying to show Job that the things that are naturally here on earth are what is important in life. All of it is here for the good of our souls and yet our so called civilizing or taming of nature is not unlike that of Job questioning God why he is made to suffer.

How is it that we can suppose that the egoic cravings of humans can nourish our starving souls when any of it has no comparison, whatsoever, to the beauty, majesty and abundance of this earth? The treasures of life are not found in the creations of man. They are found in the raw creative beauty of which we are all a part. When we see that eagle soar high above and we gasp for breath as we watch, "we" are every bit as breath-taking and none of it is because we have created our cities, monuments, and wonders. It is because our souls, like the eagles, soar above everything we believe important and look down on something so vast and wonderful. Nothing in our creative imagining comes close to its splendor.

We are the recipients of this splendor. No act or outcome in this life will change the nature of our soul in the eternities. Nothing we do here matters, so all that we need do here is embrace everything that goes on, every experience, every accomplishment, and every aspect of the life we live should be embraced in every possible way as another part of our vacation. None of us should ever feel we are victims of circumstance when we step back on to that cosmic train. We should be refreshed, invigorated, uplifted and alive from a richness of experience we may never know again, and while in infinite terms the experience is a blip on the cosmic screen, every part of this experience should leave us absolutely vibrating. What a gift it is to be here and to experience the incredible highs and lows of humankind. We should relish every moment of it.

Too many can't wait, like Job of old, to get out of life and back on board the train. Life has not been the pleasure trip it was meant to be, but that is only because in the egoic life we live and try to fit into, we lose sight of why we are here. As God spoke to Job and asked him to identify one thing in his experience that remotely compared to the splendor of this planet and everything on it, Job shrank before Him and could not. The reason is that there is no manmade thing that compares to anything on earth and in infinite terms, nothing on earth including earth itself compares to our lives in eternity.

In the last chapter of Job, the epitaph, Job is restored to his health, position, and stature that he knew before Satan physically broke him. In fact, it was greater than before. The story of Job is a metaphor for us here on earth living life that regardless of our circumstances or how we view our life experience, in the end we are restored to our unique and divine situation. If we learn to see this life, our experience, as God instructed Job to view it, nothing else matters. Nothing we do or accomplish in this life will ever surpass just being a part of life here on earth in whatever form it takes. The cosmic train leaves no one behind regardless of how the earth experience went for them. Like Job, we are all restored back to that infinite reality we all exist in. We won't be looking back as in infinity, all things blend together into one big whole, and it is wondrous. All of it is wondrous!

Life and living are the only reason we are here and all of it is to be enjoyed, but only as you choose. We cannot fail at life! There really are no illusions, only the ones we choose to accept as our condition. We can change

On Human Being

everything in our experience here in this life and we should because we get back onboard the cosmic train all too soon.

Chapter 2

Disembark; Planet Earth

Who stepped off the "Cosmic Train" is a daunting unknowing that only grows larger when we look into the night sky and see the darkness filled with tiny distant lights and ponder our unique existence in such a vast universe. We ask, "Are we alone or will we ever be able to travel such incredible distances to explore and search for others like us, or not like us?" It is a compelling, but complex mystery that challenges even the greatest scientific minds because of the inherent inability of the mind to comprehend infinity. In our lives on earth we grow to like the solidness and order of everything in our experience. Looking out into the heavens or considering infinity disrupts that order. We turn to science or religion for answers but no one can ever completely remove the mystery that surrounds our presence here...our not knowing, as it were. We may never know who stepped off that train and we will certainly never agree from a collective human viewpoint.

All we may ever be able to come to terms with in this life is that we are here and that we are unique. We seem to get that. Our own science tells us that at a basic energetic level we and everything else are the same even though we can see that we are uniquely different from other humans, other life forms and all the various forms we encounter in existence. No two things in any form of nature are exactly the same in appearance yet in our energetic make up there is no difference other than the rate at which energy vibrates. So what accounts for that uniqueness if everything is the same at the basic elemental level? Again, another mystery we may never comprehend in this reality; or will we? In the book "On Being God -

Beyond Your Life's Purpose" we are told that most of what we perceive in life is an illusion of the conditioned mind we acquire as we are taught and trained throughout our lives. That conditioning is what upholds our perception of reality even though we know so much more is going on that we are not perceptively aware of. In other words, the level of our awareness is responsible for the level of our illusion of reality. We perceive what we have accepted as reality and yet none of us accepts, or live as though, we are all the same. All things that are said to be equal do not appear to be equal. How, then, do we account for all the variety in life?

Science has developed ideas and theories about our existence and our unique selves but science tends to only consider observable facts in a strictly three dimensional sense. If it cannot be observed in these terms it is not included in the base of knowledge we claim to have about life, existence and all the other things happening. What this means is that the character and personality of humans comes from genetics, environment and other measurable phenomenon we tend to be aware of. Everything else is ruled out because it is too abstract and doesn't fit the scientific framework for proper investigation. This while knowing that things are going on far outside our ability to observe them. Such things may possibly never be understood. Science will only study what it can measure and while science attempts to imagine things outside the box of three dimensional reality it has no imagination outside it. The truth is that we will never understand the differences between humans or any other living or non-living thing in a scientific way; not fully anyway. That is because there is no way to study spiritual things unless they somehow fall into emotional or psychological areas but that is not likely. Spiritual things fall outside physically measurable norms, but most of us on some level know that there is more to us than what we see. These subtle, but real, knowing's remind us that we are part of something that is much greater than what is visible on the surface. In fact, many of us recognize coincidences and find meaning in their happening but fail to recognize that they only seem to be coincidence because they happen so infrequently. Coincidences for most of us are an infrequent look through the keyhole at a spiritual realm that is interwoven into every aspect of our lives. If we could unlock the door instead of looking through just the keyhole we would see worlds without number, others moving in and out of our reality in such a way it would startle the mind that can only see three dimensionally. We are living in a much more complex, interwoven reality than our awareness, religion, or science comprehends but we are conditioned not to see it. The question that may be asked, "So what is going on?" We have all heard the saying that we are spiritual beings having a physical experience but we live as though we are physical beings trying to become spiritual. It should be exactly the opposite. If we truly are spiritual, and we are, then it is a regression of the spiritual nature we all possess when becoming human. We have the whole scenario backwards with our ideas of purpose and meaning and that we must search to the ends of the earth to find that purpose. We live as though the search for purpose and meaning is how we find our spiritual path but it is really the opposite. We are already spiritual! Becoming human is going down from being high, not the reverse. We live life trying to work up when everything points to working down. Down should not be construed as bad or a reversal of our godlike nature but more a slowing down the pace of living as gods.

Life might be thought of as a vacation from the work of being gods on such a grand scale. Life on earth is greatly simplified from life at the speed of light – or the speed of gods, whatever that might be. We are spiritual, divine creatures taking on human form and experiencing that in a way only gods can but we live as though we must prove something here as humans in order to get back to a heavenly presence we all seem to have forgotten. We look at human existence as a lowly existence and create gods so great that we struggle the rest of our lives trying to measure up to what we already are! As gods already all we ever have to do is to embrace the human experience and simply enjoy it. You cannot attain what you already are, and we are all gods who have created this unique experience for ourselves and no one else.

Settle down and settle into the experience of human life instead of falling into the trap that we must work up to something that just isn't in play with the human existence. Get busy being human and enjoy it. Embrace every aspect of it and stop worrying about what you have forgotten about your divine nature. It will all come back if not in this life then for sure in the next one, whatever that may be. The human experience is part of a much larger happening we, as gods, are involved in. In fact, it is a happening we have created for our own benefit and it is of no benefit to run ourselves ragged trying to find some profound and significant meaning to our lives. That we are living is the meaning and as unglamorous as that may sound it is significant!

Most of us accept the uniqueness of the individuals we encounter in this life. We hear it spoken that no two people are alike but when we get to the realm of parenting this idea breaks down. Most parents will define a set of rules and guidelines that each child must conform to or else be dealt with appropriately. We are told that children need boundaries but how often do we recognize that boundaries for one may be anathema to another? We watch the frustration of parents as they struggle to get everyone of their children to conform to the same set of rules. We comment about how one child is the perfect angel while another won't do a thing we say.

As children grow we see their unique personalities and characteristics emerge and while we recognize those unique aspects the rules almost seem too tighten. Also, we see the influence of institutions begin to have an effect and, of course, if the boundaries and rules of those institutions are violated the consequences vary all the way up to expulsion or entry into new institutions designed especially for those who do not conform. While most seem to make it through this, almost every adult can look back at a time as a child where their confinement was really an internment and violated their idea of freedom. Children live life with abandoned but are systematically conditioned to live a life of purpose that is best suited for them as concluded by the collective. We even say things like "living life on purpose" and yet our parenting and institutional guidance seems to frown on any purpose that does not fit some set of rules that fit within certain boundaries.

It is unfortunate that we have gone this way since children are closer to who it is they truly are then virtually any adult will ever be. Nevertheless we structure their lives and condition them away from the knowing that they are divine. Sad to think that as they are pulled further and further away from their divine awareness, so too, are we. Few adults will not admit they are uplifted in a very special way when in the presence of a newborn baby or very young children. Additionally, adults will almost never contemplate why they feel this way. What is it in a child that pulls us toward a divine sense of awareness? How often do we hear at the birth of a child that it is a miracle?

Still we begin immediately to reshape these miracles into what we have come to accept is important in life and as they grow older the light we all notice at first is drained out of them just as it has for us. Few like to admit this but this is how it is. We teach our children to be conforming and dull. Not to be alert to the mystery of life. Alertness has nothing to do with awareness of present conditions and circumstances as we are all taught. Alertness is really being aware of what is not directly in front of our eyes. We are all born with such awareness and we are alert to it until it is replaced with what is believed to be more important.

In essence we are two individuals while sojourning here on earth. Broken down to our most basic selves there is the spiritual or god who has come to occupy the other part which is the human. The personality or character of the spiritual has always existed and is in no way connected to the genetics or environment of the human. That personality always emerges and while we would like everything to be ordered and structured the soul's personality is unique and profound and will remain that way forever. The sole basis for our experience here on earth is for the spiritual to experience the human. For many spiritually minded people we have entered a time when life must have a purpose and we drive ourselves to find it while we have somehow forgotten that our unique human form is the purpose. We have it all backwards. We look for purpose when our being here is the purpose.

If environment and conditioning is what is responsible for our personality then it is responsible to assume that we could provide the conditions and environments to have two people be exactly the same. But we can't. We know this. We can't even produce identical characteristics in identical twins. Every personality emerges on its own regardless of the conditions it is brought up in.

We see this in the lives of so many of our great, iconic leaders and teachers throughout the ages.

For instance Siddhartha was of royal dissent. Privilege beyond all others and certainly his conditioning was such that he would rule kingdoms of men as a royal. His education must have been the best that could be had and his life of privilege must have been a life others of lower class would have aspired to. In fact, it is believed that he was sheltered from everything going on outside his royal life so that he would never question that how he lived was not normal for everyone. Still, despite all his status, fortune and privilege his innate personality, his unique and divine nature had to manifest itself. For some reason as he looked at the world outside his own he recognized that the majority of people did not have anything like the life he knew. This tore at his soul to such an extent that he gave up everything he knew to live a beggar's life and be among his fellow humans among whom he was raised to be superior.

What called him to such a life that was so compelling that he would give up wealth and privilege and the very things we are conditioned to aspire to now? We are told constantly that having more frees us to be able to do and give more. We are constantly pointed toward those who have such things as Siddhartha walked away from in order to have what has come to be termed "the successful life and yet we look to him as one of the greatest of all humans having existed. In our aspirations and pursuits of what He walked away from, even now we tend to overlook what a journey it must've been for him to become the first Buddha. Instead we look at him as the Buddha and call him great and wonderful and yet if he were here now, he himself would not recognize such greatness.

The Buddha is just one example of the emergence of the personality, the god within us in spite of our conditioning to the contrary. There are so many others whom we have made famous, holy or inspiring but the greatness we credit all of our icons with is no different than what each of us possess as well. In fact, it is likely that our greatest struggles in life are the result of our human conditioning that opposes our innate, divine natures.

There are studies in the United States and likely in other countries that upwards of seventy percent of the working population are unhappy with their jobs or careers. It is probably greater than that. What does this tell us about our conditioning as humans? From the moment of our birth when everyone who observes us and is lifted up by our divine and miraculous nature we are told what is important in life. We are convinced through constant conditioning that education, career, credentials and so much more is what is important in life and we are somehow convinced that we must give up certain things to get ahead.

Getting ahead is what is important and to do so we must sometimes sacrifice an innate knowing we have inside that says otherwise. If seventy percent of the working population is unhappy with their careers how happy can they otherwise be? If the purpose of life is to enjoy the experience of living as a spiritual being having a human experience wouldn't a thirty percent or less success rate be a strong indicator that something is wrong?

It is widely believed that much of the disease and illness in the world today is caused from stress in life including the work environment. There are many descriptions of stress and ideas of how it is induced but ultimately it is the result of the rift between what the human form has been conditioned to believe and what our unique spiritual nature is. In other words, what we have come to believe is important at the physical level is fighting against the spiritual. The physical self tears at the spiritual self. It is a denial of the divine, the god that you are, and it sickens the body to the point of early failure. Stress is talked about a great deal these days and it should begin to become apparent that something about the way we have been conditioned and the way we condition our children is creating enmity between the spiritual and the human form. So much so that we are creating an epidemic of stress and bodily failure in the process.

We are taught from birth to replace what we innately are with what we are not. Parents seek every advantage they can to steer their children from their innate nature to what their particular conditioning says is important. Children grow up and struggle trying to be what parents and society say they should be. How could children not struggle? Their teeth are set on edge every time they are instructed to go against their innate nature and seek out careers or lifestyles that are more suited to the illusion we have accepted as an abundant life.

Most of us are no longer alert to what is really going on. We are very aware of what goes on directly in front of our eyes but outside that awareness we are not alert to our placement in the more expansive nature of things going on around us. It's like I can see what you are doing, but I cannot see why you are doing it." Or "I see things happening in front of me but I cannot see the effect they are having on all things I don't see." As already mentioned alertness has nothing to do with what is directly in view of our physical senses. It has to do with simply being aware that mystery surrounds us far beyond anything we sense physically. Alertness puts us in to the spectrum of mystery which is the largest part of our experience even though we are unaware in the physical sense.

    To illustrate this I had an experience with my father that made me so much more aware of the bigger picture than I had ever imagined. He fell one night and was rushed to the hospital where he was non responsive to normal physical stimulus. I had seen this sort of thing before with him and told the emergency room doctors that he simply needed to sleep some and after a little rest he would wake up and be as ornery as ever. I began to worry when, after about sixteen hours, he was non-responsive and of course the doctors were saying his situation was very dire. At the point I began to give up hope of ever speaking to him again he came around, just as I expected originally. When that happened I went back to my learned awareness that he would have these little spells but would come back as he always had before. His condition improved so he was moved to a room inside the hospital where he could be observed and cared for but without the emergency room critical care since his condition was no longer considered dire.

    We had a wonderful time for the next two days while he was kept under observation and all monitoring of vital signs indicated he was perfectly healthy. On the second day of observation he insisted I take his ring which he always wore on his left hand ring finger even though he and my mother were divorced and he had never remarried. I thought it was unusual in a way but in his old age I accepted it as just another quirky aspect of his aging personality. In handing me the ring he insisted that it had power and would protect me. I took the ring and told him I would keep it with me always which brought a smile and a nod of approval from him. We spent the rest of the day visiting and preparing him for his return to his home the next morning as he was given a clean bill of health and was signed out of the hospital's care.

He died early the next morning a few hours after I had left to return home. I was completely taken by surprise as was the hospital staff. My alertness was only aware of the information I could physically see in front of me. It was the same for all the medical staff assigned to observe and assist him. All any of us could see is the physical monitoring. None of us could see that death was swallowing him up. He, however, knew it and gave me those last two days to help me be aware of it but I was so caught up in my perception of reality that I failed to comprehend that none of what was happening was about me in any way. I was unable to see the mystery unfolding in front of me even as he was imploring me to take his ring and keep it with me always as his gesture of protecting me even after he would be gone. It was all right there in front of me. The infinite into which my Father was passing surrounded me on every side and in every way and all I could see was the physical nature of things playing out in a very superficial way. All I could make of the mysterious events playing out was "My Daddy is coming home and all would be as it formerly was."

When I look back on, what was then, a sad time I can see how completely I was surrounded in mystery and that extraneous events were pressing on me to awaken to something far more profound than what I was sensing as just a human. What happened with my father in those few short hours, was about everything seen and unseen. Mystery and physical perception; alertness is awareness of both. What we think of as mundane is wrapped in mystery but we are so busy in our world of details and routine that mystery slips quietly by.

Who we are has nothing to do with what we think. In fact, exactly the opposite is true. Who we are is what we do not think and those coincidental life experiences we all encounter from time to time are clearer expressions of what our reality is. They are also pointers to the underlying "who" that we are underneath the physical "I" we are taught to believe we are. You are unimaginable; we all are. The finite cannot comprehend the infinite and so our human expressions, intended to define us, do nothing more than limit us.

Who you are knows no physical bounds, whatsoever. The whispers of other worlds, other realities seep into our awareness when we let go of all ideas that tell us we are our physical bodies; our minds, our egos. On the other side of physical-ness lies the real you and best of all; you have always been there!

Chapter 3

Cosmic Storytelling

The common thread in all our lives is the similarities of myths throughout all of human history and within every civilization that attests that we all have a common awareness that permeates us regardless of how we are conditioned. The most common myth is that we all look to transcend our own mortality. We believe there is something greater than what we see in this existence. Our souls yearn for it and so throughout the ages, we have created our gods in such a way that they know the way of transcendence. It is as if we are all programmed from the very beginning of this earthly existence to ask the same questions about where we came from, why we are here, and what lies beyond. It is as if the gods hard wired us to ask such questions to constantly remind us that we are greater than anything we can conceive of, as three dimensional brings. We are constantly being tweaked by these questions as if to always have a door through which we can go, but only when we are ready. The great difficulty is being able to rise above the reality we have come to accept outside that door. Our attachment to life, or what we have been conditioned to see as life, is what prevents us from pushing the door open and walking through. Our acceptance of the terms and conditions of this life is what prevents us from getting the answers to those questions we ask, and yet we continue to ask them and look for ways to find answers that do not violate the rules of three dimensional reality as we know it.

We are asked to have faith that a particular path will get us to that higher "existence" we all seem to sense within. Somehow, however, we can't quite accept the idea that the substance of those things we hope for becomes the evidence of those things we cannot see. How difficult it is to be asked to believe that which we cannot see and to live in such a way that we must trust those who think they know better. How do we connect the evidence of our seeing with the hopes of things we once had before and how long must we wait and trust in the idea that comes to us from others whom we have convinced ourselves we must? Are we left to always wonder when the evidence we seek never comes?

The myths of man are a portal, a way to look, not from the inside out but from the outside in. The basic nature of all humans to know their inner essence is the evidence of our own connectedness to all of life. Mythology is an outgrowth of that which we see and don't see, but it has a basis in each one of us at a deep inner level that forces us to ask, what everyone asks, and to search for greater insight into our own divine nature. It is the common link in all of us that tries to answer the deeper questions of our existence that our three dimensional reality cannot. The twists and turns our myths take are all attempts to make that which is mortal, immortal. In other words, we are somehow raised from this plane to another by forces stronger than us.

Mortality is a constant for all of us and the idea that we all die is imposing. Not so much that we die physically in this life, but that in dying there is nothing else. Our greatest fear is that nothing more exists beyond this life and so the questions. We somehow understand that our lives, as we know them, are not all there is, but we are so thoroughly conditioned that we question everything we know at deeper levels and great fear arises because we have forgotten that we are infinite and continue on forever in some form.

Mythology gives us a basis to grab onto something outside the reality we have come to accept for ourselves and provide a nugget of hope that what we see and are is not all there is. We know innately that we are more than what is manifest here in this reality. We know this on so many levels and in so many ways, but our ultimate fear that this is all there is freezes us and lets us swim forever in a sea of doubt. Do I look at myself and wonder if I am greater than all of this or do I blindly accept that I can be what I am when I follow a prescribed outline created by the formulation of one particular interpretation of myth we all seem to know? The unknown is daunting and yet we all seem to know that there is so much more to the human creature then meets the three dimensional eye.

Our myths provide possibilities for those looming questions we ask from the depth our souls and attempts to do it in a way that makes sense in three dimensional terms, which is how we are all conditioned to be. We like the tidiness of answers when they fit into the reality we all exist in while here on earth. We are comforted when things can be proved scientifically or observationally, but we also tend to be drawn to the abstract ideas that our myths preserve in us. Somehow the gods, as in Greek mythology, provide us a sense of wonder, possibility and drama that exceeds the routines of everyday living. We like to think that our gods will pity us when down-trodden, protect us when in danger, or uphold us when in doubt. We want to know that something or someone out there has all these powers and uses them kindly and wisely to our benefit. There is security in giving over this kind of power to something greater than us and in letting ourselves be cared for by such power.

Mythology gives context and substance to our own letting go of what we truly are. Thank goodness for our myths because they have kept us connected to the idea of greatness and power even though we have forgotten that the power we give our mythic heroes and gods is our own power. We are the heroes of all mythology! There are no heroes outside what we are and when we decide to see that in ourselves is when we begin to understand that the greatness of life only exists because of "our own" greatness.

Our mythologies take on weird and wonderful twists and turns and we sometimes wonder what the gods are doing? It is this sense of wonder, perplexity and drama that attracts many of us to the plight of them. However, in spite of all the oddities of our unique cultural myths, they all remain surprisingly similar regardless of the culture. They all represent profound strength and uniqueness regardless of their origin and they are the servers of goodness, mercy and justice. We call upon them for whatever earthly needs we think we have. We credit them for all we have in this existence, and while we ascribe to them all this power to control and affect our lives, the real power lies within us individually. Their mythology is our own mythology and any power we ascribe to our heroes, gods and villains is our own power.

As long as we continue to accept the illusion of our existence, there will be myths. We cannot exist without them because it is they that keep us connected to the reality of life which is beyond everything we believe about ourselves and life on this planet. There is a greater part of us that, while mostly hidden, transcends all of our illusory beliefs. Our myths are the "voice crying in the wilderness" that allow us to, if only to fantasize, be something we just can't seem to grasp while in this life. Consequently, what we believe about ourselves, our mythological beliefs, is what we project to an outside world whose citizens do the same both individually and collectively. How we sell ourselves to others and the world is through our myths. That is why they all seem so similar.

All of us wonder about what or who we are, how we came to be and what happens after. Myths provide the link between those questions of wonderment and our current place in reality, and even though we sometimes institutionalize them, we all seem to know there is something else beyond them. Mythology does not seem to solve the "we" about "us" meaning that while the characters of our myths are individualized, the myths themselves are encompassing of the societies to which they relate. While we cannot allow ourselves to be as the gods and heroes we create, we do get caught up in their drama and we can choose whose side we will fall into – a sort of "who's on the Lord's side who" game of chance.

In some cultures, mythology is like the psychic energy that, when taken away or shattered, causes the entire society to collapse as if its very life force rested upon the myth and not the energy of its "myth believing" inhabitants. Myths deal with every aspect of our lives from birth to death and the entire range of human experience including tragedy, joy, love, hate, war, courage, tyranny etc. Our fates are determined by the mythic gods we create and give authority to. Some believe that we cannot exist without myth. It is thought to be our only connection to a spiritual nature no one seems to fully understand and no one can explain. It is the place where gods do what gods do and we as humans fall victim to whatever twists and turns those "doings" take. Myths give us characters, circumstances, events and outcomes and we accept these outcomes as our fate, sensing there is more to it than that, only we can't quite put a finger on what it is that is missing. What is missing is us.

In reality, we live two lives. The first "is" the mythical life. It is the life we want to fit into the world in general. It is the illusory life we are conditioned to view from the very beginning of life on this planet. It is the life of "I" that learns to find a place in the world outside, which is full of other "I's." Some view this as unconsciousness while others view it as consciousness. If we can agree that it is a life that is limited in its awareness of everything else going on around it, is doesn't matter what we call it. Science has proven that conscious awareness or consciousness is extremely limited to the amount of information it can process even though we know the amount of information coming into us is so great as to be overwhelming. The real problem with consciousness is "What should we be conscious of?" This is where the second life plays its part. This is the life of non-consciousness or that part of us that senses a greater reality but is not able to move that awareness into the realm of consciousness. It is what consciousness has identified as the unknown or the unknowable and because it has been identified as such, it puts little or no effort into the understanding of it. We all live these separate lives but the conscious life is so narrow and focused that it blocks out the other life that really has the greater awareness. At times, bits and pieces of it seep through the conscious filters and we glimpse the totality of life we are all a part of, but it is almost always fleeting. Our myths give us context into which we can place these experiences but again, they are only myths and fail to lead us to that inner knowing of self, the second life, that we get glimpses of every now and again.

There is a sort of war between these two lives or sets of awareness. On one hand, our conscious self connects us to the world of which it has identified itself with. That is the world as we see it through our senses and that has been narrowly defined as the realm of our identity. It takes an identity to reconcile something outside that identity into which it can place itself. In other words, I can see the world "out there" and I can place myself in that world. In placing oneself in that world, we develop an identity or self that fits to some degree in that world.

The problem that arises is that when this outer facing identity cannot reconcile the occurrences that come out of our greater awareness, using normal outer world explanations. Maybe it can be viewed as the "mythic" versus the "mystic." It is then that the focus of consciousness zeroes in on this unexplainable awareness and tries to make it fit within its known three dimensional parameters. When it cannot, then the awareness is typically defined as impossible or imaginary. Often it is reconciled to the deep, dark storage banks of the mind never to be considered again. Mythology sometimes eases the frustration of unanswered questions we all have by telling us to have faith that things will be settled in the end. In a way this is true because we all come to an awareness to all meaning sometime in our lives even if it is as we draw our last breath and exit this physical world.

Mythology never fully puts us at ease in its attempts to answer these deeper questions of life or when deep inner awareness meets outward constructs. Mythology requires a certain amount of faith if not absolute blind faith which always tends to leave us feeling cold and alone. Faith is our greatest myth. It is the ultimate shoulder we lean on in those times when deep awareness eludes us. Faith always breaks in the light of greater awareness. We often hear those who have reached profound states of enlightenment claim that just before the new awareness came that they had lost all faith. Faith, then, is a driving force that is the connective glue to our myths but it is always breakable. In other words the failure of faith is what breaks us free of our limiting beliefs. Faith drives us to break free of our myths by forcing us to give up on them!

As all myth is the projection of our inner fears, desires and concerns onto the outer world in which we live, the deeper questions of life, the inner life that is, go unanswered. In our search for answers, we cry out for myth to soothe that which scares us – that which is always left unanswered within. Our outer projections, our myths, require us to believe that somewhere or somehow, out there where we look to non-existent gods, the answers lay. Even our science, which has been very successful at dispelling so many of our myths, looks for the answers to everything "out there" with full faith that someday a theory of everything will finally be developed from which every question can be answered. Science, too, has its own myths!

We, as humans, having accepted so completely the illusion of consciousness, need mythology to help us cope with the unanswered questions of life that loom imposingly over us from time to time throughout our lives. Mythology gives us comfort when unanswerable questions bubble up from a place deep within us that we rarely acknowledge amidst the hustle and bustle of life. We can look to our gods and heroes for explanation and comfort and convince ourselves that they know all and will somehow guide us through whatever it is we question or struggle with. It is a safe way to live a life that, otherwise, seems so mysterious and illusive. Our myths give us place and hope from all that we cannot comprehend in life. Myth is the explanation of illusion we all dwell in and so plays to our conditioning whatever it is. It is the safety we seek from the dark night and it requires faith like conditioning in most cases, since our myths have become so abstract no one who thinks logically could ever accept.

Consider any of our religious traditions, be they Christian, Hindu, Judaism, Muslim, Buddhism or whatever. For some, we are saved from our sins and the impossibility to save ourselves while for others we are saved from oppression and persecution and will be raised and chosen to be above all others. Some will come and go from earth in multiple forms as they struggle over many lifetimes to "get it right" while others who are true to their myth will be exalted in endless bliss and places of glory inconceivable in this three dimensional realm. How could any of these be accepted and internalized without faith? Only an exercise of faith could allow us to believe such things and internalize them in our lives. Faith is the tool ego uses to accept myths that always look outward to something greater than ourselves. Ego asks for faith because ego has never successfully been able to explain God, or answer the questions we all ask about who we are.

The greatest evidence of this is all the religious tenets now existent on earth all contending for exclusive "rightness". Inner knowing, the discovery of God within has no need of faith or myth to explain what the ego wants us to believe. Knowing supersedes faith and dispels all myth. Any search to find the inner self will never lead to faith based conceptions. Faith is always an egoic device and that is why we must never stop searching. As long as we know our foundation is faith based, we cannot accept any conclusion that asks us to believe anything "out there" in the heavens that will eventually provide all the answers. To do so only entombs deeper an inner knowing we all can find. In other words, we replace God with false and fleeting gods. Faith is a necessary part of life and it might even be the key to finding God even though it is a device of the ego to calm the questioning or fearful mind. Faith is the ego's way of expressing that "it" (ego) has no clue.

True faith never stops searching, not even when it grows comfortable with institutional beliefs. When, or if, the search stops, we have given ourselves over to the false gods. As mentioned earlier, we have all heard it said that someone has lost their faith. You can lose faith and ultimately you must lose it to find yourself. Faith motivates us to move forward with belief in some objective but faith can always be lost and often is. Too often, faith is lost because the egoic drive to believe in something abstract becomes untenable to the true self. Perhaps even more often, we simply give up. The cost of believing is too much, so we let go or settle by simply going along with the crowd. Loss of faith takes on many forms, but true replacement of faith can only take the form of knowing and knowing only comes with the discovery of God. Your God. You!

Faith might be thought of as the motivation to fight through the constructs of ego and the illusory life we have come to accept. Faith and myth are necessary elements of the egoic life we live. We all search for basic life meanings, especially since most of those meanings are systematically conditioned out of us from birth. As long as the search of faith continues, we continue to seek out greater awareness and that is good for ultimately finding your true inner self; the god that you are already. There is power in faith, but it is partial power. Full power comes from knowing that you and any mythological God you believe in are one and the same and that you are the only god of your existence and that there are no others before you. The premise of faith is that it asks you to be blind to the unknown and accept outer sources of authority at their word. Knowing asks that your eyes always be opened to the greater awareness we all have within. Know thyself and in so doing, your awareness will comprehend all things. The so-called "theory of everything" will be found in this awareness. It is in this place that our search for myth is no longer necessary as we recognize that we are *the myth*!

Chapter 4

Faith – Our Mythological Partner

Faith is the bedfellow of mythology. But it has woven its way into the very fabric of life we live because while we can never be one hundred percent sure of our beliefs, faith holds us to them, even when they are untrue. It is the paradox of our three dimensional natures to be certain that all things are not possible while having faith that they are. The word faith is sometimes used in conjunction with the words trust and hope. We may find a person hoping to win the lottery and believing with faith unbending that it will happen, only to be disappointed when it doesn't. In extreme cases, some will lose their faith when the events they hoped for did not come to pass. "I'll never trust God again", some will say as their anger and disappointment gets the better of them. Humans are the only living things that have adopted an idea of faith mainly because of our conditioning that something outside of us is greater than us and watches over us in a kind and loving way. Our illusion creates this kind of hope within us and so we look to gods, heroes and others to solve our problems or at least see us through them and even make right in a future time or place.

Faith is like the glue that connects us to outside factors we either see or don't see but believe because that is what we have been taught to believe. Faith is a tool of ego just as caring is. We convince ourselves that whatever our mythological conditioning may be that we will be proven right, our beliefs will prevail over the beliefs of others who are as committed to theirs as we are to our own.

Faith plays into the dual nature of three dimensional life, by locking us into differing positions from others of different conditions and everyone is devoted and fixated on their own position so completely they are contemptuous of any other position. All of our religious wars have been fought over the rigidity of a "faithful" position. Our faith pulls us into positions for which there is no moral basis other than "that is how I was raised or brought up" and we accept these positions solely because someone convinced us it was right and worthy of our conviction. Faith has become the bulwark of many causes but it has also become the cause of much blindness. People believe in things that are inwardly pursued hoping they will be outwardly manifested. There is a common misconception that faith is belief in truth but the truth we find ourselves believing in is likely untrue. It might even be said that most everything we believe or say we know is untrue. As such, faith is really an idea that what is not truth can somehow become truth.

When Jesus spoke of faith, he likened it to a mustard seed. Many have taken his metaphor to mean that very little faith is needed to make big things happen. Jesus was not talking about quantity or even quality of faith, as many believe. In fact, he was not talking about faith at all when he made this comparison. He was describing something other than faith that we must all come to that exceeds faith of any kind. He was talking about knowing or "being" what you are outside of anything else you believe yourself to be. If faith is about anything, it is about inner knowing, but "knowing" supersedes faith.

The mustard seed Jesus described is ultimately a mustard tree. It has all the stuff of a mustard tree even though it is only a seed. In the world of a mustard seed, what is known and only known is that mustard seeds become mustard trees. Mustard seeds do not get wrapped around beliefs that they somehow, perhaps with faith, can become olive trees. Jesus' expression was an admonition to be what you are but in the world of humans, that is a difficult thing to do because we live in a world of egoic reality that "believes" it is something else. Most of us do not accept that we are gods nor do we believe that in any existence can we be anything like God, even though we are gods. It is not enough to simply believe, with faith, that it is so. We must find this awareness and accept that in knowing our "god-ness", we find all that God is, already exists within. We are the seed and all that is god *is* already in the seed! That is our mustard seed. A mustard seed does not wonder what it is or isn't or what it "might" become. It does not believe anything! It simply is.

Perhaps another way for Jesus to have explained this might have been "know you are God, just as the mustard seed knows it is a mustard tree". Therein you find power to overcome anything, to do anything and it costs you nothing. Humans in the illusory state we have created rarely get to see or experience who they truly are in the way a mustard seed does. We are bombarded with so many other things that we are blinded to the greatness of the "tree" within us. The mustard seed has no belief or faith. It simply is, in its purest form, a mustard tree with no illusion and no equivocation. It will do what it does and not wonder about an outcome. Now some will read this and say, "But a mustard seed doesn't have the capability of "thinking" about what it is." This should tell you something about "thinking." Our ability, as humans, to think is what leads us into the quandary of doubting our own make up. We are so caught up in egoic devices that label and define us that we have lost all sight of what we truly are. Jesus metaphor of the mustard seed is precisely about this. In other words, stop "thinking" about what you are or what you are not and simply "be!"

Here is another important point about the idea of knowing. Without attachment to our egoic ideas of what is, we release ourselves from everything that ties us to a faith based reality. Release from any beliefs releases us from anything other than "who" we are. God speaks to us at that point and the only thing we hear is a purity of essence. An essence of what we are. Only in that purity of essence do we discover the great tree within. Therein lies our true power.

Faith is a great device to aid us in finding solace amidst the noise of the world but knowing that we are the seed of God frees us from the noise altogether and allows us to grow into the greatness, the tree, that we truly are. Knowing this requires a complete letting go of everything else in our lives. Everything! Not in the egoic way that says you must give up family, job, friends, etc. and run off to be a monk in Tibet. Release from any idea that anything we have accomplished in life, own, or attach any importance to are of no value to being a "mustard seed." We must "be" gods rather than "hope" to be. Believing is not enough nor is any amount of faith going to change what "might be" from "what is".

We seem to have turned things around in our illusion. We search and train hoping that through our career, our life of goals and beliefs that we will find ourselves and find purpose and meaning to our lives, when, in fact, we find ourselves and discover the seed of God within and that purpose and meaning will take care of themselves. Find God within and you will have the seed of faith, but be the God that you are and you will move mountains.

The seed of faith has no voice. In other words, upon the discovery that each of us is god we rise above the ability of human language to describe what that means. This is "knowing." I refer to this idea of knowing a lot in my writings but I, like so many others, am remiss to be able to articulate in egoic terms, whether religious or scientific, what that means.

No one, who has come to this awareness can. "Knowing," as I refer to it, has nothing to do with the "human" aspect of our existence. It is completely detached from anything physical, which is why science and even basic human logic, have such a difficult time grasping that there is something more to our existence than what we typically see "in front" of our eyes. Yet those who have experienced the "touch" of the divine upon their physical shoulders are never the same. It is as if the awareness they had in front of their eyes is no longer there. Something else deep within holds a vision that is incomprehensible, physically and mentally, and completely overwhelms everything "out there" in the physical world. The vision renders them speechless other than for the, somewhat, vain attempts to use "metaphors" to explain it. The Tao would describe it as "knowing without knowing." In other words spiritual knowing will never be explainable by anything physical.

Faith should never be thought of as "what I want or what I can get." It applies solely to "Who I AM" That is the "works" that is spoken of by Paul the Apostle when he said "faith without works is dead." Uncovering the "who" of your existence is the essence of faith and it requires work to do it because all our lives we have been told that not only can we not move mountains but we are not worthy of the highest glory we give our gods. Our faith is a vehicle that can carry us only so far but our works must continue to unmask the identities we have surrounded ourselves with. It is in this unmasking that we draw nearer to what it is we are and it is in that knowing that mountains are moved. We are the "tree" not the "seed." The seed does not give life to the tree. The tree is always the tree and the seed knows this. "Being the seed is being the tree."

Many Christian scholars have expanded the meaning of this metaphor with ideas of "what do we do to make the seed grow?" Obviously we respond with things like plant it and water it and fertilize it and care for it and it requires these things to have it become the tree. Somehow in these various "broadened" analogies we compare these "works" of planting, fertilizing, etc. to the works we are told will, likewise, nourish us and have the object of our faith realized but none of this matters if the seed we are trying to sow is different from our true seed. In other words you cannot *become* God. Why? Because you already are God!

Faith might be better viewed as something that drives us to a point of breaking ourselves from the hold of physical reality upon us. It drives us to give up on our ideas of truth and simply give ourselves over to other forces, as we might refer to them. Many, after breaking will create new stories that include the ideas from before and maintain a new view of themselves that include the gods and hero's they believed in only now the story is altered somewhat. Faith at this point is now formed around a new story or new untruth. The pull of our conditioning almost always sneaks back into our mental picture of this new reality that we, again, must be broken of. All our lifetime of conditioned knowledge and egoic structure must be broken so that any idea of truth whatsoever is no longer held. We are literally freed from all ideas of knowledge and truth.

Faith is not about holding on to beliefs and ideas we think to be true or important. It is ultimately about letting go of everything we believe about our physical experience. *Faith is letting go!* It is never about holding on and regardless of what we place our faith in no part of it will ever be the truth we seek. The truth we seek is already within us and it requires no other effort than to find that inner awareness of who we are outside our physical natures. Faith is not believing in what is true, rather it is not believing anything we think we know at all. It is freeing ourselves from beliefs altogether and letting the essence of who we are, gods, become our awareness. This form of awareness cannot be explained. It can only be known and it is unshakeable in any reality.

Faith hooks us to our beliefs and our beliefs are the result of our particular conditioning which make them more fantasy then fact. In the light of "knowing" faith fades quickly and all desire to "know" in human terms ceases to be important anymore. Faith is acceptance that the mystery of the tree is no more important than the mystery of the seed. All that is important is the "knowing" that is without human description and physical form. True faith is a release from that which we have believed to accepting that outside of our beliefs there really exists the unbelievable!

Chapter 5

Emotions; Trees and Human Bark

A significant part of our existence, our reality, consists of the emotional states we switch from throughout the course of our day and these states subsequently give texture and form to the experience of living. We identify others as their emotional state and sometimes in describing them, we will reference such states. For instance, we might describe someone as moody, happy, full of life, vibrant, sad, depressed, angry, mean, kind, caring, fearful, and others.

Emotions are taught to us and when we recount our own lives or watch young parents raise their children, we see this teaching of emotional states. We might recall our own parents describing a situation, perhaps someone falls ill or dies, and we are told that we should be sad and feel remorse. As children, we don't fully understand these terms but as we watch other adults play out their emotions in various situations, we learn to feel sadness, anger, happiness, joy or whatever emotional reaction a given situation elicits.

Our conditioning includes the connection to events occurring in three dimensional reality and their subsequent transition into emotional states. Emotions become the strongest part of our egos in that they can rarely be dealt with in rational terms. In other words, it is much harder to change what we feel emotionally than what we know intellectually. Sometimes knowing is connected to feelings (emotions) and the ability to change is even greater. It is true that feeling is exhilarating and at times our physical bodies tingle all over with goose bumps or the hair on the back of our necks stands on end.

Events and situations that cause emotional states in us are long remembered and deeply impressed upon by our psyche and these impressions become our view of reality. It is as if the cells of our bodies, our biology as it were, holds the memory of the original experience. It is literally etched into us. We all know such times in our lives when things happened that left what we call an emotional impression on us and the recollection of such events always brings with it our emotional state at that time. Emotions as a part of our existence are a great gift of three dimensional reality. They allow us to feel a state of awareness brought about by the physical reaction we have to any given experience. We learn these states and the reactions we're supposed to have to them. Throughout the course of our lives, as experience is added upon, so too our emotional states are added upon and reinforced.

Emotions can be generally categorized as that which makes us joyful or happy and that which makes us sad or unhappy. Happy and sad creates the basic duality we find in our existence and the major creator of most conflicts. The events of our lives and their subsequent emotional states fall, in varying degrees, into one of these states. As children, we did not know such emotional states. We came to know, through conditioning, that certain acts we engaged in were met with disapproval (unhappiness) or approval (happiness) which over time have been locked into our minds and bodies in such a way that the emotional states have become a part of the way we view and respond to life. On the extreme side, as young children we may have experienced abuse or neglect by adults more powerful than us and whom we could not challenge or rebut. In such cases we develop strong emotional states such as fear, anger or frustration and because of the circumstances in which these states developed it is often impossible to ever know how they came to be. At a pre-language age the intellectual ability to articulate such emotional states did not exist and so we simply have the emotions without the explanation for them. Often these are never reconciled even as mature, well-adjusted adults. Most emotions run deep and are very personal to the point of being painful physically.

The duality at play with our various sad, happy states puts us in the realm of judging life events, emotionally, as good or bad and based on our particular conditioning that elicited those states. It puts our life on one side or another of something that is totally ego made. In fact, when you consider the age at which most of our emotional states developed we were far too young and immature to reason in any way what was going on that caused the state in the first place. At such an age we are highly susceptible to those we look to for protection and security and they, having been conditioned much the same have no other way but to share what they were led to believe and emotionally feel. It is difficult to break out of a cycle when you don't have the faintest idea that you are even in a cycle. Thus, children learn emotional states that play on the side of happy or sad depending on the circumstances they are shown and life becomes the ordeal of "sides" that we spend our lives being on this one or the other. Ego is the great divider.

One of the best ways to know how ego works in your life is to observe how much passion is involved in a particular issue you find yourself connected to. If there are two sides to an issue, and there always are in a duality, and you are passionately devoted to one or the other, ego has a tight grip on your life. Emotionality is the egoic way to make us believe that our cause or purpose is important. Passion is often looked at as something we must have when pursuing our dreams. It, too, is referred to when someone has enacted what we might refer to as great evil, e.g. "crimes of passion. Passion gives us a sense of gravity and importance for our various causes. It is our greatest display of caring which has become a noble act. This is how we come to care.

Children are not born caring. They are taught to care and what to care about. Children are actually born with *will* which is the motivation of the gods. Will is action. It is not passion or caring and you see this in children as they grow from infancy up to the ages of seven or eight. They are infinitely curious and completely without fear of any kind. They don't know fear. How could they? Fear takes training and conditioning like all other emotions. In fact, fear has become a widely used and accepted training tool to teach the duality of life which adds complication to our own navigation of it. "Others can hurt you…, fear for your life." "Don't do that or you'll be punished." Everywhere we hear fear being used as a means to condition others to do, or not do, something we believe to be wrong or right.

We also see the converse of this as well in that people will use rewards and accolades to condition us to move a certain direction. "Do this and you'll be rewarded." Guilt, which is another form of fear, is one of the ego's greatest tools to get us to accept the condition of our, so called, reality. All the emotional states we know get intertwined into a web of life that distorts and confuses the innate awareness we all possess. We confuse reality with our conditioning and say things and ask of others to follow our reasoning based on years of "getting to" the way we are.

We attach the greatest of our meaningful words to our emotions and use them as tools to control and manipulate others around us. The conditional word "if" has become one of our great guilt devices when it is attached to a statement designed to initiate guilt in us. For instance, you may hear someone say "If you respect me, you will not talk to me that way," or perhaps one of the most widely used by teenagers, especially boys, "If you love me, you'll let me." We all know what it feels like to feel guilt, sadness, joy, happiness and all the other emotional states we ascribe to the human family, but we never seem to ask where they came from. In fact, we have institutionalized all forms of emotions and created barriers around them that make them further unbreakable shackles around the situations and circumstances of our lives.

Most of us feel life through these emotional shackles and we all tend to teeter-totter between the various ups and downs we experience emotionally and these states become tightly fused to the individual we become over time. In essence, life is one big emotional experience. We look for balance, but have difficulty finding it because something opposite of what we wanted appears in our reality becoming the next "thing" in a continuous cycle of going from the state of happiness to unhappiness. With all the emotional conditioning we come to accept as reality, we begin using familiar platitudes such as "That's life" or "That's the hand I was dealt", etc. to placate our particular state.

There is much being said in the world today that we attract what we think about. We are told to think of only good things, such as abundance, good relationships, successful job or career, bigger home or car, kids that mind, non-meddling in-laws, and any number of other things we have determined will make us individually and collectively happy. We are told to think about only those things that will make us happy and by so doing we will attract them to us. We are also told that if we "feel" for things with deep emotion, even passion, they will manifest sooner as emotions engage the universe, we are told, to a much larger degree.

Who doesn't want only the biggest and best things in life, e.g. the things we have been conditioned to believe are important such as careers, homes, wealth, happy and fun relationships, mental and physical health, spiritual understanding etc.? So important have these things become in our reality that all of our identity is wrapped up in achieving them. Such has become the measure of success. Even those who would profess to help us achieve such things will use the emotions of fear and guilt to have us use their particular techniques for gaining all the things we have come to define success or a happy life as.

How often do we hear from them a confirmation of "bad economic times" in order to drive home the message that we need what they have? Fear the times "out there" but "Oh wait, I can help you!" We all tend to condition our assertions with the preface of what's wrong with something before inserting our particular viewpoint as the solution! Here's a truth: *there are no unsuccessful lives!* In human terms only, the odds of any one of us being here at this time and in our own unique place and circumstances is so remote as to defy all statistical laws. Your being here is one of the greatest miracles to have ever occurred and couldn't possibly be considered anything but successful! Even knowing this the ego wants something more to be convinced so we must spend our lives struggling to achieve something it knows will never happen and ultimately sends us into fits of emotional despair.

The egoic mind will never be able to comprehend a life without emotion. It is simply too wrapped up in the idea that emotion is what gives life feeling, richness and passion. In fact we are often told that our emotions can be a good barometer of whether our focus and intentions are good or bad. "If it feels good, do it" we are told.

How about that? I love to eat rich, sweet and gooey foods that are fattening and if used excessively, unhealthy. But I love the sensation of taste and exhilaration I feel when I eat such foods. It truly does "feel good!" I love to drink sugary soft drinks, and to eat salty snacks and treats and nothing could be finer then a Snickers bar and a Coca Cola! I love doing only certain things at my job so I will only do those things from now on. I hate cooking for my children so I will no longer do it since it does not make me feel good. I hate school but love sex. Gambling gives me a euphoric high as do various drugs. "Do that" we are told because those things make us happy and we don't want the downside of happiness to play out in anyway in our lives. Make more money because money will set you free to do more of the things you believe make you happy such as travel, fine dining, more recreation, more things, etc. Nothing could be more absurd than using the emotional sense of feeling good as a barometer for what we pursue and experience in life!

We are also told that the stronger we feel about something the more quickly it will show up in our experience. "Get emotional about your wants and desires." This, we are told, is the way to "align" our minds to the things we need to have in our lives in order to be happy, successful and ultimately fulfilled. This, however, is the essence of illusion because when we are in these emotional states we become convinced that something greater and more magnificent is just a little ways off, out there, waiting for us to set our focus on and achieve. So too are the negatives we experience. All these things play into the idea that out there somewhere is a solution to our various emotional states and that our focus on whatever it is, is the way to either enhance or overcome a particular state. This is exactly what ego wants us to believe. This is the illusion we are in and as long as we accept that life comes to us from out there somewhere in the universe we will never regain control of a non-illusory life. Our emotions tie us directly to what we think is real and the current thinking is that we are choosing between positive outcomes over negatives ones because we can emotionally control events outside ourselves.

This is how we are told the law of attraction works but what we are not told is that we do not have to live a life predicated on the choices we must make. The mind is the sole creator of the duality we experience when, in fact, we do not have to make choices. We can replace choice with knowing. That is, the intuitive knowing we all possess if we but learn to hear our own inner voice that is completely detached from anything physical. We have all heard this voice and know it, if we let ourselves remember what it was like as a child when we walked the earth without fear or any idea that we were not the creative center of the universe. We all knew this at one time, and experienced life in a way we cannot fathom as adults. Infant children have no concept of choice until we teach it to them. Infant children are without emotion until we show them, through our own responses to the "choices" we have been conditioned to identify and respond to.

Every one of us learns and eventually teaches what we have learned to others in our experience and we teach in a very absolute way. We even say things like "I don't want my children to go through some of the experiences I had. We want those we teach to avoid what we identify as our own mistakes or trials, not considering that what we are teaching them is what was taught to us. Coupled with specific teachings we are also taught how to feel about a particular situation. By observation of others close to us, who exhibit their emotional responses to life's twists and turns we in turn learn how to emotionally respond to our own set of life's twists and turns. It might be said that the only way we hurt our children is by teaching them what we believe and how to feel about those beliefs. In other words, our slants, slants them! We condition out of them what was conditioned out of us and we do it unknowingly.

We like to say "We choose our life based on our values." We like to believe that our values are what we are at our core, even though we are born into this world without any earthly values. Again, values are something we are taught and our so-called values are a reflection of those who taught us theirs. We are born gods with nothing but light and inner knowing that exceeds all the knowledge man has acquired to this point. We are conditioned to be human with earthly values and are expected to acquire emotional states which attach us to the outer world. We have come to believe that the way we see is "what is."

There is nothing wrong with finding or having happiness in our lives, but the nature of life as we have come to accept it calls for opposition in all things. This means that with the happiness we seek comes the unhappiness also. Many new age teachers and self-help gurus will tell us this is necessary for contrasts so that we know the difference between the two. This idea is not so in the spiritual form. Being spiritual means that every aspect of life experience is there to enjoy and embrace in every way possible. Life is sweet. No part of it is "not sweet" to the god within us. This is why we are here and just being here in physical form is our only purpose.

None of our emotional states have any meaning other than, we, as gods, having this incredible human experience, get to experience all the things our humanness allows us to experience. We are already greater than any of the conditions or circumstances we experience here on earth and we cannot fail in the experience! As part of our conditioning we talk a lot about success and failure but the fundamental aspect of human experience is that we cannot fail at life. Our existence is so much more than the experience of our unique humanness. Regardless of our choices there is no wrong or right. There simply is no choice that can alter the essence of what you are nor can it alter the experience you will have as a god living in a human body. Life sings; it always sings, in spite of how we feel about it or the choices we make, as humans, or what parts of it we like or dislike. Life is always honest and sings in spite of our emotional conditioning or judgments of it.

Siddhartha, who would become the first Buddha, began his spiritual life searching for the reasons for all the suffering in the world. It perplexed him and while he became enlightened, he never saw an end to suffering, violence and calamity. He even experienced great loss when his own family and childhood home was captured and destroyed by warring factions. He experienced everything life offered including physical ailments and old age. However, when he was old and coming to his own end, he told his closest followers, "Life is so very sweet." He never saw an end to suffering and violence or any of the things he sought to understand when he began his journey. He only saw the "sweetness" of it all and his life was complete. He died in peace, even though his dying may have been caused by diseased food. None of it mattered. Life, all of life, was sweet, for Buddha, but so too can it be for us, if we let go of our emotional judgments of it.

The author Haruki Murakami is often quoted with his observation that "Pain is inevitable. Suffering is optional," The mind creates suffering out of the false notion that "pain" need not be existent in our experience. It is craziness to think we can go through life without everything that it encompasses which includes pain. The unique ability of the mind, however, is to create a drama, a story that paints the walk through life as treacherous, dangerous or, sometimes, unexciting. All suffering resides in the mind! So does happiness!

Our emotions can be thought of as a thick shell that forms around us which protects us from the onslaughts of those things we believe can hurt us or the way to let in and embrace those things we believe bring pleasure. Emotions are the feedback of ego that either harden or soften with life experience. We are literally wrapped in our emotions and our bodies have been conditioned to reflect the sensations we have equated with certain experience throughout our lives. For most our emotions harden us to the things we believe are harmful to us and in the process of hardening we lose our sensitivity to the wonders that surround us.

Growing up in the Pacific Northwest, I have always had a certain affinity to trees. Washington State is referred to as the Evergreen state and it was difficult to go anywhere without having a sense of being surrounded by trees of every kind, but most of all, evergreens. As a boy, I loved walking in pine scented forests on warm summer days and smelling the richness of the soil mingled with the bark of various trees, shrubs and undergrowth. I remember thinking, as I wandered about those thick, forested areas that I could actually hear the smells. It was as if all the various scents of everything living gave off a noise or vibration that my ears could hear. And yet, it wasn't my ears that heard it. It was something deeper and more mysterious that I could not identify. It was as if my entire body vibrated at the same frequency of this buzz and mingling of so many life forms. The colors filled me with more than visual stimulation. I could hear them too.

Everything was alive but not in the ordinary sense that things live. There was a buzz to all of it that affected something else inside of me other than my physical senses. I was simply alive with an illumination and everything was a part of it. It was the dance of the living and I was caught up in it in such a way that it filled me with wonderment and awe. To be so tuned into the brilliance and loudness surrounding me, to this day, is one of the greatest experiences of my life and rarely do I feel the closeness to life I felt then.

It seemed then that the trees knew me and while amongst them, I knew them as well. I cared for them, then, as I do now. I sensed them in a way that I could almost hear them speak to me and each time this happened, I knew of their gentleness and their great connection to earth and sky. I often found myself, sitting in the cool shade they provided, wondering what it was like to reach for the sky as they did and how beautiful it must be to see the things they saw. I would also wonder what the part of them I could not see, the roots, experienced. There was as much of them in the earth as above it. I knew the trees knew the earth in a way I could not possibly know and so I asked them what it was like to know the world above and below at the same time. They answered that knowing what they know could only come from being as they are – still, quiet, strong and ever sensitive to the heartbeat of life. They always listen quietly, but steadfastly, for the sounds of every living thing. Their roots reached deeply into the earth and could feel her heartbeat tapping out a rhythmic song that soothed all who could hear it.

They told me I could hear the earth's heartbeat if I listened and was very quiet. I would press my ear against the tree and while I could not hear a rhythmic beat as they described it, I felt the warmth of the bark against my face. It was the same warmth I felt when I laid my head on my mother's lap. It was comforting warmth that penetrated my soul and I found myself sensing their life more vividly than any human. It never occurred to me that the trees I loved to be amongst were not as alive and aware as I or anyone else. I sensed their connection to the earth and air.

Like sentinels, always watching within and without. At that time, I knew nothing about the dimensionality of existence. I only marveled that the ability of trees to see into the earth and into the heavens must give them an awareness of life on earth as no other. I appreciated their tenderness toward me. They gave me shelter from the rain, shade from the sun and always security. I felt safe when with them.

I don't know the science or biology of tress. I think everyone believes they are living; however, it is not likely that science would accept that trees are conscious and aware, like humans. Conscious awareness is a product of the brain, they would tell us, and trees do not have brains. Perhaps the greatest act of the arrogance of man is to consider himself the highest of all life forms on earth. It is an egotistical view of life to think that consciousness resides only in humans and to a lesser degree that humans can judge the intelligence of so-called lesser life forms. We know that all things, whether we consider them animate or inanimate, live. Life is a vibration, a dance of particles so small that science, with all its sophisticated instrumentation, cannot detect.

We are a part of that dance that everything is a participant in. Everything on this planet, in the universe, is alive and conscious of its own dance and if we put aside the idea that, because of our brain we somehow know better, we too can experience the vibration. We participate in the vibration whether we sense it or not. Only the ego steers us away from that knowing. Odd that while all things dance to life, man, the so-called highest of all life forms on earth, has created a device that shields him from the dance that everything else in life experiences. That device is our emotions which harden with the onslaught of life experiences or soften when we perceive that experience is nonthreatening. It need not be that way, but we have let our ego create in us a self-importance that is only recognizable by other self-important egos.

When I was amongst the trees of the forest, I never felt the judgment I constantly felt among my fellow humans. I knew no shame or embarrassment and always had a rich sense of who I was at a deeply inner level that I could easily access in their presence. I wore no masks and had I done so the trees would have seen through it. As I have grown older, the strong feelings I have when among trees continues. I feel a sense of deep reverence and I am comforted in their presence. I still talk to them and they to me, although they seem more guarded than when I was a child. I think perhaps they are not as trusting of adult humans as they are of children because adult humans have not proved to be the best stewards of all things animate or inanimate. I wonder.

When I think about trees and humans now, I am struck by the definition we might give to each when we compare them. The tree, we might say, is strong, rigid, and immovable, while the human is fragile, vulnerable, and flexible. Emotionally speaking, however, the opposite is more likely the case. Unlike the tree, the ego of man has become strong, rigid and immovable; emotionally bound to thoughts and fears. The tree, like man, has a shell around it – its bark.

The bark of the tree is soft compared to the inner surface which the bark protects. However, it is the bark that is exposed to the world in which the tree stands. The bark feels the cold blast from a northern wind or the heat of a sun drenched summer day. It takes the rain in spring and the snows of winter. All that Mother Nature throws at the tree is absorbed by the bark that always stays soft relative to the inner tree. Humans, on the other hand, whose bark is the ego, become rigid, and inflexible when subjected to the barbs of life inflicted by other humans or natural circumstances. Instead of remaining soft and flexible to life, as the tree, humans build defenses and barriers that shut out anything that has caused pain, suffering and sorrow. The tree, on the other hand, is always open to life. Every aspect of it! Regardless of the perils it faces, it stands tall and erect, impeccable, living life to the very end without any hardening whatsoever toward those things it naturally faces in life.

Ego becomes so emotionally hardened that any sense of inner strength is vanquished and life becomes limited and a struggle to avoid those circumstances which caused it to harden itself originally. Ego does not live life; it avoids it. The bark of a tree embraces life in every way remaining soft, flexible and open to everything that comes its way.

We could all learn a great deal from trees and other living things. Other living things accept life in all its forms and, rather than fight against, they live with it, accepting all that life offers and basking in the light of each new day. Regardless of what each day brings, we should embrace it and revel in each spectacular moment it provides. Like my friends the trees, our bark, our egos, our emotions should weather the storms of life and never harden against it. Like the trees we should stand strong and tall, absorbing all that life brings to us and not stand against it.

As a boy and now as a man, I've always known trees to be gentle of spirit, but strong, and powerful and yet with all that strength, they stood quiet, majestic and strong. Even when the wind blows and catches their branches, they bend and sway gracefully, accepting everything about the experience they have. When the wind blows, they remain calm and gracefully move with it. They adjust to it calmly and quietly. I used to lay on my back looking up through the branches and watch them move gently in the wind and marvel at how flexible, how accepting of everything they were. It made me smile as I watched them live with ease and grace. Those were magical times and even now, I can detect an aura about them not unlike that of humans. The auras of trees, however, are always pure without any distortions; they lose no energy to life, like we humans do. Trees move gracefully with life while humans find reasons to move against it; fight it and question why.

Bark is to trees what emotions are to humans. Like bark our emotions should not become resistant to the surroundings or circumstances we find ourselves in. Instead of letting our minds create barriers to life and hardening ourselves to the rich and complex circumstances we encounter, like the bark of trees, we need to gracefully move with everything we experience and accept everything that touches us along the way.

Otherwise we miss the splendor of experience that human existence offers. I am often surprised by gurus and others who make statements about individuals who no longer serve them and that they must cut them loose from their circle of acquaintances. What a loss! "You no longer serve me!" What about our service to them? This is a hardening. Our view of life and everything that happens in our particular experience need not ever be reason to harden ourselves against it.

Emotions are the sensory conversion of physical experience into spiritual awareness. The softer they become the more of that experience we enjoy and the more expansive it becomes. If we can find a way to recognize that our emotions are an aspect of the human experience that need not become the predicate of that experience we can begin to open ourselves to a far grander sensory experience. Even those things that we find distasteful about our human experience can be gems that brighten our lives and add variety, richness and enjoyment. We owe to ourselves to be open to such vastness of experience.

Chapter 5

Cosmic Deception

In early 1980, after I had worked and scratched my way from an inspector to various levels in a quality organization, I was allowed to take a position as a quality manager for a small company located in my home town. It would be the beginning of a long career of managing quality and operations organizations for many companies I would work for in the future. In that first managerial position, I was given a book by a great man and mentor titled The New Managerial Grid by Blake and Mouton. I eagerly read the book as I was determined to be the best manager I could be. Without prior experience or a college education, I was determined to keep up with new ideas and concepts that would help me stay up with, or ahead of, those who were better educated. Reading that book would give me my very first exposure to the "Maslow Hierarchy of Needs" as they applied to workers in a typical workplace. I was fascinated by the simplicity of the hierarchy that placed basic needs, such as food, shelter, water, etc. at the base of the pyramid and the higher form of "self-actualization" at the top. In between the bottom and top levels, there were other levels which all built upon the other lower ones and allowed greater opportunities for fulfillment in life, developmental growth, and ultimately, the discovery of inner self.

As I moved through my career keeping this managerial model always in mind, I was always curious about the lack of self-actualized people I found at my level and those above me. It seemed that as I observed those who reached levels of attainment and comfort described by the hierarchy, the fewer "self-actualized" individuals there were. What I did find was what appeared to be a higher determination to achieve even more of the things they felt were important and essential to life. Even those who reached a place where the rest of the world would say they were highly successful seemed to be unsatisfied and wanting more.

I would marvel at some of the descriptions these so-called successful people would come up with to define what it was they needed to feel successful or happy themselves. It always boiled down to more and the "more" was just more grandiose versions of the same things they had already attained. As I had accepted this reality, I was sure that all of these others had simply misunderstood the concepts of the hierarchy of needs and that somehow I got it. I reasoned that when I attained financial stability and had attained all the things at the lower levels of the pyramid, I would surely "actualize" and my soul would surely stand on holy ground. I knew I would be the one to realize my spiritual nature and find the place within that would open me up to a pinnacle of mental, physical, emotional and spiritual well-being.

It never happened. It seems the further I went up the pyramid, the further away self-actualization would get. My problems, that were supposed to be going away, only seemed to get bigger and more complex with the passing of time. I reached a place where I could travel, purchase things I previously could not afford, etc. I had money to retire on and sufficient for my needs. There was also recognition in my job for outstanding work and enthusiasm and I was a "go to" individual when things needed to get done. I was physically healthy; I had presence and was considered a leader by my peers, subordinates and superiors. I had a wonderful family. I was able to provide just about anything they wanted that would enrich and

On Human Being

enhance their lives and I was a proud father and husband. Why, then, was this idea of self-actualization so fleeting? I never seemed to be able to get a hold of it, even though I met the requirements of the hierarchy of needs. My spirit was never at rest. In fact, it seemed to be worse than when I was scraping by. What was I missing and why was it that so many others I observed seemed to be no closer either?

This would bother me for thirty years. Then one day, I was reading from the works of Carlos Castaneda's Teachings of don Juan series of books, where he recounted the story of himself lamenting to don Juan about the poor, hapless state of some little boys cleaning the scraps of food from the tables of a little restaurant Carlos was observing. In the conversation that followed with don Juan, Carlos explained how sad it was for those boys. He even exclaimed to don Juan his great concern for his fellow men and that the world of those little boys was "ugly and cheap". This raised the ire of don Juan and he asked Carlos, "You think you are better off, don't you?" Carlos replied that he did and explained that "In comparison to those children's world, mine is infinitely more varied and rich in experience and in opportunities for personal satisfaction and development." Don Juan laughed at Carlos for this, explaining that Carlos had no way of knowing what kind of opportunities existed for those boys.

The real crux of the story continues as don Juan establishes that being a "man of knowledge" is the highest achievement for a human. A "man of knowledge" might be don Juan's way of describing a "self-actualized" individual. In any case, don Juan asked Carlos if anything he has done with any of his experience, opportunities or freedoms could help him become a "man of knowledge". Carlos answered no, and don Juan asked, "Then how could you feel sorry for those children?"

Cosmic Deception

I observed a similar thing while working with my Sister in a village in Honduras where she had bought property and had set up a small clinic for the people of that village and surrounding areas. There was every form of disease and malnutrition and every single person who came to her clinic would receive a dose of a de-worming medicine just for showing up. Parasites infested everyone because there was no infrastructure anywhere in Honduras that could provide basic needs as described above.

Dirt floors and stick huts packed with mud were common and trips to the river were where the villagers drank, washed clothing and dishes and bathed themselves. One day my sister and I were talking about the children who always seemed to be hanging around. I observed that they all seemed so happy and asked my sister if she thought these little ones stood a chance of ever having a spiritual awareness. She exclaimed immediately that it was not possible in the least as they were struggling with so many other issues that to discover their own divine nature would be impossible. I was surprised by her response and asked, "How do you explain that they all seem so happy?" Her response was just as immediate and similarly direct. "I don't know" she said, "it puzzles me too because they have nothing and they have nothing to look forward to!"

I was not satisfied with this answer and pressed her a bit further on the subject of spirituality. She insisted that "basic needs" had to be served before anyone could advance to a more "enlightened" state and that outside the work she was doing to help the little ones in her village few if any had any chance of having anything other than a life of poverty and disease. I remember being saddened by her assessment of those children and pondered the sweetness in their faces and their complete exhilaration with the life they were living. Not once did I ever hear a child complain of their circumstances and everywhere I saw gratitude and acceptance, happiness and joy. In fact, when I was getting ready to leave three of the young children wrote me letters in Spanish thanking me for coming to visit them and expressing how much they loved having me there with them. What moved me most; however, were their wishes for me. Each of these wonderful children wished for me to have "everything I desired" in life and to be happy. Without having any concept of how "good" I had things in my life, how abundant and full of the things that are supposed to help us become "actualized," these children were completely giving of themselves. What they gave was more than all the riches in the world.

They gave their love, their friendship and from the very depths of their souls they spoke to mine. They were without labels or identifiers. They knew nothing of their "lack" which was a label I, my sister and others had put on them. They were living life "sweetly" without any hold to an image others thought they should wear. Their "giving" to me was from the depths of someone deeply spiritual but without, even, the label of "spirituality."

They were divine and it didn't matter if they knew what that meant or not. Life for them was a treat as was my life when I was with them. I wept when I read the words of giving and concern for my happiness. Spiritually speaking these were the great ones. Amidst, the squalor, disease and rampant poverty, as we in the west would define it; I witnessed majesty as I have never seen it. I stood among giants and I trembled before them. I could no longer feel any sorrow for these children as my sorrow for them turned to sorrow for myself. I had become the judge of their existence and what I had seen for them was destroyed by what they already knew about existence. In desolation they knew more than I ever hoped to. They were humble; I was embarrassed. I was completely undressed by the "gods" of this tiny little village and I have never been the same since. My prayer since that visit has been that the children of this village never discover the labels we put on them and that their simple view of life never gives way to the noise of our, so called, "actualized" descriptions.

The "Hierarchy of Needs" is inverted. Surely spiritual awareness, which I had sought for so many years, is not a property of attainment, acclaim, and fulfillment of so-called basic needs. Spiritual awareness, self-actualization, or whatever you choose to call it is our very *first* aspect; it is the very core of our divine nature. How true the New Age statement that "we are spiritual beings having a human experience". There is nothing we must attain to in order to achieve spiritual awakening. In fact, it might be considered an arrogant assumption that we must somehow become something we are not, nor may ever be, in order to achieve higher states of awareness. One might ask, "What chance does the poor and infirm have of ever reaching higher states of awareness if they must rise above basic needs when such a possibility may never present itself in their lifetimes?" We all sense a kind of hypocrisy at such a question because we know that some of our greatest spiritual icons came from such circumstances. Some even went from incredible wealth and royalty to a life of poverty and begging as a way to find the awareness I was convinced must come some other way.

We are spiritual beings. Our first state of existence is a spiritual one and it is the human-ness of our earthly existence that conditions us to think that the human is not the *second* state but the first. The focal point of our existence, the peak of the pyramid, if you will, is our most basic knowing, and poverty and lack is equally able as is wealth and riches, or education and intellect, to drive us from or to that knowing. Even health is sometimes equated to a good spiritual life and yet we see so many who are sickly, even bed-ridden and near death who have clarity of life and a sweetness that can only come from a divine knowing and awareness.

Each of us, regardless of our own condition, is totally free. We can change ourselves in the blink of an eye and there is nothing in this life that can take that from us. Each of us is spiritual beyond our wildest imaginings. Gods we are, and gods we will always be. The so-called conditions we say or think prevent us from knowing are illusions of the mind-created reality which we accept as our nature. Nothing we possess or accomplish or attain in this physical reality will ever come close to our true value as divine beings who are crowned with glory from before time. Nothing in this life matters more than the re-discovery of that knowing which each of us possess as infinite beings. This is why it is so critical to learn how to quiet the mind from its endless chatter. The chatter upholds what the mind thinks we are, and consequently, we reinforce that over and over and over.

Ultimately, there is no hierarchy of needs. There is no a hierarchy at all. There is only "being". For most of us, that means finding the seeker, not the sought. The sought is ever present. The part of us that seeks must think about that which it seeks in order to know it when it finds it. The problem is that thinking is incapable of defining that which is sought and so will never find it. This is why we must stop seeking. Seeking equals thinking and thinking is to the sought as the clouds are to the sun. We know the sun is there, we just can't see it. What we are and have always been is ever present. It is only obscured by the clouds hovering over it. Clouds of thinking and chattering.

There is no circumstance or condition that precludes anyone from remembering their own divine nature. No attainment in physical life can assure us of an opportunity, greater or lesser, to find the God of our own nature and to reach a state of awareness that fully comprehends the unknown. We already know the answers to all of the questions. They lie within each of us and the discovery of them is a personal journey that only we as individuals can take. No teachers or guides are needed for this personal inner quest. Only quiet. In stillness, we know God; we know ourselves.

We can seek out guides, mentors and gurus to help us and give pointers but each of us, at some point, will be required to stand on our own and pass through the "refiners fire" alone. After passing through, we will know that the greatest part of our existence as humans has only been a shell. We will realize the power of our own spiritual nature and the physical aspect of us was nothing more than a vehicle to walk us through a human experience and that all of our identity with physical things is nothing compared to our unique and divine natures. The divine nature of man is found in every walk of life, in every condition, and every culture. There are no exclusions and the diversity of experience through the ages is testament that each of us can find our own unique path to God. Every minute of our lives doing whatever it is we do is the pathway to that discovery of self that knows the divine is within. Every turn, every climb, every twist of fate is the spiritual knocking on the door of the physical. All we must do is silence the mind and listen to the stillness.

There are no heroes outside what we are and when we decide to see that in ourselves is when we begin to understand that the greatness of life only exists because of "our own" greatness.

Chapter 6

What's Happening?

There is a greeting westerners have used for many years upon seeing each other that simply goes, "what's happening"? There was a television sitcom with the title "What's Happening" back in the 1970s as well. That query, as to what's happening, has in many ways become a greeting of sorts or an expression of good will at the meeting of friends or acquaintances. It has become a part of our language that asks others to look forward or backward and describe what has happened and what will be happening.

It is the nature of our mind created reality to steer our awareness away from the now that, in truth, is the only thing happening and, onto what is not happening. Most of us, in fact, are conditioned to never look at what is happening right now and so our lives begin to look like narratives of things past or future. They literally become what is not happening even though we like to believe that this not happening is what is really happening.

We see this not happening in every aspect of life. We are told from the very beginning of our lives to get this or that or be this or that. We are stood against examples of the things we are instructed to get or be and told this is how it should be. We are reminded that in our getting or being that that's when it will happen for us. While we are never told what "it" is the admonition to get it is forceful and persuasive. Most of us learn well and get caught up in the conditioning, reinforcing it for others and teaching it anew to our children. Rarely do we ever look at the reason the way we are is because we are taught to be that way.

Nor do we ask why we were taught to be that way and who taught our teachers to be the way they are. Most of us merely perpetuate what has been going on for generations, and what has been going on for generations is the minds version of what's happening.

The minds version of what is happening is, in fact, what's not happening? Consider the things we think about or talk to ourselves about on a regular basis. Most of our minds are talking without any conscious awareness of the conversation going on in our heads and the majority of that conversation has nothing, whatever to do with what's happening.

When I was working full time I would often think about what I would tell my boss about a certain situation or how I would run the company or department if I were in his or her shoes. I would create elaborate arguments and rehearse them over and over so if the situation presented itself I would be all ready to go. Sometimes I would talk out loud with others telling them what I planned to say or do if the right opportunity would appear. Typically, when situations or opportunities did appear for me to direct the conversation I had so carefully planned they didn't go anything at all like I thought they would. I would leave wondering what that was all about and I would find myself rehearsing what I should have said or could have said. Again, more unconscious conversation in my mind trying to resolve what's not happening. If I wasn't looking at the future I was looking at the aftermath of the past. My mind never stopped these discussions. It stressed me out.

Other things I would worry about were the stability of the company and about what I was sure would be layoffs or cutbacks that would not only affect me but many others as well. Again, my mind would begin to consider alternatives or solutions for events that had not happened and may or may not happen. I would stress out over these mind created scenarios and wonder and talk to myself, sometimes to a point of exhaustion. We all do this to some degree or another. We talk to ourselves about the spouse or children, schools, vacations, finances, politics, religious beliefs, the car, the house, mother, father, girlfriend's, boyfriends, sports, music, television, past events, future plans and so on. Each day is filled with these mind created discussions that are repeated over and over and over. Most of the time without any awareness that we're having them. Television, movies and other forms of entertainment are filled with dramas that parallel this obsession of the mind to be anywhere but in the present. Our lives are inundated with this kind of noise and hence we become victims to it. It happens to all of us. It is the result of our conditioning, hence our nature and often the result of that noise is anxiety and stress.

We are conditioned to look at what is not happening and make it a happening. Consider all the things we prattle on about and think about as that which has happened and we can't do anything about or it is that which we think about that has not happened. Whatever it is it is not happening! And if it is not happening why is it so in command of our lives?

There is a world of not happening, happening but that world only exists in our minds. We bring into the reality of now that non-reality of then and allow it to find a significant place in our present. We give non-reality, reality and allow it to violate the beauty and splendor of our present moment. This moment in time is all that exists in that it is completely pure in every way until we crowd it with non-reality.

What is not happening ever really happens in the present. Even when we bring the thought of it into our present moment, it is still not happening. We just allow ourselves to feel as though it is as if that somehow shows the nobility of concern for coming events, or that our worry and concern is a preparation for what is not happening. It is the emotions we allow ourselves to feel and express, through all this not happening that damages us. Isn't it interesting how we have created ways to feel emotionally when we think about all the things that are not happening in our present state? It is one thing to feel in present time but to feel for that which is not happening is to allow the body and mind to obsess and weaken over things it can do nothing about. Consider that events or circumstances we create in our minds that are not happening, impact the health of our bodies in the present! Only the mind-created reality of non-reality is capable of doing this.

We all know that the brain is an incredibly complex instrument that controls and monitors every aspect of the human body. It is also the instrument of cognition, reason and emotion. It is a great instrument of learning and memory, sensory input and sensory filtering. We hear often that most humans only use five to ten percent of the brain's capacity to compute and store information. We often hear this in conjunction with the admonition that we are so much greater then we think ourselves to be. If somehow we could tap into this unused part of the brain and use it more fully we could achieve and be so much more than we are now. On a physical level this may be true but remember we are more than just physical beings. We are spiritual beings first, housed in physical forms. Our spiritual nature exceeds any physical concepts, thoughts or thinking of the human mind. Yet it is the physical that we focus on the most. The mind is part of the physical reality we live in and as incredible as we believe it to be we're still so much more than that. Even if we were using one hundred percent of what we consider to be the capacity of the brain we are greater than that. Right now in this very moment we exceed any thought or thinking the mind creates.

Why then do we allow ourselves to be run by our thinking? This is one of the great mysteries of our time. Even in new thought circles we fall back to the mind or the subconscious mind as the great gift of human beings. Most will acknowledge the spirit but rarely is the intelligence of the spirit acknowledged as something outside human intelligence. Human thinking has the benefit of our physical senses which are vivid and loud and our minds have concocted the idea that anything that cannot be observed in some way by these senses either cannot be real or, in some cases, is simply reconciled as impossible. The irony is that all of us at one time or another have experienced things for which our mental state, the mind, simply cannot explain and yet it is as real, sometimes even more real, then anything we have ever experienced through our other senses.

The mind holds rigidly to its reality by talking incessantly about everything it has created an identity with. That is how it reinforces its reality and it does this constantly. Often it is working under the radar of consciousness but it is always working. Inexorably it locks us into what it conceives as important. Its tendency is to over complicate things and make life an endless series of struggles and trials. So successful has the mind, and the collective mind, been at complicating our lives that we find ourselves in this realm of what's not happening believing it is what is happening. In fact, much of our new age thought has focused on the trials and struggles we face as opportunities for growth in the physical sense. Clever tool, the mind, to convince us that the only way out of its devices is to accept that struggle and suffering is for our benefit and that through such things life improves.

Three dimensional life is supposed to be fun and it should not be complicated and fraught with struggle as the mind imagines it. A mind that is constantly looking outward for answers to the struggles and suffering in life will always look to what's not happening for those answers. It will create scenarios outside the present moment that projects an outcome that is not happening. It may even look to the past and claim that we must learn from those experiences even though, they too, are not happening. It is all too easy to complicate the present with what is not present. It is the common state most of us find ourselves in. Even the law of attraction has been distorted to such a degree that our wanting or desires are a product of what's not happening. Put your intention out there and the universe conspires to provide it for you. The problem with this is that it plays directly into the mind-created reality that once you have what you desire from out there you will achieve happiness, contentment or whatever it is you seek. We see this, as well, with the new age movement to find our purpose in life, the finding of which is our only way to freedom and happiness. People struggle endlessly to find a reason for being here. Finding purpose is the new what's not happening!

The implication of finding or wanting something in life is perhaps the strongest indication of the minds success at keeping us disconnected with what is happening from what's not happening. As long as we stay mired in the out there, what's not happening, we will never discover the in here. The in here is the place where time stops and no sense of wanting or desires exist. Everything just as it is, right now, is incredible and what we are is all there is and that is everything! There ceases to be complications with what was and what might be. Simply peace with the now and what's not happening quietly falls away. We have now and it is now where we have fullness.

The out there is a fabrication of the mind. There is nothing out there that can help you, hurt you, frighten you, strengthen you, heal you, satisfy you, teach you, etc. All that is needed is already here. It is within us at any given moment. You already know it. You need only acknowledge it. I Am is always present. I met a woman who had become unemployed and was desperately trying to find work. On her way home from an interview one day she saw the billboard sign of a business she said she had passed every single day for several years. She mentioned that for some reason on this particular day the sign just jumped out at her in a way she had never seen it before.

She decided to stop and apply for work there without even knowing they were hiring. She went into the office and asked and the receptionist provided her with an application to fill out. The receptionist mentioned the company was hiring certain positions and asked the woman what she did. The woman responded with her particular skill and expertise and was told by the receptionist that is exactly what they were looking for. The woman filled out the application, attached a resume and handed it to the receptionist.

In telling the story the woman spoke as if something quite unknown to her was working inside her. She even said the words in describing the events, "you know law of attraction and all of that." She said everything was unfolding in ways she had never experienced before and she believed an inner force was working for her.

By the time the woman drove home she had a message from the company asking if she could come in for an interview the next day. She immediately called and arranged for the meeting. She was excited; you could hear it in her voice as she told the story. She expressed how everything had fallen into place and how she just knew that attraction was at work in her life. She explained that she knew things were aligning her way and that she had never in her life seen things so clearly. It was a compelling story. She went to the interview the next day with a feeling she had never felt before and just knew everything would fall into place. She was taken on a plant tour by the human resource manager who explained how committed the company was to its employees. The benefits were among the best in the industry and by what she saw everything about the company was wonderful.

She was interviewed by seven or eight people during the course of the day and taken to lunch by the Human resource manager, as well. She recounted how every single interview was so pleasant and how she hit it off with everyone she talked to. It couldn't have been a better round of interviews and her connection to everyone she met was, as she described, uncanny. She explained that things could not have aligned better and she said she knew Law of Attraction was working in her behalf. She knew this was a special place and would be a place she could call home. She just knew she would be offered the job.

As she continued telling the story she explained that she left the interviews feeling "up" in a way she had never experienced before over anything, much less a job. The next day the human resources representative called her to explain that everyone who interviewed with her thoroughly enjoyed her and thought she would be a perfect fit for the position and a welcomed member of the company family. The woman was ecstatic! Everything was so right and had fallen into perfect place, as she put it. The Human resource representative extended her the offer of employment with great hopes she would join the company and begin work as soon as she could. Upon hearing the offer all of the sensations of alignment and connection stopped suddenly. She said that she was insulted by the offer. She said that even though salary requirements had not been discussed in the interview process she said she thought with how everything had gone up to that point that the "right" salary would fall into place as well. The offer was a few thousand dollars a year short of what she had previously made before being laid off. Rather than make a counter offer she told the representative she wasn't interested in the job at all. The phone call ended on that abrupt note.

Listening to this woman tell this story I couldn't help but think that she had completely missed the point of Law of Attraction. In fact, something far greater than the law of attraction may have been at play. It sounded like intuition had taken over the events of her life the previous few days and was guiding her down a perfect path. Higher powers were present and she knew it. Every door was opening but as soon as she heard their offer all the lights went out. She went back to all the things not happening, like her previous job and salary, and that became her happening! Instead of staying in the light she knew was guiding the situation she became insulted and offended because the company would dare make such an offer. Her "being offended" blinded her to even making a counter offer which likely would have been accepted. Her explanation was, "how dare they insult her the way they did." It was amazing to listen to her go from what appeared to be a spiritual high to an emotional low just in the telling of the story.

What's Happening?

I was saddened by the outcome of her story. I couldn't help but think of everything she would miss out on by not accepting the position. The friends made lifelong connections and a secure job with a company who would most likely have increased their offer if she had asked or raised her salary after a few months on the job. After all everyone loved her and she loved them. Families take care of their members and she had been accepted as a member before getting an offer to work there. I couldn't help but think of all the things aligning for her to have a perfect career with a company who would do everything to make her life more comfortable and enjoyable. All for naught because she was insulted.

We won't know all the circumstances of the story since it was only her recounting but it seemed to me that a lot of "what's not happening" was happening for this woman. Why the feeling of insult? Why not even a counter offer? Had past events in her life made her so sensitive that she would react in such a way? Was she going to be better off holding out for more money when up to now no offers had been extended? She lamented that she was soon to run out of her unemployment and she had no prospects. It is difficult not to make judgments about such a story but rarely have I listened to a story where the "bush" burned so bright. How much more do you need to be convinced you are being directed by the inner divine? Her life partner may have been working at the company or an acquaintance of one of her would be co-workers. There is no end to the possibilities she turned away from because she was offended. The light could not have burned brighter. At least in her telling of the story.

We can only speculate (what's not happening) as to what past events or future circumstances caused her to dismiss what she expressed at one point would be what she would do, e.g. work for this company.

Past events and future possibilities are not and never will be happening. They should never be brought into the reality of what's happening and what was happening for this young woman was a connection to higher light than she had previously known only to be shut off by some erroneous pull from the past into the nonexistent future. Light into darkness; happening into not happening!

It's just that; not happening. How often we let what's not happening become significant in our lives when what is happening right now is the only space we need to be present for. It is the human part of us that possesses this unique ability to make what is not happening into the consciousness of what is happening. Even our physical senses are overwhelmed by the power of the mind to create that which is not so. Somehow we must find a way to accept responsibility for what we intuitively know and never should we lose that knowing to past events in our lives that blind us to our inner awareness. Salaries, positions, recognition, awards, past and future events, etc. are all extraneous events we let cloud our inner knowing and the loss is tremendous.

We all need to let go of what's not happening and let what's happening be ALL that ever happens. Our true place in the world, "the ground upon which we are standing," is right now. It will never be any place else; neither should we.

Chapter 7

Duality – Monitoring Your Illusion

The egoic nature of man has become very sophisticated as the ebbs and flows of life change and alters with the times. We are living in a time some would call a spiritual awakening and individuals around the world are coming out of the proverbial woodwork to "awaken" or to help others to do so. It is a wonderful time to be alive and witness the outpouring of light and energy throughout the earth and it is happening in nearly every country on earth. Something is happening and it is wonderful. Ego sees this as well.

There is a nuance of ego that makes it so effective in its game of deception that most of us will never see it happening and go on deluding ourselves with whatever it is we have grabbed onto. The nuance of ego is that it creates its own counterpart to blend in with whatever cultural mood is taking place at the time, and it is so good at it that we actually believe we have found our inner self.

For instance, in the new age of spiritual awakening I alluded to earlier, a major part of spiritual awakening is about finding and connecting with the "inner self". I talk about this as well in the book <u>On Being God</u> and even make this inner identity the god of your experience. For those whose hearts have been opened to this new awareness, the ego subtly fools us into thinking that the part of us that is "connecting" to inner self is indeed the inner self. In its cleverness, ego even speaks the language of spirituality and we believe that that part of us is the newly found, enlightened part of us that was trying to find expression in our life. In its subtleness, this false identity proceeds to make everything we have or want in life okay.

Not that having or wanting are not okay, but one well-recognized spiritual leader of our time publicly expressed how nice it was that he could wear seven hundred dollar hand-crafted Italian shoes. He further expressed that he deserved such things, as do all of us, as if to make his desire to wear expensive hand-crafted shoes okay because collectively the rest of us who cannot afford such things "deserve" them. If I acknowledge that you deserve something but can't afford it that, somehow, makes it okay for me to have it because I can. Why would you say something like this? I don't understand this. If I but acknowledge your lack, albeit your deserving nature, I justify my "having". How does this help anyone? And yet this is a well-respected and great man who has done a tremendous amount to help thousands around the world.

"We all deserve" is an individual and collective indulgence, but it is also a part of the dual nature of the ego that dupes us into thinking we have found our spiritual nature when we have not. This is ego at its subtle best. God wants you to be rich is its mantra and you can have it all. Like Jesus being shown all the kingdoms of the world, including our own times, if he would but forsake his own soul. That is what ego asks of all of us. Look to me for everything and I will provide and ego continually dazzles us with new and improved enticements to keep us trapped in the illusion. And still our soul calls out and searches for more. Cleverly, the ego has convinced us that we should have the things it has collectively created and it is all ours if we forsake our own inner abundance. The price we pay is always too little but most of us hand it over eagerly. In fact, let's test how great our illusion is right now.

How real and unbreakable is your illusion of reality? The structures we have constructed for ourselves, individually and collectively, grip us in a way that reflects just how convincing our illusions about life are. We can sense the hold of illusion by performing this little thought test:

How strong is your illusion? If everything as you now know it was to be stripped away completely and you could reconstruct your life in any way you choose, what would it look like? How would your newly constructed life look in the face of this possibility? Please answer all of these questions honestly and don't hold back in any way:

- How would you be living? Remember you can put your life back together anyway you want. There are no limits and anything you want will be instantly yours. Again, how would you be living?
- What kind of work would you be doing or what career path would you choose? Would you be a senior member of your company's staff or would you have your own perfectly run company? You can "make it so" anyway you desire.
- What would your family look like? Perfect Mother and Father? In laws that you love or that never come around?
- How would your children be in this new creation of yours? Are they perfect angels; smart, bright, imaginative? Or maybe they are grown and changing the world in their own right.
- Who would your friends be or if you could choose the same friends, would they be different? Would you have more friends or would you have fewer. Would you change any of them or would the quality of your new friendships be different? Would you be different in your relationship with them?

- Where would you be living? Remember you can choose anywhere in the world and it is yours. Where is your "dream" place?
- What would your home look like? What would you add or remove from the home you are living in now.
- In America we speak of the "American Dream." What would your "American Dream" look like?
- What cars would you drive? Would you have more of them?
- Would you travel to foreign lands and vacation in exotic places around the world? Think of all the places you have always wanted to visit and enjoy. Do you have a "dream" vacation? Remember you will have whatever you can imagine!
- How would your financial situation look in this newly created reality? Would you have money in the bank, stocks, bonds, real estate holding such that you would never have to worry about financial things?
- What educational path would you have taken what degrees, honors, etc.? Pick your college, your credentials, honors or degrees. It is yours by simply thinking it. No limits!
- What organizations would you belong to?
- What social groups would you participate in; contribute your time and money to?
- How would you place yourself in your community? Would you actively participate in charities, church, schools, and other organizations where you believed you could contribute in significant ways? Would you do volunteer work, help the poor, etc.?
- How would you look and dress?

- Who would you know, or not know that you do now? Would your range of influence and social awareness be different than what it is now?
- What would the world look like in your newly created reality? What would government look like nationally, locally, etc.? How would international affairs be conducted and what, if any, part would you have in them?
- What things would you do that you don't do now?
- What things that you do now that you wouldn't do in this newly defined reality that you created?

Make this about you and be as lavish, imaginative or creative as you can. There are no wrong or right answers to any of the above questions. In fact, many of the questions may be misleading or distracting from where your thoughts and ideas would like to go. Go anywhere you want. The importance of the exercise is to honestly look at your life as it is now and determine how you would reconstruct it if you could. Anything is possible in the creation of your new life and all we are trying to accomplish by considering all these things is how set in "your" specific illusion you are.

Those who are honest will almost always assess these kinds of questions, and many more like them, and reconstruct their worlds along these lines. This is what we know, therefore these are the things we would tend to look at and change or improve if we could. In a lot of New Age thought, we are told that when we change our thinking, we can change our world. Much of that teaching tells us to identify our wants and to picture them and imagine with great emotion having anything we want. If a recapitulation of the past is unacceptable to you, consider those things you want and identify how such things would improve or better your life and circumstances.

Consider the things you have yet to achieve or desire at some point in your life. Much of our New Age thinking would have you focus your attention on such things as relationships, financial status, physical health, spiritual awareness, mental wellness among others. What do you desire in any of these areas? What do you focus on now that you want to have manifest in your currently reality? Let your mind go, even if you are certain none of these things will ever come about. It is the nature of your thinking we are looking at. The focus of your attention is key to understanding the complexity of your illusion. The personal intricacies of our lives and our dealings with family, friends, and acquaintances all factor in to how we view life. Our view of life is our illusion.

After giving some consideration to the reconstruction of your life and what it looks like in the new and improved version, compare it to the old. How is it different? Are you in a bigger house in a new location? Do you drive nicer cars? Do you have more money and freedom to do things you love, such as travel? Are you better educated? Is your career path moving in a new direction with higher position, more money and prestige? Do you participate in associations and charitable organizations? Are your children in the best schools with prospects for great futures? Are your relationships uplifting and fun and are you adored by family and other outside acquaintances? Are you fit and attractive regardless of age? Does the world make sense to you and are local and national governments doing everything exactly as you believe it should be? Are the stresses and complications you know now gone in this new life? Are you happier and more relaxed? Compare all the aspects of your newly created life with those you currently know. Now ask, "What is the difference between them?" Before continuing on really consider this newly described state you have created and how much improved your life is with all the things you have brought into your new reality. Breathe it in as if it had really happened and consider how you are feeling in this new place. Consider how much better life is now.

Now, in truth, what has really changed? For most of us, the difference can be measured in size, quantity or quality, relative to what currently is. A bigger house, more money, better relationships, etc. This is our, so called "new" illusion but it's really no different than the illusion we had before it! Our conditioning is so confining that we honestly believe that the extension of what we already know, what we already have in size, quantity and quality is what will make us happy and more content in life. We have accepted the myths that more money will give us greater freedom to do the things we want.

And what are the things we want? More of the same! A bigger, more comfortable house in the more exclusive neighborhood is still a house. The natural extension of this new dream house is an even bigger house in the mountains or on an ocean beach or perhaps a second house for the summer, or winter. Our conditioning has created the illusion that bigger is better. More of the same seems to be our motive to think ourselves into greater accomplishment or greater freedom.

We have even been conditioned to accept that greater accomplishment, more money, stature and position is the true meaning of success. Look how successful "so and so" is and we make that a marker for ourselves to emulate. "How to" books are written and the lives of the successful, as we have come to define them, are paraded in front of us as the model for how we should live our lives, and in so doing, we too can be successful. You can have manifested in your reality more things, credentials and wealth, and you will escape the travails of your current existence. Replace what you have and are with bigger and better versions of what is and you will be a success. Have or be anything you want. Visualize abundance as defined by the illusion you live in and you will bring it into existence. This is our illusion!

Here is what the illusion is not. There are no unsuccessful lives; No, not one! If we were to look at the life of Jesus in our terms today, he would be an abject failure. In gathering up his followers after his death, his apostles managed to find 120 people who believed in him. That is all he had to show for three years of absolute commitment to his teachings and hard work. Not to mention his ignominious death and burial. Buddha would be judged the same in our modern day terms. For Buddha, he was a royal prince endowed from birth with all the things we believe define success. He had it all and for some reason, he gave it all up to put himself in the midst of those who had nothing; or what we might define as the unsuccessful. By today's standards, some would say he gave up success to be a failure or that he could have done more if he had harnessed his wealth and put it to use to teach and spread his message. Most would, for sure, consider him to be crazy.

No one actually believes Jesus and Buddha were failures, yet the measure of value and worth we use to identify successful people today are the very things they put aside. If such things are the mark of success, then why would two of the most "known and influential" people in history completely fail to measure up to such standards? In fact, in the case of Buddha, why would he give up everything we define as successful after having it handed to him on a platter? These are unanswerable questions if you hold to a modern day definition of success.

Our egoic drive to create an image of success and to form a culture that recognizes earthly value, means, affluence, credential and all the other things we place such high value on, is exactly the opposite of what the Buddha and Jesus taught while they walked the earth. Neither of them sought fame, popularity or wealth and yet they lived abundant, rich and full lives. Lives on their terms. Their success was the awareness of the inner self and that awareness was their freedom.

Not the freedom we have come to define as "having means so we are free to do more" but exactly the opposite. Being free of means so they were able to "be" and consequently do things that in today's terms we call miracles and concede only they could do. Not doing more in the sense of being able to do things that give us earthly pleasure, but doing more to understand their own innate natures – their "being" which was that of gods. When we focus on the illusion of success we have created for life, we push away God. We are gods, so who is it really we are pushing away?

Success, as we have come to know it, is a highly egocentric, consequently illusory, idea we have created for collective society. In Western society, and more particularly in American society, we have even created a sort of arrogance that says that unless those of poorer circumstances are raised to the level of our definition of success, they cannot find the greater enlightenment we claim to have found. Hence the statement often heard that money or means gives us more freedom. In fact, it is now widely believed and taught that greater wealth provides more freedom. Freedom comes not in the attainment of those things we describe as successful, but in the letting go of all the illusory ideas about success we have come to accept.

"That which we hold on to holds us." The nature of ego is to accumulate, own and possess. In actuality, to truly have more freedom, we must learn to care less about the things we think freedom is and care more about what we believe it is not. Most of us believe that freedom is something we are given by a benevolent government or institutional authority that allows us to move more freely in society. We build militaries to defend our "rights" and protect our freedoms, believing that somehow freedom, having been given to us, must be protected and defended. In the political sense other collectives may try to take away that which we claim to be freedom, but the reality is that freedom is not a right we should expect to be handed to us or defended for us. The truth is we are free; always! Even under the arm of tyranny or abject slavery we are all free. We of our own free will give away our freedom to an illusion that anything in this life matters more than "who we are" outside anything we have or don't have.

The ultimate slavery, and exactly the opposite of our collective idea of freedom, is accepting that life comes with conditions or definitions we accept as true. Allowing your thoughts, your dreams, or actions to be outlined in the terms of those whom you have trusted through the course of your life, whether they be individuals or institutions, is real slavery and it is slavery of your own making. Ultimate freedom is not an inherent right to choose, it is however, to simply be that which you are outside any construct *you* have created for yourself. It is not what we are that restricts us. It is what we have come to think we are that does. Freedom is being the god that you are, and gods never make choices because they are free, by our collective definition, to do so.

When we say "we have the right to choose whatever we want" we are not describing freedom. We are describing the dual concept of choice that implies that something we have labeled as our right must be fought for, else we could lose it.

Freedom is not something that can be lost, or taken. Regardless of the condition we find ourselves in, or whatever walk of life we come from, we as gods are free. And no circumstance, power or condition can take that away from us. We often hear people, when referring to freedom, say something like "this is what I believe freedom to be" and then go on about what it is in three dimensional terms, including the ultimate right to make choices that affect their life situation. *Those who have choices have no freedom.* Living a life that is deciding the better of choices is a life of captivity and it only exists because we have allowed the illusion of our particular life to dictate a set of rules we choose to live by and call it freedom. Gods have no rules, thus no limitations and without limitations there is no choice that ever needs be made nor is there anything to be free from.

Ideology only exists in the human mind. In other words, it is a description or idea, we as humans create, of something that can only be described in human terms. Ideology does not exist in the realm of gods. Gods have nothing to defend and that is the ultimate freedom! Nothing is judged. The oppressor is just as enslaved as the oppressed when he must uphold his belief at the cost of suppressing others, while the oppressed enslave themselves by judging the oppression unfair or unjust. The two are not different and view freedom in only three dimensional terms. Freedom has nothing to do with choices and anyone who is in between two choices will not be free because he or she chose one or the other. Freedom comes not by choosing. It comes by being; knowing full well the extent of your own divine nature and knowing you are God frees you from anything that looks like a choice.

Choosing ties us to outcomes and leads to a succession of choices that, hopefully, lead up to that outcome. Being is never tied to outcomes and subsequently is free of any consequences we imagine deprive us of freedom. Freedom is really acceptance that our particular life is rich with experience that adds to our enjoyment as gods. We either move through life the victims of our choices or the recipients of a richness that accepts experience as nothing more than experience. In other words there are no right or wrong choices because choices do not exist. Freedom is knowing; knowing at the intuitive level that our lives are directed at a higher awareness than we allow ourselves to accept. True freedom is intuitive knowing. Choices are non-existent to the individual who recognizes their own divine nature. The only thing standing in the way of this knowing is our own conditioned lives that have us convinced that, not only do we not know, but that we cannot know.

Our reality is the product of what we have come to believe is important in life. Most of this belief, if we are honest with ourselves, was taught to us and is centered on the things others have taught us are important to maintaining a *safe*, life. The safe life asks that you accept the conditions of your experience and not extend outward too far, and by so doing you can expect reasonably predictable results. This is why when we are reassessing our so called wants we typically visualize or objectify bigger versions of what we already have or what others have that we would like to have in our experience. This is a safe approach and frees us from looking deeper within at the divine self that not only perceives more but sees that what we say we want is beneath the nature of our innate selves. The human moves toward safety, security and comfort while the divine moves toward adventure, richness and experience. The safe life is slavery.

We are greater than any experience or culmination of experiences yet common to our human nature is to subjugate ourselves to our experiences and determine that they are a pathway, to the greatness we know ourselves to already be. This is our greatest folly. Our illusion creates needing and wanting and both of these pull on a false duality that only exist because we see life as something out there that is needed in one sense and wanted in another. Ask anyone what they really want or what they really need and you will almost always get an answer that reflects a bigger and better version of what they already have. "I want a bigger house with a bigger kitchen or study, lots of bathrooms, bigger yard, etc." Or they may want a better job, more money and greater "freedom" to do and see things. It is part of the egoic deception that "having more, gives you more". In egoic terms, having more does give you more but it is just more stuff! It is more egocentric stimulus and the more you can acquire and possess the more adept you become at justifying it. And all it costs is your true spiritual nature.

In much of new age thought, the idea of gathering more has been extended to include purpose and meaning for life itself. There is a tremendous amount of energy being expended trying to find a reason for our being here in the first place. Finding this, for many, has replaced the gathering of *things* aspect of life, but has also taken on obsessive qualities. It seems many are letting go of the idea that they must gather things to them in favor of taking on more meaningful experiences that adds, so called, value to others.

Having and getting what's out there, whether it be shoes, cars, homes, wealth, acclaim or purpose, is always egoic. *Wanting is egoic.* Even wanting what our conditioning tells us is good and noble, such as "wanting to make a difference in the world" or other gestures to help or improve mankind. The reason it is egoic is that such "wanting" is driven by the illusion that our wanting for others what "we" think they need, want or, better yet, *deserve,* is our perception of how something should be out there. It has nothing to do with knowing who it is that dwells in us that is completely happy with everything that goes on in human experience. Who we are judges nothing; it loves everything!

Our wanting for others reinforces our illusion of what we have come to believe is what others want. We need to disconnect from what we want, or what we think others need or deserve and simply *act* because that is what the God within each of us does. It acts; that is all. It is difficult to comprehend this, because as soon as we determine what is best for someone, or decide what we must do for them, we invalidate them and ourselves as well. The god within each of us speaks to everyone regardless of how we define others physical conditions. We will all hear in our own way and respond from a place of inner knowing that will only concern us individually. It will be in this space that our reaching out will look compassionately on other gods experiencing life as they do and loving them fully regardless of their state.

None of us escape the illusion and those who seem to have mastered their lives and freed themselves from the "having," are never far from it. The pull of humanity is inexorable but that "being" that dwells within us sees no difference between the egoically created good or bad. Duality dissolves into living and experience without any judgments and it simply loves, appreciates and enjoys everything!

Chapter 8

Saviorism; Can You Really be Saved?

One of our greatest faith base deceptions and one that we all buy into in some form as humans is the mythology that something or someone is going to save us from whatever form of adversity we may face in our current experience. Throughout the ages humans have sought for outside sources to rescue us, or at least, to make fair what seems to be unfair in our existence. Judgment day and Karma are forms of this "making fair" scenario and most of our common mythological stories are rooted in the idea of saviorism. This idea rings in every aspect of our existence including our governments, local and national leaders, religious leaders, corporate leaders, etc.

No greater deception exists in human experience then the idea that we can and will be saved by some benevolent force that possesses power greater than our own. In fact, in our government and religious institutions we willingly hand over our own power as individuals so that they may save us from forces we believe we are unable to control. It has become more and more prevalent in western politics and that serves as a good example from which to illustrate this deception.

Regardless of our own individual politics, all government is seen as bad or good from the collective standpoint. Some faction sees the current leaders as their saviors while another faction sees it as doom and the cause of social problems whatever they may be. Both claim their own political saviorism as the way out of whatever dilemma they choose to embrace and blame the other as the cause for their existing problems. It is a vicious cycle which we, collectively, will never get out of because regardless of your political view no one can save us.

To use an example let's look at the phenomenon that occurred in America with the election of President Obama. Candidate Obama articulated an inspiring message to the American people and utilized social media to reach the electorate in unprecedented ways. His message of hope inspired people on every level of the population. Conservatives who would not think of voting Democratic in a presidential election did exactly that because they were so uplifted by the message of hope proffered by candidate Obama.

This breaking of ranks swept him into the presidency with a huge popular vote. Exit polls of voters from both parties spoke in fervent terms, saying they "believed" President Obama would bring a better day to the American landscape. In other words He could save us from the likes of his predecessor and all of his errant ways. It was a remarkable feat for President Obama to be able to whew so many into believing he could save us from the failures of the previous administration. But it took the idea of the collective that a savior was possible in the first place to make such an outcome happen. The people cried out, "we need a savior" and the response of the campaign of candidate Obama was, "I can save you."

There was a hope and enthusiasm amongst, not only Americans, but the world as a whole. New leadership followed by an era of prosperity and all eyes looked again to America as a leader in the world. Without making this a political statement all the expectation and hope, the freshness of a new and energetic president did not go as expected. In fact, after just a few years into the presidency the collective disillusionment was as great or greater than it had been with the previous administration. In just a few short years a growing collective cries out to be saved from him! What happened?

It is a timeless condition of the human experience. "Somebody save me!" Even with the full power of the President of the United States of America President Obama was remiss to save any of us from the perceived ills we see in the United States and the world at large and so we sit back, frustrated yet again. We say to ourselves, "I thought He was the one," but He wasn't. And so we look again for the next "savior" who may be waiting in the wings. We just know he or she is out there!

Religious institutions reflect the same kind of outward looking as well. Jews continue to look for another king David who will rise up and put down all the enemies of Israel and save them from a world that is set upon their destruction. At no time in history has any religious group looked more forward to a savior. Christians, too, look to the returning Jesus so save them and the world from those who do not believe in him, as their personal savior." The great saving device of this returning God is his swift and righteous judgment, righting all the wrongs Christians the world over have suffered.

For Muslims, Allah, will vindicate the faithful and restore the birthright they, too, believe was taken from them. Hindu's and Buddhists will cycle around in different forms until they have satisfied the requirements of God whose rules they subject themselves too. Their savior is time; endless time.

Religious institutions the world over whether they be large collective movements, small and localized, mystical, dogmatic, new age or old age all look to some force out there to equalize and make right what they collectively perceive as unfair or wrong. All that is asked of the individual is to believe that the unique collective perspective will be right. In other words, suffer now with patience and hope and ultimately you will be vindicated. There is no difference whether the collective institution is secular or religious. They all cry, "We are right and they are wrong." People go to their graves with this kind of hope, believing everything they were taught was wrong will be righted!

Human history is littered with fallen saviors who came with the power of words and ideas but failed to provide any long term solution to the plight of people or nations. In fact, history is nothing more than an endless parade of one thing not working but being overcome supposedly by something better only to fail and repeat over and over again. Winston Churchill referred to history as "just one damned thing after another." How very true.

If we can learn anything from history it is that we cannot learn from history! What we should gather from history is that nothing, no one, can or will save us. No president, political party, nation, religion, individual, philosophy or ideal can save us. We cannot be saved because there is nothing to be saved from!

Somehow the human mind, the ego has convinced us that we all need something outside of us to make us whole and complete. To protect us and make our lowliness or lack in the world a cause for equalization by some force that has power beyond our own. We are conditioned throughout our lives to accept some form of saviorism. It is as if the ego is hiding from some great unknown crime for which it must pay by accepting an outside force to resolve. It seems that the reality we all accept on some level is that guilt unworthiness, evil, etc. is the state of human awareness. It is not always aimed at our individual selves. These characteristics are often aimed at those who are not like us. Thus the collective finger pointing for our own collective ills.

Saviorism is dependency. It stems from the fear we are taught throughout our lives that we are to be perfect even though no one can describe perfection without their own unique judgment of it. We convince ourselves that no one can be perfect and that being the case the idea of needing saving is automatically formed. The idea is so pervasive it inserts itself into every aspect of our lives. It lies at the root of the karmic idea that "what goes around comes around." "Sooner or later you will get yours" even if we have to wait a long time for it to happen. God, e.g. savior will make it right in the end.

Our saviors, consequently, take on many forms. They are people, places and things. Even pills and plants save us. For instance, we look for a pill to slim us down or prevent us from overeating. Heaven forbid we simply take control of our own lives and stop eating or start eating in ways that are healthier! Instead, someone will create a pill that lets us eat anything we want and as much as we want without becoming overweight. Perhaps the pill will come along that will motivate me to work out so I can get that body I have always dreamed of! Perhaps our savior is this new job I've been expecting that will launch both a new career direction and greater prosperity.

I have a friend who is partially disabled who lamented constantly that he could not be whole until his government disability was approved. Now that his disability has come through, which was more than he anticipated; he now complains that he cannot live on the amount provided even though he does nothing to manage the money he does receive.

Can you see the subtlety of it? My friend was saved from a story he created and now he has created a new story that the amount of disability is not enough. He is now looking for a new savior to rescue him from this latest unfairness. After that a new unfairness will lurk into his awareness and he will turn to yet another savior. "If I can just win the lottery it would save me from my financial burdens." I hold to my religious beliefs accepting fully my struggles, my faith will cause God to look favorably upon me and vindicate my lowliness.

We all do this. The greatest saviors we look to are governments and religions because they attempt to right all the wrongs on a much larger scale but the nature of saviorism permeates every aspect of life and it affects everyone of us regardless of our situation or circumstances. The most subtle are our most benign daily wants and desires, particularly our relationships. How many times have we heard someone proclaim, "Oh I can't live without him or her?" Or "I just won't be able to go on if they break up with me," etc. As if life without someone could save us from life altogether!

So many of our individual stories and dramas are played out because of the insidious control our minds play that we must have something or someone in place that will make everything better. This is saviorism! It even finds its way into new age thought that tells us that we can have anything we want if we put our focus and attention onto something even though the original premise is I can be saved from the lack I now have in my life by thinking about and working toward whatever it is I lack.

"Ask, and it will be given" is a common idea in our collective thought and yet at its core is that whatever it is you ask for will only come from some outside source to whom we are all beholden. That is saviorism. In fact, the subtle implication is that all you need to do is ask and something greater than you will provide it. This thing, whatever you call it, is the kind giver of that which you do not have. It will save you from what you do not have presently.

The only way out of this condition is to accept full responsibility for everything in your life. You create your existence and you, therefore, are your own savior should a savior ever be required, which when you take control of everything in your experience will never happen! There is nothing to be saved from in the responsible life. Taking responsibility for life is recognizing that nothing in human experience is personal to you even though it may seem to be.

We create our own experience and exist only as humans for a short while that will never be anything more than the experience. When we take this kind of control over our lives we see that everything that happens is unique and wonderful even if the collective world comes to our rescue and tells us "it's not right or good." It is said that "we must be the change we see in the world." In other words, until we decide that nothing outside our own unique existence can or need save us this idea of saviorism will haunt us for the entirety of our lives. It never matters what the world thinks of us or how we view ourselves in it. Nothing that happens needs outside forces to square our experience with anyone else's or with collective thoughts and intentions.

You are the hero of your life. I am the hero of my own. There is nothing that will save you simply because you are the hero, the savior and when we all remove our judgments of the experience we each individually enjoy something unique and special that no other can or will. That is the beauty of discovering the divine within us. It knows that this experience is nothing in infinity and is only to be enjoyed as only gods can. It also knows that there is nothing in infinity from which we can or need be saved. We literally have it all. We literally are ALL!

Chapter 9

Creative Responsibility

We are responsible for life! However, much of our reality is caught up in making others responsible for what happens to us instead, especially if what happens causes a disruption of normal life. In terms of our "life" experience as humans, we are equipped with two, often conflicting, abilities. The first is our intuitive knowing. That is, the part of us that understands our place in the universe as the God of our experience and the creative center of the universe. While resident in our physical bodies, it is aware of its higher order of existence. It might be called the God that we are, but know not.

The second part is our mind. The mind is the creator of reality on this three dimensional plane. It is the creator of the ego part of us that must identify somehow with everything we perceive and even many things we do not. The mind is what takes over the intuitive nature we all possess and attempts to clarify everything in terms it understands. For the most part, the world of human existence is mind created. The mind has the amazing ability to imagine things greater than what it observes and perhaps even understands and cause things to manifest in its reality. This accounts for the great achievements of mankind throughout history, and accounts for many of the things yet to be achieved. The mind has the ability to resonate vibrationally through thought, feeling and emotion and cause to appear in reality what those thoughts feelings and emotions focus on. In other words, we, as humans, can create our experience in the world in the terms of our human thinking and have pretty much anything we desire and set our minds upon. If the thoughts (energy) emanating from our minds vibrate at the level of "having" whatever we want, then we can achieve it. This is what has come to be known in New Age thought as the "Law of Attraction."

Everyone knows the part of the law of attraction that tells us that like attracts like. We even have more scientific descriptions that tell us that energy vibrates and that the rate of vibration is what makes things what they are. For instance, the rock is a rock because its vibration is not the same as that of the tree or bird or whatever form matter has taken. Everything in the universe is energy vibrating at different frequencies such that all forms appear to be different from each other. In the vibrational sense, this is true but in the energetic sense, it is not. Everything is the same at the base level of existence. All that is different from one form to the other is the frequency at which energy vibrates. As it relates to the law of attraction, like vibration attracts like vibration. If our thoughts vibrate money and wealth then we will have money and wealth or if we vibrate stamina and health that is what we will have in our experience. That is how law attraction is said to work.

The aspect of law of attraction that we almost always overlook, even most teachers of it, is that while like attracts like, the manifestation of outcomes always comes in its own way. The universe is infinitely abundant and the giver of all things, but the way in which it gives is also infinite. No two creations are ever the same. How things manifest is the sole discretion of the universe. It gives freely and abundantly, but it always controls "how" whatever shows up appears to us. This is the point we tend to forget when we look at accepting responsibility for everything in our lives. Most of us never ask why we bring something into our particular existence, especially when we perceive it as bad, harmful or painful. Other than appearing in our experience we never acknowledge that we created it, whatever it is. Things don't happen for any particular reason. They happen because we create them. We bring them into our experience as a part of mind created experience.

In truth there is no "law of attraction." I know this is contrary to the new age thinking of today but in the reality of our experience outside the physical limitations we impose upon ourselves there are no laws. There are no rules. There is only infinite existence and in infinite existence nothing constrains anything else. Law of attraction sets before us choices that do not exist in infinity and puts the responsibility for a bad life or a good life on our physical awareness and energetic vibration. In reality forces we cannot imagine always underlie our physical experience. These are forces that we all possess but have been disconnected from because we have given away our higher awareness to lesser powers of which Law of Attraction is a part.

Being disconnected from our higher divine natures, we often fail to see our complicity in the events and experiences of our lives especially those of an unpleasant nature. It is the ego's way of having "plausible deniability" when things don't go as we expected them. In fact, ego is quick to explain why things don't go the way we think they should have. In most cases, it is because we did not plan correctly or execute the plan we created or that we did not take correct action. That tends to a biggie for the ego. Plan your work and work your plan. Working the plan, however, is fighting against a basic premise of The Law of Attraction. That is the premise that the "how's" are the domain of the universe. The "hows" are something our thinking will never control because the universe is the sole determiner of how things are to come about. We only need choose the "what" and align ourselves to it. In other words, vibrate to whatever it is and whatever action we take is correct action. If we are aligned to what we desire, any action in life will do. All that is necessary for us is to align with the "what" and take any action and it will manifest in its own way and time, often to our great surprise.

That is how law of attraction is said to work. Ask and it is given. The form, in which it is given, however, is where we get confused and begin to deny that what we experience in life is what we have attracted into it. It is wise but difficult to pay attention to the coincidences in our lives because it is they that give us a glimpse into something greater going on in our existence. Most of us have lost our intuitive abilities in favor of the more obvious five sense constructions we have come to accept as reality. The Law of attraction falls into this category. Another way to look at it might be to say that we are gods having a three dimensional human experience, but that the human has become the more dominant aspect of that life. How many of us really know when we hear the voice of God?

In spite of our human-ness, and the loss of knowing that we are divine, every inquiry, every supplication is responded to by our inner divine self. We ask and it is given every time without exception. Most of us, however, forget what it is we asked for while we are watching the answer manifest before us. In the spiritual realm, there are no coincidences. Coincidences only happen on the physical plane of reality we currently exist in. When we are closed off of our spiritual nature, we do not recognize that every coincidence is, in fact, a spiritual answer to a question or desire we expressed in a passing thought, a verbal exchange or emotional outpouring. There are no accidents in life, and spiritually speaking there are no coincidences. We create every aspect of the life we live.

For many, when looking at the so-called pitfalls, or the hardest of times in life, it is a hard thing to accept that they created it, that they are responsible for it. Especially when in the depths of despair, we are unable to see past, the circumstance manifested, to the nugget of truth and profound wonder that is right there in front of us. Most of us forget what it is we desire in the face of the answer before us.

Here's an example. Say that we have been very successful in our career such that we have access to pretty much anything and everything we could possible want in life. We have "the car" and toys and money to travel anywhere in the world and yet we feel empty and sad for some reason. We ponder for a moment if only we would somehow, some way, be happy. Nothing more than this thought and we pass it off and return back to our everyday life without ever considering it again. Months later we receive a call in the night telling us that we must evacuate our home immediately as a wildfire is bearing down on our particular neighborhood and our life is threatened. The evacuation is mandatory, so we gather the children, some clothes, some odds and ends and jump in the family car, and head over to friends or to another shelter that has been provided. A few days later, we are able to return to our home only to find it has been destroyed. Everything is gone.... Everything! What's worse, it is the only house on the block that has been taken. All others are unharmed. As you stand there looking in awe and disbelief, what thoughts begin to go through your head? Do you begin to wonder, why me? Are you filled with anger or grief at your poor, unfortunate state and do you blame God or some evil force for taking all that you worked for?

Certainly if someone came up to you in this terrible moment, and said "You created this, it's your responsibility" you would be enraged, angry, sullen and any number of other emotions, but the last thing you'd be thinking is that you created this. How could anyone ever want this in their life experience? Who wouldn't react this way? We don't ask for these specific things to happen to us, but we do ask that things in general do.

Remember that the universe owns the "how" in every creation. It is not for us to create the "how", only the "what". Remember the passing thought about happiness? Now, it is difficult to buy into the idea that losing everything you have will bring you happiness, but what about it? You threw the thought out there and went back to the life you were unhappy in. In fact, that unhappy life you built blinded you to any other thoughts about being happy. The universe responds. Always, without fail, but also as it sees fit. Let's look at this more closely.

You are living a life you once thought was the best possible way to bring about joy and happiness in your life. In fact, in everything you did, you were successful and it added to the things you could have, the places you could go. Every heart's desire supposedly being met except one and in a moment of pondering, you put into the universe the idea that your life remained sad and the quiet supplication to find happiness. Later, without ever considering such a thing again, you lose everything you owned in a fire. Remember everything you owned was not contributing to your happiness even though you continued to work hard to have it all. In an instant, it is gone and you are in despair – for what appears to be good reason! Many, if not most of us would never look at such an event as anything other than a disaster even though the universe's response to our creation was to take from us all the things we thought brought happiness but didn't. It removed them from our field of view in such a way that maybe, just maybe, we examine our life in another way.

Too often, the things we identify with in life cloud the things we should be identifying with. For many of us we would never be able to divorce ourselves from the awful tragedy of losing everything and surely not take responsibility for it. It was, after all, an act of God or happenstance that just took mine and no one else's.

Until we can comprehend that in the spiritual realm, the realm we are all a part of, there are no coincidences. Everything happens for a reason and more specifically, it happens for reasons we create. The saying "be careful what you wish for" rings true here even in those quiet moments when we consider that we actually do create our reality. Every aspect of it is ours to own and be responsible for. It's always easy to take responsibility for our lives when things fall into place and everything goes smoothly, but turn it around to disruption, chaos, loss and pain and it can't possibly be related to us. When we stop thinking in terms of life happening to us, we will begin to see how great our creative power is. We are gods, after all, and gods create!

For most of us, law of attraction is something we can wrap our minds around when things all seem to fall into place. Should things not be going as we thought then it is because of wrong thinking – easy, right? Law of Attraction is always connected, to worldly things and yet there is something far greater inside us that is really in control which most of us no longer know or accept. This is the true creator of our existence and it resides within us each and every moment of our lives. Our deepest thoughts and desires do not resonate from the mind but from inner knowing. The place where the god we are dwells is the place from which our happiness emanates. It is the place from which our godlike natures speak which unfolds as the creation of our experience. It is the place of no fear and no story. It is the place of knowing that resides in each of us and confirms what we all once knew very well. We are the creators of the Earth upon which we stand and that we are not the physical bodies we possess. We are something else that is pure and divine that dwells within these bodies for a short time only.

Each of us needs to reconnect to that otherness we all know we are and in so discovering recognize that the events of life are never personal. We are born into the circumstances of physical experience of our own creation and choosing and no part of the experience is to reshape or remold us into something we are or are not. All we have to do is find that part of us that loves every aspect of everything going on and all our judgments disappear and the richness of life experience begins to overwhelm us in spectacular ways. Responsibility for life is really acceptance of everything going on in life and acceptance is falling in love with the experience and nothing else. No part of life needs to be held accountable to our judgments about its fairness because every aspect of our existence is fair. In fact, the question of fairness doesn't even exist in a spectrum of infinity. It simply is ours for the experiencing and sheer enjoyment of the god like nature we all possess. The experience of life is never responsible to us in any way. We are responsible for it!

Embrace life and live with reckless abandon. Be life rather than a judge of it and it will open your senses in ways very few ever experience. We are life!

Chapter 10

Stream of Life

Follow a stream from its highest point, whether it is a spring releasing water from an unknown source or from the snows of winter melting and giving their life giving waters to everything below. As the stream finds its way down from its heights, it passes by or over many obstacles along its way, but it always seems to find a way. Its course often seems impossible, but as it runs into obstacles, it finds the path of least resistance which sometimes means going around obstacles or perhaps it waits patiently to fill a certain low spot that will allow its waters to eventually flow over its would-be obstruction. As we follow the stream, it will sometimes rush in great torrents down steep hillsides or spill over high cliffs into pristine pools below. Sometimes it will meander through large open meadows where beautiful alpine flowers bloom and fill the landscape with color, fragrance and brilliance. Perhaps the stream splits off and fills the meadow with small tributaries that merge back together. The sounds of the stream also tell us something about its travels in that it will gurgle as it meanders through unobstructed fields and meadows, but it rushes and roars as it surges over cliffs, down steep canyons filled with large boulders and other obstructions. As we continue our journey following the waters, we might see another stream joining ours, increasing its size and power. Still, the waters push forward, twisting and turning as needed to work its way around the landscape as effortlessly as possible. In fact, as we observe this stream, it never occurs to us that the waters are fighting their way downward. It all seems so effortless and easy. Even in those places where the river has cut its way through rocks and cliffs that, when looking at, simply does not look possible.

The stream weaves its way through a tapestry of life introducing us to all manner of trees, shrubs, plant life, and animal and insect life of all kinds. Some of the places the stream takes us are shaded from the sunlight and are cool and dark, even forbidding, while other places are sunlit and brilliant and the shadows cast on the moving water make it look different, even mesmerizing. There are places on its journey where it shoots through cracks in the rock and we see rainbows cast so close, we can touch them or we feel the cool mist on our faces. Everything about this journey is peaceful and calm and the constant rushing of the river soothes us and at times we may even find ourselves talking to the waters as if they could hear. They can!

Never do we sense, as we journey alongside the stream, that it struggles to get where it is going. It moves effortlessly, inexorably passing by all the wonders of its long journey to get to its destination which, by the way, does not exist. As it passes by life, it gives life by giving of itself so that all is refreshed, nourished and uplifted. It is a relaxed life that looks for peace wherever it goes, and it goes where it goes simply because that is where it goes. We may find evidence along the way when it changed course or with the help of natural forces it moves out of one bed and into another. Still, it matters not. The stream is not choosing a path to follow. It is simply flowing and as it flows, the path opens up, and with each new opening, new adventure, new beauty and wonder lies before it and it brushes up against all of it, content to take it all in and give back what it can in the form of life giving water.

Onward, ever onward, it moves through hills and valleys, forest and fields. Taking in but giving back. The stream gives life, but is given to life as life is given to it. Its course is never straight nor is it narrow or wide. We cannot map its exact course because a map of the stream's journey could never account for every detail the stream encounters on its way down the mountain.

The stream does not choose this way or that. It simply flows where the grade of the mountain (life) takes it and it embraces and gives back to everything it encounters on its way. Every aspect of the journey is just that – part of the journey. There is no purpose other than to serve as that part of the journey. That incredible moment is as the water passes by all that matters and all is uplifted and better for the experience. No great crossroads or turning points in this encounter or that one. Just life giving of itself for all to marvel at and enjoy. The stream moves on, as do we.

There are no perfect geometric patterns in life as we all would like to believe there is, or as our math and science teachers say. The straight path does not exist except in our imagined lives. There is no straight way to any purpose we consider to be our very own. Life is a stream! We are taught from a very early age that the shortest distance between two points is a straight line, but no part of our life on earth is a straight line. In life, the shortest distance between two points is the one that took you from point A to point B regardless of what distance you traveled or the time it took. Ego looks at life in a finite way, and in so doing, it must find order and structure that was never intended to be there.

Our true life is an infinite experience and every twist and turn, the ebbs and flows, as we call them, are never consistent with what our egos expect. This is the cause of suffering in individuals as well as in society. Ego constructs a true and ordered life and even uses sacred writings and ancient wisdom to reason with us that if we follow the prescribed path it reasons is the correct one, life will work out and flow effortlessly to the end. Those who rigidly follow their ego's prescribed course often find themselves in turmoil and needless suffering because they followed the rules and they didn't get where they were supposed to.

Life is full of Monday morning quarterbacks looking back at what went wrong with their plan or what they could have done differently to achieve the pre-planned outcome. We see this second guessing, questioning in every aspect of our lives including religion, academics, and occupations. We might hear someone exclaim, "I followed God's laws as I have been taught them", or "I worked hard and did everything I was supposed to, but why was I not protected or spared an outcome I was sure could not happen if I obeyed all the rules."

Unlike the natural flow of the stream which always finds its way, many will push against the natural course of life. They will push against it and question their misfortune. You can almost see them standing in the stream facing upward with clenched fist defying the direction of flow as if challenging it to reverse its direction and go where they command it. All it does, however, is move forward, following its natural course, either moving around you as you fight against it, or sweeping you up in its current. *Life does not care about the choices we make.* Life, like the river, flows on, embracing everything in its path, and giving back every step of the way.

If we could see our lives as a river or stream and simply flow with it, our journey would be so much more pleasant and our expectations would not get mixed up or confused with the twists and turns in life we could not see coming. The grand part of life we can all enjoy is the pure experience of it. A river has no purpose other than to flow where it will, and it is the same for us. Life flows on whether we resist it or not. Why not enjoy it?

Human ego is so busy finding or giving meaning to the process of life and finding justification and cause for everything that happens that we miss much of its inherent beauty. We pass by the works of man or nature and never see them because our focus is on understanding life rather than living it. In trying to understand it or analyze it, we miss it or it passes us by. Every bend in the stream, every change in direction is an opportunity to experience life in a new and incredible way, and particularly from our own unique perspective.

Maybe we won't experience things as others might, but what we do experience is uniquely ours and the only enrichment we need take from any experience is our own to appreciate and fully embrace. "What happens; happens." Not because we have control over life by the choices we make, but because there are no wrong choices, which is the same as saying there are no choices at all. If we participate in life without the mental anguish of deciding the better of all our various choices then anything we do, any path we follow will be good and right and un-judge-worthy. This type of participation in life removes the resistance we feel as well.

I used to tell my daughter, who would work so hard to get cast in school plays, or achieve academic success only to be disappointed over and over, that life was not fair. I would tell her that she would encounter situations throughout her life that would prove that life was unfair and that she would be mistreated along the way, even though she worked harder and harder to achieve her objectives. How naive I was and, unfortunately, the message I imparted to her was completely wrong. Not only is life fair, but it is completely honest. Life is truth therefore it cannot be dishonest. The only dishonesty in life is our own dishonesty which culminates deep within the egoic structures of the mind.

Our egoic identity is the only thing on this planet that resists the natural flow of life, to the point that what we have come to believe about ourselves and what we are is the only dishonest thing in life. Ego-constructed reality and reality are diametrically opposed to each other and we get caught up in the game of life that convinces us that life is hard and not always just or fair. Ego is always swimming against the current of life, trying to offer another kind of reasoning for the ebb and flow that doesn't always seem so pleasant.

Life is always honest and it always finds the way to bear that out. How hard we sometimes struggle to keep what we know about ourselves from ever seeing the light of day, and so we bring dishonesty to the light of life. Our lies, our dishonesty dims the light of life, and compounds our struggle against the stream that, if we would only let go of everything we hold so tightly to, would all drift out of sight and our lives would freely and effortlessly blend together with the flow of life never to be consumed in worry, doubt or the endless game of making ourselves "other" than ourselves.

Nothing in our three dimensional awareness can account for what is really happening and therein lies the greatest lie we tell ourselves. The more precise and defined we become, the less aware we are; and the more we convince ourselves that we are precise and defined, the more of our true selves we trample under foot, and the greater our lie becomes.

The lack of awareness culminates in the denial of the stream of life we all follow. It is to convince ourselves that we can make the stream of life straight and exact according to geometric rules that only hold in a manmade reality. We convince ourselves that within the sterile structure of manmade forms is the answer to who we are if we but push science to find the one simple equation that defines everything we will ever need to know.

Only the ego could have created such a lie. Only ego could convince us that straight lines can be found in nature and that a formula can be derived that will be able to predict everything we can expect for the future and give an explanation for everything that has happened in the past. Conscious awareness is a very limited awareness because of its ability to dump so much information so quickly we cannot even sense that it is happening.

As we meander or tumble through life, we tend to miss the incredible sights along the way as they are happening, but we know they were there because we think back upon them. Sometimes we look forward to the horizon out yonder and think that when we get there, things will be so much better, or all our questions will be answered. We easily look forward and backward because those are the places we can most freely and successfully lie about. In the conversation we have with ourselves, we can reminisce how much better things were "back then" or how much better they will be in some future "when".

Now, the present moment we exist in right now, is an honest moment that is pure and untainted by any thought for yesterday or tomorrow until our egoic reaction to it poisons it with untruth. Facing the present is our most daunting challenge because of its purity. In our un-pure state, we have difficulty facing the purity of present reality because being present forces us to look at ourselves without the ideological masks that we have created to shield us from the glare of present reality. Being present strips us clean of all the false definition we use to demonstrate ourselves to the world. It is a scary place for the ego. In fact, it is a place the ego cannot exist in because ego is anything but honest.

Ego needs identity. That is why it always reminds us and everyone else of its past accomplishments or projected future achievements. These are its cover; a safe haven from something that cannot be explained in its terms, its language.

The stream of life is infinite. The egoic life is finite. The two cannot co-exist. They cancel each other out. Either we are in the flow and completely truthful or we are in illusion and living a lie. The stream of life is enjoined with the world and nothing is missed along the way. The largest of egos and the highest degrees of knowledge and education cannot describe what the stream knows. Its world is the whole world and it is one with it. It knows the terrain, the hills, valley and rocks along the way and is never fooled by images condensed and printed on a map that the ego provides. It feels everything and reaches out to everything, as it gives to life, its "own" life.

Consciousness cuts away so much of life while ego tries so hard to convince us that what we are conscious of is the real nuts and bolts of life. It works hard to convince us that its view of the world "is" the world. Its view is always looking backward or forward, but never does it acknowledge the present with its billions and billions of pieces of information discernible right now to a quiet non-egoic soul.

We are in the stream of life whether the egoic self believes it or not, and the stream always moves ahead, even if we fight against the current. Our experience is an unfolding. The more we flow with life, the more a part of us life becomes. Every aspect of the terrain we pass through is our guide, our map and our journey becomes an infinite stream of intuition and awareness that consciousness no longer blots out. Our intuition and our wonderful bodies are sensory instruments available to all of us to navigate and enjoy our life experience here on planet earth.

We step off the cosmic train for a short time and we can enjoy the experience or fight against it. We choose. The ego created world is calculated and sterile and does everything it can to reduce the stimulation we all are equipped to comprehend. Granted, the comprehension is not in the language of ego, which has also been stripped away of the greater part of knowing. Our intuitive abilities need to be at the forefront of our awareness, not in the background as they often are. Tune them in and turn on the truth of real life. Real existence! Destiny is unknown, therefore, non-existent. The possibilities available to us along our journey through life are endless. Ego wants to see and plan for the end. It seeks a goal, an end that, when reached, is somehow a utopic conclusion to a well-planned life strategy.

I was speaking with a friend one evening who was looking for a catalyst of perhaps thought or an individual such as Buddha or Jesus, who by their words and deeds could change the hearts and minds of people to live in peace. He shared his thoughts about how the so-called age of enlightenment some 500 years earlier, which was ushered in by such great minds as Newton, Descartes, Pascal and others, had failed to provide the predicted "know how" to change a dark world into an enlightened one. The age of enlightenment was supposed to find "mind made" solutions to all the ills of human existence, including war, poverty, education, government, and every other aspect of life. My friend recognized the failure of the intellectual mind or so-called "enlightened mind" to accomplish anything other than to increase suffering and the carnage of war on a greater, more massive scale.

While he lamented this failure of enlightened minds to solve complex world issues, he asked me, "If the age of enlightenment is not the answer, what is the catalyst, event or individual that brings about changes the enlightenment sought but could not produce?" My answer was not what he wanted to hear. I told him that to look, in any way, to an outward cause, to an individual, or event would never bring about the changes in human existence he sought. The only change or catalyst he could ever affect was his own. I told him that we, as humans, are all a part of the stream of life, but that we each are our own stream as well. Individually, we affect the larger stream, but with human reasoning, we will likely never see it.

When we become our own catalyst, our change, we become the larger stream and it becomes us and our outlook on the conditions of the world we wish were different becomes part of a compassionate whole. When such a change takes place in us individually, everything else changes as well. My friend listened thoughtfully, but was unable to see it. His mind was convinced that something big and extraordinary was needed to alter things in the world as we know it. My response to him was that an individual transformation to higher awareness is big and extraordinary, but he would not accept that as an answer. "There must be something," he mused.

I could not help him. The majority of us look for the same thing. We look to our gods, our leaders, our parents, someone, anyone or anything that will reverse the way things are in a massive and dramatic way. We are conditioned to be this way. Heaven forbid we allow ourselves control of our own lives. That is how it was in the so-called enlightenment, when highly sophisticated and educated men determined that they could figure out anything intellectually. It continues to be a myth in the present day, yet the stream flows onward, ever onward and as long as we look for the utopic conclusion, the life strategy or catalyst that changes in a massive way those things we have determined must change we swim against the current of life. Life is, at that point, a struggle and we will never win against it. Despite our struggle and good intentions, we will be washed away in the inexorable flow of life that always moves forward. Everyone is eventually swept away in the current of life. Some hang on until the very end while others stop resisting and glimpse the beauty and splendor that is always there if we simply let ourselves get caught up in the flow.

The stream of life simply is! So too is life. Life is about being in the flow, not having or fighting for or against it. Regardless of the things we determine to be important, or the causes we choose, we struggle against or go with the stream of life but it always flows onward to an infinite destination we will never know. But we need not know because such knowing will not add one thing to the incredible beauty, abundance and wonder of our existence. We need only breathe life as it breathes us and go where it takes us.

There is no end in infinity! The stream of life is eternal life; so are you!

End

Afterword

Don't run around this world looking for a hole to hide in.

There are wild beasts in every cave! If you live with mice, the cat claws will find you.

The only real rest comes when you are alone with God.

Live in the nowhere that you came from, even though you have an address here.

    Rumi

Remember…YOU are God as "Human Being"

Be sure to visit Carl's website at: www.spiritual-intuition.com for all the latest information about spiritual transformation and awakening to new awareness.

You can also download a free copy of the E-book "Are You Listening? Addressing the Divine Within" when you sign up for the Spiritual Intuition Newsletter.

Look for Carl's newest and first novel titled: "Shaman" to be out in 2013.

For more information or questions regarding this book or any other spiritual needs please send an email to: carl@spiritual-intuition.com. We'd love to hear from you

Namaste